# Freedom Sounds

# Freedom Sounds

## CIVIL RIGHTS CALL OUT TO JAZZ AND AFRICA

INGRID MONSON

OXFORD
UNIVERSITY PRESS

2007

# OXFORD
UNIVERSITY PRESS

Oxford University Press, Inc., publishes works that further
Oxford University's objective of excellence
in research, scholarship, and education.

Oxford    New York
Auckland    Cape Town    Dar es Salaam    Hong Kong    Karachi
Kuala Lumpur    Madrid    Melbourne    Mexico City    Nairobi
New Delhi    Shanghai    Taipei    Toronto

With offices in
Argentina    Austria    Brazil    Chile    Czech Republic    France    Greece
Guatemala    Hungary    Italy    Japan    Poland    Portugal    Singapore
South Korea    Switzerland    Thailand    Turkey    Ukraine    Vietnam

Published by Oxford University Press, Inc.
198 Madison Avenue, New York, New York 10016

www.oup.com

Oxford is a registered trademark of Oxford University Press

Library of Congress Cataloging-in-Publication Data
Monson, Ingrid T. (Ingrid Tolia)
Freedom sounds : civil rights call out to jazz and Africa / Ingrid Monson.
    p. cm.
Includes bibliographical references (p. ) and index.
ISBN 978-0-19-512825-3
1. Jazz—1951–1960—History and criticism.   2.   1961–1970—History and criticism.
3. Jazz—Social aspects—United States.   4. Jazz—Political
aspects—United States.   5. African-Americans—Civil rights—United
States—History—20th century.   I. Title.
ML3508.M65 2007
781.65'1599—dc22      2007003541

The publication of this book was supported
by the Lloyd Hibberd Publication
Endowment Fund of the American
Musicological Society

9 8 7 6 5 4 3 2 1
Printed in the United States of America
on acid-free paper

*For Okolo M. Ewunike,*
*Sonja D. Williams,*
*and Solveig K. Daffinrud,*
*with all my heart*

# Acknowledgments

M Y FIRST ACKNOWLEDGMENT must go to Bernice Johnson Reagon and Charles Neblett, whose participation in the "Miles Davis, the Civil Rights Movement, and Jazz" conference, co-organized by Gerald Early and me in 1997, was crucial in developing my understanding of the civil rights movement. Wayne Field's thoughtful questions to these former members of the SNCC Freedom Singers, elicited a remarkable and moving line of recollection that communicated to the audience something that I doubt anyone who was there will ever forget, and which launched me into a broader research direction. Or perhaps I should go back further, to the mid-1970s when I first heard Bernice Reagon sing in Madison, Wisconsin, and wore thin the grooves of her remarkable album *Give Your Hands to Struggle* (1975 [1997] Smithsonian Folkways CD SF40049; originially released on Paredon records). I thank all the participants at that conference, who came to Washington University in St. Louis in May 1997 including Randy Weston, Bernice Reagon, Charles Neblett, Orrin Keepnews, Dan Morgenstern, Richard Davis, Sonny Fortune, and A.B. Spellman.

I must especially acknolwedge Billy Higgins and Jackie McLean, who are no longer with us, as well as Tony Williams, who had agreed to participate in the event, but died two months before it took place. Oscar Brown Jr., whose recollections of *The Freedom Now Suite* were so crucial to chapter five, is also no longer with us. These passings remind us of how quickly the first hand memories of the the 1950s and 1960s are receding from view. I thank each and every person I interviewed including Abbey Lincoln, Max Roach, Nat Hentoff, Art D'Lugoff, Ron Carter, Ira Gitler, Dan Morgenstern, Val Coleman, Marvin Rich, Ronald Moss, Orrin Keepnews, George Russell, Clark Terry, Randy Weston, and Roswell Rudd. May your voices never be forgotten.

There is always much more than the gathering of information that one takes away from interviews or personal conversations with musicians, journalists, and activists who were professionally active in the 1950s and 1960s. I'd like to mention a few examples from my experiences researching this book.

The interview I conducted with Abbey Lincoln in 1995 shook me up to my very core. I thank Ms. Lincoln for inviting me to her home and talking at length with me, as well as for our long conversation in 2001 that brought me up to date and set me straight on her views of history. The laser precision of her insights into the human heart and the honesty with which she recounted her story had an impact that still resonates. I thank Richard Davis for having taken a job at the University of Wisconsin in 1977 and encouraging me as a trumpet player, as well as for the various interviews he has granted over the years. Do you remember calling me at 6:30 A.M. in the fall of 1977 to find out whether I had been practicing?

I thank Clark Terry and his family for including me in a family dinner after the remarkable interview he gave me in St. Louis in 1997. The story of integrating NBC's Tonight Show band, that he related inspired me to dig even deeper into the interplay between race and economics. Marvin Rich seemed surprised that anyone remembers his remarkable service to the fundraising efforts of CORE, but I will always remember it.

There are personal connections that have deepened over the writing of this book. In this regard, I want to acknowledge George and Alice Russell for their deep support and our times together, and Randy Weston for his huge heart and mind, as well as his commitment to Africa. I want to thank Nat Hentoff for asking year after year, "Is your book done yet?" and for traveling to Boston to interact with my students (they were spellbound!). I have always hoped that this book might be seen in the tradition of Hentoff's remarkably honest and racially perceptive jazz writings of the 1950s and 1960s.

And then there is Max Roach, who talked to me for a couple of hours, while desperately trying not to give me specific information that had been contractually committed to his autobiography. In the spring of 1999 he performed in Boston with a band featuring lots of brass, which reminded me of *Deeds Not Words* and underscored my conviction that his gifts as a composer are often overlooked.

## Funding and Assistants

I would like to thank the American Council of Learned Societies for a post-doctoral fellowship in 1994–95 that enabled me to begin this project. I thank Deans Edward Macias and James McLeod at Washington University in St. Louis for honoring me with the Earle H. and Suzanne S. Harbison Faculty Fellowship that enabled me to begin the organization of the conference, "Miles Davis, the Civil Rights Movement and Jazz" in 1996. I thank Gerald Early for putting his weight behind our successful grant to the Missouri Humanities Council and Adele Tuchler for her great administrative expertise and energy. That was quite a year!

Harvard University made possible my sabbaticals in fall 2001 and fall 2004, which led to the completion of this manuscript. I thank the Departments of African and African American Studies and Music for hiring me in the first place.

There are several research assistants, who helped gather an enormous amount of material from jazz periodicals and African American newspapers. Judith Mabry did the lion's share of this work in academic year 1996–97, which included more than her fair share of managing interlibrary loan requests. You were truly amazing! Mona Chitkara was particularly helpful with my search of African American periodicals and Gabriel Solis helped enter many of these materials into database software (as well as do more interlibrary loan requests).

## Librarians

Although I did not write down the names of the many librarians who helped me through archival materials I would like to acknowledge the staffs of the following libraries: Special Collections, University of Arkansas, Fayetteville, Arkansas, The Music Division at the Library of Congress, the Schaumburg Center, and the State Historical Society of Wisconsin.

In addition I would like to personally thank Vincent Pelote, Esther Smith, and John Clement of the Institute of Jazz Studies at Rutgers University; and Brad Short, Head Librarian, Gaylord Music Library, Washington University in St. Louis.

## My Students

In addition to those students who served as research assistants, I would like to especially thank the class members of two iterations of my course "Jazz and the Civil Rights Movement" taught at Harvard University in Spring 1999 and Spring 2002. The open dialogue and debate we had on race, politics, and music profoundly affected the final shape of this book. You helped me to clarify my thinking as I tried to respond to your questions, comments, and perspectives. We argued, we laughed, we listened, and your energy amplified mine.

Spring 1999: Daniel Baer, Samantha Bent, Emily Bianchi, Austin Brentley, Terence Carter, Jeffrey Chaput, Jessy Fernandez, Amma Gharty-Tagoe, Rodney Glasgow, Chandra Ho, Ayana Johnson, Julian Jordan, Jarred Kennedy, Gail King, Franklin Leonard, David Lyczkowski, Desiree Lyle, Anish Melwani, Kawaun Sankar, Natasha Sokol, Justin Steil, Shatema Threadcraft, Elizabeth Walker, Megan Whyte, Carine Williams, Daniel Yates, and Charles Zerner.

Spring 2002: Ablorh Akuorkor, Jay Bacrania, Michael Baly, Joseph Charat, Thomas Crahan, Andrew Crocco, Michaela Daniel, Caleb Epps, Alison Fisher, Vasugi Ganeshananthan, Jessica Gould, Preston Golson, Peter Karlin, Osborne Jackson, Kelley Johnson, Douglas Logigian, Ian Mackenzie, Laney McClain, Nathalie Miller, Michael Nguyen, Mwashuma Nyatta, Okwudiri Onyedum, Gregory Padgett, Chartey Quarcoo, Petra Rivera, Fred Smith, Jonathan Smith, Macani Toungara, John Woody, and Yohance Young.

## Editors

I would like to thank Maribeth Payne, who was music editor at Oxford University Press when I signed on. I would also like to praise the excellent team at Oxford, which has finally gotten this manuscript to press—Suzanne Ryan, Norman Hirschy, and Stephanie Attia.

## Colleagues, Friends, and Family

For an academic one's colleagues are like the members of the band. Your ideas, just can't come to full fruition without the stimulation of their ideas and responses. I would like to mention some of the many colleagues whose thoughts have influenced my own. Jean and John Comaroff, whose combined intellectual electricity could light New York City, made an indelible contribution to my analysis of power and politics. The give and take with my colleagues in African and African American Studies since my time at Harvard has also been crucial in the larger perspective on race that has emerged in my work, including especially, Henry Louis Gates Jr., Cornel West, Lawrence Bobo, Evelyn Higginbotham, Michael Dawson, Suzanne Blier, Randy Matory, and Werner Sollors. My colleagues in Music have also been an inspiration including Kay Shelemay and Christopher Hasty. My former colleagues at Washington University in St. Louis should also be mentioned—Craig Monson, Dolores Pesce, Hugh Macdonald, Robert Snarrenberg, Richard Fox, Gerald Early, Rafia Zafar, and Leslie Brown. I must also mention my colleagues in the remarkable Jazz Study Group at Columbia University. These amazing gatherings, twice a year, have made an enormous contribution to jazz studies that goes far beyond the published volumes of essays. This was true interdisciplinary community of the likes I had never before experienced. My memories of the conversations at our meetings were my background music as I wrote this volume. Bob O'Meally, Farah Jasmine Griffin, Robin D. G. Kelley, Sherrie Tucker, Krin Gabbard, Maxine Gordon, C. Daniel Dawson, Christopher Washburne, John Szwed, Guthrie Ramsey, and Jacqui Malone are among those I talked to most.

There are certain friends whose shared interests in music, politics, and race have led to ongoing conversations on these topics over decades. Among these are Becca Pulliam, Don Byron, Toby Emmer, Patti Sunderland, Bambi Schieffelin, and Sherrie Tucker.

It is customary to put one's family members last, but this location is not an accurate representation of their importance. Okolo M. Ewunike, my spouse and unflagging supporter, always seems to inspire me to do better than I can. My mother, Sonja D. Williams, has *always* been there through thick and thin and for *everything*. I absorbed her compassion, intellectual curiosity, and introspection. My aunt, Solveig Daffinrud, has always had a fiery sense of fairness and justice, as well as an unbridled sense of humor, that has deeply affected me. My sister, Ellen Monson, always cuts to the chase, has a deep sense of justice, and, with her husband Ken Petren, a deep love of the outdoors. And lastly, a call out to the next generation, my nephew Alex Nelson Petren, who gave me the strength and joy to make it through the final sprint to the finish line.

# Contents

# Freedom Sounds

# 1

## Introduction

OUTRAGED BY THE television images of white mobs and Arkansas National Guardsmen blocking the enrollment of nine African American students in Little Rock's Central High School in September 1957, Louis Armstrong called a reporter while on tour in Grand Forks, North Dakota, then sounded off on racial injustice: "My people—the Negroes—are not looking for anything—we just want a square shake. But when I see on television and read about a crowd in Arkansas spitting and cursing at a little colored girl—I think I have a right to get sore—and say something about it."[1] Armstrong criticized President Eisenhower for his foot-dragging during the crisis, described Governor Orval Faubus as an "uneducated plowboy," and withdrew in protest from a planned State Department tour of the Soviet Union. "The people over there ask me what's wrong with my country. What am I supposed to say? The way they are treating my people in the South, the government can go to hell."[2]

Armstrong was widely praised for his outspokenness by several fellow performers and public figures including Jackie Robinson, Eartha Kitt, and Pearl Bailey. In jazz circles, however, many musicians were surprised because Armstrong was not known for his political militancy, but rather for his tendency toward an accommodating onstage persona. This political outspokenness, which was something new for Armstrong, occurred a few months after he had been publicly criticized in the African American press—along with Duke Ellington and Nat King Cole—for continuing to accept engagements at segregated theaters.[3] Armstrong probably realized that he did not need the State Department to be an ambassador for jazz, since in May 1956 he had made a wildly successful visit to the Gold Coast

3

(now Ghana) for the production of Edward R. Murrow's film *Satchmo the Great.*[4] Armstrong performed for soon-to-be President Kwame Nkrumah and was overwhelmed by the enthusiastic reception he received in Africa.[5]

Armstrong's commentary on Little Rock links several issues: the domestic struggle for civil rights, the politics of the U.S. State Department jazz tours, and his own recent experience performing in Ghana in 1956.[6] The trumpeter's story encapsulates the principal task of *Freedom Sounds,* which is to elucidate how these three larger social forces—the civil rights movement, the cold war, and anticolonialism—affected jazz and jazz musicians in the years between 1950, when the NAACP Legal Defense fund began the legal battle leading to *Brown v. Board of Education,* and 1967, the year John Coltrane died. The musical achievements of these years are among the most sacred to jazz musicians and their audiences and include the extraordinary contributions of John Coltrane, Miles Davis, Charles Mingus, Thelonious Monk, Ornette Coleman, Sun Ra, Art Blakey, Sarah Vaughan, Bill Evans, Sonny Rollins, Gil Evans, and Max Roach (to name only a few). This golden age of modern jazz established the aesthetic standards by which succeeding generations of jazz musicians have continued to measure themselves in the early twenty-first century, as well as a set of symbolic meanings that remain central to the identity of the genre.

The larger questions posed here are what combination of factors (and combinations of combinations) made this music possible? What effects, direct and indirect, did the struggle for racial equality have on aesthetics, the sense of mission musicians brought to their art, the diversity of music played and composed, and the symbolic meanings attached to the art form? What role did world affairs, especially African independence and anticolonialism, play in how African Americans came to envision their political and cultural liberation? In what ways did the ideas of aesthetic modernism mediate between music and politics?

Louis Armstrong's protest of the events in Little Rock also reminds us that moments of political activism were not confined to those musicians known for their outspokenness, such as Max Roach, Abbey Lincoln, and Charles Mingus. The theme of politics and music in jazz has a long history, with both African and non–African American constituencies advancing claims for the social and political significance of music. Jazz improvisation has been cast as a quintessentially democratic and uniquely American art form, as well as an enduring symbol for freedom.[7] It has been called a universal colorblind art, celebrated for defying the racial status quo, and lauded as an inherently rebellious and progressive art form. Free jazz has been championed as the embodiment of revolutionary black nationalism, as well as a path toward deeper spiritual truth, universality, and internationalism. Jazz has been celebrated as the triumph of African American aesthetics in American music and as the ultimate embodiment of black pride, Afro-modernism, and genius.[8] The music has perhaps been all of these things, though not at the same time and not to all constituencies.

In *Freedom Sounds* I am particularly interested in the arguments and debates that defined the scope of jazz as an aesthetic practice, a social community, and an economic livelihood—that is, what people fought about as well as agreed upon. Many of these arguments were about race and racism, even when the ostensible subject of discussion was something else, like harmonic choices or swinging. My aim is not only to capture the multiple points of view expressed about music and politics but also to understand the social and musical logic that informed them.

In addressing issues of race and culture *Freedom Sounds* extends a trend toward social and cultural histories of jazz that has been under way since the early 1990s. The works of Burton Peretti, Scott DeVeaux, William Kenney, Samuel Floyd, Ronald Radano, and David Stowe have contributed substantially to a historiography that has drawn attention to the structural role of Jim Crow segregation in shaping the emergence and practice of jazz in its most canonical years from early jazz to the mid-1960s and challenged the unquestioned status of modernism and biography in jazz history.[9] The jazz artist as the iconoclastic hero, the nonconformist, the transcendent and self-determining subject, and the social critic is so tied up with the symbolic legacy of the music, especially since World War II, that it is difficult to challenge the primacy of these images without seeming to betray something fundamental and sacred about the music.

Yet far more is to be gained by viewing modernism historically and contextually, I maintain, than by continuing to accept its aesthetic presumptions as timeless truths. The familiar narratives of jazz historiography about the fifties and sixties have emphasized genius and heroism and the inexorable march toward the beauty of modern art. In doing so, they have been extraordinarily successful in legitimizing jazz and bringing greater respect and dignity to its artists. The many biographies, autobiographies, discographies, encyclopedias, and synoptic accounts of modern developments in musical style honor the individual achievements of the greatest icons of the music, and compile an enormous amount of information on individual musicians and the recorded legacy of the music they have left behind.[10]

Nevertheless, a literature focused primarily on the individual tends to lose track of larger trends and historical circumstances shared across broader social constituencies. The parallels between debates in the civil rights movement and those in jazz constitute one such larger circumstance that *Freedom Sounds* investigates. During the civil rights movement, the intractable conflicts that emerged over race, leadership, strategy, and policy goals were quite similar in many respects to the arguments over race, power, aesthetics, and economics that took place in jazz. Another way to think of this is that the civil rights movement and jazz musicians drew from a common set of discourses (or ideas) that shaped the way disputes were conceived and the way in which various constituencies chose to put their ideas into practice. One irony of this period (which I take as a point of departure) is that, just as musicians were perfecting their relationship to modernism and most likely to declare the autonomy and transcendence of their art, they were simultaneously most likely to find themselves buffeted by the political forces around them, both domestic and international.

### The Structural Role of Jim Crow

Any account of the politics of race in jazz during the 1950s and 1960s must surely begin with a recognition of the structural significance of Jim Crow policies for the musical world. To begin with, the history of this music called jazz, from its origins through the golden age, is coextensive with the history of Jim Crow segregation. In this sense, Jim Crow functioned as a structural condition over which the emergence of the genre took place, and its effects were not limited to the South. Shortly after *Plessy v. Ferguson* (1896)—the Supreme Court decision that established the doctrine of separate but equal—Buddy Bolden's band dazzled New Orleans with a distinctive sound that heralded the synthesis of ragtime, blues, spirituals, classical music, marches, and popular song that became jazz. At the other end of the period under study, the passage of the Civil Rights Act of 1964 and the Voting Rights Act of 1965 (which dismantled the legal basis for racial segregation) saw the recording of John Coltrane's *A Love Supreme,* the flourishing of Miles Davis's second great quintet, and the experimentalism of Sun Ra's *Heliocentric Worlds.*[11] This is not to suggest that Jim Crow *caused* jazz but to recognize that, throughout the establishment and flourishing of the genre, discriminatory practices in the music industry and society indelibly shaped everyday life for musicians and their audiences. Segregation also concentrated a great deal of African American musical talent in the "racially expected" genres of jazz, blues, and gospel since opportunities in other genres, such as classical music, were limited.

White musicians also had to face the color line, although in a more selective sense. After leaving the clubs and bandstands on the "black side" of town, for example, white musicians and audience members were still eligible for the taken-for-granted rights and privileges of whiteness at midcentury (like hotel rooms, voting, radio and TV broadcast, and membership cards in white unions). Many were not fully aware of the impact of white privilege on their ability to cross the color line, get a meal, or find employment in a band that worked on television, and hence were quite unprepared for the political and racial tensions of the 1960s. Some came to resent the additional prestige and symbolic authority that blackness acquired in jazz during these years and in the early 1960s turned to charging reverse racism (a topic that is explored in chapter 7). Others were radicalized by the racial injustice they observed and found in the politicization of the music the inspiration to develop their own social consciences. An underlying premise of this book is that, during these years, everyone in the world of jazz had to cope with the politics of race in one form or another, whether through denial, engagement, withdrawal, strategic confrontation, cathartic rage, resentment, celebration, or sublimation.

Although multiple factors beyond race were clearly affecting the music—economics, recording technology, class, talent, gender, ethnicity, modernism, anticolonialism—the legal legacy of Jim Crow often elevated race to the category that trumped all. At moments of conflict, broader constellations of social factors were often reduced to or projected onto the single variable of race. The challenge for this volume is both to acknowledge the historical salience of the category of race in the history of jazz and also to delineate the way in which it is complicated by other sociological variables (such as class and gender) and the history of interracial debate.

## Legal Definitions of Race

*There are white Americans so to speak and black Americans. But any*
*fool can see that the white people are not really white, and that*
*black people are not black.*
—Albert Murray

Although jazz musicians and their audiences generally accepted the obviousness of whether someone was black or white, it is important to
recognize that defining and maintaining the line between the races was a
major preoccupation of the Jim Crow years. The so-called one-drop rule
of racial definition, which held that any traceable black ancestry was
sufficient to render a person legally black, is something that developed in
tandem with the codification of Jim Crow segregation laws of the late
nineteenth century. According to F. James Davis, the fraction defining
"who is black" fluctuated widely from century to century and from state to
state and tended toward smaller proportions in the late nineteenth and
early twentieth centuries. From 1785 to 1910, for example, a mulatto or
"colored person" in Virginia was defined as someone with one-quarter or
greater black ancestry.[12] From 1910 to 1924 Virginia lowered the portion to
one-sixteenth. After 1924 Virginia declared that a white person was legally
required to have "no trace whatsoever" of black ancestry and no more than
one-sixteenth Native American heritage.[13]

These changing legal definitions redefined many formerly "legally
white" people as black. As George Schuyler reported, in 1940 a person of
one-eighth African American heritage could legally marry a white person
in Nebraska, Maryland, Louisiana, Missouri, Mississippi, or South Carolina. The same marriage, however, would violate the miscegenation laws
in Arizona, Montana, Virginia, Georgia, Alabama, Oklahoma, Arkansas,
and Texas.[14] It is important to recognize the remoteness of the ancestry
needed to be considered "colored": A person who is one-eighth black has
seven white great-grandparents and one black great-grandparent.

The one-drop rule was designed to maintain white purity and domination by assigning any intermixture to the legally subordinate category.
The rule assuaged Southern white paranoia about the danger of "invisible blackness" by eliminating the category of mixed heritage by fiat. The
strict binary racial classification of Jim Crow attempted to legislate a clear

division in a society that was far more hybrid than segregation laws admitted. Historically speaking, "colored" persons included many mixed ancestries—not only black-white but also black–Native American and black-Asian. Although "mulatto" came to mean strictly black-white intermixtures, in the eighteenth century the term also included black–Native American and European–Native American combinations.[15] In addition to masking such intermixtures, the one-drop rule during the Jim Crow era also collapsed ethnic and cultural distinctions within populations of African descent. The impact of Caribbean populations of African descent (Cuban, Haitian, Puerto Rican, and Jamaican, for example), as well as that of the Creoles of color in Louisiana, are among the streams of cultural influence obscured by the system of binary racial classification.

In the social policy of the United States, ethnic distinctions among European immigrant groups were also collapsed by the emphasis on binary racial classification. As the historical literature on the social construction of "whiteness" has documented, the various European ethnic groups composing white America—from German to Irish to Italian—*became* collectively "white" through a process of marking their boundary from "blackness."[16] The one-drop-rule, in other words, also consolidated the category of "white" by focusing on the legal definition of "blackness."

In general the jazz world of the forties, fifties, and sixties accepted definitions of black and white that were consistent with the framework of the one-drop rule. The fact that many black persons were white in appearance nevertheless confounded the enforcement of Jim Crow laws, a circumstance that some jazz musicians used to their advantage. Tenor saxophonist Earle Warren, for example, was light enough to "pass for white" for the purposes of purchasing food for the Count Basie band while on tour in the South. Members of Darlings of Rhythm (a predominantly African American all-women's orchestra) also managed to turn the vagaries of the racial divide against Jim Crow. White musicians put on "nut brown powder" to darken themselves when performing in predominantly black bands in the South, rendering themselves sometimes darker than their lighter-skinned black band mates. When white trumpeter Toby Butler was arrested for violating Georgia's segregation laws, the African American leader of the band (Jessie Turner) confused the authorities by insisting that Butler was her first cousin. Since the one-drop tradition made it entirely possible that Butler *was* Jessie Turner's cousin, the police released her.[17]

## Culture and Hybridity

*American culture, even in its most rigidly segregated precincts, is patently and irrevocably composite. It is, regardless of all the hysterical protestations of those who would have it otherwise, incontestably mulatto. Indeed, for all the traditional antagonisms and obvious differences, the so-called black and so-called white people of the United State resemble nobody else in the world so much as they resemble each other.*

—Albert Murray

Situations of such cultural hybridity (mixedness, mulattoness) present daunting challenges to cultural analysts committed to neither denying difference and its structural persistence nor reifying culture into a biologically based essentialist paradigm of race. It is important to remember that mixedness may or may not be visible since, as Naomi Pabst has argued, there is a difference between "light-skinnedness" and "racially distinct parentage, which is not always marked by light skin." In her view (and in Murray's quote in the epigraph to this section), mixedness or hybridity "simply is and always was," and categories are invariably "impure" and "already crossed."[18] If legal definitions of race in the United States artificially simplified a hybrid, mixed heritage, however, it is also true that a real and persistent color line exists that continues to define everyday social experience and perceptions in the United States.

My position presumes that culture is a dynamic process of synthesis through time, even without the complicating factor of cross-cultural hybridity, because cultures must reproduce themselves over time. Even in the hypothetical case of a purely endogamous, isolated cultural group, notions of cultural authenticity, identity, and legitimacy must necessarily be re-created and passed on in a process of intergenerational transmission, negotiation, contestation, and synthesis. Each generation must respond to unpredictable historical circumstances (weather, illness) and apply cultural principles to new historical situations, often subtly transforming them in the process. This is akin to what Amiri Baraka had in mind when he spoke of the "changing same."[19] What a community accepts as an authentic cultural expression in any given generation may consequently change over time in response to historical circumstances and communal debate—a social process not unlike improvising. This is not to deny that core issues and problems recur in every generation, but to emphasize that creative and individual responses to the same problems continually arise.[20]

Since the word "culture" is often used as a code word for "race," I would like to be clear from the beginning that I take as my point of departure an anthropological concept of culture. More specifically, it is one that is informed by practice-based directions in anthropological theory emphasizing (1) culture as emerging from social practices in a process of contestation and engagement (which occurs over time, that is, history), (2) culture as inevitably mixed and partially overlapping with other cultures around it, and (3) cultures as not bound neatly to space or geography but rather mediated by recording, print, and broadcast media. Culture, then, is not simply about race or ethnicity, but also about the definition and redefinition of collectivities (including races, identities, classes, ethnic groups, genders) through various kinds of social practice, such as playing music, arguing about race, living in the same neighborhood, attending religious services, watching television, marriage, and political activism.[21]

People can and do share many social practices without sharing ethnicity or race, but these everyday activities of social life inevitably take place within the larger social structures of economics, law, and nation that, as we have seen, in the United States of the mid-twentieth century, continually reinscribed race as the single most important cultural, legal, and economic boundary marker. In talking about culture and race in this volume, then, it is crucial for us to keep in mind that, although the sociological variable of race often predicts the sharing of crucial kinds of social experience in the United States, race alone is not what makes culture; rather, it consists of configurations of social experience, gender, class, values, and history.

The problem only gets worse when we consider the impact of cross-cultural contact over time. In thinking about cultural groups that have interacted and mutually influenced one another, several crucial questions arise. What are the power relations that shape the contact or cultural overlap? Who profits from the contact? Is an area of cultural overlap enforced or voluntary for the participants? When does a borrower have a right to claim ownership? Which set of cultural values shapes the process by which divergent cultural elements and practices are shared and synthesized? Which values and ideologies, in other words, are dominant and hegemonic?

In the abstract it is possible to imagine a society in which cultural borrowing and synthesis proceed with relatively little anxiety over the contemporary reshaping of tradition, but in the world of jazz at the mid-twentieth century, racially stratified debates over authenticity, legitimacy, and white appropriation were highly polarized. The discourse of aesthetic modernism provided both a meeting ground for musicians from divergent backgrounds and a means of asserting deep cultural differences. From the early 1950s to the mid-1960s a general shift took place from a colorblind ideology on race within the jazz community to the assertion of a black-identified consciousness on the part of many African American musicians and their supporters. This discursive change closely parallels comparable developments in the civil rights movement, black nationalism, and black power (and, indeed, makes little sense without considering these contexts). If jazz ideology in the late forties and early fifties stressed integration and modernist aesthetic uplift, by the early sixties, many jazz musicians stressed cultural self-determination and the rejection of mainstream American culture.

However, this ideological shift in the jazz community was not simply a response to larger political issues, but also a reaction to everyday economic imbalances in the music industry, the inability of liberal, color-blind presumptions to address them, and the in-between status of jazz improvisation as neither popular nor classical music. In moments of power struggle—such as competition over jobs, pay scales, recording contracts, nightclub gigs, print media attention, and television and film contracts—the jazz world often divided into racialized debates over the relative merit of black and white performers. Arguments over who swung and who was the most innovative were often tacitly about race despite the insistence of the combatants that they were "colorblind."

At the same time, blackness acquired a new level of dignity and prestige in jazz—among white audiences, as well as black—as the astonishing musical achievements of individuals such as Miles Davis, John Coltrane, and Thelonious Monk were read against the backdrop of the struggle for civil rights and racial justice. If freedom and excellence were the goals, the synthesis of African American musical traditions and modernism accomplished by these musical visionaries symbolically encapsulated the dreams of the civil rights and black nationalist movements in ways that leading white musicians could not. Despite the common assumption that only the "music itself" should count in the evaluation of excellence, musicians, audiences, and critics responded to the entire complex of sound, image, and cultural symbolism.

## Black Nationalism and White Resentment

Many popular descriptions of the spectrum of liberal political opinion on race in the 1950s and 1960s divide the landscape into two opposing camps, those supporting integration and those advocating black nationalism. In this narrative, integrationists supported nonviolence, colorblind evaluations of individuals, and working within the framework of a liberal democracy to seek legal redress and compensation for racial injustice. Mainstream civil rights organizations such as the National Association for the Advancement of Colored People (NAACP), Congress of Racial Equality (CORE), and Southern Christian Leadership Conference (SCLC) are usually associated with this position. Black nationalists, on the other hand, emphasized black economic and political self-determination, cultural autonomy, and, in some cases, separatism. The Nation of Islam, Malcolm X, the Black Panther Party, US, and many other black liberation organizations are generally associated with this perspective.

As political scientist Michael Dawson has argued, the history of African American political ideology is far more complicated than this dualistic framework allows. What is key to keep in mind throughout this volume is that black liberal political ideology, as well as black nationalist (or other radical) political thinking, differed substantially from white liberal political opinion, especially on the questions of the accountability of the individual to the larger community and economics.

Since the role of individualism and individual expression plays such a central role in jazz aesthetics and the economic disparities between black and white performers during the 1950s and 1960s proved so contentious in interracial debates, I begin by presenting a brief summary of Dawson's analysis of the history of African American political ideology. If mainstream liberalism in the United States has emphasized, above all, individualism and equal opportunity in the pursuit of life, liberty, and happiness, black liberalism has consistently differed in two key dimensions. First, it has stressed not only equality of economic opportunity but also equality of outcome. African Americans have expected that equality of opportunity should lead to gaining a fair share of the American economic pie. In music, the sense that African American excellence ought to translate into a fair economic return (one proportionate to the aesthetic contributions of African Americans) was a particularly strong concern during the 1950s and 1960s.

Second, African Americans have viewed their individual possibilities as linked to the fate of their larger racial community to a greater degree than other ethnic groups in the United States. Because African Americans have had minority status within a winner-takes-all form of democratic representation, the importance of collective responses to issues of community-wide importance has been an enduring theme in African American history. This emphasis on communal and collective bonds, Dawson argues, runs counter to mainstream individualistic liberal thought, and, furthermore, has been important in the thinking of black liberals such as Martin Luther King Jr., as well as black radicals from Malcolm X to Amiri Baraka.[22] One important consequence of this collective orientation is that the African American community, through its activism and its periodicals, often held black performers to a high standard of political accountability.

Black nationalism (and black radicalism more broadly) has also been more variegated than popular understandings convey. According to Dawson, the key components of black nationalism since the time of Martin Delaney have placed an emphasis on black autonomy and varying levels of economic, social, and political separation from white Americans. While some organizations (for example, the Communist Party and the Nation of Islam) have emphasized the importance of establishing a separate black state, separatism, nevertheless, has *not* been the defining issue for black nationalism. More widely supported aspects of black nationalism include economic self-determination, cultural self-definition, and the development of autonomous black-led organizations. In the twentieth-century, black nationalism emphasized the special place of Africa as a historical, cultural, and spiritual homeland. Black Marxism, in addition, emphasized the connection between the U.S. struggle for racial justice and the national liberation struggles of the formerly colonized nations.[23]

The breadth of African American political opinion is important to keep in mind as one observes the fractious charges and countercharges between white and black jazz musicians during the 1960s. African American emphasis on collectivity and the need to redress a history of economic discrimination were often taken as racially exclusionary or separatist by liberal whites, who appealed to the language of individualism and universality in an attempt to deflate the importance of black communal loyalties. Since an interest in collective self-determination was apparent in both African Americans who supported mainstream civil rights organizations and those who endorsed more radical organizations (from the Nation of Islam to the Black Panther Party), considerable interracial miscommunication took place (and continues to do so) over this issue.

Although most writing in jazz and African American studies has emphasized the changing consciousness of African Americans in response to the events of the civil rights movement and black radicalism, I suggest there was a corresponding change among racially liberal and radical whites. Many young progressive whites were inspired by the political activism and moral example of the civil rights and black power movements and began to evaluate themselves by some of the ethical standards they espoused. As political and cultural histories of the 1960s have often observed, it is no accident that the antiwar movement (Vietnam), the women's movement, and the gay liberation movement (and later countercultural movements) took the organizing tactics and moral rhetoric of the civil rights movement as a point of departure in articulating their own political strategies and demands for human rights. Just as Robin Kelley has argued for African American activists—that self-transformation and the ability to dream were just as much a part of the civil rights movement as the lunch-counter sit-ins and voter registration drives—so too did many young whites see rejecting the racial status quo of their parents' generation as key to their own self-transformation and moral vision.

Between 1950 and 1967 many white musicians, critics, and their audiences began to embrace more fully than previous generations African American musical and cultural standards as a benchmark for evaluating themselves aesthetically, morally, and politically. This is a crucial point in opening an alternative framework for thinking through several interracially tense questions in jazz studies, including (1) why the canonic figures in jazz, whether chosen by African or non–African American critics and musicians, are predominantly African American; (2) whether jazz is best thought of as African American music or American music, and (3) whether white participation in jazz has essentially amounted to appropriation, imitation, and cultural theft. The ultimate problem, it seems to me, is how to acknowledge the depth of the African American cultural impact on mainstream American musical and cultural aesthetics without denying the hybridity of the music and the complexity of the recursive relationships between black and nonblack jazz players. In chapter 3 I propose a framework for considering these issues.

The years during which I researched and wrote this book have witnessed an enormous growth in what I term the "white resentment narrative" in jazz history and criticism. The last chapter of Gene Lee's *Cats of Many Colors,* for example, rails against African American discrimination against white musicians in jazz. An often-cited essay by Terry Teachout accuses Wynton Marsalis and Jazz at Lincoln Center of antiwhite bias in hiring and programming, while suggesting that there is an overemphasis on African Americans in jazz history that can be explained only by an excess of black nationalist thinking and political correctness.[24] Richard Sudhalter, in *Lost Chords: White Musicians and Their Contribution to Jazz, 1915–1945,* takes it one step further by arguing that emphasis on the African American roots of jazz amounts to a "black creationist canon" that, in his view, obscures the simple multicultural truth that "black and white once worked side by side, often defying the racial and social norms of their time to create a music whose graces reflected the combined effort."[25] The former position is considered ideological while the latter is presented as historically accurate.

Nevertheless, these writers make use of liberal, individualist ideology to argue for a colorblind or race-neutral perspective that views music itself as above and beyond politics. Moreover, the argument is made with ideological purpose, that is, to redress an alleged grievance—that white musicians have been left out of jazz history and, when included, have been considered to be less authentic. As we will see, the current wave of white resentment narratives in jazz revisits similar debates that took place in the jazz community during the early 1960s as the musical world was politicized by the events of the civil rights movement and as African Americans increasingly demanded a more central place in jazz history. Although the jazz community has long been thought of as one characterized by greater interracial collaboration than has occurred in the rest of American society, it has less often been noted that it was among the first social scenes to develop the discourse of reverse racism.

My own position on ideology and politics is that no one stands outside the flow of the ideas, ideologies, discourses, and political interest in the world around us or fails to draw on ideas larger than themselves in making a case for one version of history or another. Since the writing of history is always an interpretive act (and in jazz history it is certainly not difficult to find works that draw drastically different conclusions from the same set of "facts"), I believe that it is better to be explicit about one's interpretive decisions and take pains to establish the ideological, political, and cultural contexts that make wildly different ideological positions plausible than to pretend that one is just presenting the facts—musical, historical, or otherwise.

## Modernism and Modernity

In the 1950s and 1960s jazz successfully constructed itself ideologically, musically, and symbolically into a modern art music, even if the institutional trappings of this status did not come into being until thirty to forty years later. The relationship between jazz musicians and their publics with regard to the discourse of modernism is consequently a crucial theme underlying much of this volume. I am particularly interested in understanding how issues of race mediated between the aesthetic and political views of the modern. At the most general level, African Americans were more likely to see an inherent connection between music and politics than their white counterparts, who more frequently accepted the art-for-art's-sake argument that music was ultimately individual and above and beyond politics. Yet a desire to be "modern" (in a sense including not only musical craft but also an entire "authentic" persona mixing aspects of rebellion, originality, social criticism, progressiveness, and being "true to oneself") was an aspiration articulated on both sides of the color line.

The idea of the modern in jazz has accomplished various kinds of musical and political work throughout the history of jazz, some of it consonant with its uses in European art music, some of it decidedly dissonant. Although jazz has since its inception been considered a modern music, considerable debate has taken place throughout its history about whether its folk, popular, or art music qualities should be emphasized; about which label—"highbrow," "middlebrow," or "lowbrow"—is most appropriate to describe it; and about the musical standards by which it should be judged. The interest that both European and American modernist composers showed in jazz in the 1920s and 1930s, as well as the tendency of European audiences to recognize the "art" in jazz and to treat its musicians accordingly, encouraged many jazz musicians to think of themselves as artists in a bohemian high art sense.[26] The conditions in the music industry under which they labored, however, were decidedly those of music for popular entertainment, with all of the racial stratifications of the early to mid-twentieth century intact.

The success with which swing music conquered the marketplace in the 1930s and 1940s made it a commercial popular music, even though many of its musicians always considered it to be something above and beyond. Its advocates generally pointed to the sophistication of the music in harmonic, rhythmic, and technical terms, as well as the creative beauty of improvisation, to justify this sensibility. On these modernist criteria of form and content most musicians, black or white, generally agreed.

Bebop musicians extended the embrace of modernism by adding their disdain of the popular, as well as their interest in the same hallmarks of avant-garde modernism that interested "high art" experimental composers: formal experimentation and theoretical exploration; a politically vanguardist stance and the rhetoric of progress; and an alternation between the celebration of intuition and rationalism as the basis of art. Yet bebop did not embrace one of the most significant markers of avant-garde musical modernism: the break with tonality. Indeed, jazz after World War II arguably developed the most sophisticated and interesting tonal language of the twentieth century. The attempted break with tonality came later, in the free jazz of the early 1960s.[27]

Since the topic of modernism is enormously broad, ranging from the entire history of Western thinking since the Enlightenment (in philosophy and social theory) to the specifically aesthetic movements of the twentieth century, including (to name only a few) surrealism, dada, constructivism, serialism, and jazz, it will be useful to draw some distinctions from the outset. Wherever possible I use the term "modernity" to refer to the expansive sense of Western thought since the Enlightenment and "modernism" to refer to the specifically musical and aesthetic aspects of jazz as musical art. Nevertheless, in the broader literature the words "modernism" and "modernist" can swing both ways. Where I intend the expansive sense, I explicitly say so.

Since historians, social and critical race theorists, anthropologists, and postcolonial theorists have argued for the last two decades that the concept of race and racism is deeply rooted in the history of the Western modernity, the parts of this volume that pertain to race and political history draw most heavily on the broader concept of modernity. I have found it helpful to think of the modern in this expanded sense as an overlapping family of discourses expressed in political, aesthetic, economic, historical, and technological domains. If ideas of truth, transcendence, universality, freedom, autonomy, subjectivity, and progress are common across all of these categories, each one contains, in addition, a more particularized set of themes. The political domain has emphasized individual rights, the self-determining subject, secularism, progress, revolution, and nationalism; the economic field has emphasized industrialization, commodification, alienation, and the free market, as well as systematic critiques of the market system such as Marxism. The historical sphere has been invested in progress, teleology, rationality, and origins, while the technological realm has emphasized science as a mode of rationality. In aesthetics, what I am calling modernism includes a constellation of ideas about form and content, abstraction, individuality, iconoclasm, rebellion, the autonomy of art, authenticity, progress, and genius.[28]

Although the broader project of modernity has celebrated individual freedom and the emancipatory potential of reason, the flourishing of slavery and imperialism concurrently created a far different experience of the modern for Africans, African Americans, and colonized populations. For Paul Gilroy this position at the vortex of the most glaring contradiction between modernity's professed ideals and its actual practice is critical in our understanding of the relationship of black political movements to the Western intellectual heritage: "A concept of modernity that is worth its salt ought, for example, to have something to contribute to an analysis of how the particular varieties of radicalism articulated through the revolts of enslaved people made selective use of the ideologies of the western Age of Revolution and then flowed into social movements of an anti-colonial and decidedly anti-capitalist type."[29]

The civil rights movement drew upon the universalizing legacy of modernity to advance its cause. Civil rights attorneys emphasized the modern principles of political democracy, equality before the law, and individual freedom to highlight the gap between the rhetoric of equality and the actual denial of citizenship rights to African Americans. Similarly, bebop musicians drew upon broadly accepted ideas about the modern artist and universal musical standards to argue for the inclusion of African American musicians in the top ranks of modern music. Simply embracing aesthetic modernism, in this sense, was viewed as being of political consequence.

In Gilroy's view, this position of being both inside and outside of modern Western culture (like Du Bois's "double consciousness") is one of the defining conditions of the Black Atlantic and fostered the development of black music and arts as a "counterculture of modernity." By this he means a musical practice that was committed to the "idea of a better future" and embodied the style of agency that would be necessary for political transformation.[30] Nevertheless, black artistic expression in jazz also looked to the ancient past and religion as a source of cultural renewal, critique, and empowerment, often expressed in myths and rituals of an idealized African past. James Hall has suggested that the spiritual interests of musicians like John Coltrane should be seen as part of an "antimodern" stream in African American thought that both provided a deep critique of modernity and validated African American longings for community and nationhood. Robin Kelley's *Freedom Dreams* has argued further that African American interest in a redemptive vision of Africa cannot simply be dismissed as romantic or utopian but rather should be seen as central to the development of an African American notion of freedom that is more than materialist.[31]

Whether this impulse is viewed as operating outside the legacy of Western modernism or as a counterculture of critique residing partly within and partly without it, *Freedom Sounds* shares with Hall's and Kelley's analyses the view that the turn toward non-Western modes of spiritual expression and ritual enactment in the jazz world was connected to an identification with both the anticolonial struggles of the emerging non-Western nations (in Africa and Asia) and the cultural heritage of the African continent in particular.

## Intellectual Antecedents and Theoretical Frameworks

### African American Studies

The flourishing of African American studies since the 1960s has made available to contemporary jazz scholars a "paradigm-shifting" body of work on African American social and cultural history, the civil rights movement, and interracial dynamics that was simply not available to writers working in the 1960s and 1970s. Recognition of African American studies as a resource for rethinking the questions that are asked of jazz history, music criticism, and cultural criticism has been a growing theme in recent scholarship not only because of its power to redress past exclusions, but also because of the interdisciplinary affinity between the analytical problems raised by African American experience (double consciousness, racial oppression, hybridity, slavery, the underside of modernity) and the interpretive issues emphasized by poststructural and postmodern critiques of contemporary thought and society. The past fifteen years have witnessed an explosion of interdisciplinary scholarship on jazz that includes work from the fields of literature, music, history, ethnomusicology, dance, anthropology, film studies, diasporic studies, gender studies, and art history. One of the crucial themes common to this emerging literature on jazz cultural studies is attention to the issues of race, power, and internationalism.[32]

As both Mae Henderson and Wahneema Lubiano have argued, African American intellectuals have been writing about these issues for the last hundred years in ways that anticipated the theoretical concerns of contemporary cultural studies, anthropology, poststructuralism, and postcolonialism.[33] I have been particularly interested in the writings of those who early on placed African American history and the struggle for racial justice in an international and African diasporic context, such as W.E.B. Du Bois, Marcus Garvey, and Paul Robeson, as well as those who engaged actively with the field of anthropology, including Du Bois, Zora Neale Hurston, Katherine Dunham, St. Clair Drake, and Amiri Baraka.[34]

As Faye and Ira Harrison have argued, W.E.B. Du Bois ought to be counted among the intellectual ancestors of anthropology by virtue of his ethnographic methodology in *The Philadelphia Negro*, his dialogues with Franz Boas on race and culture, and his lifelong interest in Pan-Africanism. He has, in addition, been acknowledged for his formidable impact on the fields of sociology and history.[35] Because so many African American intellectuals operated on the margins or outside of academia altogether, it has been difficult for them to gain recognition for the resonances of their work with now widely utilized interdisciplinary paradigms in the humanities and social sciences. Du Bois's emphasis on global context, for example, and his role in developing Pan-Africanism as both an idea and a political movement demonstrated a broadness of vision that would be at home in the company of contemporary discussions of the African diaspora and globalization. His concept of "double consciousness" raised issues of cultural hybridity and the relational construction of identity that remain central to debates in cultural studies and poststructuralism.[36]

A similar case could be made for the relevance of Amiri Baraka's *Blues People* to the fields of ethnomusicology, social theory, and the current interdisciplinary renaissance in jazz scholarship.[37] Baraka's analysis of African retentions in African American music and culture demonstrates a deep engagement with Herskovits's *Myth of the Negro Past,* an anthropological work that put to rest the idea that Africans arrived in the United States without culture and without history. Baraka cites many of Herskovits's examples of African retentions in black religious, musical, and daily life that can arguably be said to emanate from Dahomean and Yoruba culture.[38]

Yet more important than the specifics of particular African retentions in Baraka's analysis or indeed the many outdated historical facts cited in the text is his flair for creative social theorizing that combines anthropological understandings of syncretism with a Marxist conception of the dialectic. From anthropology comes the idea that African cultural continuities underlie the myriad ways in which African Americans have modified and reshaped European cultural forms, and from Marx and Hegel comes the idea of a dialectical synthesis in which the encounter of opposing forces will yield something "that must contain both ideas." Throughout *Blues People* Baraka applies these two concepts to the history of black music to yield spectacularly insightful comments on the meaning and significance of the music.[39]

Baraka opened *Blues People* by stating that his task was "a strictly *theoretical* endeavor" designed to investigate his central hypothesis: that music reveals something of deep cultural significance about the nature of African American existence in America, and, by extension, the nature of American society as a whole.[40] I have argued elsewhere that Baraka ought to be recognized for his contributions to theorizing the relationship between music and race and that it is a mistake to view *Blues People* as a simply an artifact of cultural nationalism.[41] By drawing attention to the shifting relationships between music and the symbolic and emotional meanings attached to it by various social groupings, Baraka did what many scholars are trying to do today—that is, analyze the role of music in shaping and affirming various kinds of social identities and its role in political and cultural resistance. The study of cultural identities (that is, the relationship among personal experience, racial and gender hierarchies, economics, and symbolic meanings attached to various forms of cultural expression) has been an enduring theme in recent work in African American studies, cultural studies, ethnomusicology, anthropology, and postcolonialism.[42]

Du Bois and Baraka are just two African American intellectuals who have emphasized the central importance of music in African American cultural life. A fuller treatment of the relationship of jazz to African American intellectual history can be found in Eric Porter's elegant *What Is This Thing Called Jazz.*[43] My goal here is to establish that there are long-standing linkages between African American thought and broader theoretical debates in the social sciences and humanities.

## Social Theory: Discourse, Structure, Practice

*Freedom Sounds* is less a traditional history than a critical essay on the relationships among the music, racism, and society in a particular historical period and what we have to learn from them. It is more concerned with explaining why the history of the music has always been contested ground— with issues of race tending to provoke the most incendiary debates—than with providing an exhaustive chronological narrative of the period. It is more interested in asking why such a profound proliferation of musical creativity occurred during a period of heightened political intensity, why the participants in stormy polemical battles cared so deeply, and why the core fights and disputes that emerged during the 1950s and 1960s have been so remarkably durable in their discursive shape and lingering animosities.

I have been particularly interested in the linkages between African American theorizations of race, identity, music, and politics and an eclectic mix of more often cited academic social theoretical literature that has been influential in the humanities and social sciences in the last quarter of a century. The literature that has influenced me the most includes the poststructural work of Michel Foucault, the sociology of Anthony Giddens, the practice theory inaugurated by Pierre Bourdieu, and the anthropology of Jean and John Comaroff and Sherry Ortner.[44] The concepts in this body of work have helped me keep the big picture in mind while sifting through the contradictions and paradoxical details that abound in the everyday lives of musicians. For I am ultimately less interested in establishing that jazz musicians of the 1950s and early 1960s were heroes and geniuses (something that has been demonstrated over and over again in the jazz literature) than in understanding how they navigated such contested social terrain in the process of earning that reputation.

Three basic social theoretical concepts circulate throughout the book and require some explanation: discourse, structure, and practice. Like all interpretive frameworks and analyses, this one is partial and incomplete and not meant to be an end in itself. These concepts are rather like the chord changes on a lead sheet: They serve as a general point of departure but can never be mistaken for improvised solos themselves, with all of their quirky and beautiful particularity.

By discourse, I mean ideas that are expressed most typically in language, are deployed in the process of framing arguments and justifying positions, and possess the authority and prestige to order how we think about the world. This is discourse in a sense that was put forth by Michel Foucault, and it is most useful in conjunction with his notion of discursive formations—constellations of discourses that together form networks of ideas that shape the ideological landscape and nature of debate in a particular historical period.[45] In jazz of the fifties and sixties a set of ideas about the modern artist is particularly important in understanding how jazz musicians chose to define themselves. By making themselves into artists and rebelling against the role of entertainer, jazz musicians made use of culturally prestigious discourses (art, the modern, genius) to assert a higher status for the improviser's art.[46] Likewise, the discourse of race had profound effects on how musicians defined themselves and on their interpretation of the role of the modern artist. In general, understanding how various constituencies within the jazz world appealed to the discursive formations of race, modernism, and modernity is crucial to the intellectual project of *Freedom Sounds*.[47]

My usage of discourse departs from Foucault, however, by conceiving of music itself as a discourse. How can this be? Music is full of ideas that are evaluated by audiences and musicians, that acquire authority and prestige within particular aesthetic landscapes, and that are perceived to "say something" substantive about human experience and feeling. They furthermore function within constellations of musical ideas (styles) that form a context in which they are evaluated and perceived. Just as linguistic discourses form an interrelated matrix of meaning, so do the musical utterances of jazz improvisers form a larger network of musical meanings that are invoked and commented upon in the course of performance. When I speak of music as a discourse, I do not mean simply "talk about music" but also the relationships between the sounds themselves and the symbolic, social, political, and personal meanings that individuals, collectivities, and institutions construct for them. If Charlie Parker's virtuosity, Dizzy Gillespie's flatted fifths, and Kenny Clarke's rhythmic bombs came to signify an attitude and a politics, we must ask for whom and by whom such meanings were created. The "music itself" is not external to a social and political account but rather a central player in the dialogue between art and meaning.[48]

By structure, I mean the social structures, laws, social categories, technologies, and economic systems that define the terms of social experience for large groups of people. The demographic categories used in social analysis such as race, gender, class, ethnicity, sexual orientation, educational level, and place of residence form one aspect of structure. Legal codes governing what is permitted and prohibited to members of various social groups and the system of economic exchange also form durable yet malleable configurations that shape what is possible for individuals. Although structures, as Anthony Giddens and William Sewell remind us, change through an accumulation of intended and unintended consequences in the course of social reproduction, structures change far more slowly than practices.

My understanding of social structure is informed by the thinking of Anthony Giddens, who views structure as dual, that is, as "both the medium and the outcome of practices which constitute social systems."[49] By this he means that structures shape what people can do, but, conversely, what people do also shapes the reproduction and transformation of structures. This is, in part, because the actions of individual agents have both intended and unintended consequences that undermine the stability of the system. For Giddens, an interplay always exists between structure and agency in the creation of social life. The choices individuals make in their everyday life, how they orient themselves to particular ideas and ideologies, and what actions they take on their behalf are all viewed as critical components to the making of both social structures and history.

Yet, there is always a collective component to agency since people must be able to coordinate their efforts with others to create collective projects. Furthermore, existing social structures empower individuals differently, according to their place in a configuration of social hierarchies and institutional organizations. As William Sewell has noted, "the agency of fathers, executives, or professors is greatly expanded by the places they occupy in patriarchal families, corporations, or universities and by their consequent authority to bind the collectivity by their actions."[50] Hence, it is important to consider the social categories to which an individual belongs, as well as a person's position within institutional organizations. Of particular importance for jazz in the 1950s and 1960s is the structural persistence of Jim Crow practices in the music industry (including segregated unions, traveling conditions, performing venues, wages, and opportunities to appear in film and television). Black and white musicians occupied different positions within this racially defined institutional and economic structure that musical communion alone could not alter.

Despite the strength of both discourses and structures in defining the lead sheet over which the improvisation of social life takes place, it is ultimately practice that is of greatest interest in this volume. Practice is the third term—the wild card—for it is what people choose to do given the particular structural and discursive configurations in which they live. Practice is about agency in everyday life, that is, the implementation of cultural ideas, values, and structures through various kinds of social action. Practices can take many forms—musical, economic, sexual, ritual, and so on, but key to their difference from discourse is their stress on embodied knowledge and action. Pierre Bourdieu, a central figure in the development of practice theory, asserted that every society transmits embodied patterns learned by emulation of the actions of others (rather than transmitted by discourse) that serve to develop "practical mastery" of social life.[51]

Bourdieu had in mind the practical competence necessary to navigate everyday life within a particular culture, but its easy extension into the practicing of musicians is not hard to see. The activity of practicing—mastering scales, rhythms, harmony, patterns, repertory, and style by repeating passages over and over again—is simply part of what it is to be a musician. Once musicians have this musical knowledge "in their fingers" (and ears), they may no longer have to think consciously about the things they drilled into their bodies through practicing. Thus mimesis and repetition—of live or recorded sources—lead to embodied knowledge and the freeing of the conscious mind for creative aesthetic discovery and expression. For the improvising jazz musician, the true test has always been not the knowledge demonstrated through words but that put into musical practice on the bandstand.[52]

In social theory, the idea of practice as social action is particularly useful for moving beyond a deterministic understanding of how structures and discourses shape social life and in mediating between micro- and macro-levels of musical and social analysis. Although the social categories one occupies may be given—black, white, man, woman, rich, poor—through the creative deployment of various kinds of practices, an individual just might succeed in doing a whole host of things that are not predicted by the social categories to which they belong.

Indeed, aesthetic practice in twentieth-century America—musical practice in particular—has been extremely important in imagining a freer society than the one we inherited. In the late 1940s and early 1950s jazz drew upon a multiplicity of aesthetic perspectives in fashioning individual sounds, including the African American vernacular aesthetics, the aesthetics of the American popular song, the aesthetics of classical music, and also, for some artists, African diasporic sounds such as Afro-Cuban sacred and secular music, Nigerian talking drums, and Trinidadian calypso. Individual musicians, regardless of their ethnic home base, can and did exercise aesthetic agency by exploring musical aesthetics from both within and beyond their expected ethnic categories.

Cultural and social anthropologists who developed the idea of practice theory, in the sense in which I am using it here, have used it to move beyond an older concept of culture as bounded, holistic, and homogeneous and toward a concept that keeps difference, overlap, and contingency at the center.[53] In music, the idea of music as a musical and social practice has long been a productive theme in the field of ethnomusicology, where it has informed social constructionist work on a wide range of world music genres.[54] Timothy Taylor's work on global popular music and technology has been particularly important in bringing this perspective to popular music studies.[55] In my own work, practice theory served to ground my approach to the music in *Saying Something* in my use of the practice-based literature of linguistic anthropology and African American literary studies to talk about jazz improvisation as interactive, emergent, and socially communicative. In more recent work I have been interested in how musical practices and processes in their polyphonic complexity may offer a better theoretical model for thinking through the cross-cultural complexities of music and globalization than some current social theories.[56]

## Practice in Recent Jazz Studies

Practice in the sense used here has had a growing presence in recent work on African American music, most notably in the work of Travis Jackson,

Guthrie Ramsey, and Nichole Rustin. Jackson has used the idea of practice in talking about jazz improvisation, genre boundaries, and musical and spiritual flow from this vantage point.[57] Ramsey's use of practice theory to talk about how people "negotiate the system" in their everyday lives, as well as his evocative term "community theaters" to describe the spaces (such as churches, schools, and dances) in which "everyday blackness" is practiced, has offered a compelling portrait of how music and cultural identity are interwoven across a wide spectrum of African American musical genres.[58] Rustin has creatively applied a practice-based understanding of identity to address intersections of race and masculinity in Charles Mingus's life and move beyond understanding W.E.B. Du Bois's idea of double consciousness as an internal "split" forcing black subjects to see themselves through the eyes of another. For Rustin, Mingus's artistic practice (and personal self-understanding constructed through it) was about actively embracing the multiple selves he describes in *Beneath the Underdog* rather than a quest for creating an overarching superego.[59]

Rustin's work reminds us also of the close intersection between race and gender in the jazz musician's quest for self-determination and personal authenticity. If a key component of masculinity is the "will to self-determination" as Rustin argues, the close connection between black nationalism's stress on self-determination and its gendered expression becomes more legible in the individual lives of jazz musicians for whom respect and recognition were hard won.[60]

Ultimately practice is a flexible idea that helps describe individual relationships to social forces and ideas beyond any one person's control. Freedom in jazz, after all, is that feeling of improvised musical self-determination that is both the joy and challenge of every improvised performance. It is here that jazz, black nationalism, and modern subjectivity meet: in everyday practices and performances as intimate as love itself, yet as connected to real-world aspirations for freedom and justice as the knee bone is to the thigh bone.

# 2

# Jim Crow, Economics, and the Politics of Musicianship

THE MUSIC BUSINESS until the mid-1960s was astonishingly segregated. Musicians, critics, record producers, booking agents, and club owners all worked within a hierarchical entertainment industry whose institutional configurations, power relations, and racial conventions had been forged during the consolidation of the popular music industry in the 1930s. It is important to keep in mind a number of features of the music industry between the 1930s and 1960s. First, the recording and broadcast industries were consolidated after the Great Depression. The 1930s witnessed the emergence of the major labels (Victor, Columbia, and Decca) and the national radio networks (NBC and CBS) that dominated the broadcasting market. These corporations formed a durable, interlocking web of economic relationships through which music was recorded and distributed.

Second, the copyright system rewards songwriters and publishers, not performers. Performance (or artist) royalties on recordings or wages for performing on recordings amounted to little compared to the mechanical and broadcast royalties that songwriters and publishers earned.[1] The U.S. Copyright Act of 1909 was predicated on the assumption that works requiring copyright protection were notated compositions rather than recorded performances or improvisations that took them as a point of departure. Indeed, it was not until February 15, 1972, that an amendment to the act extended federal copyright protection to sound recordings published on or after that date.[2] By these rules, when Miles Davis recorded "My

Funny Valentine" by Rodgers and Hart in 1956, mechanical royalties were paid to the songwriters and their publisher, but Davis's unique version of the tune was not copyrightable. When Davis's performance was heard on radio or TV, additional broadcast royalties were earned by the songwriters and publisher and collected by the American Society of Composers, Authors, and Publishers (ASCAP). In the 1950s and 1960s many jazz musicians formed their own publishing companies and more assertively negotiated for writer's credit on their compositions, but, even so, it is difficult to imagine a copyright structure less suited to protecting the art of jazz improvisation.

Third, although recording contracts made provisions for artist royalties, the terms of standard contracts all but ensured that most would never see a royalty check. Artist performance royalties were (and still are) calculated as a percentage of the retail price less taxes, duties, and percentages for packaging and breakage. Since royalty rates in jazz generally ranged between five and ten percent and full recording costs (including any advances) were recoverable from this amount, it is not surprising that many musicians received bills for outstanding recording costs rather than artist royalties. In 1960, for example, Charles Mingus received a royalty statement from Atlantic Records dunning him for $1,644.81, the difference between royalties earned on U.S. and foreign sales of *The Clown* ($45.93) and his advance ($1,690.74). It was not until 1968 that Mingus's Atlantic royalties on three albums—*The Clown, Blues and Roots,* and *Oh Yeah!*—moved into the black.[3]

Fourth, the American Federation of Musicians (AFM), which had had segregated locals since its founding in 1896,[4] controlled access to the highest paying gigs in the music industry (studio and broadcast work) through licensing and certification agreements with broadcasters (radio and later TV), recording companies, booking agents, theaters, and the film industry.[5] The AFM experienced its greatest level of power and influence under the presidency of James Caesar Petrillo (1940–1958), who waged war against the effects of "canned music" (recordings) on the economic livelihood of musicians. Petrillo also presided reluctantly over the "amalgamation" of segregated AFM locals that began with merger of Los Angeles Locals 767 and 47 in 1953.[6]

Because AFM contracts with broadcasters were administered by the white locals, virtually all staff radio jobs and sponsored radio series broadcasts in the 1930s and early 1940s were held by white musicians or bands.

Sponsored radio programs, which featured a band or group of bands on a regular basis under the sponsorship of a corporate advertiser, were crucial in establishing the national reputations of white bands such as those of Benny Goodman and Tommy Dorsey. Prominent black bands, such as those of Duke Ellington, Count Basie, and Louis Armstrong, could be heard sporadically on late-night programs broadcast live from clubs and ballrooms, but it was not until 1946, when Nat King Cole's trio aired a weekly fifteen-minute sponsored broadcast on NBC, that the color bar in a prime time radio series was broken.[7]

White AFM locals also controlled the contracting of major hotel venues, which allowed some bands the luxury of engagements that lasted a week or two rather than the more typical "one-nighters." As Scott De-Veaux has documented, racially stratified access to these "location" jobs ensured that black bands toured more than white bands. They exhausted themselves in the process and faced the never-ending hassles Jim Crow posed for travelers—nonexistent hotel rooms, difficulties in procuring food, and lack of toilet facilities on the road. Musicians stayed in boarding houses or private homes in the black community, slept on the bus or in cars, ate take-out food (the all-American drive-in likely having its antecedents in rear take-out windows for "colored" customers), and usually went into the theater from the back. Successful bandleaders, such as Duke Ellington, sometimes booked private Pullman cars to avoid the worst of Jim Crow indignities in the South, but these strategies often generated added white hostility toward successful northern musicians.[8]

One of the greatest misconceptions about Jim Crow is that it was an exclusively Southern phenomenon. Until the 1960s, however, musicians could just as easily encounter back-door policies for black musicians, segregated dances, rules against fraternizing with white customers, segregated hotel bookings, and difficulty in restaurants in New York, California, Kansas City, Las Vegas, Boston, or Chicago.[9]

## Challenging Jim Crow in Jazz

The jazz press of the forties published many indignant articles and editorials about continuing Jim Crow policies in the music business that illustrate the development of a pro-integration discourse in the jazz world that mobilized the ideas of democracy, equality, and protest on its behalf.

It was not uncommon for commentators to invoke World War II as a means of emphasizing the contradiction between the United States' war effort for democracy abroad and continued Jim Crow at home. In November 1943, not long after race riots in Los Angeles, Detroit, and New York, *Metronome* published an angry editorial directed at Henry Schooler (owner of Hollywood's Aragon ballroom) that protested the banning of Negro orchestras in his establishments: "What a filthy action to take at this time, when American boys, by the literal million, are risking their lives in what they believe to be the defense of equal rights for all."[10]

In early 1946 *Down Beat* applauded the dismissal of charges against Cab Calloway after an incident at Kansas City's Pla-Mor ballroom. The editors, once again invoking the war, explained that "Calloway, accompanied by a colored friend, Felix Payne Jr., who had just returned from 18 months of service in the Indo-China theater, went to the Pla-Mor ballroom to visit Lionel Hampton, at the latter's express invitation." Calloway was pistol-whipped by an officer employed by the club—so severely that he required seven stitches in his scalp—and was then charged with three criminal offenses including disturbing the peace, public intoxication, and resisting an officer. The editorial continued by praising Hampton for refusing to play after the incident, thereby forfeiting his guarantee and percentage for the night and forcing the management to refund admissions charges to the patrons. *Down Beat* also congratulated the patrons themselves, many of whom had applauded Hampton's decision to end the night's performance.[11]

During the summer of 1946 *Down Beat* reported a number of racial incidents, at least two of them involving New York musicians. Sarah Vaughan and her fiancé, George Treadwell, were beaten up in New York near the West Third (now West Fourth) stop on the Sixth Avenue subway line. The two had been on their way home from the Cafe Society when they were assaulted by a gang of twenty-five young white men. In this case the police quickly arrested two leaders of the gang. The police were not so cooperative, however, when a cab driver refused to drive bassist Carleton Powell uptown. Powell insisted that the driver take him to a midtown police station, where, on June 12, 1946, he was severely beaten by police officers who claimed that the bassist had stabbed one of the officers with a knife. Powell and the Civil Rights Congress disputed this version of events, and the publicity surrounding the case generated much sympathy from fellow entertainers. A delegation consisting of writer Dashiell Hammett, bandleader Charlie Barnet, and actress Betty Garrett presented a petition from several hundred performers to the deputy police chief, explaining that denial of taxi service was a common problem in show business and that they expected police protection rather than brutality when faced with such refusal.[12]

In the same issue, *Down Beat* reported two other incidents under the headline "Jim Crow Stuff Still Spreading!" The first concerned Toby Butler, a white woman trumpeter who was detained in Georgia for touring with a black all-woman orchestra known as the Darlings of Rhythm.[13] She was released after Jesse Turner, the leader of the band, told Georgia authorities that Butler was her relative. The second incident involved the filming of the Charlie Barnet orchestra for the Monogram picture *Freddie Steps Out*. As was customary, the music was recorded before the band was filmed, and Al Killian and Paul Webster, both African American, were featured on a version of "Southland." On the day of the filming, however, Killian and Webster were not allowed to appear on camera, a decision made by Monogram business officials over the head of Barnet and producer Sam Katyman. In an editorial devoted to the matter, *Down Beat* attacked the film industry for its racial policies. Hollywood, it argued, "has done nothing to promote the type of morality so vital to the attainment of the ideals that distinguish our way of life, like, for example, demonstrating the ethical and constitutional axiom that all men are inherently equal."[14]

## Mixed Bands

In the early 1940s opportunities began to emerge for top African American musicians to work for white bands, often at substantially higher wages. Although Teddy Wilson's appearance with Benny Goodman's trio at the Congress Hotel in 1936 is often cited as the first widely publicized performance by a black performer with a white band, other bandleaders, including Fate Marable, Benny Carter, and Charlie Barnet have been mentioned as earlier examples of the mixed band. Indeed, it was not uncommon in early jazz for white musicians to play with black performers in black venues; controversy ensued primarily when the mixing occurred in prestigious white venues. Wilson's appearance with the Goodman trio—a group with whom he had previously recorded—was thought to be more acceptable than a performance with the big band. The trio (and later quartet with Lionel Hampton) appeared separately from the full band, but by the end of 1937 was a regular feature of Goodman's performances and broadcasts.

In 1938 Lionel Hampton became the first African American to appear with the full Goodman band despite the fact that since 1934 Goodman had employed several African Americans behind the scenes as arrangers and composers, including Fletcher Henderson, Jimmy Mundy, and Edgar Sampson. In the forties, Gene Krupa, Benny Goodman, Charlie Barnet, and Artie Shaw were among the bands that included prominent African American artists in their band, such as Billie Holiday, Roy Eldridge, Cootie Williams, Lena Horne, Sid Catlett, Frankie Newton, Charlie Christian, and Al Killian. The advent of integrated bands, however, was a mixed blessing for many black bands since they became subject to raids by higher-paying white bands.[15]

During this period, "mixed" usually meant what later would be called "tokenism"—for example, one or two African Americans playing in an otherwise all-white band.[16] While employing African American artists, many white bandleaders found they had much to learn about the pragmatics of Jim Crow, as Roy Eldridge's painful experiences on the road with Gene Krupa and Artie Shaw illustrate. In 1951 the trumpeter returned from a year in Europe and vowed to Leonard Feather that there would be "no more white bands for me."[17] Eldridge explained that, while working in California with Krupa in the early forties, he was seldom able to stay at the same hotel as the rest of the band and was often left to his own devices to locate accommodations, which were usually isolating distances away from his bandmates. Night after night hotel managers made flimsy excuses about why a room that had been reserved for him was unavailable.

Moreover, the venues at which they played were often just as problematic. In Norfolk, Virginia, he was handed a bucket of water rather than be allowed to use the washroom with the other band members. In addition, when he was performing a feature there with white singer Anita O'Day, authorities required that the two be on opposite sides of the stage on separate microphones. At the Hollywood Palladium, Eldridge described being under the watchful eye of the bouncer, who allowed him to sit at tables with celebrities, but intervened if he socialized with ordinary white patrons. Since Eldridge's features such as "Let Me Off Uptown" and "Rockin' Chair" were among the most popular in the band's repertory, Eldridge chafed at the contrast between how he was treated on stage and off: "Man, when you're on the stage you're great, but as soon as you come off, you're nothing."

After a while the pressures took a toll on Eldridge's nerves. While touring in California with Artie Shaw, he was barred from entering a ballroom as he arrived to go to work, despite that fact that his name was on the marquee. Although Shaw later made the doorman apologize and got him fired, Eldridge related that, in the aftermath of the altercation, he had been reduced to tears in the midst of the performance. After also being denied admission to a San Francisco auditorium where they were performing, Eldridge left the Shaw band despite the fact that he felt well treated by Artie and his band members. "It's not worth the glory, not worth the money, not worth anything," he concluded.[18]

A few weeks later Lena Horne begged to differ with Eldridge's pessimistic view of mixed bands and his ostensibly anti-integrationist conclusions. Horne assured *Down Beat* readers that Feather had probably caught Roy on a bad day and that "I hope others will not be influenced by his decision, if he really meant what he said, because we can't lick a problem by running away from it." Horne did not disagree with Eldridge's description of the kinds of treatment that African Americans experienced, but saw the indignities as part of what must be endured in the process of "breaking down age-old prejudices." She also praised the efforts of white bandleaders, including Charlie Barnet, Benny Goodman, Gene Krupa, Tommy Dorsey, and Red Norvo, whom she saw as "pioneers" in racial matters: "Many times when I was singing with Charlie Barnet I wanted to quit for the same reasons Roy mentions. I might have, too, had it not been for the wonderful support I always got in every way from Charlie and the boys in the band."[19]

Eldridge's comments evidently upset some *Down Beat* readers, for a month later Frank Holzfeind, manager of the Blue Note in Chicago, who was present at the original interview, assured readers that "Roy wasn't on any soap box" but had simply expressed his opinion "with the same emotion that he would had Leonard asked him whether we won or lost on the races." In an effort to downplay the impression that Eldridge might be a "crusader," Holzfeind explained that Roy's comments had been lifted from a perfectly "pleasant conversation with a friend." *Down Beat* readers were much more comfortable with Lena Horne's position on mixed bands, but Eldridge's comments and readers' ambivalent reactions foreshadowed more intense debates over integration in the musical community of the early sixties.[20]

## Mixed Audiences

Diversifying the membership of bands was only one dimension of the Jim Crow problem in jazz since many mixed bands continued to play for segregated audiences. If mainstream opinion in the jazz world by the mid-forties held that the move toward mixed bands was a good thing, the politically militant wing began to hold bandleaders accountable for accepting contracts at segregated performance venues. In 1947 Norman Granz, founder of Jazz at the Philharmonic (JATP), sent a plea to thirty bandleaders including Gene Krupa, Cab Calloway, Woody Herman, Artie Shaw, Billy Eckstine, Sammy Kaye, Jimmy Dorsey, Duke Ellington, and Count Basie, asking them to include an antidiscrimination clause in their contracts. Granz offered the JATP clause as an example: "It is the essence of this agreement that there is to be no discrimination whatever in the sale of tickets and that there is to be no segregation of white people from Negroes. In the event of any violation of either of these provisions by you, the management of the hall or anyone else, Mr. Granz has the privilege of refusing to give the concert, in which case you will forfeit one-half of the contract price to him."[21]

Paul Robeson's use of such a clause and a similar campaign in the theater industry were among Granz's models. Among those who offered enthusiastic support for the idea were Count Basie, Charlie Barnet, Coleman Hawkins, and Artie Shaw.[22]

Robeson's prestige cannot be overestimated as an inspiration to many in the entertainment industry. His highly successful appearance as Othello on Broadway in 1943 and 1944 was viewed as a watershed event in the entertainment world, and many jazz musicians took notice, including Dizzy Gillespie, who attended opening night. For the first time a black man had been cast in a major production of what was considered one of the greatest roles in theater. When Communist Party member Ben Davis Jr. ran for a seat on the New York City Council in late 1943, Robeson performed a scene from *Othello* at a victory rally organized by Teddy Wilson. Other performers participating in this all-star show were Coleman Hawkins, Billie Holiday, Pearl Primus, Hazel Scott, Mary Lou Williams, and Ella Fitzgerald. Not long after, twelve thousand people turned out for a forty-sixth birthday celebration for Robeson on April 16, 1944, at the armory at Thirty-fourth Street and Park Avenue in New York. Among the performers were Count Basie, Duke Ellington, and Mary Lou Williams.

As one of the most prominent voices in the forties, Robeson also directed the attention of mainstream civil rights leaders to African struggles against colonialism, a topic that chapter 4 deals with more fully.[23]

Like Robeson, Granz viewed an antidiscrimination clause as part of a long-term effort to force reluctant club owners and theater managers to change their Jim Crow policies. Granz had achieved some success in Los Angeles through his Sunday jam sessions at Hollywood clubs, at which he insisted there be no segregated seating plans or exclusion on the basis of color. Once managers realized that nonrestrictive policies could actually generate additional business, several clubs stopped excluding African Americans. Granz's first major Jazz at the Philharmonic concert was held in 1944 as a benefit for twenty-one Mexican youths who had been convicted on various charges stemming from the "zoot suit" riots of 1943. Its tremendous success led to a series of eighteen concerts held at the Philharmonic Auditorium in Los Angeles.[24]

In addition, JATP coupled its concert tours (which included many of the best-known musicians in jazz, including Coleman Hawkins, Helen Humes, Buck Clayton, Flip Phillips, and Buddy Rich) with an explicitly activist stance against racial discrimination. Other benefit concerts were done for the Fair Employment Practices Commission (FEPC) and for organizations working for antilynching legislation. Granz also started a series of JATP fan clubs, issuing charters only to those groups that opened membership to persons of all races, nationalities, and religions.[25]

By the early 1950s a sizeable portion of the jazz world clearly felt that it was imperative for jazz musicians on both sides of the color line to oppose segregation in jazz. A discourse linking jazz and integration became an article of faith for many musicians and in the process coupled jazz with a moral stance and politics that shared the goals of the emerging mainstream civil rights movement. This idealized understanding of music as a potential space for true democracy and equality, however, was often undercut by the day-to-day economic realities of the music business.

## The American Federation of Musicians

Most jazz instrumentalists who recorded and toured in the 1950s and 1960s were members of the American Federation of Musicians (AFM) despite the fact that the union had a reputation of doing little for jazz musicians.[26] They joined because they had to in order to perform in major jazz venues and to record their music. From the 1940s through the 1960s, when James Petrillo and Herman Kenin served as president, the AFM had considerable clout. The AFM had licensing agreements with broadcasters, recording companies, clubs, booking agents, and the film industry, which required affiliated employers to use union members and observe AFM minimum pay scale guidelines and work rules regarding overtime, transportation, and cartage.[27]

Individual locals set pay scales for club dates and recording sessions within their jurisdictions. In order to remain signatories in good standing, employers, in addition to observing the minimum scale and work rules, were required to pay a percentage of the payroll to various union funds supporting pensions, disability benefits, and performance work for un- employed musicians.[28] A typical nightclub gig in New York in the early 1950s required four sets of forty minutes, with twenty-minute intermis- sions between sets. In 1951 the scale for a sideman working in a New York club was $125 per week (six days of work) for four sets a night.[29] Leaders were paid double scale. The minimum for single-night engagements was $20 for the first four hours.[30] By this standard, an extremely busy band member who worked forty to fifty weeks a year could earn an annual income of $5,000 to $6,250 in 1951, substantially above the 1950 median white family income of $3,445.[31] Most jazz musicians worked substantially less than this. A musician who worked between ten and thirty weeks a year could expect to earn from $1,250 to $3,750. In Los Angeles the scale for sidemen on full-time jobs in 1951 ranged from $85 to $130 per week.[32]

Standard AFM recording session agreements set a minimum scale for three hours and overtime thereafter. In 1955 New York's Local 802 re- quired a minimum of $42 per three-hour session, a rate that increased to $51.50 per session in 1960.[33] Since a twelve-inch LP generally required three sessions (or two sessions plus overtime), a musician in 1960 might expect to earn approximately $150 for playing as a sideman on an album. Many jazz recordings, however, were made in New Jersey (for Prestige and Blue Note), whose AFM locals likely set standards less favorable than those of Local 802. Recording companies were supposed to pay the local, and after collecting its share for union funds, the union was supposed to pay the musician. In practice, the recording companies sometimes paid the musicians directly (at times offering the excuse that the musician in question was leaving town). As long as the union received its percentages for funds and taxes, the AFM did not object.[34]

The union enforced its terms by sending delegates to club dates and recording sessions to spot-check membership cards and observe working conditions. Jazz sessions and club dates were never the union's top priority, since much more revenue was at stake in contracts for television and radio broadcasts, jingles, and Broadway theatrical productions. The names of many well-known jazz musicians nevertheless appear in the minutes of the trial and executive boards of Local 802, sometimes for infractions discovered by the union delegate or sergeant at arms and sometimes with regard to the grievances they filed against clubs, bandleaders, or recording companies who failed to pay. The most common violations for musicians included playing for less than scale, failing to file contracts with the union, hiring nonunion musicians as sidemen, failing to deposit a transfer when relocating from one union jurisdiction to another, and working on one's day off.

The Trial Board of Local 802, which in the mid-1950s had eight members, functioned like a court that ruled on cases brought before it. For example, *B. Schwarz vs. Horace Silver* was filed in early 1955 by the sergeant at arms (B. Schwarz), after he discovered that bassist Doug Watkins was working with Silver's band in New York on a delinquent card from Detroit's Local 5. Silver and Watkins pleaded guilty; Silver received a reprimand, but Watkins was fined $10.[35] Thad Jones also ran afoul of the sergeant at arms and was brought before the Trial Board for having failed to deposit a transfer from Local 5 while playing in New York, and for playing Birdland on his day off. Other musicians who were pursued in the mid-1950s over failure to deposit transfers include Elvin Jones, Philly Joe Jones, Red Garland, Clifford Brown, Melba Liston, Red Mitchell, and Hampton Hawes, all members of prominent jazz groups.[36]

Although the Trial Board seems to have gone after prominent African American musicians for transfer violations disproportionately, it also served as the body before which a musician could file grievances against bandleaders and club owners. In May 1955 Idrees Sulieman filed charges with the union against Buddy Rich after the drummer had reneged on a promise to hire him. Sulieman dropped the charges after Rich agreed to hire him as promised. Doc Cheatham, Maurio Bauzá and recording delegate Frank Baristo filed charges against Gil Fuller after he failed to pay them for a recording session he had told them was for Mercury Records. Fuller had booked the studio himself and slipped out the back with the tapes without paying. For this and for bouncing checks to the union, Fuller was expelled from the organization.[37]

In addition, Herbie Mann and Michael Babatunde Olatunji filed charges against promoter Don Friedman for failure to pay wages owed, Gil Evans made a nonpayment claim against Joe Termini of the Jazz Gallery, and Count Basie and Louis Prima were both charged with failing to pay scale to sidemen on club dates.[38] Clubs who failed to pay their percentages to the union's trust or welfare funds found themselves named on the National Defaulters or Unfair Lists published monthly in the *International Musician* until they paid in full. The Jazz Gallery, Eddie Condon's, and Basin St. East were among those in repeated violation, and Roulette Records had its recording license revoked for failing to pay musicians.

The paper trail provided by union records provides some insight into the kinds of economic issues that caused conflict for the working musician of the 1950s and 1960s, as well as how musicians turned to the union to redress grievances pertaining to payment for performance. The generally low regard for Local 802 no doubt reflected its lack of interest and effectiveness in improving conditions and wages for the improvising musician. As Orrin Keepnews recalled, the union had a reputation of "being for the union" first and foremost. It is important to remember that, although Local 802 was integrated in terms of membership, the highest-paying performance work in New York (broadcast, Broadway theater, and studio work) went to white musicians since the contractors were usually white. Ultimately Local 802 did not take action on behalf of African American musicians who sought to cross the racial barrier in studio work. It took a systematic campaign on the part of the National Urban League, for example, to open the doors of NBC TV to trumpeter Clark Terry.

In the late 1950s AFM contracts required that each network (NBC, ABC, CBS) maintain a staff of approximately 175 musicians. Although CBS and ABC employed a handful of African American musicians, NBC remained all white. The National Urban League (NUL) researched the situation, asked NBC to explain why there were no African American musicians on staff, and was told that there were not enough black musicians qualified to play on television. In 1958 the organization developed and circulated a questionnaire that asked professional musicians of stature to recommend personnel they thought would be qualified to serve as staff musicians at NBC. Clark Terry's name was among those most frequently mentioned by those polled, and he credits the National Urban League, not the AFM, with enabling him to work as a staff musician at NBC in 1959.[39]

Getting hired was one thing; being welcomed another. Terry recalls that "it felt strange being a token. . . . I knew I had to walk the straight and narrow" because the network would be looking for any infraction. In 1962 the NUL pressured NBC to hire a second African American, so Terry was asked to recommend the "right" kind of trumpet player: "He had to be married. He had to have a family. He had to be a lead trumpet player. He had to be a soloist. He had to be beyond reproach. He had to be properly dressed. He had to be one that got along with everybody. He just had to be everything."[40]

Terry recommended Snooky Young, who took leave from the Count Basie band to accept the position, and the two of them played for the *Johnny Carson Show* in Skitch Henderson's band. Six months later Aaron Vee, the contractor who had hired them both, approached Terry to say that they were going to have to let Snooky Young go.[41] Vee claimed that Young did not get along well with Skitch Henderson, but Terry felt that this was "the biggest lie ever told" and that they simply wanted to return to the racial status quo now that the "heat was off" from the Urban League: "The two of us came to work on time. We'd sit in our chairs fifteen, twenty minutes ahead of time. When it was time to hit we were ready. We had cologne and stuff. We were immaculately dressed. There were creases in our clothes, shoes shined, clean shirts, hair combed, shaven, which is a lot more than you could say of the other guys. So I knew he was just using this as an opportunity to go back to normal."[42]

When Terry told the contractor he could have his all-white orchestra again and walked out, Aaron Vee begged him to return. Terry recalls advocating strongly on behalf of Snooky Young by threatening to take the story to *Ebony* magazine unless Young remained with the orchestra: "Just remember, Aaron, Snooky and I both used to not know you and we both have taken offense but good. Matter of fact I'd be delighted to just give you back what you had together and not be a bother. But first of all, I want you to know that Bob Johnson, my very dear friend Bob Johnson, is one of the chief writers for Johnson publications. He would be delighted to have this story."[43]

Terry prevailed but did not tell Snooky Young about the incident until years later. It took persistence, agitation, and threats to persuade NBC to change its hiring policies for staff musicians. As Terry's example illustrates, the AFM, including its integrated locals, did not play a leading role in challenging long-standing contracting practices that negatively impacted its African American members, even though some union officials were sympathetic.[44] Rather, political organizations affiliated with the civil rights movement, such as the National Urban League and the Congress of Racial Equality (CORE) took the lead in making fair employment demands on behalf of musicians.

## Desegregating Los Angeles

The pivotal challenge to the AFM's policy of segregated unions took place in Los Angeles in the early 1950s. Prior to this campaign New York's Local 802 and Detroit's Local 5 were the only integrated locals in the American Federation of Musicians. The AFM's practice of separate locals dated to its founding in 1896, when the Great Western Union (later Local 197) was chartered in St. Louis.[45] Chicago's Local 208, the largest and best-known African American local was formed in 1902, after Local 10 denied membership to black musicians. At least nine major international unions explicitly prohibited Negro membership, but the American Federation of Musicians was among five AFL unions that admitted black members in auxiliary locals. In 1943 there were 673 AFM locals, of which 631 were exclusively white, 32 black, 8 who admitted African Americans in subsidiary groups, and 2 with integrated memberships.[46]

The campaign for desegregating Los Angeles locals 767 and 47, which took three years to complete and was conducted with little support from the national organization, illustrates the issues at stake in union desegregation. Los Angeles musicians were more supportive of integration than musicians in many other cities, in part because members of Local 767 (the African American local) perceived a significant potential for expanded work opportunities through Local 47 (the white local). Los Angeles, after all, was the center of the film industry and a center for network television as well. In the early 1950s *Billboard* reported soaring revenues earned by Local 47 members from television and film. In 1955 the seven major

Hollywood film studios paid $2.768 million to 303 contracted musicians, or an average of $9,135 per musician. This is nearly twice the 1955 median white family income ($4,613) and three and a half times the median black family income.[47]

Building upon existing professional relationships between black and white musicians, many of whom had played together in clubs along Los Angeles's Central Avenue, some members of 767 (the black local) and 47 (the white local) began to meet informally to discuss the possibility of merging the two unions. According to Britt Woodman and Buddy Collette, Charles Mingus played a prominent role in raising the issue among Local 767 musicians. Mingus and Woodman had learned from white musicians what they had long suspected: Members of Local 47 were paid more for work at the same clubs than members of Local 767 and had a six-day work week instead of Local 767's seven-day week. They also confirmed that white contractors who controlled studio work in the motion picture industry discriminated against African American musicians, often using as an excuse their (untrue) presumption that black musicians could not read music. Since Local 47 also controlled the hiring of the major theaters in Los Angeles, such as the Million Dollar Theatre, Local 767 members had little opportunity to compete for the best jobs in Los Angeles.[48]

Occasionally a contractor from Local 47 would call a 767 member, as drummer Lee Young was in 1940 when he played a one-time job on the *Camel Caravan,* an NBC radio broadcast. "When it was over, the guys were applauding, and the leader told me that I had the job for thirteen weeks."[49] However, when Young showed up for work the following week, the contractor reneged on the offer. According to Art Farmer, if an African American musician was offered a job in a venue controlled by Local 47, like Billy Berg's or the Swing Club, a "special dispensation" had to be procured. Local 767, on the other hand, had no objection to Local 47 members who worked in Central Avenue clubs.[50]

In addition, other circumstances affecting Local 767 contributed to an interest in amalgamation. After a two-year slump in the dance band business, which affected the African American local more deeply than the white, Local 767 was in a weakened financial position and had difficulty attracting new members, who saw little benefit in joining the union. Since Local 767 could not provide the same wage scales, protection, and benefits as Local 47, many younger musicians thought it was better to be nonunion than a member of the segregated local. The prospect of joining Local 47 was attractive to them because they felt that their chances of securing high-paying jobs in the motion picture industry and television "would be no worse, and probably would be better" after amalgamation. The symbolic aspect of amalgamation was also an important factor in the tilt toward integration. As *Down Beat* correspondent Charles Emge reported, "Negro musicians here feel that their best interests are not served by the existence of a separate union group, which is in itself a symbol of the segregation principle to which all Negroes and many whites object."[51]

Many musicians in Local 767 were nevertheless skeptical that amalgamation would result in improved opportunities and conditions for black musicians. Union officials, including President Leo Davis, stood to lose their jobs and adamantly opposed the merger. Some expressed concern that they would be a minority with inadequate representation in the combined local and were reluctant to give proceeds from the sale of the Local 767 union hall to Local 47. Others did not want to lose the sense of community and camaraderie that had grown up around the union hall. Big Jay McNeely, who felt that in the end the merger offered no benefit, remembers Local 767 fondly: "We had our own local, we had our own money, we owned the building. If I was on the road traveling and got into trouble, they sent me money.... We'd probably be better off now with that local, you see."[52] Nevertheless, the dominant perspective at this pre–*Brown v. Board of Education* moment held that, with two separate unions, Local 767 would always be getting the leftovers rather than a full piece of the action.[53]

An outgrowth of the meetings between the pro-merger members of both locals was an interracial Community Symphony Orchestra that played Monday-night concerts at Humanist Hall (Twenty-third and Union) to raise money and generate publicity for the amalgamation campaign. Buddy Collette, Britt Woodman, and Red Callender were among the African American musicians who participated. Appearances with the orchestra led to Collette's becoming the "Jackie Robinson" of the television networks after Jerry Fielding heard him play at Humanist Hall and hired him for Groucho Marx's television show *You Bet Your Life* in 1950.[54]

Fielding became a prominent supporter of the amalgamation effort in Local 47 and began hiring other black musicians for television programs, including Red Callender and Gerald Wiggins. The move generated a great deal of hate mail to NBC in 1952, and Fielding, whose real name was Feldman, soon found himself subpoenaed to appear before the House Un-American Activities Committee despite the fact that he was not a Communist. Groucho Marx then dropped him. Several other musicians working for amalgamation were also subject to rumors of Communist influence, including William Douglass and Buddy Collette.[55]

The success of the Community Symphony Orchestra on Monday nights inspired the inauguration of Sunday-afternoon jazz concerts and jam sessions at Humanist Hall. Josephine Baker, Harry "Sweets" Edison, and Nat King Cole were among the performers who appeared and spoke before large audiences on behalf of merging the two unions. The musicians still needed a strategy to move the issue within the union bureaucracies. During the summer of 1951 they began circulating a petition among members of Locals 767 and 47, formally requesting that the leadership of both locals undertake the necessary steps to merge the unions. Members of Local 767 also decided to run a slate of pro-amalgamation candidates for union office, including Benny Carter for president. At a special membership meeting on the amalgamation question held in November 1951, the membership of Local 767 went on record as favoring the merger.[56]

The election, also held in November, resulted in a considerable victory for the pro-merger slate. Although Leo Davis, who opposed the amalgamation, defeated Benny Carter for the presidency, the merger forces won heavily in the trustee and director positions. Benny Carter and Marl Young became trustees, John Anderson and Russell McDavid were elected directors, and Bill Douglass won the vice presidency. Since the board of directors comprised four officers, three trustees, and two directors, the pro-merger group had won a five-to-four majority. Shortly thereafter, members of Local 767 approved a resolution calling for immediate action on the issue of amalgamation and elected a committee to meet with officials of Local 47, including Benny Carter (who chaired the committee), Marl Young, Leo Davis, Paul Howard, Harvey Brooks, Estelle Edson, and Buddy Collette.[57]

The leadership of Local 47 had indicated informally that it would not oppose the amalgamation, but by May 1952 snags over initiation fees, seniority, and death benefits emerged during negotiations. Local 47 initially wanted each member of Local 767 to pay a $100 initiation fee, the same as it charged new members and transfers. Local 767 members, who had already paid a $25 initiation fee as members of the segregated local, did not believe they should be charged the same fee as transfers from distant locals, especially since most of them would be continuing in jobs they already had rather than competing for new jobs with Local 47 members. Local 767 proposed that its current assets be transferred to Local 47 in lieu of initiation fees.[58]

After thirty years of union membership, musicians became eligible for life memberships requiring them to pay no further dues, so seniority also became an issue. Older musicians, in particular, wanted to make sure that their years of membership in Local 767 would be counted toward life membership in Local 47. Marl Young proposed that the date of 767 enrollment count as the date of enrollment in Local 47 for purposes of life membership.

Another age-related concern was the death benefit. In both locals, all members who were over forty when first joining the union were ineligible for the death benefit—$400 in Local 767 and $1,000 in Local 47. Negotiators for Local 47 did not want to cover Local 767 members who were over forty at the time of amalgamation. After determining that two-thirds of the Local 767 membership was under forty, Young proposed that those over forty continue to be covered at the old rate of $400—to be financed from the sale of Local 767's assets and that those under forty be eligible for the $1,000 benefit in Local 47. According to Marl Young, the leadership of Local 47 did not believe these issues could be worked out, but the negotiating committee kept insisting that the proposal be put to a vote of the Local 47 membership. Meanwhile, Local 47 members who favored the merger, including George Kast, Gail Robinson, Joe Eger, and Seymour Shelkow, began a campaign to convince Local 47 members of the advantages of amalgamation.[59]

When difficulties first emerged in the late spring of 1952, Benny Carter placed a positive spin on the negotiations by emphasizing that the discussions with the Local 47 board members had been "not only friendly but completely cooperative" and that "the main thing is to eliminate the principle of segregation," something on which the leaderships of both unions were in agreement. Later in the summer, when Local 47's board of directors sent a counterproposal to Local 767 that did not permit conversion of life membership in 767 to life membership in Local 47, made no provision for death benefits for life members, asked for a $51 initiation fee from all 767 members, and refused to accept Local 767's assets in lieu of initiation fees (because they claimed the move would make them liable to legal suits from 767's members), Carter's tone became more aggressive:

> Inasmuch as we have offered to turn over the assets of Local 767 (close to $20,000), which will virtually cover the dollar value of new initiation fees, and our members, upon affiliation, will immediately begin paying the same dues and taxes on engagements as all other Local 47 members, there can be no sound basis for this stand. If the officials of Local 47 are sincere in their statements to the effect that they honestly favor the elimination of the present racially segregated union for musicians here, they will submit our proposal to their own membership by means of the usual procedure—a special or general meeting called for this purpose.[60]

Writing in his dual capacity as a member of both the official committee of Local 767 charged with negotiating the merger and the more informal Committee for Amalgamation comprising members of both locals, Carter emphasized a series of points for *Down Beat* readers that indicate some of the deeper reservations the integration forces faced within Local 47. Carter denied that those who favored amalgamation were trying to force people to "change the patterns of their social or professional lives" or that Negro musicians expected or desired any "special representation" within Local 47: "A Negro musician would have the same right—but no more right—to become a candidate for office as any other member. He could expect to receive the support in an election of part—not necessarily all—of his fellow Negro members. He would receive the support—if he warranted it—of his white fellow-union members."[61]

Assuaging fears that Negro musicians would immediately move in on "fields of employment in which some of our Local 767 members feel they do not now have equal opportunity" (i.e., lucrative jobs in film and TV), Carter went so far as to say that the members of the Committee for Amalgamation did not expect that a racially integrated union would change access to these jobs immediately. "Our sole aim," he emphasized, "is the elimination of segregation along racial lines from the structure of our own union organization, because we believe that such a move will create a stronger union of greater benefit to all of its members—white and Negro."[62]

Several points of anxiety have recurred in debates over affirmative action (and related strategies to redress racial imbalances) both during and after the civil rights movement: how to achieve democratic representation in mixed organizations in which African Americans are far outnumbered; white fears that people of color were asking for special privileges rather than a level playing field; white feeling that black civil rights organizations wanted to move too fast in their demands for racial equality; and the transfer of racial anxiety onto ostensibly financial (or other administrative) concerns.

In the end, the Local 47 membership voted for amalgamation in December 1952 and accepted the terms of Local 767's proposal.[63] The only remaining hurdle was to get the approval of the International Executive Board (IEB) of the national AFM, which had been following the merger negotiations closely. John te Groen from Local 47 and Marl Young from Local 767 went to New York to meet with James C. Petrillo about the merger proposal. Charles Bagley, a member of the IEB and vice president of Local 47, objected to the merger agreement, claiming that the only way to achieve integration under union rules would be for Local 767 to completely dissolve. Young discovered that he had not seen the ongoing correspondence between the white union, the black union, and the national body over the terms of the merger. Sensing that Bagley and te Groen were trying to undermine the merger, Young called George Kast, a leader of the integration forces within Local 47, who persuaded Local 47 members to protest the subterfuge. Meanwhile, Petrillo and the national organization affirmed the legality of the terms of the merger under AFM bylaws. When the merger finally went into effect on April 1, 1953, Los Angeles became the first victory in a much longer process of desegregating the AFM; it became something like the *Brown v. Board of Education* case of the music world.[64]

Yet, like *Brown v. Board of Education,* it was one thing to establish the principle of desegregation and quite another to achieve its hoped-for benefits. Did black musicians find that opportunities in film and studio work increased after the amalgamation of the unions? Solid statistics are hard to come by, but it seems that a few prominent African American musicians found increased opportunities in the studios and films, but most jazz musicians continued to find the studios a closed shop. White contractors remained the principal gatekeepers to triple-scale session work in the film and recording industries, and most of them continued to rely on their own particular network of acquaintances. Many musicians told Lowell Dickerson that they felt that amalgamation did little for the majority of African American musicians in Los Angeles.[65] Indeed, it has remained a common complaint among African American jazz musicians nationwide that contracting practices for elite recording, film, and Broadway jobs have tended to favor white union members.[66]

Nevertheless, several of the African American musicians who had been prominent in the struggle for amalgamation were among those who found some success in the studios. Benny Carter, who was already known as a film composer and arranger due to his work on *Stormy Weather* in 1943, wrote for eight films between 1951 and 1957, including *An American in Paris* (1951), *The Snows of Kilimanjaro* (1951), and *The Sun Also Rises* (1957). Buddy Collette, who continued as a member of the band for Groucho Marx's television show, also worked heavily as a studio musician during the 1960s and 1970s; he played with Frank Sinatra and was a staff musician for the Danny Kaye, Carol Burnett, and Flip Wilson television shows. It is difficult to track the extent of jazz musicians who worked in studios in the 1950s and 1960s since industry regulations did not require listing them on album credits until the early 1970s (and then only for rhythm sections).[67]

Buddy Collette maintained an active performing career as a jazz musician and a studio musician: "It was like living in two worlds. There were the so-called jazz guys, who only did the clubs on a Friday or Saturday night, or a jam session, and they'd be trying to borrow a couple bucks from you. Then I'd meet this other group of people—studio players—and they were talking about building and selling homes. Right away you'd get a feeling: 'Now this is more inviting. I could stay in LA and wouldn't have to go out on the road.' "[68]

Although work in the nightclubs and concert halls carried more prestige among jazz aficionados (and produced the recognized innovators in the tradition), the more anonymous world of the studio offered one of the best paths to financial security.

## Desegregating the National Organization

The desegregation of the American Federation of Musicians nationally is closely tied to the integration of the San Francisco and Chicago locals. In December 1956, not long after the Supreme Court decision that ordered the desegregation of Alabama buses in the wake of the Montgomery bus boycott, San Francisco's Local 6 (the white local) voted against merging with Local 669 (the black local). The national AFM, which had avoided an unequivocal position on desegregation, now faced a situation in which a white local was explicitly blocking a request for amalgamation from the African American local. In 1945 Local 669 had been granted an independent charter as a result of Petrillo's decision to end subsidiary status. In 1956 it had 350 members (Local 6 had more than 4,000), the majority of whom were African American but who included Chinese, Portuguese, Japanese, and a few white members as well.[69] The amalgamation of locals 669 and 6, which took more than four years to accomplish, ultimately required a change of leadership in the national organization, the threat of a suit by the state of California, and the union's intervention in the negotiating process.[70]

The victorious Los Angeles musicians took the lead in raising the issue of desegregating the AFM at the national level. In early 1957 they formed the Musicians Committee for Integration with Marl Young as its chairman. The membership abounded with high-profile artists, including Nat Cole, Benny Carter, Earl Bostic, Wild Bill Davis, Ernie Freeman, Johnny Otis, John Collins, Joe Wilson, Eddie Beal, Rozelle Gayle, Gerald Wiggins, Buddy Collette, Bill Douglass, Barney Bigard, and Red Callender. In June 1957 they introduced a resolution to the national convention in Denver encouraging AFM locals to integrate on their own initiative but empowering the International Executive Board of the AFM to order integration. Petrillo and the national convention sidestepped the resolution by referring it for study to the office of the president, a move widely regarded as a parliamentary maneuver to delay movement on the question indefinitely.

At the same meeting an opposing petition signed by sixty black delegates, representing twenty-eight Negro locals (a majority), took the position that integration should not be forced on the locals. The first signature on the counterpetition was Harry Gray, president of Chicago's influential Local 208. The Chicago local did not see major advantages in merging with Local 10 since it already controlled a sizeable number of venues in its own right and had established minimum scales equivalent to those in Local 10. African American musicians were nevertheless frozen out of the same types of employment as they were in New York, premium hotel venues, television and radio, and studio work.[71] Petrillo's support for those opposed to "forced integration" reflected his dual status as president of the AFM and Chicago's Local 10. As president of Local 10, a position he had held since 1922, Petrillo had formed a working relationship with Harry

Gray, president of Local 208, with whom he had an understanding regarding the division of musical turf in Chicago.

The Musicians Committee for Integration was incensed by Petrillo's stance at the 1957 convention, despite the fact that many African American locals supported it. In the fall they requested that Petrillo make a public statement of support for ending membership restrictions based on race. The committee also asked him to inform all of the locals that, effective November 1, 1957, (1) membership requirements based on "race, creed, color, or national origin" would be invalid; (2) traveling musicians could deposit their credentials in the local of their choice in jurisdictions with two locals; (3) members who moved into a jurisdiction with two locals would be able to join the local of their choice; and (4) members who lived in a jurisdiction with two locals could elect to transfer their membership to the other local by paying the existing admission fee without taking a competency exam. After receiving no response from the president, the committee notified Petrillo in December that they intended to bring the issue of integration before George Meany, president of the AFL-CIO.[72] When asked whether he feared Petrillo's wrath, Marl Young replied, "Frankly, I don't care . . . and I just don't give a damn. . . . We're the ones who're mad; because we're fed up to the teeth with getting the runaround from him. I believe that Meany will show more interest in us. If *he* doesn't, then we're going to court."[73]

At the time there was much anti-Petrillo sentiment in Local 47 not only over the issue of segregated locals but also with respect to the mandatory five percent of earnings deducted from payments to studio musicians that the AFM directed to the Musicians Performance Trust Fund (MPTF). The MPTF, the fruit of Petrillo's victory in the aftermath of the recording ban between 1942 and 1944, funded performance jobs for unemployed union members displaced by the use of recorded music. Studio musicians, an elite group within the AFM, resented the reduction in their earnings caused by this tax and wanted the five percent returned to the musicians who earned it. A group led by Local 47's Cecil Read (and including Marl Young) had actively opposed Petrillo's position on the MPTF since 1956. Read's group ultimately sued the AFM over this issue, formed a separate union known as the Musicians Guild of America (MGA), and won bargaining rights in a National Labor Relations Board (NLRB) election in 1958. In advocating for its position, the MGA pointed not only to the MPTF but also to the continuing legacy of Jim Crow in the AFM. The MGA rejoined the AFM in 1960.[74]

In 1958, caught amid the conflict over the integration of locals and legal battles over the MTPF, James Petrillo resigned as president of the AFM. The new president, Herman Kenin, also stalled on union integration until 1959, when the California attorney general threatened to file suit over the integration of the San Francisco unions. The segregated locals in San Francisco had long been a source of embarrassment. When subsequent merger negotiations between the boards of the two locals came to a standstill over issues of representation and finances, Kenin sent in a committee of three negotiators, including William Harris, AFM international vice president; Stanley Ballard, international secretary, and George Clancy, international treasurer. Over a four-day period in February 1960 they hammered out an agreement that guaranteed Local 669 three representatives in the administration of the amalgamated local—a coordinator to the president, a coordinator to the secretary, and a member of the executive board. Local 6 also absorbed the assets of Local 669. Once again issues of representation and finances dominated in negotiations over amalgamation.[75]

In 1960 an AFL-CIO directive that required its member unions to desegregate created additional pressure on the AFM president to put an end to segregated locals. Although Kenin was said to be more supportive of integration than his predecessor, he was also reluctant to go toe to toe with Petrillo, now president of Chicago's Local 10. A younger generation of Local 208 members now agitated for the integration of Local 10 and viewed Harry Gray's understanding with Petrillo as not in their best interests.[76]

## Creating Chicago's Local 10-208

Not until James Petrillo was defeated by Bernard Richards for the presidency of Chicago's Local 10 in 1963 and a campaign by CORE urged desegregation did Kenin ultimately press Local 10 to merge with Local 208. Local 208's representatives Harry Gray and William Everett Samuels were not willing to agree to a merger plan that did not guarantee Local 208 members representation on the governing bodies of the merged union. Although Los Angeles Local 767 had been willing to risk a lack of representation on Local 47's executive board in the interests of accomplishing integration, Local 208 was not. Since Bernard Richards, president of Local 10, refused to accept anything more than consolidated membership, Local 208's insistence on representation led to a protracted struggle.

When the unions failed to merge in March 1964 as Kenin ordered, he and the International Executive Board proposed their own terms for a merger that was to begin immediately and be completed by January 1966. Kenin's proposal gave Local 208 something akin to proportional representation on the leadership bodies of the new Local 10-208. Until January 1966 a merged local 10-208 would be governed by a joint executive board with the understanding that Local 208 members would not serve after that time. Members of Local 208 would instead elect new representatives in 1965 to ten (out of twenty-six) leadership posts on various governing bodies and committees in the merged union. This number was less than Local 208 had requested, but its members ratified the terms of the merger in May 1964.

Local 10, however, voted against the plan despite considerable pressure from Kenin and the AFM national convention. Appealing to a classic white resentment discourse, Richards and his supporters complained that setting aside board positions for Local 208 members constituted reverse discrimination. Their additional claim that, under Local 10's merger proposal, African American musicians, who would be a numerical minority in the merged organization, would likely be denied representation on leadership bodies and thus disenfranchised, was discounted. Kenin responded by placing Local 10 in legal trusteeship and sending a representative to force the implementation of the plan.

When Local 10-208 formally merged in January 1966, more than twenty segregated locals still remained in the American Federation of Musicians, but the tide had turned. By the early 1970s the AFM imposed integration on unions that were reluctant to merge, including Philadelphia's Local 274, the second largest African American AFM local. That local, which already had a more integrated membership than the white local, opposed a merger with Local 77. As a result, the national AFM cancelled Local 274's charter. This move failed to lead to a substantial increase in black membership in Local 77, however, because many African American musicians simply left the union entirely.

By the early 1970s many African Americans had become skeptical of the idea that integration was the answer to the problems of racial inequality. As is apparent in the case of the American Federation of Musicians, integrating with white organizations often meant becoming a numerical minority, which in turn led to forfeiting the self-determination and self-governance that had existed in the segregated locals. Affirmative action policies, which emerged from the political practice of civil rights organizations, were meant to redress this imbalance by insisting on guaranteed levels of representation. This tension between a desire for equal access to mainstream institutional organizations and the desire for self-determination remains a powerful factor in African American relationships to the political ideologies of black nationalism and liberalism, as Michael Dawson's work underscores.[77] To the extent that participation in integrated organizations leads to a lack of African American representation in leadership positions and governance, black nationalist political strategies will always remain an attractive alternative.

## The Civil Rights Movement and a Politics of Musicianship

About the time that musicians in Los Angeles began to discuss the integration of locals 767 and 47, Thurgood Marshall presented the first of the five school integration cases (from Kansas, Virginia, South Carolina, Delaware, and the District of Columbia) that would be argued collectively before the Supreme Court under the name of *Brown v. Board of Education of Topeka.* After defeats in all five cases in 1951 and 1952, the first arguments before the Supreme Court were heard in December 1952. Failing to reach a decision, the justices announced that they would hear further arguments in December 1953. In the meantime, Chief Justice Fred M. Vinson died unexpectedly of a heart attack, and President Eisenhower named Earl Warren, then governor of California, to the post.[78]

On May 17, 1954, the Supreme Court ruled unanimously that "in the field of public education the doctrine of 'separate but equal' has no place." Although a ruling on the constitutionality of school segregation had been much anticipated, the public was quite unprepared for a unanimous decision one way or the other. In the early months of 1954, Chief Justice Earl Warren had made it his mission to persuade the four initial holdouts— Justices Clark, Frankfurter, Jackson, and Reed—that a decision of this magnitude would require an overwhelming majority to win popular support. Although many Southern states initially announced their intention to comply with the *Brown* decision, Eisenhower's failure to publicly endorse the ruling, as well as his support of state rather than federal initiatives to implement the decision, ultimately played into the hands of its opponents. In October 1954 the first White Citizens Council was formed in Mississippi for the express purpose of fighting desegregation. It would soon have branches all over the South.[79]

Although the prestige of the National Association for the Advancement of Colored People (NAACP) was greatly enhanced by its victory in the *Brown v. Board of Education* decision and the organization consequently gained an enormous number of members, by 1956 several state governments had launched a systematic campaign of repression against the group. That year, Louisiana, Alabama, and Texas obtained injunctions ordering the halt of NAACP operations within their borders, while South Carolina made it illegal for teachers to be members of the organization. In some states NAACP offices were bombed; other states passed laws requiring that the NAACP divulge its memberships lists, a move designed to facilitate reprisals against the organization's members, who risked job loss, foreclosure, denial of credit, harassment by White Citizens Councils, and violent reprisals. By 1957 the organization faced litigation in eight Southern states (Louisiana, Texas, Arkansas, South Carolina, Georgia, Tennessee, Florida, and Virginia), and Alabama had successfully outlawed the NAACP. Aldon Morris has argued that the campaign of intimidation and harassment against the NAACP was a crucial factor in the rise of the modern civil rights movement, for it left an opening for mass-based, direct-action organizations. Although by the 1960s the NAACP had acquired a stodgy, conservative image in the eyes of a younger generation of activists, in the mid-1950s many people considered the NAACP to be a subversive, possibly Communist, organization.[80]

The Montgomery bus boycott, which began in December 1955, when Rosa Parks refused to relinquish her seat to a white patron, is often taken to be the founding event of the nonviolent direct-action tactics of the modern civil rights movement.[81] The organizers of the Montgomery boycott, however, had taken inspiration from an earlier bus boycott in Baton Rouge, Louisiana, in 1953. The Baton Rouge movement, organized by the Reverend T. J. Jemison, had successfully organized a free car service to carry boycotters to their places of employment, a tactic that was to be crucial in the success of the Montgomery boycott. When Martin Luther King Jr. and the Montgomery Improvement Association (MIA) began organizing substitute transportation for the boycott, they called Reverend Jemison first. Unlike the NAACP strategy, which depended on lengthy appeals through the legal system, the Baton Rouge and Montgomery boycotts relied first on the mass mobilization of citizens in a particular area and only later on legal tactics.

Perhaps the most remarkable thing about the Montgomery boycott was the universal compliance of the African American population, despite what the White Citizens Council called the white boycott—the denial of "credit, supplies, sales and all other forms of economic sustenance to Negroes identified as anti-segregation activists."[82] The year-long public drama of the boycott, which included harassment ticketing of car pool drivers for every imaginable traffic infraction, and bombings of the homes of Martin Luther King Jr. and E. D. Nixon, proved that, with common purpose and conviction, African American citizens could effectively organize to undermine Jim Crow. After the Supreme Court affirmed a lower court ruling in November 1956 (to the effect that Alabama's state and local ordinances requiring segregation on buses were unconstitutional), the effectiveness of mass-based direct action was powerfully demonstrated.

Now, more than fifty years after the Montgomery bus boycott, it is difficult to appreciate the bravery and valor of the African Americans whose mass defiance of segregation laws so inexorably tipped the balance toward the ultimate legal victory of the civil rights movement. As Bernice Reagon (a veteran of the civil rights movement and former member of the Student Nonviolent Coordinating Committee [SNCC] Freedom Singers) has emphasized, nonviolent direct action was anything but passive: "Today when they say nonviolence, it is so romanticized. It feels so passive. You think about the placing of the only thing you have to offer, your life . . . that's another level. To walk out of your house and walk in the street facing down the powers that be in your local community with your body, it's war-stancing of the most aggressive, offensive kind. And that is what it is very important to know about these people who acted in the civil rights movement."[83]

## More Than a Politics of Style

In a similar way the defiance and resistance of jazz musicians has often been confused with a romanticized politics of style that views music's relationship to the civil rights struggle as mostly symbolic. Here the defiant attitude of musicians, combined with formal innovations that smashed aesthetic norms, have been viewed as the heart and soul of the relationship between music and politics. The history of the desegregation of the American Federation of Musicians and of performance venues presented in this chapter illustrates that the interplay between politics and music had a far more practical quality as well. This more everyday quality of the link between political struggle and music is visible especially in the economics of the music industry and union contracting of recordings and performances. Without the external pressure of the civil rights organizations, the American Federation of Musicians would not have desegregated when it did, nor would Clark Terry have been hired as an NBC staff musician when he was.

The direct action politics of the civil rights movement frequently coupled public protest with economic boycott in order to negotiate greater access to economic and educational opportunity. Demands for hiring African Americans in nonmenial positions, for example, were a central demand of the Birmingham campaign led by the Southern Christian Leadership Conference (SCLC) during the spring of 1963. Through a combination of mass political protest, boycott, and assertive negotiation with businesses in downtown Birmingham (which succeeded in dividing white elites), civil rights activists agitated for both economic opportunity and the desegregation of public accommodations. The economic, as well as symbolic, aspects of racial justice were an integral component of the mainstream civil rights movement and frequently the means through which local civil rights campaigns were won.[84] This is not to suggest, however, that the symbolic power of the civil rights movement should be underplayed but rather to emphasize that its moral vision was nourished by its practical insight into the economic, as well as moral, vulnerabilities of its opponents.


## Moral Exhortation


Yet among the greatest challenges for the organizers of the civil rights movement was summoning the courage to act. At a conference addressing the relationship between music and the movement held at Washington University in Saint Louis in May 1997, Bernice Reagon offered a powerful explanation of why music, especially singing, was an especially practical component of civil rights organizing. She asked us to envision African

American communities in which the local activists were a small minority who, with the help of one or two civil rights organizers from elsewhere, hoped to inspire their justifiably fearful neighbors to march for the right to vote. One component of the effort was the logical argument that, in those parts of the South where African Americans outnumbered whites, black voting would be key to transforming the power structure: "But when you go and talk to a particular person about actually who is going to be in the first group? It does not make sense unless you are prepared to die. Unless you are prepared to lose *everything* you have. And many people *lost* everything they had."[85]

Singing, according to Reagon and Charles Neblett, also a veteran of the SNCC Freedom Singers, helped civil rights activists to overcome fear, continue marching despite the threats and violence, and sustain their participation in the personal transformation the civil rights movement required: "In many cases [it was] very dangerous and so periodically you'll call back to headquarters in Atlanta and you gather. You always gather and you announce the gathering in the singing. The singing and the power of the singing echoes the intensity with which you have been living your life. And it's a way in which you can announce to each other where you have been and celebrate what you've been doing and also celebrate that you're in fact alive to be together again."[86]

The moral example of the civil rights organizers could be both challenging and intimidating. As Bernice Reagon explained at a conference celebrating the work of SNCC organizers, "When you organize, you *bother* people." Organizers kept coming back to the homes of the reluctant until they were ready to do almost anything to get the organizer to leave them alone. Moral exhortation, goading, and shaming were all among the tools that activists used to mobilize the justifiably reluctant into becoming part of the greater collective struggle. In Reagon's view, a song is a "mini-symbol" of that personal transformation: "You cannot raise a song and not *feel* yourself change." Put another way, "The singing suspends the confusion and points to a higher order, sometimes long enough for you to execute the next step. Therefore, singing will not set you free, but don't try to get free without it."[87]

One effect of the moral example of the civil rights organizers on professional music was the heightened expectation that African American musicians would take a stand in support of the movement. As the examples of Nat King Cole, Louis Armstrong, and other performers illustrate, the consequences of failing to live up to the standards of the African American community were particularly harsh for African Americans. Yet as the civil rights movement escalated, white musicians, too, were expected to take a stand.

## Nat King Cole

The case of Nat King Cole illustrates the way in which new standards of professional behavior for African American entertainers were articulated against the backdrop of the *Brown* decision and the Montgomery bus boycott. In April 1956, in the early months of the boycott, Nat King Cole was performing with Ted Heath's band at the Municipal Auditorium in Birmingham when six white men jumped up on stage and "bopped him around in true hoodlum fashion." The young men objected to Cole's appearance with a white band and had been put up to the deed by the Alabama White Citizens Council. Rather than eliciting sympathy from the African American press, Nat Cole, who was not badly hurt, was roundly denounced for having accepted an engagement in a segregated theater to begin with. The Supreme Court had ruled that "segregation in the American way of life is unconstitutional and therefore unlawful" and that Cole thus did not have the right to break the law "by hiding behind the outlawed laws of Alabama." It particularly galled the African American community that, after the incident, Cole had announced that he would continue to play Jim Crow venues, had "made statements which tended to disassociate himself from the overall Negro struggle against segregation," and had declined to press charges against his attackers.[88]

Despite the fact that Cole was among the most revered of contemporary African American performers, the African American press was harsh. An editorial in the *New York Amsterdam News* found Nat King Cole's attitude intolerable, especially in light of the sacrifices made concurrently by the people of Montgomery: "The Negroes of Alabama today are making all kinds of sacrifices to show the white people down there that they despise segregation. And it seems to us that the least a Northern Negro can do is either join with them in their fight, or stay away from there and let them conduct the fight alone."[89]

The editors held Cole to a different standard than the rank-and-file Negro visitor to Birmingham who "cannot force a white hotel to give him a room no matter how militant he may be." Cole's case was different because he had something to sell—"his musical talents and his voice"—that the white people of Birmingham wished to purchase. His decision to sell them under terms that were "humiliating to King Cole and the race to which he belongs," despite the fact that he was an entertainer of sufficient stature to demand his own terms, was something that the *Amsterdam News* flatly condemned. To Cole's protest that he had to live up to contracts that had already been signed, the editors responded, "we've heard that one before from too many colored performers." Cole was also held up as an example to other African Americans in his position: "We submit that King Cole was wrong and that all other Negroes in his positions are wrong who do the same thing. And they should be condemned by Negroes for upholding such a wrong."[90]

As if this weren't enough, the editorial was accompanied by an unflattering cartoon (titled "There Was a Boy...!") that depicted Nat Cole as a minstrel figure smiling and tossing bills and coins into the air while seated on a pile of money. Directly across from him was the figure of a strong, upstanding African American wearing a tag reading "SOLD" and gripped by an enormous fist labeled "BIAS." The *New York Amsterdam News* also pictured on its cover a patron at the Shallimar bar breaking copies of Cole's recordings with the approval of the bar's owner. Several businessmen in turn inaugurated a boycott of Cole's recordings in their establishments.[91] The intensity of the disappointment in Nat Cole was directly proportional to the esteem in which he was held in the African American community. One of the striking things about the treatment Nat Cole received in the African American press was that he was held to an especially high standard *because* he was beloved.[92]

In late May 1956 Leonard Feather reported that Cole had been assaulted twice: once by the white men in Birmingham and once by the black press. The denunciation Cole had received, he explained, had been partially in response to an erroneous article in the *New York Post* that claimed that Cole had refused to join the NAACP. Despite the fact that Cole had immediately wired the NAACP to correct this misimpression, the initial article's allegations provoked a chain reaction in the Negro press. Feather argued that, despite Cole's refusal to turn down Jim Crow venues, he was still a victim of racism. "Unlike Perry Como," he had been confined to minor roles in movies, could not get his own television show, and had experienced bigoted threats from neighbors who wished to scare him out of his Los

Angeles home.[93] The attack on Cole, Feather implored, had gone too far.[94] In the same issue of *Down Beat* Nat Hentoff took a harder line: "No artist of whatever color should encourage Jim Crow in this manner."[95]

Attempting to clarify his position on racial matters, Cole himself wrote a letter to the editors of *Down Beat*. "First of all," he began, "I would like to say that I am, have been and will continue to be dedicated to the complete elimination of all forms of discrimination, segregation and bigotry." As proof of his support of the NAACP he mentioned that "only last November" he had played a benefit for the Las Vegas chapter of the organization and that he had sent a letter to Roy Wilkins offering to help the NAACP in whatever way he could. Cole also announced that, as of that date, he was subscribing as a life member of the NAACP. Indeed, after the beginning of the lunch-counter sit-ins in 1960, Cole's name was frequently to be found on the rolls of entertainers performing benefits for the organization.[96]

Cole was certainly not the only musician who had performed at benefits for the NAACP and yet found himself denounced for playing to Jim Crow audiences. In 1951 members of the NAACP chapter in Richmond, Virginia, picketed a concert by Marian Anderson, long known for her commitment to breaking down the color barrier. This so infuriated Duke Ellington, who canceled a concert there the following week under threat of renewed picketing, that he spoke out publicly. Commenting that it was a "disgraceful" way to treat a great singer and person such as Marian Anderson, Duke questioned "why they pick out a Negro's investment and destroy it rather than the whites'." "Why boycott the Negro artists," he continued, "when they do not boycott Tommy Dorsey and the symphony"? Ellington, who had lost $4,000 on the cancellation, was particularly incensed since he had only recently raised $16,000 for the national NAACP at his Metropolitan Opera benefit concert.[97]

The moral climate after *Brown* and the Montgomery bus boycott clearly had an effect on the terms of the debate over mixed bands and mixed audiences. If in the mid-1940s playing with a mixed band was taken as a sign of a progressive racial attitude, by the mid-1950s a performer had to refuse to play to segregated audiences to meet the rising moral standards of the civil rights movement. This standard was far more expensive for performers to meet than that of mixed bands and was not without its internal contradictions. The public shaming of Nat King Cole, for example, singled out an African American performer when dozens of prominent white performers who played at the same venues went unscathed.

Nevertheless, African American performers seemed to be held especially accountable within the black community in the increasingly politicized racial climate of the post-*Brown* years.

Although the leading edge of the civil rights movement and the jazz community wanted performers to refuse Jim Crow audiences, it was actually quite common for jazz musicians to play in segregated venues as late as the early 1960s without much uproar. In late 1956 *Down Beat* writer John Tynan was shocked when told by the management of the Dunes in Las Vegas that he and other members of the press were not to invite Count Basie or any of his sidemen to their tables during intermissions, but he did not criticize Basie for having accepted the engagement. The furor over Cole and segregated audiences in the mid-1950s was led by the black press, although various jazz writers, including Nat Hentoff, began to publicize Jim Crow policies in clubs and the white musicians who accommodated them.

In September 1955 Hentoff reminded *Down Beat* readers that Jim Crow policies were also found in the North. Citing the example of an Ohio night club that refused to hire black musicians, Hentoff lamented that "a few of our better known white jazzmen continue to play the room even though they're fully aware of the club's policy." Without naming any names, Hentoff was particularly aghast that "one of the more respected trios in modern jazz" had recently played there, as well as a widely known traditional pianist. The problem, he continued, was not restricted to this club alone. Many bookers and musicians had informed him about so-called jazz rooms that "operate under the same kind of restricted covenant." Articulating an increasingly common point of view within the jazz world, Hentoff concluded that "it is shameful that these places should still exist—and should still receive support from some musicians and some members of the jazz audience."[98]

## Dave Brubeck

Compared to the black press, the jazz press was slow to embrace the criterion of refusing to play for segregated audiences as a sign of racial progress. Norman Granz emphasized this issue after *Down Beat* lavishly praised Dave Brubeck's decision to cancel a tour of Southern colleges and universities rather than replace his African American bassist, Eugene Wright. An article by Ralph Gleason presented a detailed account of the tour cancellation in mid-February 1960. Brubeck had originally planned a twenty-five-date tour, but after refusing to sign contracts that contained "lily-white" clauses about the composition of the band, he was left with ten performances. Brubeck had apparently not made the fact that his band was integrated explicit in the first round, for after he sent a telegram to the ten remaining locations explaining the group's racial composition, only three institutions—the University of Jacksonville, Vanderbilt University, and the University of the South (Sewanee, Tennessee)—were willing to accept an integrated group.[99]

Brubeck was indignant, canceled all shows at institutions that did not allow mixed bands, and forfeited in the process some $40,000. He appealed to Southern jazz fans to pressure colleges and universities "to make special provisions" for jazz performances: They had, after all "played Little Rock last year and were the first integrated jazz group to play there after the high school episode. There was no problem at our concert." They had also played without incident at East Carolina College the night before they left on their State Department tour. Paul Desmond said he felt sorry for the kids down South but quipped that perhaps not all was lost: "The State Department could send us on a tour through the South!" Eugene Wright also found the situation to be deplorable: "It's a shame we can go and travel all over the world and have no problems and come home and have such a silly problem." A month later Ralph Gleason lavishly praised Brubeck's stance: "My hat, if I wore one, would be off to Dave Brubeck right now. He's done a great thing for all of us and we—members of all races—owe him a debt of gratitude."[100]

Norman Granz was unimpressed. After containing himself for several months, he wrote to *Down Beat* to communicate the position on mixed audiences he had taken since 1946: "Here is the crux of the matter: at no time did I see any guarantee that even if Brubeck had been allowed to appear with the mixed group ... he [would] have been playing before a mixed audience, and the latter, I submit, is far more important than the mixed group." Although he could forgive Brubeck's well-meaning naiveté, he found "the tragic lack of understanding by the so-called writers of jazz who don't know a damn about the realities of life" less forgivable. Holding up mixed bands as a laudatory example made no sense to him in light of his own experience with JATP:

You see, I had the same experience when I formed Jazz at the Philharmonic. I never had any trouble playing anywhere in the

South with a mixed group, and I mean anywhere. The important thing was that I had a clause in my contract in advance that said I could play with a mixed group and that I would play only before nonsegregated audiences, and it was with that point of view that we managed to break down segregation and established in many cities a precedent for mixed audiences, which is the heart of true integration.[101]

In Granz's perspective, understanding the "realities of life" meant understanding the everyday practical consequences of Jim Crow in the music industry. The more mundane aspects of a musician's life, including membership in the American Federation of Musicians, contracts, travel, and the racial composition of bands and audiences, illustrate the racial fault lines around which individual artists negotiated their careers. Between World War II and the 1960s jazz musicians inevitably confronted choices around these issues that implicitly or explicitly constructed a politics of musicianship. In response to shifting historical circumstances, such as World War II, *Brown v. Board of Education,* and the Montgomery bus boycott, debates about segregated locals, integrated bands, and mixed audiences took on heightened moral overtones, as musicians, many of whom were invested in the notion that the world of jazz was more advanced on racial issues than American society at large, evaluated each other's performances not only onstage but also off. Despite aesthetic modernism's view of art as something above and beyond politics, again and again jazz musicians were pulled into the fray.

Under the proliferation of styles in the 1950s, including cool jazz, hard bop, West Coast, modal jazz, and third stream, simmered a field of interrelated political, economic, and ethical issues that linked jazz to broader developments in American society. Jazz musicians of the 1950s embraced various forms of modernist musical sensibility through which many contrasting claims for jazz were articulated. On the one hand, racial divisions were transcended by emphasizing the lofty achievements of jazz as an art equivalent in stature to Western classical music. On the other hand, modernist aesthetics asserted the genius of African American musical artists as proof of the absurdity of racial prejudice by linking artistic achievement to political assertion.

Not everyone agreed on the meaning of "true integration," which became especially apparent in the world of jazz in the early 1960s. For

African Americans the primary goal of integration, which then had the rather narrow meaning of outlawing Jim Crow, was to expand economic and educational opportunities for black people. Black Americans wanted access to jobs, housing, and other appurtenances of the good life. Interracial communion was secondary. To the extent that eliminating de jure segregation did not expand opportunities, many African Americans were open to alternative ideologies that sought empowerment through the strategies of autonomy and self-determination.

White fans tended to view integration differently. In the fifties white, predominantly male, college students flocked to jazz, many of them finding in the music a way to escape the stultifying expectations of a suburbanizing America—where young men were expected to provide for families with stay-at-home moms, submit to the demands of bureaucratic organizations, and be patriotic. For many white musicians and fans, jazz offered a swinging alternative, where the mainstream rules of family and work could be defied and reshaped in dialogue with what was imagined as a more liberating model of African American masculinity and style. Interracial communion was consequently an important component of white liberal identification with an idealized, integrated jazz community. Economic opportunity was secondary to a shared commitment to true art and its attendant nonconformism. These racially stratified differences over the goals of integration and the meaning of musical art brewed quietly in the fifties, not to emerge into an intense and fractured dialogue until after the Greensboro lunch-counter sit-ins in 1960.

# 3

## Modernism, Race, and Aesthetics

I F, AS AMIRI Baraka has argued in *Blues People*, bebop represented the triumph of African American musical artists over the commercialism of mass-marketed white swing, the news was lost on the 1950s' readers of *Down Beat* and *Metronome*. In the readers' polls conducted by both magazines, Stan Getz was the number one tenor saxophonist for ten consecutive years, Shelley Manne was the first-place drummer in seven out of ten polls in *Down Beat,* and Stan Kenton's arranger Pete Rugolo often took top honors in the arranging category. In the eyes of the broader American public, jazz in the early 1950s had a decidedly white face.

As the decade progressed, a shift from white to black winners occurred on at least some instruments. From 1950 to 1955 Bill Harris, a trombonist with Woody Herman, earned top honors, but after that J. J. Johnson dominated the field. Bassist Eddie Safranski of the Kenton orchestra earned the number one spot in *Metronome* from 1950 to 1954 but for the rest of the decade was superseded by Ray Brown. Vibist Milt Jackson took top honors beginning in 1955, but Terry Gibbs was the winner from 1950 to 1954.

On other instruments, such as the alto saxophone, a shift took place over the course of the decade from black to white—from Charlie Parker (who would likely have dominated had he lived) and Johnny Hodges to Paul Desmond. In the piano category, *Down Beat* readers cast their votes consistently for two African American artists—Oscar Peterson and Erroll Garner—while *Metronome* readers also included Lennie Tristano, George Shearing, and Dave Brubeck among the first-place finishers.

The readers of *Down Beat* and *Metronome* diverged most significantly in their evaluation of trumpet players. Dizzy Gillespie and Miles Davis dominated the fifties in the eyes of *Metronome* readers, while *Down Beat* shifted loyalties from Maynard Ferguson and Chet Baker to Miles Davis. Among vocalists, African Americans Ella Fitzgerald and Sarah Vaughan dominated the female vocal category, while the preferred male singers moved from Billy Eckstine to Frank Sinatra in the same period. The only women instrumentalists to make the top five in either publication were Marjorie Hyams, who placed fourth on vibes in *Down Beat*'s 1950 poll, and Mary Lou Williams, who placed fifth on piano in *Metronome*'s 1953 poll.[1]

The listening preferences of the predominantly white readership of jazz magazines illustrate several points. First, an enormous gap exists between the historically recognized canonic jazz figures of 1950s' jazz and the actual listening tastes of the 1950s' public. John Coltrane did not appear among the top five tenor saxophonists until 1959, when he emerged shortly after Sonny Rollins's first appearance on the list in 1958. Drummer Max Roach was consistently rated number two throughout the decade, and Art Blakey went unrecognized in the top five until 1957 (in *Metronome*) and 1958 (in *Down Beat*). Thelonious Monk appeared among the top five pianists in 1958 and 1959, while Red Garland, Miles Davis's pianist, never turned up at all.

Second, while many of the African American winners offered a "cool school" sound, including (arguably) Miles Davis and the Modern Jazz Quartet (MJQ), white readers were also able to embrace the hard bop sound of J. J. Johnson and the swinging bass lines of Ray Brown and Paul Chambers. Third, although there is no consistent racial trend throughout all of the instrumental categories, the preference of magazine readers for white saxophonists modeled on the lighter tone and horizontal playing style of Lester Young is striking.

Jazz critics in the same period ranked African American musicians higher than their readers. The participants in *Down Beat*'s annual critics' polls (which began in 1953) were far less impressed with the Stan Kenton Orchestra, the Dave Brubeck Quartet, trumpeter Chet Baker, and drummer Shelly Manne than were participants in the *Down Beat* readers' poll. Thelonious Monk was voted the top pianist from 1958 to 1961; the Ellington band won the big band category more often than any other group; and the Modern Jazz Quartet dominated the combo competition. From 1953 to 1955 Stan Getz took top honors on tenor sax, but for the rest of the decade Coleman Hawkins, Sonny Rollins, and John Coltrane dominated the instrument from the critics' point of view. Rather than Paul Desmond, the critics preferred Charlie Parker, Benny Carter, and Cannonball

Adderley on alto sax, although Lee Konitz won in 1958. The critics also placed Max Roach first on drums in 1955 and from 1958 to 1961. In white drummers they preferred Buddy Rich to Shelly Manne, especially in the first part of the decade. The critics, it seems, had somewhat "blacker" tastes than their readers.[2]

The covers of *Down Beat* magazine reveal another trend from white to black. In 1950 approximately twenty-two of twenty-six covers featured white performers, whereas only four included black performers.[3] In 1967 *Down Beat* featured seventeen covers with black performers and nine with white performers. Latinos or Asians were, with few exceptions, virtually nonexistent. Figure 3.1 diagrams the racial breakdown of those featured on the cover of *Down Beat* from 1950 to 1967. When a gender breakdown is added (see figure 3.2), it becomes apparent that the shift from predominantly white to predominantly black covers also resulted in gender realignment. White women were included on fourteen covers in 1950, but in 1967 they were included on none at all. This is largely due to decreased coverage of popular song repertory in *Down Beat*. The women on the covers of the early 1950s' issues included Peggy Lee, Patti Page, and Doris Day—singers not usually considered jazz singers today. African American women such as Ella Fitzgerald or Sarah Vaughan were of marginal visibility throughout.

What should one make of these racial trends? Can the blacker aesthetic preferences of white critics be read as a residue of a greater interracial dialogue existing within the jazz community as has so frequently been

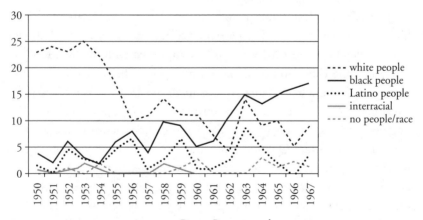

FIGURE 3.1. *Down Beat* covers by race.

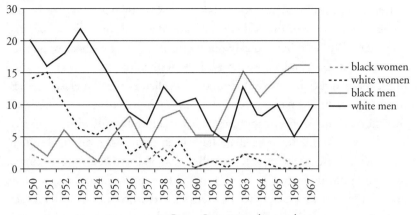

FIGURE 3.2. *Down Beat* covers by gender.

claimed? Is the shared aesthetic ground between white critics and leading black musicians proof of the objectivity and universality of musical standards as the ideals of modernist art claim? Is that same shared terrain evidence of the impact of African American music on mainstream aesthetics?

In more recent jazz historical literature, the apparent blackening of aesthetic standards in jazz during the 1950s and 1960s has been cast as something of a black nationalist plot of the post–civil rights era. Richard Sudhalter's book on the history of white jazz musicians and Terry Teachout's sharp criticism of Jazz at Lincoln Center have both suggested that the shift in the historical literature toward African American musicians in today's literature is simply ideological rather than musical.[4] I contend that something far more complicated and interesting took place that demands a substantial reframing of the way we think about modernism, race, and aesthetics in jazz.

At the center of the problem is the relationship between so-called black and white aesthetic styles in jazz of this period. The larger aesthetic and representational shift during this time was in many ways the outcome of an ever-present competitive contest between black men and white men over who would define the aesthetic center and meaning of the music. Yet, defining a black or a white aesthetic in musical terms has always been difficult since counterexamples and exceptions to any definition have not been hard to supply.

Indeed, there is likely no topic more certain to elicit firestorms of invective and counterinvective in jazz than the idea that jazz has both a white sound and a black sound. Jazz, after all, as one line of argument goes, is universal—a colorblind art music open to all who master its repertory, improvisational mode of musical creation, and demand for individuality and originality. But, as others quickly point out, it is a music whose origins are in African America and whose most central aesthetic components are rooted in the blues and that elusive rhythmic flow called swing. To erase that aesthetic history in the name of universalism, many contend, is a whitewash that allows white people to appropriate black cultural forms with impunity.[5]

The basic terms of this debate have been part of the discursive air in jazz since at least the swing era, when Benny Goodman became the King of Swing and Ellington and Basie were the Duke and the Count, respectively, despite their creative priority.[6] Nevertheless, the problem is much older, dating to when enslaved Africans first arrived in the seventeenth century and fledgling white Americans first began to notice the musical gifts of the new arrivals. During the Great Awakening and the era of the camp meeting, missionizing evangelizers commented mostly on their singing, declaring the slaves to have melody in their souls and an ear for music "above all the human species."[7] To these early observers, the music unquestionably sounded very distinctive. Nevertheless, when black congregations transformed the hymns of Isaac Watts and John Wesley in performance and later invented their own Christian texts and melodies, which became known as spirituals, there were those, such as George Pullen Jackson, who wished to claim that the repertory was of European origin.[8]

In the early to mid-twentieth century, African American jazz musicians self-consciously took up the mantle of the modern artist as a means of legitimating their music and as part of a broader-based transformation of African America from rural to urban. This effort brought with it the inexorable demand for full citizenship and inclusion in modernity's promise of equality and justice for all. Bebop musicians and civil rights activists mobilized the language of merit, universal justice, and transcendence to demand entrée and recognition in mainstream American society, one in the language of art, the other in the language of politics.

Yet, as in all things pertaining to race in the United States, the idea of the modern artist was a double-edged sword. If it enabled African American musicians to partially break out of a race-based, second-class citizenship by appealing to merit and genius, it also provided a rhetoric through which white musicians could insist that the music be understood as colorblind and dismiss those who emphasized its black heritage as reverse racists. This basic discursive framework has shaped the way in which debates over race and jazz have been argued since the mid-twentieth century. The music tends to be cast as either universal or ethnically particular, colorblind or fundamentally black, with many jumping from one side to the other depending on the contextual situation. In a music as cosmopolitan as jazz, which draws on multiple aesthetic streams, how can history both account for the many musical elements that circulated and inspired across the racial boundaries and give just credit for the profound expansion and innovation of the jazz aesthetics in these years led by African American icons like Miles Davis, John Coltrane, Charles Mingus, and Ornette Coleman?

In this chapter I offer a framework for moving beyond the familiar standoff between blackness and colorblindness through a particular version of social constructionism. The aesthetic contest between the styles of so-called cool jazz and hard bop serve as historical examples. I argue that the musical landscape of modern jazz in the mid-twentieth century can be viewed as a palette consisting of five broad aesthetic streams: (1) the aesthetics of African American vernacular musics as expressed in jazz, blues, gospel, and R&B; (2) the aesthetics of American popular song as descended from Tin Pan Alley and musical theater; (3) the aesthetics of modern classical music; (4) the aesthetics of Africa and its diaspora; and (5) the aesthetics of other non-Western musics, most notably in this time period, India.

The crux of the argument is that individual jazz musicians drew from one or more of these aesthetic perspectives and often combined them in novel ways to produce an alternative aesthetics of modernism at once more populist than its European art music counterpart, yet committed to articulating its elite position relative to the more commercial genres of R&B and rock and roll. The ultimate victory of hard bop styles in defining the aesthetic center of this canonic period in jazz, I suggest, represents a blackening of modernist aesthetics, which would ultimately serve as a standard against which any player of jazz would be evaluated. Following the usage of Baker, Ramsey, and Werner, I call this aesthetic Afro-modernism.[9]


## Color-Coded Styles

The main musical styles of the 1950s—cool, hard bop, third steam, soul jazz—have long been color coded. Cool, West Coast, and third stream have typically been associated with white players, while hard bop and soul jazz have been linked to black musicians. So-called West Coast and cool jazz, with their preference for thinner timbres, relaxed time feels, and lyrical melodies have generally been taken as a "whiter" sound, while hard bop and soul jazz, with their prioritization of heavier timbres, blues inflection, and hard, driving rhythmic feels have generally been cast as "blacker." Historians have long noted the ill fit of these categories, with West Coast ignoring the hard-driving California sounds of Dexter Gordon, Wardell Gray, and Hampton Hawes (and the East Coast origins of Stan Getz), and "cool school" failing to account for the aesthetic range of musicians such as Miles Davis and Milt Jackson.

Since African American musicians have expressed themselves in styles ranging from the lusciously smooth tone of Johnny Hodges playing "Day Dream" to the ear-splitting intensity of John Coltrane on *Ascension,* from the passionate blues of Charlie Parker on "Parker's Mood" to Duke Ellington's hauntingly relaxed feel on *Reminiscing in Tempo,* it is difficult to accept an aesthetic framework that requires evaluating the performances with a greater preponderance of blues elements as always blacker.[10] Indeed, one of the limitations of rigid musical definitions of blackness in music is that they underplay the aesthetic range of the types of music that African Americans have played, as well as the importance to the history of black creativity of the synthesizing encounter between black and white musical repertories. This forging of an Afro-modernist sensibility through the creative fusion of black aesthetics and modernism, I maintain, is one of the most influential achievements of jazz in the twentieth century.

In jazz of the 1950s and 1960s African American musicians often deployed the aesthetic resources of Western modernism, as well as black vernacular music to assert themselves as artists. This is not simply a matter of deferring to "white values," as the later rhetoric of Black Power might phrase it, but also of putting modernism to work in the aesthetic struggle to keep innovating and the political struggle to gain higher status and power for black music and culture. This is what Paul Gilroy is talking about when he speaks of black Atlantic music as a "counterculture of modernity" and what Amiri Baraka spoke about when he suggested in 1961 that African American musicians had a necessary relationship to aesthetic modernism by virtue of living in the West: "We are, all of us, moderns, whether we like it or not."[11]

By the same token, white musicians of the 1950s and 1960s had a wide variety of relationships to African American musical aesthetics and modernism. Pianist Lennie Tristano's abstract improvisational approach on "Wow," which de-emphasizes the rhythm section and places a premium on the precision of the horns, is something quite different from Stan Getz's sound on "Dark Eyes."[12] Despite Getz's whiteness, his bluesy performance is much closer to a sound ideal shared by many African American performers of the era and, in comparison to Tristano, shows greater sensitivity to the call-and-response dimensions of African American aesthetics. White musicians of the fifties, it seems, also had a variety of relationships to the musical legacy of black music and Western modernism but filtered, instead, through the social experience of being white. Stan Getz's ten years as number one tenor saxophonist in the *Down Beat* readers' poll was widely perceived among African Americans as the product of advantages white musicians had in getting coverage in jazz publications, even though many black musicians admired and respected Getz as an individual for his playing.

Perhaps the greatest difference between black and white musicians in the 1950s ultimately lies in the fact that the latter had access to structural white privilege, no matter what their individual relationship to the blues and African American aesthetics more broadly, while black musicians experienced structural racial discrimination, no matter what their individual relationship to Western modernism and mainstream culture. American social structure and the economic structure of the music industry with its de jure and de facto segregation of black and white ensured this.

This point, which has caused much confusion, emphasizes a disjunction between an individual's self-conscious identity (whether ethnic or political) and that person's treatment as a citizen within the larger sociology of race relations in the United States. If an African American's degree of black consciousness was evaluated and often harshly judged by other African Americans in the 1960s, the fact remained that even the person with "faulty consciousness" (the so-called Uncle Tom) experienced racism. Conversely, the "advanced consciousness" of the racially progressive white person did not alter the fact that public accommodations laws in the South and segregated practices in the North conferred certain benefits upon white musicians, whether they actively desired them or not. The ability of African Americans to play classical music or sing in the crooning style of Bing Crosby or the ability of white musicians to play the blues and swing in a convincingly black manner did not affect the more impersonal physical characteristics that were used to draw the legal racial line. Whether one experiences white privilege or the daily frustrations of racism is not so much a moral question, in other words, but an everyday social condition.

Aesthetics, however, are more malleable, mobile, and pluralistic than social structures despite their roots in particular cultural communities and geographic locations. Regardless of one's cultural and social home base, in other words, it is possible to make choices to engage and participate in a variety of aesthetic traditions. I call this process of active musical self-fashioning *aesthetic agency*. Such musical cosmopolitanism has long been a hallmark of jazz musicians, who have generally emphasized their breadth of listening and musical appreciation, and the music of this golden age in jazz history is replete with examples. But there are limits to the efficacy of an individual's aesthetic choices; they cannot by themselves alter the underlying social condition.

## On Black and White Sounds

Of the many definitions of black musical aesthetics offered in the last few decades, some have emphasized musical traits, while others have highlighted a constellation of factors including cultural history, musical structures, and religious sensibility.[13] The most prominent definitions have been those offered by Albert Murray's "Blues Aesthetic," Samuel Floyd's "Ring Shout Aesthetic," and Olly Wilson's "Heterogeneous Sound Ideal." For Albert Murray, the blues aesthetic is simultaneously a musical sound and a psychological and spiritual balm that enables people to keep the blues of everyday life at bay. The feeling, in his view, is just as important as the specifically musical traits of the blues. In Murray's words, "The blues counteragent that is so much a part of many people's equipment for living that they hardly ever think about it as such anymore is that artful and sometimes seemingly magical combination of idiomatic incantation and percussion that creates the dance-oriented good-time music also known as the blues."[14] The interrelationship between the vocal and the percussive seems crucial here, and Muddy Waters's 1950 recording of "Walkin' Blues" offers one of many possible illustrations of what Murray means. Here the percussiveness is supplied mainly by the intensity of Muddy Waters's acoustic guitar.[15]

In choosing the blues as a template, Murray privileged the secular over the sacred sphere as the space of freedom, even though a considerable part of his book *Stomping the Blues* talks about their interconnection. This tends to erase the contribution of black women to African American aesthetics, since their greatest musical contributions in the early twentieth century were in the sacred sphere, as Evelyn Higginbotham has pointed out.[16] Samuel Floyd inverts Murray's secular/sacred hierarchy by viewing African American musical aesthetics since the eighteenth century as descending from the aesthetic of the "ring shout," a genre inseparable from dance and religion. Here the sacred takes priority, but that interrelationship between the voice and time flow remains the same. Floyd's perspective directs us to the sacred vocal literature in African American music, much older than the blues and full of "calls, cries, and hollers; call-and-response devices...blue notes, bent notes, and elisions; hums, moans, grunts, vocables, interjections and punctuations."[17]

The Alan Lomax recordings of traditional secular and sacred African American singing in the 1930s and 1940s, as well as the later recordings of Georgia Sea Islander singers (made in 1959 and 1960), have often been used as examples of what the singing of the ring shout in the eighteenth and nineteenth centuries may have sounded like. Excerpts from "Sign of the Judgment" and "Run, Old Jeremiah" illustrate the musical organization of the genre, which features call and response between a song leader and a group, with rhythmic accompaniment provided by handclaps and/or a broomstick or other percussion.[18] "Sign of the Judgment," which is sung at a slow pace, features a transition between the final intoned words of the preacher's sermon and the beginning of group singing. "Run, Old Jeremiah" is sung at a much faster pace and includes foot stamping, as well as handclapping.

The vocal timbres, slides, and groans sung by the Georgia Sea Islanders and two singers (Joe Washington and Austin Coleman) from Jennings, Louisiana, illustrate one of the central components of Olly Wilson's "heterogeneous sound ideal"—a preference for timbral contrasts and a melodic style that delights in a vocalized sound quality. Excerpts from Ornette Coleman's solo on "Blues Connotation" and Stanley Turrentine's solo on Jimmy Smith's "Prayer Meeting" also provide examples of this timbral quality in jazz.[19]

The remaining criteria in Wilson's conception of the heterogeneous sound ideal, which situates black musical aesthetics in the African diaspora, emphasize the temporal organization of the music. They include (1) a preference for cross-rhythm that emerges from "the interplay of fixed and variable rhythmic units" (such as the rhythm section and soloist), (2) a call-and-response structure that exists simultaneously at several levels of the musical structure (as on Count Basie's "Volcano"), and (3) the tendency of the music to generate bodily involvement on the part of musicians and audience members.[20] Indeed, most works on African American musical aesthetics emphasize the groove-and-feel elements of the music (among them swing) and often leave the topic of harmony and its relationship to African American aesthetics unaddressed.[21]

Among the many performances that could illustrate the heterogeneous sound ideal is Lee Morgan's solo on "Moanin'." Morgan's blues-inflected trumpet line replete with bends, scoops, and dramatic registral sweeps proves that it does not take a saxophone or a voice to give a vocal quality to a melodic line. This is just the kind of exuberant, bluesy playing that has earned Morgan the reputation of being the quintessential hard bopper and the absolute embodiment of "badness."[22] From a trumpeter's perspective the bravado to open a solo on a smeared high concert D and then repeat the pitch strong and loud three times in the first five measures boasts of chops of an extraordinary kind. Morgan's phrasing in call and response with Bobby Timmons's comping and Blakey's hard swinging shuffle feel—with strong backbeat, gorgeously timbred ride cymbal and hi-hat—tend to make all but the most resistant want to pat their feet.

There is no parallel literature that attempts to define the musical characteristics of a white mainstream musical aesthetic, but I would like to suggest that the ideas of what sounded "white" in 1950s' jazz stem from two main aesthetic streams—American popular song and classical music—as well as from judgments about the ways in which white musicians failed to live up to aspects of African American aesthetics, usually swing or emotional presence. Even though the definitions of "white sound" tend to be less explicit than those of "black sound," the judgment of sounding white mobilized a similar combination of aesthetic criteria, including vocal style, preferred instrumental timbres, and rhythm.

One legacy of mainstream popular song in the United States is the lyrical singing style known as crooning, which usually meant a round, smooth vocal tone, the use of expressive vibrato, and a sentimental emotional tone. Bing Crosby and Frank Sinatra (both white) were among the most famous crooners of the mid-twentieth century as their smooth and romantic versions of "Pennies from Heaven" demonstrate.[23] By this definition, however, Billy Eckstine and Nat King Cole (both black) must also be included among the crooners. Eckstine's velvety performance on "Blue Moon," as well as Nat Cole's joyful version of "Sweet Lorraine," remind us that crooning was one of many accepted and appreciated singing styles among African Americans of the 1940s and 1950s.[24]

The crooning sensibility leaves its mark in jazz instrumental style most obviously in the performance of jazz ballads, in which musicians have reveled in the more romantic, sentimental, introspective, and "softer" sides of musical expressivity.[25] This reminds us that, whether musicians were considered primarily to be in the hard bop or cool jazz camp, the wide range of repertory expected of the jazz musician—from up-tempo swinging tunes to ballads—complicates the reduction of any particular musician's aesthetic to simply hard or soft, black or white. Among the many implications of the stark contrast drawn in sonic stereotypes of black sounds and white sounds are its gendered associations. Here African American aesthetics are coded as manly and virile, and the white aesthetic by contrast is coded as feminine or, at least, less virile.

The debate over hard bop and cool jazz in the 1950s often had a chain of metaphorical oppositions churning just below: hard/soft, black/white, male/female, emotional/cold, and, nonintellectual/intellectual. The musical dispute often focused on saxophone sounds as exemplary of the contrasts between styles. The light-toned, smooth-timbred sounds of Stan Getz and Paul Desmond (both white) were often contrasted with the edgier, bluesier saxophone styles of Sonny Rollins, Sonny Stitt, and John Coltrane (all black). Getz's performance of "On the Alamo" and Desmond's rendition of "Pennies from Heaven" illustrate saxophone styles coded white in the contemporary literature.[26]

However, the complexity of the sonic relationships among African American and non–African American musicians is complicated considerably by the fact that many of the 1950s' white saxophonists modeled themselves on two of the most admired black saxophonists of the previous generation, Lester Young and Johnny Hodges. Young's light-toned yet impeccably swinging solo on "Tickletoe," as well as Hodges's romantic, crooning style on "Day Dream," make audible the interconnection between the fifties' white saxophone styles and the earlier African American saxophonists.[27]

The limits of any rigidly fixed definitions of black and white aesthetics are particularly apparent here. It would be absurd to suggest, after all, that Johnny Hodges and Lester Young are less black because the white saxophonists of the 1950s were inspired by their sounds. Yet the historical dynamic of non–African Americans exploring "yesterday's blues" points to a deeper recurrent cultural dynamic—a time lag between the first appearance of a style among African Americans and its diffusion beyond racial borders.[28]

Shared musical qualities, then, are not just a matter of musical traits coexisting at some point in time but also implicate the historical processes of circulation and recirculation by which the commonalities were established. Although it has been typical to refer to such processes as reciprocal, it would be more accurate to think of them as recursive—in other words, where the result of one interaction is drawn upon in the next.[29] If "reciprocal" implies free exchange on a level playing field, I mean "recursive" to imply exchange on playing field that is shaped by various forms of social stratification over time. How to describe this recursiveness between black and white remains a central problem in American cultural and political history, and, in many ways, music remains a particularly compelling window into its depth.

## Modernism and Colorblindness

The usual means of explaining musical traits that were shared across the color line in the mid-1950s was to suggest that the music was "colorblind." Yet a look at how the discourse of color blindness was deployed in jazz periodicals of the 1950s goes a long way toward explaining why many African American jazz musicians began to emphasize the differences between the aesthetic styles of black and white players rather than their overlap. As Jon Panish has stated, the discourse of "colorblindness" tended to "exaggerate the permeability of racial boundaries during the postwar era" by failing to address the power relationships involved in an economic and ideological climate in which "color evasiveness" was often used to silence African American perspectives on the meaning of the music.[30] This is not to suggest that the expression of colorblind sentiments was disingenuous or that genuine moments of interracial harmony on the bandstand did not occur, but rather to emphasize that structural racial stratification persisted after the performances were over.

In the remainder of this chapter I discuss the connection between modernism and the two most important aesthetic streams that figured in the debate between cool jazz and hard bop—classical music and rhythm and blues (especially the gospel-inflected rhythm and blues of the 1950s). On the classical musical side figure the stories of the *Birth of the Cool* sessions, Lennie Tristano, Dave Brubeck, and the Modern Jazz Quartet. On the rhythm and blues side are those of Horace Silver and Art Blakey.

## Colorblindness in Practice

*Jazz is America's own. It is the music that grew out of a young and vigorous melting-pot nation. It is a product of all America, deriving much of its inspiration and creation from the Negro people. Jazz holds up no superficial bars. It is played and listened to by all peoples—in harmony, together. Pigmentation differences have no place in jazz. As in genuine democracy, only performance counts. Jazz is truly the music of democratic America. It is an ideal medium for bringing about a better understanding among all peoples.*

—Norman Granz

Norman Granz's comments epitomize the colorblind ideal as it was often expressed in the jazz world of the late forties and fifties. The fact that these comments appeared in *Crisis* (the official organ of the NAACP) illustrates the compatibility of this perspective with the leading civil rights organization of the 1940s and 1950s. Here jazz is offered as the ultimate American music, both democratic and capable of acting as a moral force in the construction of cross-cultural understanding. It is also portrayed as a meritocracy, where the only thing that matters is the quality of the music, a presumably objective category.

Granz coupled colorblindness with active opposition to Jim Crow in the music business. The Jazz at the Philharmonic concerts and package tours that Granz sponsored beginning in 1944 were self-consciously integrated events and featured top names in the field, who often played extended jam sessions and cutting contests. Dizzy Gillespie versus Roy Eldridge, Bill Harris contra J. J. Johnson, or Ben Webster meets Flip Phillips might have been featured on any given night.[31] Gillespie expressed reservations about Granz's aesthetic penchant for putting two or three trumpeters on stage to "battle one another's brains out" but emphasized the importance of the excellent working conditions Granz provided for

JATP musicians. Unlike other promoters, Gillespie explained, "Norman Granz gave jazz musicians 'first class' treatment. You traveled 'first class,' stayed in 'first class' hotels, and he demanded no segregation in seating."[32]

Nevertheless, colorblindness could also be used to put African Americans on the spot. Perhaps the most famous example is Leonard Feather's blindfold test with Roy Eldridge in July 1951, titled "Little Jazz Goes Color Blind." The trumpeter listened to ten bands, four of which comprised exclusively white or black musicians; the remainder included at least one African American. He mistook George Shearing's English white bassist and drummer for black, correctly identified Eddie Condon's trombonist and drummer as black, could not tell whether the integrated band on Miles Davis's *Venus de Milo* (from the *Birth of the Cool* sessions) or the all-black quartet of Billy Taylor was white or black ("they could be Eskimos for all I know"). Nor, for that matter, was he confident about whether the piano duo of Duke Ellington and Billy Strayhorn was black or white. Based on the ten selections Feather presented, Eldridge was forced to concede that Feather had won the argument: "I guess I'll have to go along with you, Leonard—you can't tell just from listening to records."[33] But Feather purposefully chose examples in which the musical boundaries were not clear in order to demand that Eldridge get on board the colorblind wagon. Rather than view white ability to play jazz as a blackening of mainstream musical style, colorblind discourse of the day preferred to claim that the ability to swing and play the blues could be divorced from any necessary connection to blackness and African Americans.


## Birth of the Cool

Various crossings of the color line in the fifties and sixties have often been celebrated as evidence of new racial attitudes, especially in contrast to the greater segregation of the bandstand during the swing era. Stan Getz's hiring of Horace Silver, Dave Brubeck's quartet with bassist Eugene Wright, pianist Bill Evans with Miles Davis, Ornette Coleman's choice of bassist Charlie Haden, Louis Bellson drumming for Duke Ellington, and Roswell Rudd in Archie Shepp's band are among the racial border crossings that have been cited in evidence. Yet there is probably no more influential and conspicuously integrated musical project than Miles Davis's *Birth of the Cool* sessions. The *Birth of the Cool* is particularly important not only for the integrated cast of musicians but also for the "cool" aesthetic position it established, which later came to be viewed as the white side of the typical black versus white sound stereotypes of the 1950s. In the binary logic that characterized racial thinking in the United States, if hard bop was black, then the cool sound was white, regardless of the number of influential African American musicians who also played in a cool manner. The album titled *Birth of the Cool* was not compiled until 1957, although the music had been recorded in 1949 and 1950. The tracks were first released as 78s, and none of the titles included the word "cool."[34]

The *Birth of the Cool* sessions grew out of a group of musicians who met in Gil Evans's basement apartment (on the corner of Fifty-fifth Street and Fifth Avenue in New York) to exchange musical ideas and theories with potential application in jazz composition. Among the participants were John Lewis, George Russell, John Carisi, and Miles Davis. Gil Evans had been arranging for the Claude Thornhill orchestra and had written several highly respected arrangements of bop standards, including *Anthropology* and *Thriving on a Riff.* In 1947 Evans approached Miles Davis about arranging Davis's composition *Donna Lee* for the Thornhill band. Miles granted permission but asked in exchange that he be allowed to study Evans's scores. Davis provided insights of his own, as well as the impetus to turn theory into practice, and organized rehearsals to try out ideas that emerged from more informal musical discussions. Among the goals of the group were the development of a writing style that retained the immediacy of improvisation, the creation of fresh sonorities through innovative instrumental combinations, and the production of a more seamless integration between the written and the improvised components of an arrangement.

The revolving group of musicians, many drawn from the Thornhill band, rehearsed regularly in 1948 and in October played a two-week engagement at New York's Royal Roost. Davis secured a recording contract from Capitol Records despite the reluctance of the company's three principal producers. Twelve sides were recorded in three sessions held in 1949 and 1950, each with slightly different personnel and racial representation. The first recording session (January 21, 1949) featured two arrangements by John Lewis ("Move" and "Budo") and two by Gerry Mulligan ("Jeru" and "Godchild"). The band itself included two black musicians (Max Roach and Miles Davis) and seven white musicians (Kai Winding, Junior Collins, John Barber, Lee Konitz, Gerry Mulligan, Al Haig, and Joe Shulman). Three members of the band had been members of the Claude

Thornhill orchestra, including Bill Barber, Lee Konitz, and Joe Shulman; Miles Davis had worked with Al Haig while a member of the Charlie Parker band.[35] In 1949 a predominantly white band under the leadership of a black man was certainly newsworthy.

The band for the second session (April 22, 1949) included five African Americans (Miles Davis, J. J. Johnson, John Lewis, Nelson Boyd, and Kenny Clarke) and four non–African Americans (Gerry Mulligan, Lee Konitz, John Barber, and Sandy Siegelstein).[36] The arranging and compositional talents of Gerry Mulligan, Gil Evans, John Carisi, and John Lewis were featured on "Venus De Milo," "Boplicity," "Israel," and "Rouge," respectively. The final session, held on March 9, 1950, retained the same ethnic proportions and featured the compositions and arrangements of Gerry Mulligan ("Rocker," "Darn that Dream"), Gil Evans ("Moon Dreams"), and Miles Davis ("Deception").[37]

The *Birth of the Cool* bands could not have been more integrated had an affirmative action officer been doing the hiring, yet the favored way of explaining the composition of the bands was to say that race was irrelevant. Music was the higher, more universal principle. As Miles Davis explained his hiring of Lee Konitz on alto sax, "I wouldn't give a damn if he was green with red breath. I'm hiring a motherfucker to play, not for what color he is." Later in the fifties Davis was quoted as saying, "Music has no color: It's a raceless art. I don't care if a musician is green as long as he's talented."[38]

The link between the discourse of colorblindness and modernist aesthetics in jazz was forged through the notion of music itself as a higher principle than race. Yet the critical standards of classical music were the ones usually mobilized to establish what was modern. André Hodeir's analysis of the "cool tendency" in jazz (first published in the United States in 1956) illustrates the centrality of modernist aesthetic values, especially those of progress, experimentation, purity, and objectivity.[39] Hodeir's analyses of four *Birth of the Cool* sides—"Boplicity," "Israel," "Jeru," and "Godchild"—assimilate modern jazz to the standards of European art music rather than question the universal applicability of those criteria.[40]

Demonstrating modernist faith in progress, Hodeir argued that the cool tendency represented the "furthest point reached to date in the evolution of jazz." He described the musical attributes of the cool sound in relation to the more "violent" sonorities of swing and bebop, established by figures such as Roy Eldridge, Coleman Hawkins, and Charlie Parker. In Hodeir's genealogy of cool, Benny Carter, Teddy Wilson, and Benny

Goodman were the first proponents of a more sober conception of jazz, while Lester Young provided the ultimate model for a smoother, more relaxed approach to swinging.[41] To his credit, Hodeir recognized the problematic aspects of prevailing racial sound stereotypes in jazz: "Sharp attacks, rough timbre, hard touch, and vibrato had for a long time been regarded as essential characteristics of the Negro's sonority, whereas they were actually just characteristics of the hot idiom. Lester Young deserves the credit for showing that it is possible to avoid almost all these features and still produce authentic jazz."[42]

In Hodeir's opinion, cool jazz musicians, such as Lee Konitz, played with an even wispier tone color than Young, virtually eliminated vibrato from their sounds, avoided sharp accents and attacks, rarely played loudly, and were closer in sonority to the European conceptions of "purity of sound" than bebop players. Turning his attention to phrasing, he found that, with the exception of Miles Davis, cool players generally lacked rhythmic imagination when compared to bebop. Davis's asymmetrical phrases, which shift points of accent from bar to bar, in his opinion, are rhythmically more interesting (and show his debt to bebop and Charlie Parker) than the more symmetrical phrasing of soloists such as Stan Getz, Zoot Sims, and Al Cohn.

A positive evaluation of asymmetry (and counterpoint) is also stressed in Hodeir's analysis of the "two incontestable masterpieces" of the *Birth of the Cool* sessions—"Boplicity" and "Israel." "Boplicity," a Gil Evans arrangement of a Miles Davis thirty-two-bar AABA tune, features a B section in the second chorus that is extended to ten measures; the first six present an orchestrated paraphrase of the melody, and the last four highlight a solo phrase by Miles Davis that teases the listener into anticipating a full-blown solo (1:26–1:43). Instead, Davis's phrase transitions smoothly into the lead melody of an orchestrated paraphrase of the A section (1:44–1:57). The listener expects Davis's solo at the top of the third chorus but instead hears a call and response between Davis and the orchestrated accompaniment that gradually gives way to an unobstructed solo on the second A section (1:58–2:12). This passage provides an excellent example of the close interweaving of written and improvised segments in the *Birth of the Cool* arrangements.

Formal experimentation is another dimension highly prized in Hodeir's analyses and many subsequent discussions of the *Birth of the Cool*.[43] Hodeir describes Gerry Mulligan's "Jeru" as even more "revolutionary" than "Boplicity" because of its formal asymmetries and changes of meter. The B section of the first chorus (Hodeir calls it the "exposition") of the AABA form includes four bars of 4/4, three bars of 3/4, three bars of 2/4, and four bars of 4/4 (0:22–0:45). The A section that follows is nine bars instead of eight. By emphasizing formal variety Hodeir implicitly places Mulligan's and Evans's arrangements in the company of great modern European composers, such as Stravinsky or Schoenberg, who also shunned the obviousness of regular symmetrical forms. The formal innovations in these arrangements, as well as the impressionistic use of parallel voicings in unusual instrument pairings (French horn and tuba, alto and baritone sax, trumpet and trombone), all point to the modern *sophistication* prized in these works. Hodeir's critical evaluation appropriated the language of modernism and formal musical analysis to assert the right of jazz to be included in the category of "serious" music.

André Hodeir's analysis stressed the Apollonian qualities of the *Birth of the Cool* (restraint, balance, subtlety, sophistication) as opposed to the more Dionysian flavor of bebop (unrestrained, orgiastic, intense, exuberant). Both sides of this Nietzschean dialectic are components of modernism— the true artist ideally "harnessing Dionysian energy with Apollonian order and systemization"—and both are arguably ingredients in white and black relationships to modern jazz.[44] In the racial logic of the postwar period, however, the Dionysian side of the opposition was almost always coded black. In the chain of implicit oppositions operating in the aesthetic discourses of the 1950s, composition, intellectualism, and Western classical music were coded as white, while improvisation, emotional expressiveness, and the legacy of the blues were coded as black. Either principle could be invoked to claim the status of "artist," but in some contexts the former principle carried greater prestige, whereas in others the latter trumped all.

## Jazz and Classical Music

When arguing with classical musicians and composers, jazz musicians on both sides of the color line found invoking the Apollonian qualities of jazz to be a useful mode of defense. Connoisseurs of classical music often delivered backhanded compliments to jazz, praising the vitality of the genre but lamenting its "serious limitations" especially in the arena of unity and form. Composer Aaron Copland's comments on the "progres-

sive jazz" of the early 1950s (i.e., Stan Kenton and other experimenters such as Charles Mingus, Lennie Tristano, and George Russell) illustrate this point: "Progressive jazz has been freed of harmonic limitations. . . . Now its main trouble is a lack of unity in expressive content, by failing to drive home a unified idea. Progressive jazz composers don't always know, expressively, what they're trying to do. They seem to be distracted by amusing things along the way."[45]

Copland seems to have reserved the elevated status of "composer" for classical music alone. In his view, the jazz field was "full of arrangers posing as composers." Copland singled out George Russell, for one, as having written good material but said that it was "a little on the arranger's side."[46] Sympathetic classical composers, such as Gunther Schuller, responded to the background presumption of the inferiority of jazz by taking pains to demonstrate the unity and compositional brilliance in the works of jazz composers and improvisers. Schuller's first essay on jazz, published in 1957, is tellingly titled "The Future of Form in Jazz." Offering Ellington's "Creole Rhapsody" and "Reminiscing in Tempo" as early examples of formal innovation in jazz composition, Schuller identifies the masterpieces of form in contemporary jazz (that is, of the 1950s): Charles Mingus's "Pithecanthropus Erectus" and "Love Chant," John Lewis's "Django," and George Russell's "Lydian M-1."[47]

It is not surprising that in the late forties and early fifties such emphasis was placed on comparing leading jazz musicians to modern classical composers, for to do so was to claim a right to higher cultural status for jazz and a new uncompromising identity for the jazz musician. Improvisers freely advertised their interest in modern classical music, which functioned as a symbolic marker of urban cosmopolitanism and musical sophistication. Nat Hentoff's "From Bird to Berg" offered something of a hip classical listening list for the early 1950s' *Down Beat* audience (prepared with the assistance of pianist Teddy Wilson). The specific works recommended (which remain common favorites among jazz enthusiasts) reveal a great deal about the sort of classical music and musicians that jazz musicians identified with. Readers were advised to check out Stravinsky's *Ebony Concerto, Symphony in Three Movements, Le Sacre du Printemps,* and *Petrouchka;* Bartók's *Concerto for Orchestra* and *Sonata for Two Pianos and Percussion;* Hindemith's "Music for Brass and Strings;" Alban Berg's *Wozzeck* and *Concerto for Violin, Piano, and Thirteen Wind Instruments;* and Varèse's "Ionisation" and "Density 21.5". Hindemith's *Kleine*

*Kammermusik* was favorably compared to Miles Davis's *Birth of the Cool* sides. Also making the list were J. S. Bach and Gabrielli. If Debussy and Ravel were of primary interest in the twenties and thirties, the younger generation of musicians embraced Stravinsky and Bartók, two modern composers known for their jagged, driving rhythms and incorporation of folk elements. As a Russian and a Hungarian, respectively, Stravinsky and Bartók were marginal Europeans, viewed somewhat differently than composers from Germany, France, and Italy.

Having developed an interest in classical music in the late 1940s, Charlie Parker counted Stravinsky, Schoenberg, Prokofiev, Hindemith, Ravel, Debussy, Wagner, and Bach among the composers he admired. After visiting Paris in 1949, he considered embarking on the formal study of classical music with famed composition teacher Nadia Boulanger and Marcel Mule (a classical saxophonist). In 1954 Parker approached Edgard Varèse about the possibility of compositional study. According to his biographer, Parker was convinced that the study of classical music would help him advance his art.[48] Part of the symbolic cachet of European classical music to African American musicians at this time no doubt had to do with the relatively nondiscriminatory treatment musicians experienced while traveling in Europe and the greater artistic respect that continental audiences displayed for jazz. A specifically European conception of the modern artist held great appeal.

### African Americans and Classical Music

African American musicians have generally been caught between a rock and a hard place when it comes to classical music. On the one hand, a cosmopolitan display of knowledge enabled artists such as Duke Ellington to resist white stereotypes of the folk musician—that untutored, instinctual "noble savage" to which Moldy Fig critics were so attached.[49] On the other hand, musicians who embraced classical music ideals and incorporated references to the European tradition faced at least two types of critical response. First, interest in classical music by jazz musicians was often taken as an admission that jazz innovations were *derived* from European sources.

After Charlie Parker expressed his admiration for Bartók, his interviewer asked how many of Parker's innovations in bebop before 1945 were the product of "spontaneous experimentation" and how many were the result of "adaptation of the ideas of your classical predecessors, for example, as in Bartok?" Since Parker was unfamiliar with classical music in the formative years of bebop, he bridled at the suggestion: "Nothin'—not a bit of the idiom in which music travels today, known as progressive [bebop] music, was adapted [from] or even inspired by the older composers."[50] Second, within African American communities, an overemphasis on classical continuities in the music was considered by some constituencies as pretentious or indicative of insufficient pride in African American roots. The Modern Jazz Quartet faced such criticism during its long career.

The dilemma was definitely not new. Duke Ellington, responding to those who compared him to Bach, Ravel, and Stravinsky, offered a cogent explanation for his ambivalent reaction to such praise:

> If I seem a little shy about being displayed on a critical platform with the classical big shots, let me also dispel the notion that I hesitate to place the jazz medium in a top musical category. Jazz, swing, jive and every other musical phenomenon of American musical life are as much an art medium as are the most profound works of the famous classical composers. To attempt to elevate the status of the jazz musician by forcing the level of his best work into comparisons with classical music is to deny him this rightful share of originality. Let us remember that many "long-hair" composers (still current) freely admit that they have been influenced by the jazz idiom. . . . Music, like any other art form, reflects the mood, temperament and environment of its creators.[51]

To the extent that the comparison with European composers simply assimilated jazz to the presumed superior standards of classical music, it failed to recognize the alternative Afro-modern standards jazz proposed for American music. That jazz as an art form articulated its own musical vision—by developing expressive and improvisational principles rooted in a wide variety of African American musics—challenged the hegemony of European musical standards in American music. Modernism in jazz was most successful when it infused improvisation with its sonorities, harmonic extensions, and virtuosity *without* undercutting these improvisational and expressive principles.

Indeed, one way to read the debate over the merits of black versus white jazz musicians that suffused the pages of jazz publications in the fifties is as a contest over which set of criteria—those of European high art music or those of Afro-modernism—should serve as the ultimate arbiter of excellence. White musicians, who were often defensive over the charge that they did not swing or play with enough emotion, often stressed the principles of modernism (such as the structural, compositional, or technical sophistication of their work), which were less dependent on African American musical principles. Nevertheless, many African American musicians also sought validation through the cultivation of aesthetic principles developed in European art music traditions.

Classical music was certainly not a foreign language to jazz musicians, especially those who played instruments prominently used in European art music such as trumpet, clarinet, piano, and bass. As one of the consequences of the Jim Crow line in European art music, many classically trained black musicians had few alternatives but jazz or R&B. Pianist John Lewis, trumpeter Miles Davis, and bassists Ron Carter, Richard Davis, Charles Mingus, and Art Davis are among the many African American musicians of this generation with formidable classical credentials. The virtuosic technique cultivated in classical study—whether through private instruction, conservatory training, mentoring by a more experienced musician, or self-instruction—as well as theoretical and conceptual knowledge, were resources that came to be expected of jazz musicians. Indeed, learning about the structural properties of music was prized and celebrated in the late 1940s and early 1950s.[52] Moreover, musicians on either side of the cool jazz/hard bop debate—from Horace Silver, Benny Golson, and Quincy Jones to Gil Evans, Lennie Tristano, and Stan Kenton—have repeatedly cited the importance of studying harmony and composition. In fact, if there is a musical "bridge discourse" between Afro-modernism and classical music, between cool jazz and hard bop, I would argue that it is harmony.[53]


## Lennie Tristano

Perhaps the most appealing promise of modernism to jazz musicians was that musical merit rather than race or class would determine whose achievements would be recognized and celebrated. Implicit in this stance was the idea that universal colorblind musical standards existed and could be fairly applied to the work of jazz musicians. Technical and structural musical standards such as complexity, virtuosity, harmonic sophistication, and form were supposed to prevail rather than who one was. The success of Dave Brubeck and Lennie Tristano and their portrayal in the jazz press of the 1950s illustrate that, despite the best intentions, modernism alone could not level the playing field.

Lennie Tristano was perhaps the strongest white contender for the status of innovator in a field of competitors resoundingly dominated by African American musicians (Charlie Parker, Dizzy Gillespie, Thelonious Monk). Tristano's experiments with counterpoint, his technical mastery, and his abilities as a composer caught the attention of several prominent African American artists, including Charles Mingus, Max Roach, George Russell, and Charlie Parker. As Brian Priestley has noted, they respected the fact that Tristano was a thinker and a teacher, as well as a virtuosic technician. Tristano's inability to get along well with many African American musicians and his reputation for a cold, prickly personality and racial prejudice are well known despite the fact that he taught his students to model themselves on an African American pantheon of heroes: Louis Armstrong, Earl Hines, Roy Eldridge, Lester Young, Charlie Christian, Charlie Parker, and Bud Powell.[54]

Among the things that irritated many African Americans about Tristano was the fact that the jazz press presented him as a modern master of Apollonian virtue, while ignoring the intelligence and sophistication of the presumably more Dionysian African American pantheon of innovators. *Metronome*'s feature on Tristano in August 1949 was titled "Master in the Making," and Barry Ulanov's prose fell all over itself in emphasizing Lennie's modern difference: "It became apparent that Lennie's was not only an inquiring mind but an instructed one, that in the realms of literature and philosophy, as in music, he was not content merely to feel something, that he had to explore ideas, to experience them, to think them through carefully, thoroughly, logically until he could fully grasp them and then hold on to them."[55]

By drawing attention to Tristano's intellectual credentials, including his American Conservatory degree and study of composition, Ulanov championed Tristano's qualifications to lead a "bright new era of jazz." By suggesting that other jazz musicians were "content merely to feel," Ulanov's colorblind language nevertheless played on the racial stereotype of African Americans as all emotion, little intellect. The white mind was the "instructed one," so just who might the reader have inferred was the "uninstructed one"?

Ulanov's view of Tristano is somewhat ironic since the centerpiece of Tristano's teaching later became learning by ear and developing emotional melodic expression.[56] Ulanov, who later became an English professor at Barnard College, praised qualities in Tristano very much like those highly valued in the academic intellectual circles of which he was a part.[57] Ulanov identified with Tristano—that is, found validation of his own values—in Tristano's aesthetic. A month later Ulanov wrote another ode to Tristano, this time focusing upon his Capitol recordings.[58]

Tristano's "Intuition" and "Digression" have long been cited as forerunners to free jazz since they had no preset plan other than the order of the instrumental entrances. There are no drums on these tracks, for Denzel Best (an African American musician) had another gig and had to leave the recording session early. The performances have more affinity to the sound of modern classical chamber music than they do to Ornette Coleman's *The Shape of Jazz to Come,* largely because they forsake many of the melodic, timbral, and rhythmic qualities that have been crucial to African American aesthetics as defined by Murray, Floyd, and Wilson.

One of the reasons "Intuition" and "Digression" sound classical (and to some observers "white") is that Tristano actively avoided the interactive call-and-response organization that featured so prominently in the definitions of black aesthetics presented earlier in this chapter.[59] Tristano also rejected the timbral inflections and phrasing of blues and gospel and instead focused upon long, uninterrupted melodic lines, often in a timbrally blended unison. The double-timed bridge on "Wow" (0:21–0:31) aptly illustrates the precision of the Tristano Sextet, while also demonstrating the band's aesthetic distance from the "vocalization of sound" component of African American aesthetics. Although bebop phrasing also emphasized long lines, in Tristano's band the drums did not interject many bombs, nor did Tristano's horn players create cross-rhythms through offbeat accentuation or vary their timbres as widely as did Parker or Gillespie.

"Intuition," which is substantially more interactive than "Wow" or "Crosscurrent," illustrates Tristano's interest in freely improvised counterpoint. The melodic lines are long and continuous and are layered on top of one another in contrapuntal style and rhythmic phrasing consistent with the ideals of modern classical music. The lack of emphasis on cross-rhythm and call and response subjected Tristano to the charge that his music did not swing, while his preference for homogeneous timbres in the unison performance of his melodic lines struck many listeners as expressively cold.

It is important to recognize that many white listeners and critics objected just as vociferously to Tristano's lack of attention to the expressive standards of African American aesthetics. Writing in 1951, Bill Coss lamented the constrained role of Tristano's rhythm section, which included Max Roach (an African American) and bassist Clyde Lombardi: "When they seemed about to interject some spirit of continuity and definiteness into the performance, they found themselves alone in a kind of stone edifice as cold and unyielding as the metaphor is meant to imply." Tristano's music was in his opinion "as tangible as an algebra problem" and lacked emotional depth. Coss accused Tristano of fostering "a sophomoric cult and an ever-broadening, in-grown, other-world snobbishness which has no justification in relation to reality." Defenders claimed that Tristano's music was all about feeling but used more refined expressive means than the "growling and howling" more typical of R&B. (The racial coding of black aesthetics as vulgar and primitive could not be more transparent.) Tristano's attention to melodic development, control, and virtuosity, in the opinion of his fans, produced a qualitatively different, but no less intense, emotional experience.[60]

It is crucial, from the point of view of cultural analysis, to recognize that a portion of the white listening audience had assimilated many aspects of African American aesthetics into their expectations and preferences for jazz as a genre. Their criticisms of Tristano and Brubeck were similar to those of many of their African American counterparts who found the music of the leading white contenders less than emotionally satisfying. The internalization of these Afro-modernist standards as a recursive element in their own aesthetics, I suggest, was important in the gradual blackening of musical tastes among jazz aficionados during the civil rights years. The aesthetic dilemma for jazz and modernism in the 1950s revolved around the extent to which musicians would accommodate themselves to classical musical standards of expression (tone color, phrasing, formal organization, rhythmic approach), in the process "elevating" the music to Euro-American highbrow tastes, and the extent to which they would deploy African American call and response organization and improvisational principles to breathe new life into contemporary definitions of musical modernism itself. If the early fifties placed a great deal of emphasis on the former, by the early 1960s the triumph of the latter was in full swing.

## Dave Brubeck: Looking the Part

Dave Brubeck, like Lennie Tristano, was viewed by many observers as lacking in the expressive resources of the African American tradition deemed essential for a genuine jazz feeling. As Leonard Feather opined, "Many musicians have whispered (but are afraid to repeat aloud, because it is impolitic to attack a reigning idol) that Brubeck, for all his academic qualifications and harmonic ingenuity, never has borne any message for them; that he is not primarily a swinging pianist, and that the truest jazz talent of the group is Paul Desmond."[61]

In the early stages of Brubeck's career, his classical credentials were championed by Barry Ulanov, who once again saw the possibility of elevating jazz to classical music:

> More than any other contemporary jazz musician, Dave is directed in his playing by his studying background. You're not always aware of the impending M.A. degree under Milhaud. You don't always know that this man has devoted hours to counterpoint, harmony, theory, composition, and related disciplines. But the signs are plentiful. A little canon here, a bop fugue there. A little melodic development somewhere else, a grand exposition elsewhere still. The texture is out of the great classical composers; the base upon which it rests is jazz motion.[62]

Early *Down Beat* articles stressed Brubeck's "double life" as a classical composer and jazz musician. Since he was never a proficient reader of music (by his own admission), he was in many ways far less appropriate than John Lewis or Miles Davis as an example of the jazz musician who was skilled in classical music. Brubeck, after all, was nearly dropped from the undergraduate music program at College of the Pacific after it was discovered that he could not sight-read. He could write music and did well in harmony but could not perform from the printed page. When it came to performance, Brubeck had always been an "ear musician" like Wes Montgomery. The dean agreed to keep Brubeck in the program on the condition that he promise "never to pursue a career in teaching music."[63] (It is difficult to imagine that a nonreading African American student would have been accorded such lenience.) Brubeck, nevertheless, looked the part, and his competence in classical music was presumed.

Brubeck's limitations in classical music may have been among the factors that led him to later distance himself from it. Although Brubeck initially viewed jazz performance as a way to build up a backlog of ideas that he could then use as a composer, by mid-1954 he had his own criticisms of the contemporary composition scene: "I've now come to believe that any music that expresses emotion is the only music that's going to live. And jazz certainly does that. In their intellectuality, most of the contemporary composers, including most of the 12-tone system writers, are getting too far from the roots of our culture. And for American composers, our roots should be in jazz. So I hope that what I do eventually write has more of a jazz influence in it than any other influence. But I do not think there is any necessary dichotomy between jazz and what is called 'serious music.' "[64]

For Brubeck, jazz was a creative and emotionally liberating space for his musical development despite the fact that arbiters of jazz sensibility found his San Francisco–based aesthetic to be removed from the vitality of the New York scene and the expressive resources of African American musical traditions. In many ways Brubeck's heart was in the right place, something that is most clearly revealed in a two-part article he wrote for *Down Beat* in 1950 titled "Jazz's Evolvement as Art Form." Brubeck argued that jazz had an aesthetic energy of its own that required "an emotional awareness outside the bounds of traditional critique." Far from arguing for greater emulation of classical music, Brubeck emphasized the "mixed parentage" of jazz and suggested that exploration of African music offered a way to invigorate the genre. He also suggested that the composer who wished to use jazz as a source should "go to the fountainhead—to the original blues, spirituals, and ragtime—so that his music will not be victimized by the usage of a cliché of one of the short-lived eras of jazz."[65]

## *Time* Magazine

On November 8, 1954, Dave Brubeck became the first jazz musician to be featured on the cover of *Time* magazine. Although critics had been ambivalent before, after this the gloves came off. Leonard Feather argued that

Duke Ellington should have been on the magazine cover first, and several years later Brubeck admitted that he agreed. Ellington had been the first to congratulate Brubeck on the honor, and, as Brubeck recalled, "that even made me feel worse."[66]

The *Time* article was racially coded, celebrating Brubeck as a sign of "a new kind of jazz age in the U.S." Unlike the jazz age of the twenties, " jazz as played by Brubeck and other modernists (Gerry Mulligan, Chet Baker, Stan Getz, Shorty Rogers) is neither chaotic nor abandoned. It goes to the head and the heart more than to the feet."[67] As if the racial coding were not clear enough, the author went on to describe jazz as having emerged from slave chants, blues, work songs, and "gaudy Negro funeral parades." The article then described King Oliver, Sidney Bechet, and Louis Armstrong as players who "blatted their way from the cemetery playing 'High Society' or 'Didn't He Ramble.' "[68] Brubeck's popularity with college students across the country seemed to promise a jazz that would be more upscale, less interested in social protest, and whiter.

The *Time* article seemed almost calculated to fan the flames of racial resentment, for it also bragged that Brubeck's expected income that year would be $100,000 and included a picture of Brubeck's custom-built home in Oakland, California. To many jazz aficionados, Brubeck's income and lifestyle seemed to be grossly out of proportion to his artistic contributions to the genre. After a barrage of criticism, Brubeck protested that critics were treating him unfairly: "You'd think I'd betrayed jazz by getting on *Time*." As he explained some years later, "I didn't try in any way to get the *Time* cover. I went along with what was happening, and immediately there was a cry of protest from all sides."[69] Brubeck saw himself as being criticized for "not, of all things, being a Negro!"[70] That *Time* editors viewed Dave Brubeck as more suitable for the cover of the magazine than Duke Ellington or Louis Armstrong illustrates the racial advantages of whiteness at midcentury. Although Brubeck is partially Native American in ancestry, this was not known publicly at the time.[71]

Musically, Brubeck was criticized for not swinging, and some questioned whether his music was really jazz. Among Brubeck's many musical defenders were several African Americans, including Charlie Parker, Mary Lou Williams, Billy Taylor, and Charles Mingus. Some of Brubeck's most insulting critics were white, among them Leonard Feather, John Mehegan, Eddie Condon, and Tony Scott.[72] Critics were ambivalent about classical music influences in jazz, and Brubeck's success highlighted the persistence of racial stratification in the music business. The titles of Brubeck's albums—from *Jazz Goes to College* to *Dave Digs Disney*—though effective from a marketing point of view, seemed to underscore the gap. Leonard Feather commented on racial disparities in the music business by comparing Brubeck to the Modern Jazz Quartet, the black equivalent of a classically influenced, clean-cut, and respectable ensemble: "On the one hand, you are delighted that an intelligent, ambitious, clean-living, and talented fellow like Brubeck can win so many fans and, in effect, do so much for jazz; on the other hand, you are distressed that an intelligent, ambitious, clean-living and talented fellow like John Lewis, mentor of the MJQ, can have accomplished so much more, musically, while gaining so much less ground, economically."[73]

## The Politics of Respectability

The Modern Jazz Quartet accomplished a synthesis of jazz and classical music that may be the peak achievement of the cool jazz and Third Stream movement in jazz.[74] If Brubeck was at times somewhat ambivalent about classical music, John Lewis and the Modern Jazz Quartet embraced the encounter wholeheartedly. Their "chamber jazz" style featured John Lewis's compositions and a delicate interplay between Lewis on piano, Milt Jackson on vibes, Percy Heath on bass, and Connie Kay on drums. Voted the best combo eight times between 1953 and 1961 in the *Down Beat* critics' poll, the MJQ was an African American ensemble whose music successfully crossed over to white audiences with a predilection for the aesthetics of classical music, while retaining enough swing and improvisational excitement to earn the respect of jazz lovers. Theirs was a precise but conservative jazz whose very elegance and sophistication demanded that white audiences respond to them as the intelligent, dignified men they were.

In many ways the Modern Jazz Quartet practiced a musical "politics of respectability" that combined both a conservative and subversive impulse.[75] In its embrace of classical musical standards of excellence, the Modern Jazz Quartet seemed to want to prove to an audience beyond the African American community that they too were learned in matters of form, thematic development, fugal writing, and harmony. Their music did not question the universal applicability of these standards but rather demonstrated that they could improvise compellingly within them and bring the complex chromatic melodies of bebop and the emotional poignancy of the blues into a musical environment replete with formal control. They dressed impeccably, carried themselves with forbearance, and with every note demonstrated that theirs was a music that belonged not in a nightclub but rather in the concert hall (Ralph Ellison once described their appearance as "funereal").[76] In a social climate that associated jazz musicians with heroin addiction and dissoluteness, the MJQ confronted white audiences in the United States and Europe with a conservative black masculinity that they seldom realized existed. As Milt Jackson recalled, "The idea was to raise the stature of jazz, which had become... stigmatized just by the name itself and was put down. For me, jazz is on the same level as classical music, which everyone respects in all countries."[77]

For John Lewis, who had studied music at the University of New Mexico and received a master's degree from the Manhattan School of Music in 1952, the MJQ offered an ongoing environment in which to develop his formidable skills as a composer, which are especially evident in pieces like "Django" and the fugal "Vendome."[78] If pieces like "The Queen's Fancy" seemed rather pretentious in their invocation of baroque musical styles and if the fugal subjects and answers in "Vendome" and "Concorde" sometimes replaced African American approaches to call and response, the MJQ also took the swing-era practice of swinging the classics to a new compositional level. Yet, despite their privileging of classical aesthetic values pertaining to form and timbral color, the music of the Modern Jazz Quartet often contained some unarguably swinging solos by both Milt Jackson and John Lewis.

In the 1950s the critical reaction to the Modern Jazz Quartet was quite positive but nevertheless ambivalent about whether what the group played was really jazz. The reigning in of the drums and the understated emotional tone of the group (in other words, the lack of emphasis on two central components of African American aesthetics) left many reviewers respectful but puzzled. "There are also times... where effect seems almost more important than the feeling," wrote one reviewer, while another found irony: "The filigree that the quartet uses from time to time serves as an ironic contrast to the intense swinging that goes on within these admittedly sometimes-flowery frames." Saxophonist Don Byas felt that the arrangements of the MJQ departed too much from the jazz tradition but admired the individual players in the group anyway. He saw a commercial purpose behind the group's classical focus.[79]

In 1956 Kenny Clarke, the group's first drummer, delivered perhaps the most scathing critique of John Lewis:

> I will surprise you, perhaps, by claiming that he detests jazz. He can play jazz fantastically if he wants to, but he doesn't like to. What he likes is Bach and Chopin. It's insane to say that I was bored in the MJQ. I wanted to play jazz, but there was no way with those damned arrangements. So I left. Milt Jackson is a marvelous jazzman, but he has his hands tied in the MJQ. He suffers a lot from never having the chance to really play. I think that in the end he'll leave, like me.[80]

But Milt Jackson did not leave, at least not until he had spent twenty-three years in the group. Although Jackson recorded many celebrated albums with top hard bop players of the day, including Miles Davis, John Coltrane, Thelonious Monk, Cannonball Adderley, and Wes Montgomery, and no doubt had been invited many times to join other ensembles on a regular basis, he remained with the MJQ.[81] He must have found something musically and personally satisfying in the way the group practiced the politics of respectability. Although the balance between African American and classical music aesthetic standards in the MJQ may have been weighted too heavily toward the latter in the historical context of the emergence of hard bop, the desire of many classically trained jazz musicians to have that competence publicly acknowledged has been deep and ongoing.[82]

## Modernism and African American Aesthetics

As the work of Guthrie Ramsey and David Rosenthal has shown, the emphasis on jazz as an art music in jazz historiography has often obscured the extent to which the music was interconnected to rhythm and blues and other popular African American musics.[83] This is particularly true of hard bop styles of the 1950s and early 1960s, which were performed in neighborhood clubs, taverns, and other sites of "everyday blackness" that Ramsey has argued served as "community theaters."[84]

Although the advent of bebop is generally taken as the historical moment that jazz became an art music and lost its popular following, Rosenthal provides a persuasive case for the ongoing popularity of jazz in black communities throughout this period.[85] The styles of jazz that were popular in African American clubs and taverns may have been dismissed by Martin Williams as "The Funky–Hard Bop Regression" and suspected of being "anthems for a black middle-brow" audience by Amiri Baraka but were a beloved part of everyday life in the African American communities of northern cities such as Philadelphia, Detroit, New York, and Chicago.[86]

The cross-fertilization of African American styles that took place in such venues occurred in several ways. To begin with, many of the most respected names in jazz began their careers playing in rhythm and blues bands. Benny Golson played with Bull Moose Jackson and Screamin' Jay Hawkins; John Coltrane worked for Eddie "Cleanhead" Vinson, Jimmy Johnson, and Earl Bostic; Clifford Brown worked in Lionel Hampton's band, as well as Chris Powell's Blue Flames.[87] The R&B bands of the early 1950s often featured saxophone solos replete with showboating antics such as "walking the bar" and writhing on the floor in the heat of musical passion. Working the crowd into a frenzy through a slowly building solo that teased and prodded toward an inexorably cathartic climax was part of the art of this musical extroversion. This was the era of bands with horns and before the electric guitar replaced the tenor saxophone as the solo instrument of choice. In many ways the hard bop of Horace Silver and Art Blakey built on the musical legacy of the riffing Kansas City bands (Count Basie and Jay McShann) and as developed and extended by bands like Louis Jordan's, with its hard-driving shuffle-feel and jazz-based instrumentation. Hard bop combined the extroversion and exuberance of these populist styles with the instrumental artistry and harmonic sophistication of bebop.

## Hard Bop Aesthetics

The quintessential hard bop band is of course Art Blakey and the Jazz Messengers. The prominence of Blakey's drumming and its exemplary swing, fire, and intensity have long been the focus of any discussion of the group. Blakey's drumming—which was louder than that of Max Roach or Kenny Clarke and more given to exploiting the hard-driving shuffle-feel of R&B and often prodded soloists to greater fervor through well-timed riffs, press rolls, and other drum interjections—was sometimes criticized for overshadowing soloists. Blakey's drumming frequently drew attention to the lower-pitched drums in the set—the tom-toms and bass drum—and freely incorporated Afro-Cuban and Latin drumming patterns in a manner that established new standards for modern jazz drumming.[88] In describing the aims of his music, Blakey commented in 1953, "We'll certainly play modern, but we want to get the people to follow the beat and let the horns do what they want to. Once they follow the beat they'll be able to follow the horns too."[89]

Yet to view the reclamation of blackness in hard bop aesthetics as simply a matter of rhythm or the greater prominence of blues inflection in solos would grossly underestimate the importance of composition and harmony in the hard bop redefinition of the jazz mainstream that took place in the late 1950s and early 1960s.[90] Think of the many compositions that Horace Silver, Benny Golson, and Bobby Timmons added to the jazz repertory—"Ecaroh," "Horace Scope," "Doodlin,'" "Along Came Betty," "Killer Joe," "Are You Real," "Moanin,'" and "Dat Dere"—or those provided by the more experimental wing of hard bop (Charles Mingus, John Coltrane, Thelonious Monk, Wayne Shorter)—"Haitian Fight Song," "Wednesday Night Prayer Meeting," "Syeeda's Flute Song," "Equinox," "Epistrophy," "Evidence," "Ping Pong," "Speak No Evil," and "Armageddon." This repertory combined interest in the various components of the heterogeneous sound ideal with sophisticated harmonies and compositional innovation. Jazz musicians were no longer content to confine their repertory to jazz standards from the Tin Pan Alley and musical theater traditions; instead, they created an original repertory that became the jazz standards of later generations. In contrast to the writing of the Modern Jazz Quartet or Dave Brubeck, many of these composers were less interested in structural shapes and counterpoint taken from the Western classical tradition than in combining musical processes and emotions from the broader African American and Afro-Caribbean traditions, harmonic sophistication, and formal innovation that served to create more space for extended improvisation.

## Riffs, Vamps, and Composition

Two key elements of hard bop compositional style illustrate the interconnection of harmony and rhythm in hard bop aesthetics: riffs and vamps. *Riffs* are short, repeated melodic or rhythmic figures that appear in a wide variety of musical roles (for instance, as melodies in their own right, in call and response, and as layers in accompaniment textures). The Count Basie band compositions "Sent for You Yesterday" and "Volcano" illustrate the multifaceted possibilities of the riff.[91] Riffs are sometimes continuously repeating figures with little space between repetitions; when these appear in the bass line, they are usually called *ostinatos.*

Horace Silver's "Horoscope" (later called "Horace Scope") illustrates one way that melodic riffs and harmony reinforced one another in hard bop compositions. In a variation on blues practice, the chords shift each time the riff figure is repeated, endowing the melody with new harmonic color each time. In "Horoscope," however, the harmonic progression over which the riff is played is more modern than the blues.[92]

Figure 3.3 shows how the E natural that anchors the riff functions as a ♯9 of a D♭7 chord in the first bar, a ♭5 of the B♭7 on the second, and the 5 of the A7 chord in the third measure.[93] Blakey's drumming accents this pitch when the harmonies change. The riff thus helps drive the harmonic progression to a satisfying closure. Another excellent example of this approach is Thelonious Monk's more canonic composition "Thelonious."[94]

Horace Silver also makes use of riff figures in his almost Monkish-sounding solo on "Horoscope." At several points Silver uses the repetition of a riff to create a delightful dance of rhythmic displacement (1:04–1:14, 1:28–1:35, 1:49–1:55). This classic property of the riff—that its length does not coincide with the length of a bar and thus will begin in a different place with each repetition—is something that Thelonious Monk's compositions took great advantage of.[95] The displaced accents projected by a riff are a crucial resource in the creation of the syncopated cross-rhythms so highly prized in jazz aesthetics.

*Vamps* are repeating figures (usually two to four bars in length) that may include an oscillation between two harmonies, a short, repeated harmonic progression, and a bass ostinato or a pedal-point figure. They es-

FIGURE 3.3. Horace Silver, "Horoscope." Used by permission. Music by Horace Silver, copyright by Ecaroh Music.

tablish a harmonic context with a rifflike rhythmic quality, are usually open ended in length, and most typically are found in introductions and codas. During the 1950s and 1960s, however, they came to be integral textual components of the compositions themselves.

Benny Golson's "Killer Joe" is a classic example of a hard bop vamp tune. Its vamp consists of an alternation between two chords, plus a repeating bass line, and it serves as both an introduction and an accompaniment texture in the A sections of the AABA form.[96]

The rhythm of McCoy Tyner's piano chords feature a shout-like dotted quarter-eighth figure (aka the Charleston rhythm), while the bass line has an ostinato quality not far removed from some of the repeating bass lines found in the R&B of the 1950s. Lee Morgan's "Sidewinder" is another classic vamp-based hard bop tune that uses a bass line more obviously connected to the R&B tradition; Wayne Shorter's "Ping Pong" provides another example of a vamp based on the Charleston rhythm.[97] The wide variety of vamp figures found in the jazz at this time made sonic links to popular African American genres, as well as to Latin music. This was a key part of the soulful flavor of music.

Take Bobby Timmons's "This Here," which is built on a gospel vamp in 6/4.[98] The vamp serves as both as an introduction and accompaniment figure and in so doing defines the feel of the piece. The hypnotic qualities of these vamp figures later reached their artistic apotheosis in the great rhythm section of John Coltrane—McCoy Tyner, Jimmy Garrison, and Elvin Jones. The growing presence of the "gospel tinge" in hard bop must certainly have been encouraged by the popularity of Ray Charles's music. Charles's reliance on gospel piano vamps in "Come Back Baby," "What Would I Do without You," "A Fool for You," "Hallelujah, I Love Her So," "That's Enough," and "Tell All the World about You," must surely have had an impact on the populist stream of hard bop music through its presence on the jukeboxes of African American clubs in the 1950s. In addition, several jazz musicians played in Charles's bands, including drummers Connie Kay (of the MJQ) and Panama Francis, saxophonists David "Fathead" Newman, Cecil Payne, and Hank Crawford, and trumpeter Marcus Belgrave. That jazz critics tended to write about performances in higher prestige and whiter social settings like Greenwich Village clubs and concert hall performances no doubt helps explain the comparative lack of attention to the interconnections between jazz and R&B.[99]

Another aesthetic stream in strong evidence in the rhythms and vamps of Horace Silver and Art Blakey is Latin music, Afro-Cuban in particular. A montuno-like vamp figure, for example, serves as the accompaniment feel for the Latin sections of Silver's "Ecaroh." [100] In the 1952 piano trio version, Silver oscillates between two altered dominant chords that are voiced to bring out a half-step alternation between Ab and G and a tenth between the bass and the bottom of piano voicing. Art Blakey plays a mambo bell pattern rhythm (in 2–3 clave), and Gene Ramey plays a two-bar Latin ostinato pattern (figure 3.4). [101]

As in Dizzy Gillespie's "Night in Tunisia," Latin sections often alternated with swing sections in hard bop recordings. In "Split Kick," from 1954, Blakey plays the same mambo bell pattern, while Silver articulates the changes with a bass line in the tumbao rhythm (dotted quarter–dotted quarter–quarter). Although the "Latin tinge" has been a part of the jazz language since its earliest history, a ramping up of the Afro-Cuban presence in hard bop is particularly revealed when vamp patterns are explored. [102]

Another aspect of hard bop composition that is germane to the larger argument of this chapter is the flowering of two- and three-part horn writing. Composers such as Horace Silver, Benny Golson, Wayne Shorter, and Joe Henderson created rich harmonizations and counterlines that have become deeply embedded in mainstream jazz. The Jazz Messengers' 1956 recording of "Ecaroh," for example, features Donald Byrd's trumpet and Hank Mobley's tenor sax voiced in perfect fourths placed on the seventh and #9 of the underlying harmony. Other notable horn writing can be found on Benny Golson's "Are You Real," Joe Henderson's "Home-stretch," Lee Morgan's "Desert Moonlight," Nelson's "Stolen Moments" and "Teenies Blues," and Wayne Shorter's "Master Mind" and "Ping

FIGURE 3.4. Horace Silver, "Ecaroh" vamp. Used by permission. Music by Horace Silver, copyright by Ecaroh Music.

Pong." Although the line writing in these pieces is usually consonant in the context of jazz harmony (featuring many thirds and sixths), at their best these small-group arrangements delight the ear by amplifying the extended colors of the harmonies with superb voice leading.


## Harmony and Blackness

The place of harmony in African American aesthetics, I believe, is crucial in moving beyond the excessive stereotyping of black music as primarily characterized by rhythm, as well as the overattribution of the harmonic elements in the music as white. To say that the African American musical aesthetics are hybrid and combine aspects of European and African musical resources does not, in my opinion, go far enough in accounting historically for the impact of black music on American culture, for it neglects to recognize the long history and originality of African American harmonic practice. As histories of the subject prior to the twentieth century have noted, African American music was more likely to be identified by its vocal style and harmonic gift than by rhythm.[103]

At the turn of the twentieth century W.E.B. Du Bois and James Weldon Johnson viewed the spirituals as the Negro people's greatest gift to American culture, and recent scholarship has credited African American a capella singing as the source of the barbershop quartet, a genre until recently thought of as quintessentially white. This is the recursive quality of cultural exchange, in which a cultural resource borrowed from one group becomes indigenized and transformed over time and in that new state is borrowed back by the first group.

Marshall Sahlins has described the borrowing and transformation aspects of a similar process in a colonial context as "the indigenization of modernity"; that is, the incorporation of a borrowed cultural resource becomes a means of articulating difference down the line. Specifically, in a globalized world, local changes that result from contact with modernity often produce influential local diversities that acquire different symbolic inflections in the new context. With colonialism and imperialism in mind, Sahlins argues that culture has been an important weapon in response to domination: "And how else can the people respond to what has been inflicted on them except by devising on their own heritage, acting according to their own categories, logics, understandings?" Yet this "devising" of heritage is seldom about simply returning to origins; instead, it deploys aspects of modernity in the self-fashioning—using the master's tools in the struggle against him, in other words.[104]

In terms of musical history, this is simply to argue that in African America contact with Western harmony produced distinctive harmonic practices that were developed and transmitted (often aurally) by African American musicians, who performed within African American cultural settings, especially the church. Among these chacteristic means of presenting harmony are vamps and riffs, plus the harmony of the blues with its proclivities toward altering the dominant, and the thick, extended voicings of the gospel choir.[105]

In the twentieth century, aspects of these harmonic practices heard variously in blues, gospel, jazz, rhythm and blues, and congregational singing were then selectively borrowed back by enthusiastic white (and other non–African American) musicians eager to incorporate that aesthetic feeling into their musical projects. The expressive power of these harmonic (and often simultaneously rhythmic) musical devices is especially apparent in the populist stream of hard bop music (Horace Silver, Jimmy Smith, Cannonball Adderley, Gene Ammons). To the extent that these musicians modernized the harmony of rhythm and blues, boogie woogie, and gospel and rejoiced in establishing an intensified improvisational language, they cultivated a modern African American art music that thrived somewhere between the classical aspirations of cool jazz and everyday popular music.

## Aesthetic Cross-Dressing and Cultural Polarization

There is perhaps no stronger proof of the dominance of African American aesthetics in jazz than the phenomenon of white musicians who long to have their sound confused for black. White musicians as stylistically diverse as trombonist Jack Teagarden, pianist Bill Evans, trumpeter Chet Baker, drummer Stan Levey, pianist Russ Freeman, baritone saxophonist Pepper Adams, and alto saxophonist Art Pepper have been cited as evidence that white people "can too" swing and play the blues. The fundamentally defensive posture taken by advocates for white musicians in this racially charged discourse simply confirms the centrality of the African American legacy in shaping the musical aesthetics of the mainstream jazz tradition. White musicians who earned the approval of their African American colleagues with regard to their jazz abilities have usually been proud to have their "soulfulness" recognized. Not every white jazz musician has longed for such approval, but the phenomenon of the "white Negro" has been an enduring presence in twentieth-century American culture.[106] This is particularly apparent in the popular music of today, when, as Krin Gabbard has recently argued, "It is more difficult to find white performers who *do not* imitate black people than it is to find those that do. To see and hear a young white pop singer today is to witness a nuanced channeling of blackness, from the husky-voiced melismas of Christina Aguilera to the forcefully articulated rap performers such as Eminem."[107]

Yet there has been an enormous reluctance to recognize the presence of the blues and swing in the musical vocabularies of white (and other non–African American musicians) for what it is: an assimilation of African American aesthetics into the very center of mainstream American aesthetic practices. A recursive rather than reciprocal concept of cultural exchange is useful here, too. If Western harmony was indigenized in African American musical traditions and practices, as I have argued, in some ways swing was indigenized or localized by white bands when it was adopted in the popular swing music of the 1930s and 1940s and subsequently passed on through predominantly segregated social networks (as described in chapter 2). This transmission through networks largely distinct from African American communities, unions, and performance spaces had the effect of localizing the musical practices of jazz for non–African American social settings and endowing them with a different symbolic force. This localization was often called "dilution," "imitation," or "stealing" by later African American commentators (in part to emphasize the unequal economic playing field on which this took place).

The popularization of swing rhythms by white dance bands nevertheless established an extremely visible tradition of white jazz practice that subsequent white musicians have cited to authenticate their claim that they too have jazz "ancestors" and that swing and the blues are therefore color-blind. Indeed, historical evidence that places white musicians in the company of African American and Creole musicians in the earliest days of jazz has repeatedly been used to question the African American origins of jazz.[108] A deeper historical analysis would need to account for the power relationships of that early white presence, the way in which the Latin tinge complicated the color line, and the nature of recursive cultural exchange, as well as its prevailing direction.

What I am arguing is that, just as harmony functioned as a bridge discourse between classical music and black vernacular musics, swing and the blues served as linking discourses between Afro-modernism and American popular music. The big difference is that the white localization of the blues and swing was not as frequently borrowed back into African American musical practice at a later point in time Rather, in response to the commercial and popular success of white jazz musicians, which was viewed by many as depriving African American musicians of a fair economic return on their creativity, many African American jazz musicians of the 1950s and 1960s seemed determined to emphasize and develop black difference rather than witness a repeat of the 1930s, when Benny Goodman was crowned the King of Swing. The racialized power differentials in the music industry, in other words, led to a dynamic that offered African American musicians a choice between emphasizing difference and earning recognition as black artists or emphasizing sameness and having the history of African American leadership in the music erased in a sea of colorblindness.

The renewed emphasis on black difference in the aesthetics of hard bop was often heard at the time as angry, militant, and masculine. In describing Lee Morgan's exceptional "badness," Rosenthal says that "what Lee possessed and Cannonball lacked, at least by comparison, was *malice.*" Furthermore, it made his colleagues "sound like a bunch of sissies beside him."[109] The assertive sound of the music combined with titles that referenced black culture, politics, and Africa—"Dat Dere," "Moanin,'" "The Sermon," "Cornbread," "Freedom Suite," "Fables of Faubus," "Wednesday Night Prayer Meeting," "Freedom Rider," "Appointment in Ghana," "Dahomey Dance," "Africa," "Black," "Tell It Like It Is"—all invited the listener to contextualize the music in relationship to African American culture, the unfolding civil rights movement, and African independence. It was not until after the Montgomery bus boycott, the independence of Ghana, and the desegregation crisis in Little Rock, after all, that the full flowering of hard bop took place. Many African American musicians, it seems, rejected the discourse of musical colorblindness and preferred instead a musical modernism that drew attention to blackness. The use of musical culture as a weapon in this larger struggle for political and cultural recognition is hardly surprising. As Sahlins has said, "the cultural self-consciousness developing among imperialism's erstwhile victims is one of the more remarkable phenomena of world history in the later twentieth century."[110]

# 4

# Africa, the Cold War, and the Diaspora at Home

*We were all aware. The black community was aware of
what was going on in Africa because we were looking
around for some help.*

—Max Roach

THE 1960S ARE usually associated with black Americans' development of pride in their African roots, yet even a cursory examination of African American intellectual history reveals that, throughout the twentieth century, the domestic civil rights struggle was consistently viewed as intertwined with the fate of Africa and anticolonialism more broadly. For instance, W.E.B. Du Bois's lifelong interest in Pan-Africanism, which included participation in seven Pan-Africanist conferences between 1900 and 1945, as well as his eventual emigration to postindependence Ghana, put forth a Marxist analysis of racism and colonialism. Marcus Garvey's United Negro Improvement Association (UNIA), which riveted Harlem in the 1920s, stressed migration back to Africa, black entrepreneurship, and a spiritual vision of black global unity made manifest in the slogan "One Aim, One God, One Destiny." Malcolm X, whose rise to public prominence in the early 1960s galvanized black people across the nation, in many ways combined and updated the messages of both Du Bois and Garvey to an increasingly militant younger generation outraged by the violence against the civil rights movement. Malcolm X also became an in-spiration to the leaders of many newly independent African nations.[1]

The U.S. State Department also shared an internationalist view of the civil rights movement but with a vastly different political objective. In the early 1950s the State Department grew increasingly concerned that do-mestic racial relations were having a negative impact on the Cold War. More specifically, it worried that the dozens of countries on the verge of independence from Western colonial powers (most of them with non-Caucasian populations) would view racism in the United States as a strong reason to ally with the Soviet Union rather than the West. Indeed, the Soviet Union often pointed to U.S. racial policies as evidence of the hy-pocrisy of the United States's claim to be leader of the free world.[2]

The lives of jazz musicians intersected with these global political cur-rents in a variety of ways that are explored in this chapter: (1) the career of Paul Robeson; (2) the State Department jazz tours, which began in 1956; (3) musical projects that were inspired by events on the African continent, the independence of Ghana in 1957, and the admission of sixteen African nations to the United Nations in 1960; and (4) the influence of African and Afro-Caribbean immigrants in the musical landscape of New York and California.

## Paul Robeson

In the 1940s Paul Robeson was tremendously admired by many jazz musicians as a singer, actor, and political activist. Robeson's highly suc-cessful appearances as Shakespeare's Othello on Broadway in 1943 and 1944, for which he earned the Donaldson Award for best actor of the year and the NAACP's Spingarn medal for outstanding achievement by a black American, were followed closely by the jazz community, including Dizzy Gillespie, who attended opening night. For the first time in the United States, an African American had been cast in a major production of one of the most famous roles in the Western theatrical tradition. Paul Robeson had also been known since the 1920s as a great singer of African American spirituals and international folk music, as well as for his refusal to sing operatic and classical repertory.[3]

In the 1940s Paul Robeson connected the domestic struggle for civil rights to an anticolonialist perspective through his work with the Council on African Affairs (CAA). As Penny Von Eschen has documented, in the early and midforties the CAA sponsored many rallies and benefit concerts in New York City that drew attention to anticolonialist issues, including the annexation of Southwest Africa (now Namibia) by South Africa. Many well-known jazz musicians appeared at these events. Robeson's forty-sixth birthday celebration on April 16, 1944 (which also marked an anniversary of the CAA), included performances by Count Basie, Mary Lou Williams, and Duke Ellington. Robeson's speech at the event emphasized the need of colonial peoples for self-determination and called for international solidarity.

One of the CAA's most widely publicized events in the forties was the Big Three Unity Rally to support famine relief in South Africa. Held at Madison Square Garden on June 6, 1946, the rally drew nineteen thousand people. Mary Lou Williams appeared on a roster that included the Golden Gate Quartet, Pete Seeger, Paul Robeson, Josh White, and Sonny Terry. Later in the year Duke Ellington collaborated with John Latouche on "Beggar's Holiday," a musical theater piece performed as a benefit for the Council on African Affairs on Christmas night. When Ben Davis Jr., a Communist Party member, ran for a seat on the New York City Council in late 1943, Robeson performed a scene from *Othello* at a victory rally organized by Teddy Wilson. Among other performers participating in the all-star show were Coleman Hawkins, Billie Holiday, Pearl Primus, Hazel Scott, Mary Lou Williams, and Ella Fitzgerald. Another enthusiastic admirer of Robeson was Charlie Parker, who was known to go out of his way to hear any Robeson performance. In 1951, after Robeson's passport had been revoked by the State Department, Parker even sought Robeson out at Chicago's Pershing Hotel because he wanted to shake his hand and tell him personally, "You're a great man."[4]

In the 1930s Robeson became interested in African culture and politics while in London, where he met several future leaders of the African independence movement, including Kenya's Jomo Kenyatta, Ghana's Kwame Nkrumah, and Nigerians Nnamdi Azikiwe and K. O. Mbadiwe.[5] In London he also became acquainted with Jawaharlal Nehru's sister Vijaya Lakshmi Pandit, who discussed with him anticolonial efforts in India. In 1937 Robeson and Max Yergan founded the International Committee on African Affairs, which was reorganized in 1942 as the Council on African Affairs. The organization's objectives were to educate the American public about Africa and facilitate the studies of African students in the United States.[6]

In the few years between the end of World War II and the beginning of the Cold War in 1947 under President Truman, a broadly anticolonialist analysis of World War II and its implications for the domestic civil rights agenda was supported by not only leftists but also more mainstream civil rights voices, including those of then city councilman Adam Clayton Powell Jr.; Walter White, executive director of the NAACP; and Mary McLeod Bethune of the National Council of Negro Women. The popular legitimacy of an anticolonial internationalist perspective had been encouraged in 1945 by the founding of the United Nations, whose organizing conference included much debate over how colonial subjects should be represented.[7]

Within six months of the conference two major gatherings were held to discuss the rights of African colonial subjects and develop a means for representing them in the United Nations. First, W.E.B. Du Bois organized a meeting of several organizations to discuss proposals that had originated at the Pan-African Congress held in Manchester, England, in 1945, and the African Academy of Arts and Research (AAAR) held another.[8] The AAAR was headed by Kingsley Ozoumba Mbadiwe,[9] a Nigerian who had been encouraged to study in the United States by activist newspaper editor Nnamdi Azikiwe. Dizzy Gillespie met Mbadiwe in New York in the midforties and later did a benefit concert for the AAAR at the Diplomat Hotel with Max Roach, Charlie Parker, and a group of African and Cuban drummers. In his autobiography Gillespie spoke about doing several concerts for the organization: "Those concerts for the African Academy of Arts and Research turned out to be tremendous. Through that experience, Charlie Parker and I found the connections between Afro-Cuban and African music and discovered the identity of our music with theirs. Those concerts should definitely have been recorded, because we had a ball discovering our identity."[10]

By 1950 Paul Robeson's passport had been revoked for his outspoken criticism of the Korean War, and by 1951 W.E.B. Du Bois had been indicted as an unregistered foreign agent for his work against the Cold War. Both were suspected of being Communists. Liberals, who had previously allied themselves with the work of the CAA, began leaving the organization in 1948, which isolated the anticolonialist perspective on civil rights on the Left. In the war against Communism, many African American leaders saw an opportunity to press for domestic civil rights. Since the Soviet Union pointed to racism in U.S. racial policies as a reason for the colonized nations to support a Communist vision of the future, many liberal African American leaders, including Walter White, argued that antidiscrimination measures at home were essential in the fight against Communism. This new argument—that anti-Communism and civil rights were allies—is the logic that underlay the Eisenhower administration's decision to launch the State Department's Cultural Presentations Program (CPP) in 1954.

As Von Eschen has observed, the United States emerged as a global power between 1945 and 1960 at the same time as forty countries representing a quarter of the world's population (800 million) cast off colonialism and gained their independence. The United States wanted these newly emerging nations to ally with the West, not the Soviet Union. In 1956 the State Department was persuaded that jazz was an important tool in achieving this diplomatic objective.[11]

## The State Department Cultural Presentations Program

The Cultural Presentations Program (more informally known as the State Department tours) began in 1954 as the President's Special International Program for Cultural Presentations and was overseen by the Bureau of International Educational and Cultural Affairs of the Department of State. The department had been following the success of touring Soviet cultural groups at festivals and fairs in various regions of the world, especially in generating support among the young. In August 1954 President Eisenhower asked Congress to approve a President's Emergency Fund for the purpose of establishing a cultural exchange program capable of demonstrating the superiority of the cultural values of free enterprise.[12] The sum of five million dollars was appropriated, half of which was designated for cultural presentations and the other half for U.S. manufacturers to attend international trade fairs. Two years later the program was given full legislative sanction at the same funding level under the International Cultural and Trade Fairs Participation Act of 1956 (PL-806). A 1961 report evaluating the program explained that the initial impetus of the program had been competition through culture and that it had targeted two audiences—the intellectual leadership of nonaligned nations and those segments of youth showing the "greatest promise of eventual leadership"[13]

The Bureau of Educational and Cultural Affairs (CU)[14] designated the American National Theatre and Academy (ANTA) as its professional agent for administering the program. A privately supported membership organization chartered by Congress in 1935, ANTA had already been assisting the State Department in international exchange, most recently for the Berlin festivals held in 1951, 1952, and 1953. The International Exchange Service (IES) of ANTA, headed by Robert Dowling, set up advisory panels in music, dance, and drama and charged them with evaluating and selecting performing groups for the International Exchange Program (IEP), also known as the Cultural Presentations Program. Members of the original Music Advisory Panel, who served on a volunteer basis, included composers William Schuman, Virgil Thomson, and Howard Hanson; Paul Henry Lang and Jay Harrison of the *New York Herald Tribune;* Harold Spivacke of the Library of Congress; Carleton Sprague Smith, director of the Music Division of the New York Public Library; Edwin Hughes of the National Music Council; and Al Manuti, president of Local 802 of the American Federation of Musicians.[15]

Among the groups and people that toured under the auspices of the State Department in 1954 and 1955 were the American Ballet Theater, organist E. Power Biggs, the New York Philharmonic, the Jose Limón dance group, a production of *Porgy and Bess,* and baritone William Warfield. The State Department also included sporting events in its conception of cultural exchange. During these same years the Harlem Globetrotters, the AAU track team, and the skiing team of the University of Denver were among the sports groups sent abroad.[16]

In early 1955 the Music Advisory Panel (MAP) was asked to consider Harry James as a potential performer to send abroad. Some members of the panel did not feel comfortable judging popular music and suggested that they needed a jazz expert on the panel. The ambivalence of the panel members about jazz and popular music was apparent when one of the ANTA officials attending the meeting took the position that a popular music group should never be sent abroad until a symphony orchestra had been heard first. "We are known all over the world for jazz," he remarked, "We are trying to indicate that we have other music." Harold Spivacke, on the other hand, took the position that since "the Russians have made a point of associating us with lowdown jazz, and use it as propaganda against us . . . we should say we are proud of it."[17]

By November 1955, after Congressman Adam Clayton Powell Jr. urged the State Department to include jazz in its cultural exchange programs, the panel stated that "there is a sudden great interest in the field of jazz." They approached Marshall Stearns, president of the Institute of Jazz Studies at Hunter College, as a possible panel member and asked him to initiate negotiations with major artists. Although the classical music panelists included three well-known classical composers—Virgil Thomson, Howard Hanson, and William Schuman—jazz artists of an equivalent stature (such as Duke Ellington or Louis Armstrong) were apparently never considered as potential judges. At the December 20, 1955, meeting of the music panel, Stearns officially joined the group as special consultant on jazz projects for the first time and named the bands of Louis Armstrong, Dizzy Gillespie, Duke Ellington, Count Basie, and Stan Kenton as the five best groups in jazz.

After one panel member inquired whether "these Negro bands have white players too" (they did), the panel decided that the jazz projects ideally should be "mixed color groups." The panel's first choice for the inaugural State Department jazz tour was Louis Armstrong, but panel members felt that he was too expensive, and, besides, he was busy with a movie project (Murrow's *Saga of Satchmo*). Duke Ellington was the second choice, but "unfortunately he refuses to fly" (as did Count Basie). Dizzy Gillespie was next in line, earning double-edged praise from the panel that ultimately reveals the vortex of contradiction and ambivalence into which the International Exchange Program pulled jazz: "Gillespie is an intelligent comedian, cultivated, with novelty acts, and his musical material is interesting. A tour is therefore recommended for him."[18]

Eight years later, despite the extraordinary success of the jazz tours, the State Department was still delivering backhanded compliments: "Most Jazz performers have been outstanding in their willingness to take part in demonstration and clinic sessions outside of their scheduled appearances. Jazz is certainly no substitute for the great symphonies, but must be kept in its own context. Its use offers a challenge in the proper spacing and balancing of presentations in all the performing arts."[19]

## Dizzy Gillespie and the Cool War

In November 1955, Adam Clayton Powell Jr. held a press conference on the steps of the House Office Building in Washington, D.C., to announce the State Department's intention to send jazz performers abroad on goodwill tours. "Instead of talking about a cold war," he quipped, "we can call it a 'cool war' from now on." Out came Dizzy Gillespie onto the steps of the building, holding up his trumpet to add, "The weapon that we will use is the cool line," and then blew a few for the delighted CBS newsreel crew. *Down Beat* described the State Department's official support for jazz as "a Utopian dream come true." Citing the enthusiastic support of Theodore Streibert, chief of the U.S. Information Services (USIS), Powell explained that he had convinced the department that "instead of emphasizing ballet dancers and classical music, they can get real value out of spending the vast majority of the money on jazz and other Americana such as folk music, mambos, spirituals, American-Indian dances, Hawaiian music, and so forth."[20] The new openness of the State Department to the possibility of sending jazz musicians abroad may also have had something to do with the *Brown v. Board of Education* decision (something they wished to advertise) and the lynching of Emmett Till in September 1955 (something whose negative impact in the international sphere they wished to counteract).

In early February 1956 the State Department officially announced that Dizzy Gillespie's band would be the first jazz group sent abroad under ANTA's International Exchange Program, although a contract was not signed until a few weeks before the first concert of the tour on March 27. The State Department had originally planned to begin the tour in Bombay, but a few weeks before the scheduled appearances, Nehru announced a firm policy of nonalignment with either the United States or the Soviet Union. The State Department canceled appearances in India and quickly made arrangements for the tour to commence in Abadan, Iran. Gillespie's first tour proved so successful that the State Department asked him to do a second one to Latin America later that summer (see table 4.1).

At this point in the program the department apparently scheduled tour dates as something of a reward for cooperative countries. As Gillespie recalled, "Our tour was limited to countries which had treaties with the United States or where you had U.S. military bases: Persia [Iran], Lebanon, Syria, Pakistan, Turkey, and Greece. We didn't go to any of the countries the U.S. didn't have some sort of 'security' agreement with."[21]

Gillespie, who had been performing mostly in small groups, saw the State Department invitation as an opportunity to work with a big band without the ordinary financial risks involved with booking a large ensemble. Since he was about to head for Europe with Jazz at the Philharmonic, he asked Quincy Jones to put the band together while he was away. As Gillespie put it, the band fitted the program's preference for mixed

TABLE 4.1. Itineraries of Dizzy Gillespie's two State Department tours in 1956

| First Tour, Mar.–May 1956 | | Second Tour, July–Aug. 1956 | |
|---|---|---|---|
| Mar. 27–30 | Abadan, Iran | July 25 | Quito, Ecuador |
| Apr. 2–5 | Dacca, Pakistan | July 26–27 | Guayaquíl, Ecuador |
| Apr. 7–11 | Karachi, Pakistan | July 28–Aug. 4 | Buenos Aires, Argentina |
| Apr. 14–17 | Beirut, Lebanon | Aug. 5 | Montevideo, Uruguay |
| Apr. 18 | Damascus, Syria | Aug. 6–12 | Rio de Janeiro, Brazil |
| Apr. 19 | Aleppo, Syria | Aug. 13–15 | Sao Paulo, Brazil |
| Apr. 23–25 | Ankara, Turkey | Aug. 16–18 | Belo Horizonte, Brazil |
| Apr. 27–May 5 | Istanbul, Turkey | Aug. 19 | Santos, Brazil |
| May 7–8 | Belgrade, Yugoslavia | Aug. 20–21 | Sao Paulo, Brazil |
| May 9–10 | Belgrade, Yugoslavia | **Tour total** | 49 performances |
| May 12–21 | Athens, Greece | | |
| **Tour total** | 54 performances | | |

"Dizzy Gillespie Itinerary, Near and Middle East," CU subseries 1, box 9, folder 11, "Performance Records G–P," 1956.

ensembles: "We had a complete 'American' assortment of blacks, whites, males, females, Jews, and Gentiles in the band." The band included, among others, Melba Liston, Ernie Wilkins, Quincy Jones, Phil Woods, Walter Davis Jr., Charlie Persip, and Frank Rehak.[22]

With Quincy Jones in charge of preparatory rehearsals, a program was developed that presented a concise musical history of jazz. Quincy Jones, Melba Liston, and Ernie Wilkins were responsible for the arranging and contributed original charts as well, including Liston's "Annie's Dance" (based on a theme by Grieg) and "My Reverie" and Quincy Jones's "Q's Tune." The first half of the concert began with Dizzy Gillespie on bongo drums and Charlie Persip on drum set demonstrating African rhythms. Herb Lance followed, singing several spirituals such as "Sometimes I Feel Like a Motherless Child" and "Joshua Fit the Battle of Jericho." These were followed by an old-time blues and a small group playing "When the Saints Go Marching In" in New Orleans style. Dizzy and the full band continued with a series of arrangements illustrating the development of the big band and summarizing jazz trumpet styles. Among the compositions they played were Duke Ellington's "Mood Indigo," Benny Goodman's "King Porter Stomp" (arr. Fletcher Henderson), Jimmie Lunceford's "For Dancers Only," Roy Eldridge's "Rockin' Chair," and Count Basie's "One O'Clock Jump," which were scored from the original recordings. To illustrate how bebop musicians wrote new compositions over the chord changes of existing standards, Gillespie simultaneously played "Groovin' High" and "Whispering."

The second half of the concert included more contemporary arrangements of "Stella by Starlight" (arr. Melba Liston), "Cool Breeze," and "A Night in Tunisia." Herb Lance sang "Lucky Old Sun" and "Seems Like She Just Don't Care," and Dottie Saulters's repertory included "Birth of the Blues," "Make Love to Me," "Gabriel," "All God's Children," and "Born to Be Blue." Gillespie also featured a small group doing bebop numbers such as "Shoo Be Doo Be," "Sunny Side of the Street," and "Begin the Beguine." Charlie Persip was featured on an arrangement of "The Champ." Marshall Stearns, who had advocated for Gillespie on the Music Advisory Panel, accompanied the band on the tour as a lecturer on jazz history and an all-around band boy.[23]

Quincy Jones remembers an official from ANTA as "arrogant and condescending": "He came to rehearsal and stood in front of the band in a preppy wool suit and bow tie, and gave us advice in a flat, patronizing voice, saying, 'I have nothing to tell you except that when you're abroad, you're representing our country. So please indulge in your various idiosyncrasies discreetly.' . . . This kind of talk got our jaws tight. We were good and pissed off, but like the black soldiers in World War II, we kept on keepin' on."[24]

The opening concert on March 27 was at the Taj Theatre in Abadan, Iran, where Dizzy Gillespie and his All-Stars performed before Princess Shahnaz Pahlavi, daughter of the Shah of Iran. Most of the predominantly Muslim audience had had no previous exposure to jazz and were more disconcerted by the mixed-gender composition of the band than its mixed ethnic membership. Melba Liston on trombone and Dottie Saulters on vocals performed with men in clothing considered immodest by Muslim standards. As the band played its history of jazz section, the audience was extremely quiet, seemingly apathetic and puzzled. But then, according to a reporter from the *Pittsburgh Courier,* a "miracle" took place. The audience started to "catch the beat," awkwardly at first, and by intermission "the theater was as hot as any American jazz spot." On subsequent concerts in Abadan, the education process proceeded more quickly, as fans from previous concerts returned and led the way in participation.[25]

The first night in Dacca (now Dhaka, Bangladesh), according to Marshall Stearns, was a "colossal flop" as the band played to a small audience in a city with no jukeboxes and very few radios. Gillespie, who was disconcerted to have mentioned Louis Armstrong during the concert and received absolutely no response, commented later, "When you call Louis's name and nobody answers, you know you're in trouble." By the third or fourth concert word had spread (with the help of the USIS), and the band was playing to packed halls.[26]

In Karachi, Pakistan, Dizzy played with a snake charmer, a terrific photo opportunity that provided several widely circulated photos of Gillespie's bell in the face of an upright cobra while a fifteen-foot-long python lay across his shoulders. When the cobra suddenly hissed and attacked the horn, Gillespie remembers doing a "world record backward broad jump" away from the snake. Although the cobra was defanged, Gillespie was "almost scared bopless," as a *Courier* reporter put it, especially when he found out the following day that many supposedly defanged snakes were not. This led to a popular jazz community legend that Dizzy was so bad he could even charm a cobra.[27]

Throughout the tour Gillespie and his band participated in jam sessions with local musicians and befriended people outside the elite audiences that the State Department intended them to impress. The desire of many band members to make contact with people outside embassy circles at times caused tension between the State Department and the musicians. In Ankara, the band arrived at the Turkish American Club, where an outdoor jam session had been arranged for which only well-heeled people seemed to have tickets. Gillespie noticed a group of young "ragamuffins" peering in through the outside wall and is reported to have said, "Man, we're here to play for all the people," a remark overheard by a USIS official. When asked why he had not yet joined the jam (which had already begun), Gillespie explained that he was not going to play until the young people had been let in. The ambassador hemmed and hawed but finally agreed to Dizzy's demand.[28]

Quincy Jones recalls that the elites at embassy events often ignored the musicians and that the conditions that musicians endured while traveling were part of Gillespie's protest: three months of "110 degree heat, crappy food, swarming with flies, no showers, no baths, dysentery, constant traveling, and this was the thank-you we got."[29]

Gillespie and his band members also enjoyed meeting local musicians. In Ankara Gillespie met Muvaffak Falay, a Turkish trumpet player who had listened to jazz recordings but had never heard a live American musician. Gillespie was so touched by Falay's enthusiastic response to him that he had the State Department get a cigarette case engraved with the words "In Token of the Brotherhood of Jazz" and presented it to him the following night during the concert. At times Gillespie sought out local musicians, including a single-stringed violin player in Dacca (Dhaka) and a sarangi player in Karachi. In Turkey, Quincy Jones met Arif Mardin, who later achieved fame with his musical arrangements for Aretha Franklin.[30]

One of the more powerful things experienced by the musicians who went on the State Department tours was the feeling that they were extending the reach of jazz to the whole world. Stearns expressed a common sentiment when he stated after watching a Karachi crowd get into the groove, "There's something universal here." Although the jazz musicians knew very well that they were being used to serve U.S. interests in the Cold War (this was part of their briefing from the State Department), they took pride in their power to reach overseas audiences in a way that classical music could not and pursued their own visions of cultural ambassadorship. Jazz, in their view, offered an alternative, more democratic vision of American society, and the musicians enjoyed enacting a sense of solidarity and diasporic interconnection with people outside the European orbit. They did not view their participation in the program as an aspect of Western cultural imperialism but as an alternative to it.

The musicians considered it a great honor to have been selected by the State Department, and representing the United States was something they felt they could do without compromising their integrity. As Dizzy Gillespie recalled, "I sort've liked the idea of representing America, but I wasn't going over to apologize for the racist policies of America. . . . I know what they've done to us, and I'm not gonna make any excuses." Gillespie's personal desire for the tour was to bring people together through music, and this goal worked well for the State Department, which was delighted with his band's willingness to meet with people, engage in jam sessions with local musicians, hand out free tickets, give away instruments to promising local musicians, and even buy clothes for young fans who sat outside the door of theaters every night to listen but could not afford a ticket. "Yeah, I was very honored to have been chosen as the first jazz musician to represent the United States on a cultural mission, and I had a good time." The tour was so successful—way beyond State Department expectations—that they immediately signed him up to do another one, this time to South America, which took place from July 25 to August 21, 1956.[31]

Everywhere the band went the musicians were asked many questions about racism in the United States. The Montgomery bus boycott, which throughout 1956 was widely covered by the international press, was taking place during both tours. Many audiences were impressed that Gillespie not only had an interracial band but also was the leader. "That was strange to them because they'd heard about blacks being lynched and burned, and here I come with half whites and blacks and a girl playing in the band. And everybody seemed to be getting along fine." Trombonist Melba Liston encountered numerous questions from women in the Middle East about "how in the world I could be running around there traveling and single when they were so subjected over there." Her appearance with the band evidently inspired "a bunch of the sisters over there to demand a little more appreciation for their innate abilities."[32]

Gillespie ultimately spoke frankly about U.S. racial problems but took his own success as a sign of racial progress: "We have our problems but we're still working on it. I'm the leader of this band, and those white guys are working for me. That's a helluva thing." This sentiment could not have more perfectly fit the State Department's objective of presenting African American success as a counterweight to negative Soviet publicity on racial relations in the United States. A more critical voice, however, was that of W.E.B. Du Bois, who said, "Some of our best scholars and civil servants have been bribed by the State Department to testify abroad and especially in Africa to the success of capitalism in making the Negro free. Yet it was British capitalism which made the African slave trade the greatest commercial venture in the world; and it was American slavery that raised capitalism to its domination in the 19th century."[33]

One irony of Gillespie's success as a U.S. cultural ambassador is the fact that he was once a card-carrying member of the Communist Party— not out of political conviction, he explained, but because in the late thirties he played many racially mixed "communist dances" and other events with bassist Cass Carr in New York while awaiting permission to join Local 802 of the AFM. After much proselytization, he said "I signed one of those cards; [but] I never went to a meeting." Nevertheless, had the State

Department realized that Dizzy had ever belonged to Communist Party USA or realized the extent of his sympathies for Paul Robeson, they likely would not have sent him abroad.[34]

## Finances

Although the State Department was gratified by the success of the Gillespie tours, Southern segregationists and more conservative cold warriors found much to criticize. One letter to the editor of the *Savannah Georgia News* saw in the jazz tours evidence of Communist infiltration of the State Department. Along with the appointment of what the writer claimed were "unqualified" African Americans to policy-making positions in the State Department,[35] the fact that the Gillespie band was paid $2,150 per week (more than President Eisenhower's salary of $2,000 a week, the writer claimed) was viewed as pandering to black Americans at taxpayers' expense, something the Reds must have planned. Since criticism of the government for overpaying performers was common to those voicing criticism of the tours, the finances of the tours deserve some examination.[36]

On its tour through the Middle East the Gillespie band was actually paid $1,950 per week, a sum that was distributed among twenty-one persons, including administrative personnel, plus a $15 dollar per diem per person (an average of $197 per person per week). Anticipating a net loss on the concerts, the International Exchange Program agreed to pay transportation ($30,000) and the difference between income earned by concerts and expenses up to a maximum of $62,000 for the approximately nine week tour.[37] Congress consequently appropriated $92,000 for the tour in March 1956. The band agreed in principle to perform a maximum of fourteen performances per week, although they actually played about six performances per week on their first tour. The band also agreed, "by reason of the room scarcity in the countries," to be housed two to a room. Concerts were booked with the help of ANTA, the State Department, and Shaw Artists Corporation, Gillespie's booking agent. Government funding protected against financial loss up to a specified maximum figure (in the case of Gillespie's first tour, $62,000). The contracts had provisions for curtailing tours should it be discovered during a tour that losses were greater than expected.[38]

Gillespie's Latin American tour was paid $2,500 per week for a group of twenty (an average of $125 per week [$235 with per diem]). The department scheduled nearly the maximum number of engagements per week on this tour since the band performed forty-nine engagements in a four-week period (approximately twelve performances per week). The State Department's salary budget appeared to be based on simple union scale (a minimum wage) despite the fact that they were asking the top bands in the country to perform. Bandleaders who had been approached by the State Department about tours in 1955 and 1956, including Louis Armstrong, Duke Ellington, and Count Basie, told the *Pittsburgh Courier* that they could not afford to play for what the government was offering and that "as musical ambassadors they expect more than scale." The department was, in some cases, offering up to $1,000 per week less than what these bandleaders were earning in the private sector. In Louis Armstrong's case the difference was even larger. On commercially booked gigs in 1956 Armstrong's earnings averaged $5,000 per night. Armstrong had offered to do the State Department tour for $1,500 a night guaranteed, but the government found this figure too high despite the fact that it was playing classical musicians at higher rates than this.[39]

The Gillespie tours were actually quite a bargain for the State Department since later tours offered far better terms. It apparently took some time for the government to appreciate the value of jazz as a diplomatic commodity and adjust its payment schedule accordingly. Wilbur De Paris, who led an eleven-week tour to Africa from March 4 to May 17, 1957, was paid $2,000 per week, plus a $15 per diem for an eight-person ensemble (an average of $355 per week). A four-week tour of Poland and Yugoslavia in April 1957 paid the nineteen-person Glenn Miller Orchestra $10,000 a week (an average of $526 per person per week), a figure that apparently included per diem payments.[40]

Figures from Herbie Mann's tour in 1960 and Louis Armstrong's tour to Africa in 1960 and 1961 provide some idea of the way fees were distributed in professional ensembles. Herbie Mann's fourteen-week tour across the African continent was budgeted at $4,600 per week. Of this, Mann earned $1,200 per week, vibist and arranger Johnny Rae $350, bassist Don Payne $275, trumpeter Doc Cheatham $300, trombonist Willie Dennis $300, conguero Patato Valdez $325, and bongoist José Mangual $325. Seventy-three percent of the weekly gross ($3,400), in other

TABLE 4.2. A comparison of selected State Department tour budgets

| Performer | Dates | Destinations | Number of Performers and Administrative Personnel | Maximum Number of Performances per Week | Budget per Week |
|---|---|---|---|---|---|
| Dizzy Gillespie | Mar. 27–May 21, 1956 | Iran, Pakistan, Turkey, Syria, Yugoslavia, Greece | 21 | 14 | $1,950 plus per diem |
| Dizzy Gillespie | July 25–Aug. 21, 1956 | Ecuador, Argentina, Uruguay, Brazil | 20 | 14 | $2,500 plus per diem |
| Wilbur De Paris | Mar. 4–May 17, 1957 | Sudan, Ghana, Nigeria, Liberia, Congo, Kenya, Tanganyika, Libya, Ethiopia, Tunisia, Morocco | 8 | | $2,000 plus per diem |
| Glenn Miller Orchestra | Apr. 1–24, 1957 | Yugoslavia, Poland | 19 | 10 | $10,000 |
| Dave Brubeck | Mar. 6–May 9, 1958 | Poland, Turkey, India, Ceylon, Pakistan, Afghanistan, Iran, Iraq | 6 | 9 | $4,000 |
| Herbie Mann | Dec. 31, 1959–Apr. 5, 1960 | Sierra Leone, Liberia, Nigeria, Mozambique, Rhodesia, Tanganyika, Kenya, Ethiopia, Sudan, Morocco, Tunisia | 10 | 8 | $4,600 |
| Louis Armstrong (cosponsored by Pepsi) | Oct. 25–Dec. 4, 1960; Jan. 10–29, 1961 | Cameroun, Congo, Uganda, Kenya, Tanganyika, Rhodesia, Togo, Ivory Coast, Senegal, Mali, Sierra Leone, Liberia, Sudan, Egypt | 12 | 6 | $10,000 |
| Benny Goodman | May 30–July 9, 1962 | Soviet Union | 24 | 6 | $10,000 |

"Projects Completed and Approved for Assistance, from beginning July 1954 through June 1965, FY 1955, through FY 1966," CU subseries 1, box 2, folder 9, "Cultural Presentations Program, Projects Completed and Approved for Assistance, 1954–1966."

words, was paid out in salaries. Administrative and miscellaneous expenses, including a company manager, an accountant, uniform upkeep, insurance, a personal manager, and payroll taxes, made up the remainder. Louis Armstrong's tour to Africa from October 24, 1960, to December 1960 and January 19–29, 1961, was budgeted at $10,000 per week for seven performers and five administrative personnel, forty-eight percent of which was budgeted for performers' salaries: Armstrong (including expenses for his wife) $2,000 per week, Barney Bigard $560, pianist Billy Kyle $420, Trummy Young $550, drummer Danny Barcelona $420, bassist Mort Herbert $420, and vocalist Velma Middleton $420. Armstrong's entourage included a valet; his doctor, Alexander Schiff; a band boy; and a personal manager. Later tours not only paid more but also required fewer performances per week. Table 4.2 summarizes these figures.[41]

To place these figures in perspective, remember that classical musicians were generally paid higher salaries by the State Department. Rudolf Serkin earned $3,000 per concert for the four concerts he performed in India from November 25 to November 29, 1956. Violinist Joseph Fuchs earned $700 per concert, plus $250 per week, during a tour of Central and South America from May 24 to July 7, 1957; Marian Anderson was paid $1,100 per concert during her tour of Norway and Germany from September 19 to October 23, 1956; and William Warfield earned $2,500 a week on a tour of the Middle and Far East from January 6 to March 13, 1958.[42]

### Demographics and African Destinations

Between 1956 and 1969 the State Department sponsored twenty-eight tours featuring jazz groups and R&B groups (table 4.3). Sixteen tours were led by African American bandleaders (57%), but since several musicians undertook more than one tour, eleven African American bandleaders were sponsored. Twelve tours were led by white musicians (42%), but since three musicians undertook two tours apiece, seven bandleaders were supported. The chosen ones were Dizzy Gillespie, Wilbur De Paris, Louis Armstrong, Cozy Cole, Duke Ellington, Earl Hines, Randy Weston, Charles Lloyd, Oliver Nelson, Junior Wells, Buddy Guy, Benny Goodman, Dave Brubeck, Woody Herman, Jack Teagarden, Red Nichols, Charlie Byrd, and Paul Winter. The stylistic spread of the bands ranged from New Orleans jazz to bebop, with the notable absence of four of the

TABLE 4.3. Department of State Cultural Presentations Program, jazz tours completed, 1956–1969

| Date | Performing Group | Destinations |
|---|---|---|
| 1956 Mar. 27–May 21 | Dizzy Gillespie | Iran, Pakistan, Turkey, Greece, Yugoslavia, United Arab Republic |
| 1956 July 26–Aug. 21 | Dizzy Gillespie | Ecuador, Argentina, Uruguay, Brazil |
| 1956 Dec. 6–Jan. 17, 1957 | Benny Goodman | Thailand, Singapore, Burma, Japan, Hong Kong, Malaysia, Cambodia |
| 1957 Mar. 4–May 17 | Wilbur De Paris | Africa: Sudan, Ghana, Nigeria, Liberia, Congo, Central African Republic, Kenya, Tanzania, Ethiopia, Libya, Tunisia |
| 1958 Mar. 6–May 9 | Dave Brubeck | Poland, Turkey, India, Ceylon, Pakistan, Afghanistan, Iran, Iraq |
| 1958 Aug. 10–31 | Woody Herman | Panama, Venezuela, Colombia, Ecuador, Chile, Bolivia, Paraguay, Brazil, Jamaica, Honduras, Guatemala |
| 1958 Sept. 26–Jan. 21, 1959 | Jack Teagarden | Afghanistan, Pakistan, India, Ceylon, Burma, Thailand, Laos, Vietnam, Cambodia, Singapore, Malay, Philippines, Hong Kong, Taiwan, Korea, Japan, Okinawa |
| 1959 Dec. 31–Apr. 5, 1960 | Herbie Mann | Africa: Sierra Leone, Liberia, Nigeria, Mozambique, Rhodesia, Nyasaland, Tanzania, Kenya, Ethiopia, Sudan, Morocco, Tunisia |
| 1960 Jan. 4–Mar. 30 | Red Nichols | Greece, Turkey, Cypress, Palestine, Jordan, Iran, Afghanistan, Pakistan, India, Ceylon, Nepal, UAR, Syria |
| 1960 Oct. 25–Dec. 4 | Louis Armstrong | Africa: Cameroun, Congo, Uganda, Kenya, Tanzania, Rhodesia, Nyasaland, Togo, Ivory Coast, Senegal, Mali, Sierra Leone, Liberia, Sudan |
| 1961 Jan. 10–29 | Louis Armstrong | Egypt |
| 1961 Mar. 12–May 27 | Charlie Byrd | Venezuela, Brazil, Uruguay, Paraguay, Argentina, Chile, Bolivia, Peru, Ecuador, Colombia, Panama, Costa Rica, Nicaragua, Honduras |
| 1962 Feb. 6–July 13 | Paul Winter | Haiti, Mexico, Guatemala, El Salvador, French West Indies, Nicaragua, Costa Rica, Chile, Panama, Colombia, Ecuador, Peru, Bolivia, Argentina, Uruguay, Paraguay, Brazil, British Guiana, Venezuela |
| 1962 May 30–July 9 | Benny Goodman | USSR |

TABLE 4.3. (*continued*)

| Date | Performing Group | Destinations |
|---|---|---|
| 1962 | | |
| May 31–June 4 | Louis Armstrong | Chile |
| 1962 Oct. 15–Mar. 7, 1963 | Cozy Cole | Africa: Morocco, Senegal, Volta, Niger, Liberia, Ivory Coast, Dahomey, Congo, Chad, Central African Republic, Cameroun, Ghana, Togo, Guinea |
| 1963 Sept. 6–Nov. 22 | Duke Ellington | Near East, South Asia, Syria, Jordan, Afghanistan, Indonesia, Turkey, Ceylon, Pakistan, Iran, Iraq, Lebanon, India |
| 1965 Sept. 5–24 | Paul Winter Sextet | Brazil |
| 1966 Mar. 31–Apr. 9 | Duke Ellington | Africa: Senegal |
| 1966 Apr. 1–June 8 | Woody Herman | Africa: Tanzania, Uganda, Congo, Ivory Coast, Algeria; Yugoslavia, UAR, Romania |
| 1966 July 7–Aug. 17 | Earl Hines | USSR |
| 1967 Jan. 16–Apr. 9 | Randy Weston | Africa: Algeria, Cameroun, Gabon, Ghana, Ivory Coast, Liberia, Mali, Morocco, Niger, Senegal, Sierra Leone, Upper Volta; Lebanon, Egypt |
| 1967 Oct. 12–22 | Charles Lloyd | Poland, Czechoslovakia, Romania |
| 1967 Nov. 13–Jan. 20, 1968 | Junior Wells | Africa: Dahomey, Cambodia, Togo, Central African Republic, Chad, Mali, Niger, Upper Volta, Ivory Coast, Liberia, Sierra Leone, Guinea, Senegal |
| 1968 Apr. 1–May 26 | Charlie Byrd | Korea, Japan, Afghanistan, Pakistan, India, Nepal, Ceylon, Philippines |
| 1968 Apr. 29–June 23 | Charles Lloyd | Okinawa, Hong Kong, Thailand, Laos, Malaysia, Singapore, Philippines, Taiwan |
| 1969 Mar.–Apr. | Oliver Nelson | Africa: Cameroun, Central African Republic, Chad, Niger, Upper Volta, Senegal |
| 1969 Apr. 24–June 14 | Buddy Guy | Africa: Congo, Tanzania, Malagasy Republic, Mauritius, Zambia, Malawi, Kenya, Uganda |

Compiled from "Tours Completed from Beginning of Program in 1954 through June 1968 (FY1955–1968)," CU subseries 1, general and historical files, box 3, folder 10, "Cultural Presentations, Lists of Groups, 1954–1968"; "Projects Completed and Approved for Assistance from Beginning July 1954 through June 1962: FY 1955 through FY 1963," CU subseries 1, general and historical files, box 1, folder 39, "GTIC, Cultural Presentations, 1962–1965," 1–21; "Randy Weston Sextet, Itinerary," CU series 2, performing arts subseries 1, performers, box 31, folder 23, "Weston, Randy (American Jazz in Africa) (1 of 4)," n.d.; "Wilbur De Paris, Final Itinerary," aerogramme, Nov. 25, 1966; CU subseries 1, general and historical files, box 9, folder 10, "Performance Records A–F," 1957; "Herbie Mann Jazz Band" (itinerary), CU subseries 1, general and historical files, box 9, folder 11, "Performance Records G–P," 1960.

most talked-about musicians of the day: Miles Davis, John Coltrane, Charles Mingus, and Thelonius Monk.

The Music Advisory Panel certainly discussed these musicians, as well as many others, but its choices reflected the program's desire for musicians who would "present well" at diplomatic events and had name recognition among embassy officials around the world, whose musical tastes were generally formed before bebop.[43] For a time, performers and their groups were given letter grades evaluating their suitability as "Jazz ambassadors."[44] In December 1959, the panel, whose jazz experts included Marshall Stearns and John Wilson, gave Max Roach a C and in April 1960 gave Miles Davis a dual grade—A minus for his music but a C for "personal behavior."[45]

The absence of African American members on the Music Advisory Panel was well known in the jazz world. In 1963 jazz critic Don DeMichael wrote to Lucius Battle, the executive secretary of the Cultural Presentations Program to nominate Duke Ellington, Coleman Hawkins, or Ralph Ellison to a vacant seat on the panel. It was not until 1967, however, that an African American—Julius Willis, a folk music expert—was appointed to the music panel. Gunther Schuller joined the group as a combined jazz and classical music specialist that same year.[46]

The African continent was an especially important destination for African American bands sponsored by the State Department. Eight of the ten tours with African destinations were led by black bandleaders (table 4.4). Particularly notable are Wilbur De Paris's tour in 1957, which began with Ghana's independence celebrations, Louis Armstrong's visit to the Congo shortly after its independence (and just before Patrice Lumumba's disappearance and assassination), Duke Ellington's presence at Leopold Senghor's First World Festival of Negro Arts, held in Dakar in April 1966, and Randy Weston's exceptional tour of the continent in 1967. The symbolic value of African American musicians in counteracting the United States' well-deserved reputation for racism was particularly strong for U.S. embassies in Africa. That this strategy was apparently effective is clear in the following report from the U.S. Embassy in Addis Ababa, Ethiopia, in May 1957, which describes the effect of Wilbur De Paris's visit:

One Ethiopian Body Guard officer . . . expressed surprise, while talking with a member of the band, to learn that the musician had just purchased a new home and that he owned his own automobile.

TABLE 4.4. State Department tours to Africa, 1956–1969

| Date | Performing Group | Destinations |
|---|---|---|
| 1957<br>Mar. 4–May 17 | Wilbur De Paris | Africa: Sudan, Ghana, Nigeria, Liberia, Congo, Central African Republic, Kenya, Tanzania, Ethiopia, Libya, Tunisia |
| 1959<br>Dec. 31–Apr 5, 1960 | Herbie Mann | Africa: Sierra Leone, Liberia, Nigeria, Mozambique, Rhodesia, Nyasaland, Tanzania, Kenya, Ethiopia, Sudan, Morocco, Tunisia |
| 1960<br>Oct. 25–Dec. 4 | Louis Armstrong | Africa: Cameroun, Congo, Uganda, Kenya, Tanzania, Rhodesia, Nyasaland, Togo, Ivory Coast, Senegal, Mali, Sierra Leone, Liberia, Sudan |
| 1962<br>Oct. 15–Mar. 7, 1963 | Cozy Cole | Africa: Morocco, Senegal, Volta, Niger, Liberia, Ivory Coast, Dahomey, Congo, Chad, Central African Republic, Cameroun, Ghana, Togo, Guinea |
| 1966<br>Mar. 31–Apr. 9 | Duke Ellington | Africa: Senegal |
| 1966<br>Apr. 1–June 8 | Woody Herman | Africa: Tanzania, Uganda, Congo, Ivory Coast, Algeria; Yugoslavia, UAR, Romania |
| 1967<br>Jan. 16–Apr. 9 | Randy Weston | Africa: Algeria, Cameroun, Gabon, Ghana, Ivory Coast, Liberia, Mali, Morocco, Niger, Senegal, Sierra Leone, Upper Volta; Lebanon, Egypt |
| 1967<br>Nov. 13–Jan. 20, 1968 | Junior Wells | Africa: Dahomey, Cambodia, Togo, Central African Republic, Chad, Mali, Niger, Upper Volta, Ivory Coast, Liberia, Sierra Leone, Guinea, Senegal |
| 1969<br>Mar.–Apr. | Oliver Nelson | Africa: Cameroun, Central African Republic, Chad, Niger, Upper Volta, Senegal |
| 1969<br>Apr. 24–June 14 | Buddy Guy | Africa: Congo, Tanzania, Malagasy Republic, Mauritius, Zambia, Malawi, Kenya, Uganda |

Compiled from "Tours Completed from Beginning of Program in 1954 through June 1968 (FY1955–FY1968)," CU subseries 1, general and historical files, box 3, folder 10, "Cultural Presentations, Lists of Groups, 1954–1968"; "Projects Completed and Approved for Assistance from Beginning July 1954 through June 1962: FY 1955 through FY 1963," CU subseries 1, general and historical files, box 1, folder 39, "GTIC, Cultural Presentations, 1962–1965," 1–21; "Randy Weston Sextet, Itinerary," CU series 2, performing arts subseries 1, performers, box 31, folder 23, "Weston, Randy (American Jazz in Africa) (1 of 4)," n.d.; "Wilbur De Paris, Final Itinerary," CU subseries 1, general and historical files, box 9, folder 10, "Performance Records A–F," 1957; "Herbie Mann Jazz Band," (itinerary), CU subseries 1, general and historical files, box 9, folder 11, "Performance Records G–P," 1960.

He later told an Embassy staff member that while he had read of American Negroes having such material possessions, he had doubted this was true. He told the staff member that he had now revised his opinion of the status of Negroes in the United States. He said he would not have believed these facts had not the American Negro told him himself. . . . The general aura of good-will generated by this visit of an American Negro musical group was extensive, and the spirit of cooperation engendered by the visit has enabled the Embassy and USIS to establish new and valuable contacts."[47]

Nevertheless, the State Department tours had both intended and un-intended consequences, as musicians asserted their goals for the tours and confronted the attitudes of State Department personnel. Randy Weston's report to the State Department on the strengths and weaknesses of his 1967 tour, for example, included many recommendations for improving the effectiveness of the trips and exposed the racial attitudes of the State Department escort officer who accompanied the group in its travels:

That kind of attitude (and we noticed it in a few of the local U.S. personnel, too) inhibits goodwill between the peoples of any given country and the United States and tends to weaken the good im-pact of a tour. These negative attitudes were very upsetting to us, whenever we encountered them (either in our own escort or in local U.S. personnel), and made our job—and *theirs*—more difficult than it should have been. It is a shame that the United States ever sends people with what we (and many Africans) consider to be "colonial" mentalities any place overseas, for they make a very bad impression on nearly everyone who meets them.[48]

## Louis Armstrong in Ghana

While Dizzy Gillespie was touring the Middle East for the State De-partment, Louis Armstrong and his All-Stars were being filmed in Africa for *See It Now*, a television program produced by Edward R. Murrow and Fred W. Friendly. The television material was later expanded into a doc-umentary film titled *Satchmo the Great*.[49] In the film, which features footage of Armstrong on tour in Switzerland, France, England, and Ghana, Murrow describes Armstrong as an "ambassador with a horn," which serves to underscore the fact that, long before the State Department tours, Armstrong had already established himself as "Ambassador Satch." When Armstrong arrived in Accra, Ghana, in May 1956, he was greeted at the airport by a crowd of ten thousand, including a band playing a high-life piece in his honor called "All for You, Louis." Louis descended to the tarmac, trumpet in hand, and walked over to join the overjoyed band. He and his wife Lucille were later whisked away to lunch with Prime Minister Kwame Nkrumah, who within a year would become independent Ghana's first president.

After lunch, Armstrong played an outdoor concert at Accra's largest park to an audience estimated at nearly one hundred thousand.[50] The film footage shows an enthusiastic and dancing crowd as far as the eye can see. At an evening concert Armstrong dedicated Fats Waller's [What did I do to be so] "Black and Blue" to Prime Minister Nkrumah, who was so moved by Armstrong's tribute that he is captured teary eyed on film. Nkrumah had become a fan of Armstrong when he was a student at Lincoln University near Philadelphia in the late 1930s.

The following day seventy tribal chiefs and their drummers and dancers performed for Armstrong at Achimota College in Accra. Seated outside underneath umbrellas to protect him from the sun, Armstrong listened to a wide selection of traditional music from Ghana's many ethnic groups. The delegation of chiefs presented him with a specially designed talking drum to commemorate his visit to Ghana, and Armstrong later remarked that "every time I listened to these cats beat it out on them tribal drums I kept saying to myself, 'Satch, you're hearing the real stuff.'" An Ewe woman dancing before him reminded him strongly of his mother, Mary Ann. "She danced and sang like my mother, and when I went over to talk to her she even held her head like Mama used to hold hers and before long I was calling her 'Mama.'" Armstrong, it seems, experienced a new-found sense of membership in an African diaspora. "After all, my ancestors came from here, and I still have African blood in me." Only a few years earlier, he had ridiculed a Babs Gonzalez record for "trying to take every-body to Africa."[51]

Armstrong's visit to Ghana came at a crucial time for Nkrumah's Convention People's Party (CPP), which faced an election in July that would determine whether it would be the party to govern the Gold Coast during the transition to independence. The CPP favored a centralized state under the leadership of Nkrumah, while the National Liberation Movement (NLM) favored a federal system that would ensure representation of Ghana's principal regions and ethnic groups. The CPP offered a vision of national unity that downplayed ethnic differences and autonomous political structures, while the NLM was widely perceived as an Ashanti-dominated movement. Although the NLM charged the CPP with corruption and dictatorial tendencies (charges that would later be borne out), the CPP's message of a modern national unity, which de-emphasized tribal differences and would later embrace a vision of pan-African unity, ultimately carried the election.[52]

Armstrong's appearance before the tribal chiefs at Achimota College may have been designed to demonstrate the CPP's support of traditional culture, thereby undermining the NLM's criticisms of Nkrumah, while at the same time presenting Armstrong as the embodiment of a black modernity to which the CPP aspired. While American commentators found in jazz's international success evidence of a universal musical language, African audiences across the continent seemed to view black American jazz musicians as sophisticated examples of African progress. If going to Africa provided Armstrong a feeling of authentic connection to his ethnic roots, jazz gave many African audiences a sense of the possibilities of an urban modernity. It did not matter to the Ghanaians that Armstrong's repertory and style were considered outdated by younger American musicians; to the audiences in Accra, he was a modern king.

After the Convention People's Party victory in the election of July 17, 1956,[53] Ghana's formal independence from the British Empire was set for March 6, 1957, a development widely heralded as portending the total dismantling of the colonial system in sub-Saharan Africa. The State Department was keenly aware of Ghana's impending independence, as well as the success of the Armstrong visit the previous May. By December 1956 word had reached the Music Advisory Panel of ANTA that the State Department wanted to select a suitable jazz group to attend the independence ceremonies in Accra. Having ruled out paying a fee acceptable to Armstrong, the panel considered Billy Taylor with percussionist Cándido Camero, Wilbur De Paris (who had a less expensive New Orleans combo), and pianist Erroll Garner. Since funds were not available for a trip to Accra alone, they booked Wilbur De Paris for the independence ceremonies, plus a two-and-a-half-month tour of the African continent (March 4–May 17) that included well-attended stops in Ghana, Nigeria, Liberia, the Belgian Congo (now the Democratic Republic of the Congo), Kenya, Senegal, Ethiopia, the Sudan, Libya, Tunisia, and Morocco. The itinerary overlapped, in part, the destinations of Vice President Richard Nixon's diplomatic tour of Africa, which included Ghana's independence ceremonies, as well as Morocco, Liberia, Uganda, Ethiopia, Sudan, Libya, Italy, and Tunisia.[54]

The choice of De Paris, in retrospect, seems peculiar since neither his appearance at Ghana's independence ceremonies nor the African tour received anywhere near the level of publicity given Dizzy Gillespie's tours in 1956, despite the political importance the State Department placed on Africa. In Ghana, De Paris was overshadowed by the lingering effects of Armstrong's visit in May. Although "Ambassador Satch" was personally invited to the festivities, he was unable to attend due to other performing commitments. Instead, Lucille Armstrong attended in his place and brought along a copy of *Satchmo the Great.* The film was screened before an audience that included President Kwame Nkrumah, Vice President Richard Nixon, and the Duchess of Kent. Although everyone enjoyed the film, the audience evidently chanted "we want Satchmo." When Nkrumah confided in Mrs. Armstrong that he was worried about the scheduled dance with the Duchess of Kent (since he did not know any Western ballroom dances), she came to the rescue by teaching him the waltz and the foxtrot. Lucille Armstrong's activities were widely mentioned in the African American press, but Wilbur De Paris received hardly a word.[55]

Other public figures who attended the independence ceremonies were Reverend Martin Luther King Jr.; Ralph Bunche, undersecretary general of the United Nations; Congressmen Adam Clayton Powell Jr.; and Charles Diggs. The U.S. government wanted to communicate to African audiences that Americans supported African independence—but perhaps not too loudly. President Eisenhower was notably absent from the festivities. As with John F. Kennedy's call to Coretta Scott King while Martin Luther King Jr. was in jail (and Robert F. Kennedy's subsequent call to a Georgia judge) during the 1960 presidential campaign, the government apparently hoped that coverage would be minimal in white newspapers but maximal in the black press.[56]

Ghana's independence was in fact widely celebrated in African American newspapers, many of which sent correspondents to Accra. Among them were Alex Rivera, Marguerite Cartwright, and J. A. Rogers of the *Pittsburgh Courier* and Ethel Payne of the *Chicago Defender*. To commemorate the event, the *Courier* published a thirty-two-page special supplement that included feature stories about Ghana's history, personal profiles of Nkrumah, and many ads and editorials congratulating Ghana on its triumph. Ghana's independence was taken not only as a harbinger of the demise of colonialism on the African continent but also as a beacon of hope and challenge to the American civil rights movement.[57] In the minds of many African American commentators, the success of Ghana could "prove," once and for all, the worthiness of people of color:

> But the significance to American Negroes is more than the extension of a greeting or a hand of welcome. This is because the ancient empire of Ghana was the land of the forefathers of most American Negroes. Traced through the centuries, the majority of American Negroes are Ghanaians whose cultural roots have been destroyed, a new people who have lost touch with their original culture and civilization and have failed of full acceptance in the new society where they find themselves. Are American Negroes an inferior people? Can they meet the full challenge of modern, Western civilization? We American Negroes look to Ghana to furnish the answers to these questions.[58]

The acceptance of the notion that Africans and African Americans needed to "prove" their equality was stated even more explicitly later in the *Courier* editorial: "When we, American Negroes, shake hands with Ghana today, we say not only 'Welcome!' but also, 'your opportunity to prove yourself is our opportunity to prove ourselves.'"[59]

J. A. Rogers, whose illustrated "Your History" columns had been acquainting the *Courier*'s readers with African American history for quite some time, observed that Accra, Ghana's capital, compared "most favorably with any U.S. metropolis of comparable size" with its "splendid railroad depot," "busy wharves," "fine motels," movie theaters, and eight daily newspapers printed on modern presses. The big difference was that in Ghana this infrastructure was run by Africans. Rogers's tone, like that of the *Courier* editorial, responded to the American presumption of African backwardness by explicitly asserting Ghana's competitiveness in modern ways. At Achimota College, he stressed, "courses are the same as those given in leading American and European universities."[60]

The week before Ghana's independence celebrations, Louis Armstrong found himself lambasted in the *Pittsburgh Courier* for playing to segregated audiences, much as Nat King Cole had been in 1956. George Pitts felt that "it's about time high-salaried Negro entertainers started doing something about being forced to play before segregated audiences in the South." Calling for a contract clause that would void any booking before a segregated audience (similar to the one suggested by Norman Granz and Paul Robeson), Pitts quoted a statement by Armstrong that smoothed over the problem of segregated halls: "Man, the horn don't know anything about it. I'll play anywhere they'll listen." Pitts found statements like these "sickening."[61]

Two weeks after Pitts's criticism, another article appeared in the *Courier* denouncing several entertainers for appearing before segregated audiences. "Stay Out of Dixie!" William Nunn exclaimed, singling out Louis Armstrong, Nat Cole, and Duke Ellington in particular. The public shaming of Armstrong in the black press in the months before Little Rock may partially explain why he chose to speak out publicly for the first time during the Central High desegregation crisis.[62]

In July 1957 *Variety* reported that a State Department tour to the Soviet Union was in the works for Armstrong for the following spring. When Armstrong sounded off in September, accusing Eisenhower of allowing Governor Orval Faubus to run the country, he explained his decision to back out of the State Department tour: "The people over there ask me what's wrong with my country. What am I supposed to say?" The State Department was conspicuously quiet, evidently wanting to leave the door open for Armstrong's eventual participation in the Cultural Presentations Program. Here, after all, was proof that the domestic racial situation did indeed have a negative impact on U.S. foreign policy objectives. In 1956 and 1957, it seems, the domestic and international political issues combined to link the African continent, the State Department, Little Rock, and jazz as the music found itself of considerable symbolic value to a variety of constituencies.[63]

## Art Blakey's Diaspora

As Norman Weinstein has documented, references to the African continent can be found in musical works throughout the history of jazz, from

Eubie Blake's "Sounds of Africa" (1899), Clarence Williams's "Senegalese Stomp" (1926), Duke Ellington's "Liberian Suite" (1947), and John Coltrane's "Africa Brass" (1961) to Randy Weston's "Khepera" (1998).[64] Indeed there are far too many recordings on African themes between 1950 and 1967 to do justice to the repertory here. Instead I would like to follow some of Art Blakey's and Randy Weston's major projects referencing Africa from 1953 to 1962 for what they reveal about the interconnectedness of African musical projects in jazz with both historical events on the African continent and Afro-Caribbean musics and musicians at home. For, although African musicians such as Babatunde Olatunji from Nigeria and Asadata Dafora from Sierre Leone played an important role in making jazz musicians aware of the richness of African musics, the most famous African projects of the 1950s and early 1960s were often realized through the participation of top-flight Afro-Caribbean musicians.

Art Blakey's "Message from Kenya," for example, is a duet with percussionist Sabu Martinez, a young American-born conga player whose primary inspiration was Chano Pozo (the Cuban dancer and percussionist whose collaboration with Dizzy Gillespie on "Cubana Be Cubana Bop" and "Manteca" inaugurated the Cubop movement).[65] When Pozo was killed in 1948, Martinez was asked to take his place in Dizzy Gillespie's band. Martinez collaborated with Art Blakey on several of his most famous African and diasporic projects, including *Orgy in Rhythm* (1957), "Cu-Bop!" (1957), *Drum Suite* (1957), and *Holiday for Skins* (1958).[66] The most striking thing about "Message from Kenya" is that, although the title references the African continent, Martinez's conga playing and chanting invoke Changó and Yemoja, two of Santería's (Lucumí's) Orishas.[67] Martinez sets the pace on conga, and, throughout his opening solo, Blakey seems determined to make his tom toms sound like a set of low-pitched congas. The one part of the drum set he never touches throughout the four-minute performance is the snare drum.

The Afro-Cuban connection is also apparent in Blakey's drumming on the remainder of the *Horace Silver Trio* album, on which "A Message from Kenya" appears. Blakey's solo on "Safari" (1:55–2:09), for example, opens with a congalike pattern played on the toms (figure 4.1).[68] This gesture is followed by some inspired pitch-bending that transfers the elbow-on-the-drum technique of conga players to the drum set.[69]

Why was the message from Kenya and not Cuba? It is hard to say for sure, but, throughout much of 1953, coverage of the Mau Mau uprisings in

1:55

FIGURE 4.1. Art Blakey, "Safari," tom-tom pattern, transcribed by I. Monson. Used by permission. Music by Horace Silver, copyright by Ecaroh Music.

Kenya frequently appeared in the news. The Mau Mau, whose principal base of support was the Kikuyu people, emerged in the wake of unsuccessful attempts to secure land reform from the British colonial government. In 1952, in response to desperate economic conditions in the countryside, the Mau Mau (or Kenya Land and Freedom movement) sought to reclaim expropriated territory by driving whites off the land through lethal violence and sabotage. The British used the movement to discredit the broader independence movement, most notably Jomo Kenyatta, who was imprisoned by the British from 1952 to 1959 on the false charge of masterminding the Mau Mau. Blakey's was not the only reference to Kenya; in 1958 Machito and his Afro-Cubans recorded an album titled *Kenya,* which featured several jazz soloists, including Julian "Cannonball" Adderley, Doc Cheatham, Joe Newman, and Eddie Bert. The liner notes draw a parallel between Kenya and Machito's musical explorations: "For just as Kenya stands for the new Africa, it represents here in this collection of sides the newest in Afro-Cuban jazz."[70]

Three and a half weeks before Ghana's independence celebrations (in March 1957) Art Blakey recorded an album titled *Ritual* for Blue Note Records. In a verbal introduction to the title track, he recounted his trip to the African continent:

> In 1947 after the Eckstine Band broke up we took a trip to Africa. I was supposed to stay there three months and I stayed two years, because I wanted to live among the people and find out just how they lived, and about the drums especially. We were in the interior of Nigeria. And I met some people they call the Ijaw people who are very, very interesting people. They live sort of primitive. The drum is the most important instrument there. Anything that happens that day that is good, they play about it that night. This particular thing caught my ear for the different rhythms."[71]

The most remarkable thing about these comments is Blakey's explicit admission that one of the reasons he went to Africa was to learn "about the drums especially." In later years Blakey went to great lengths to deny that music was a motivating factor for his travel to Africa or that he had ever touched a drum while on the continent. In one of the most detailed accounts of his African sojourn Blakey told two French interviewers in 1963, "For two years, I immersed myself solely in philosophers, religion, and Hebrew and Arab languages. I do not remember having played an instrument even one time during this entire period."[72]

Later, Blakey's denials became even more emphatic: "I didn't go to Africa to study drums—somebody wrote that—I went to Africa because there wasn't anything else for me to do. I couldn't get any gigs, and I had to work my way over on a boat. I went over there to study religion and philosophy. I didn't bother with the drums, I wasn't after that. I went over there to see what I could do about religion."[73]

Yet, in 1957, on the eve of Ghana's independence Art Blakey chose to let the world know that he had been to Africa even though he neglected to mention that he had actually spent most of his time in Ghana, not Nigeria. Blakey could not have been in Africa for two full years since his recording history places him in the United States in March and October of 1948.[74] Given Blakey's many contradictory and enigmatic statements about his experiences in Africa, it is hard to fully accept the programmatic description of *Ritual* he provides. When asked why Blakey verbally denied Africa, Randy Weston emphasized that Art was a legendary storyteller whose words were less important than what he played. "Art was the one," Weston emphasized, who inspired Weston's own musical explorations of African music in the 1950s.[75]

For the title track, "Ritual," recorded on February 11, 1957, Blakey reconfigured the band into a pseudo-Afro-Cuban rhythm section with Jackie McLean, Spanky DeBrest, Sam Dockery, and Bill Hardman on lead cowbell, supporting cowbell, maracas, and claves rather than their usual alto sax, bass, piano and trumpet, respectively. Like West African master drummers, who lead from the lowest-pitched instrument, Blakey once again emphasizes the low-pitched tom toms in his solo. The evocation of Cuba in this piece is entirely atmospheric since the valiant efforts of the band members as percussionists are certainly not up to the standards of Afro-Cuban percussion. A little more than a week later Blakey recorded an album for CBS called *Drum Suite,* which included Sabu Martinez on bongo and Cuban conguero Cándido Camero.[76] It included three heavily Cuban pieces titled "The Sacrifice," "Cubano Chant," and "Oscalypso."[77]

For *Orgy in Rhythm,* which was recorded the day after Ghana's independence ceremonies (March 7, 1957), Sabu Martinez organized a full Afro-Cuban rhythm section. In addition to Sabu, the percussionists included Carlos "Patato" Valdés (spelled "Potato Valdez" on the album cover), José Valiente, Ubaldo Nieto, and Evilio Quintero. Patato Valdés had immigrated to New York from Cuba in the early 1950s, and he became especially known for his work in the bands of Machito and Tito Puente. Nieto had also worked with Machito and appeared on Dizzy Gillespie's 1954 recording *Afro.*[78]

*Orgy in Rhythm* also included four drum set players—Blakey, Art Taylor, Jo Jones, and "Specs" Wright. Both Jones and Wright also played timpani on the album, which features extended drum solos over Afro-Cuban vamps and the haunting flute work of Herbie Mann. Later, under State Department sponsorship, Mann would play with Machito's band and tour Africa with an ensemble that included Machito veterans Patato Valdés and José Mangual.

The atmosphere of the album is folkloric, as musical projects such as these were often described, and there were many of them in the 1950s, including most famously Tito Puente's *Puente in Percussion* (1955) and *Top Percussion* (1957). "Toffi" features Art Blakey singing an African-style chant in call and response with a chorus, as well as extended solos on piano, flute, and percussion, all over a repeating bass ostinato in six that is paired with a 6/8 (12/8) Afro-Cuban clave pattern that is usually associated with sacred repertory. This is the so-called long bell version of the pattern (figure 4.2) It is notated here in 12/8.[79] The Afro-Cuban percussion section affords the jazz drummers a chance to take extended solos against an interactive accompaniment rather than solo alone, as is more usual in jazz bands.

"Buhaina Chant" begins with timpani and flute paired in an out-of-time introduction that is followed by a solo voice that leads into the up-tempo percussion descarga (as improvised jam sessions are called in Latin

FIGURE 4.2. Long-bell pattern, from Art Blakey's "Toffi," transcribed by I. Monson. Used by permission of EMI.

music). The musical plan of the introduction is quite similar to the exotic opening of Pérez Prado's *Voodoo Suite* (1954), with its rumbling timpani and chanted vocal. Although the title *Orgy in Rhythm* delivers on the stereotyped associations of drums, Africa, and sexuality, Blue Note's cover art was quite tame (a photo of Blakey seated at the drum set), especially in comparison to the scantily clad black female dancer on the cover of Prado's *Voodoo Suite.*

The Latin percussion section on *Holiday for Skins* (1958), also organized by Sabu Martinez, featured a very young Ray Baretto, Chonguito Vicente, Victor Gonzalez, Julio Martinez, and Andy Delannoy. Baretto had joined Tito Puente's band in 1957, and Vicente was a mainstay of the Tito Rodríguez band. Like *Orgy in Rhythm, Holiday for Skins* allowed a group of drum set players (Blakey, Philly Joe Jones, and Jo Jones) to solo over bass and percussion accompaniment.

The religious flavor of Santería (Lucumí) is especially in evidence on "Dinga," a piece that includes a chanted invocation to Elegua, the Yoruba Orisha of the crossroads. Elegua is always the first Orisha to be saluted in the *oro del igbodu,* a series of musical rhythms to honor the Orishas. The flowing, rhythmic feel established by the percussion section at the opening is called *bembé,* also the name of the central public ceremony in Santería in which it is typically used. Its full texture is built up entrance by entrance. A bass line enters first, setting up the expectation of a 3/4 or 6/8 meter (figure 4.3, entrance 1), similar to what occurs in "Toffi."[80]

When the first cowbell enters, it establishes a two-against-three feel against the bass (entrance 2). After this pattern stabilizes, the second cowbell player enters with the short-bell version of the Afro-Cuban 6/8 clave pattern (entrance 3). Soon a two-pitch conga rhythm enters (alternating an open and a slapped tone), which subdivides the two sides of the two-against-three feel (entrance 4). A second conga rhythm enters (entrance 5) a few moments later and subdivides the three sides of the cross-rhythm. The chant to Elegua enters over this composite texture. "Dinga" echoes Sabu Martinez's "Simba," which was recorded in April 1957 (especially in its chant to Elegua), as well as Tito Puente's venerated album, *Top Percussion,* recorded in July 1957. Three of the eleven percussion pieces on the album ("Eleguara," "Bragada," and "Obarisco") use the same rhythmic feel as "Dinga" except that there is no bass part. All also invoke the Orishas.[81]

Blakey's rejection of these recordings has obscured their significance in jazz history. Blakey claimed that the musicians' egos and competitiveness

FIGURE 4.3. Art Blakey, "Dinga," percussion entrances, transcribed by I. Monson. Used by permission of EMI.

got in the way of achieving the musical experience he was seeking: "On my record date I called all these drummers. You would tell one, 'Take a solo here and we will play background.' Well, the first drummer would take a solo and it would be so damn long the next guy would have no chance to play. He'd be trying to show the other drummers how much he knew. But put us all together and we knew nothin.' It was a novelty at the time, but it just didn't happen."[82]

Critics were also ambivalent about these recordings. Dom Cerulli, writing for *Down Beat*, gave *Orgy in Rhythm* three and a half stars, finding "the effect . . . more that of a travelog sound track than of a jazz session." He found the album halfway between "religious and/or tribal music" and jazz and argued that the latter selections were the most valid. Don Gold, on the other hand, praised *Ritual* highly. In his opinion, the album featured "Blakey firing more intercontinental missiles than the Russians dreamed existed." He nevertheless drew upon common Western images of Africa at the time: "It's all quite fascinating, in its savagery."

In addition, *Metronome*'s reviewer Jack Maher, continuing on the trope of African savagery, found volume two of *Orgy in Rhythm* to be "less bloody than his [Blakey's] first." Maher thought that drummers would be particularly interested in the record. In what would become a common inference later on, he heard hostility in the African sound: "The main reservation we have about this album is wild and frightening hostility Blakey and Taylor show as they seem intent upon beating heads in and the rumble filled background." *Holiday for Skins* was given two and half stars by *Down Beat*'s reviewer, who found it a "scant offering indeed" and asked "how many Africanesque chants can one stand?" He noted somewhat sarcastically that fans of drum solos would nevertheless probably find it the "apotheosis of everything." None of the reviewers mentioned African independence as a context for Blakey's recordings, but these predominantly white writers were not likely to have been avid readers of the *Pittsburgh Courier, Chicago Defender,* or *New York Amsterdam News,* which throughout the 1950s covered news from the African continent and publicized the visits of Haile Selassie, William V. S. Tubman, and Kwame Nkrumah to the United States in 1954 and 1958.[83]

## Africa at Home

The participation of veterans of the Machito, Tito Puente, and Tito Rodríguez bands in projects such as Art Blakey's *Orgy in Rhythm* and *Holiday for Skins* remind us that the musical landscape of the 1950s was defined not simply by West Coast jazz, hard bop, rock and roll, and rhythm and blues but also by the mambo craze. The Palladium at Fifty-third and Broadway was the most famous venue where Latino, African American, and white audiences mingled, but both the Apollo Theater and the Savoy Ballroom also held regular mambo nights in the 1950s. Calypso also had its place on the listening menus of mainstream and African American audiences long before the calypso craze of 1956, which was set off by Harry Belafonte's album *Calypso.*[84]

The invisibility of the Spanish- and English-speaking Caribbean in the cultural history of American popular music is partly due to the fact that the dominant racial ideology required assigning people of Caribbean descent to one side or the other of the black/white color line.[85] Since Caribbean people range from white to brown to black, the cultural distinctiveness of the various ethnic groups (Cuban, Puerto Rican, Trinidadian, Jamaican, Haitian) was often rendered invisible to a broader American audience. Although Afro-Cuban musicians could sometimes argue that they were "Spanish" and not "black" and be successful at receiving service in Southern Jim Crow restaurants, the more visible the African ancestry, the more likely the American public would view the person as black.

Yet, an interest in Latin rhythms was not confined to African American jazz musicians. Both Stan Kenton and George Shearing, two prominent white musicians, were also caught up in the mambo craze of the 1950s. Kenton even recorded a tribute to Machito in 1947 and went with his arranger, Pete Rugulo, to seek musical advice on Cuban music from Mario Bauzá and René Hernández. Kenton's use of Latin music seems divorced from any interest in the African diasporic political implications of the type that interested Art Blakey and Randy Weston, but he did hire prominent Caribbean musicians of color as did Shearing. Kenton's musical practice infused Latin rhythms into a big band sound with symphonic aspirations.[86] George Shearing's band of the 1950s included Afro-Cuban percussionist Armando Peraza, as well as bassist Al McKibbon, an African American who became heavily involved in Afro-Cuban music after working with Chano Pozo in Dizzy Gillespie's band. Shearing's small group efforts on pieces such as "Call Mambo," "Afro No. IV," and "Estampa Cabana" (all from 1958) illustrate how thoroughly he had studied secular dance rhythms of Cuban music, including montuno patterns.[87]

Musically what distinguishes the self-consciously Africanist aspirations of Art Blakey's projects is the use of the 6/8 clave feels of Afro-Cuban sacred music. Although Blakey also used the secular dance rhythms of the mambo in his Jazz Messenger recordings of, for example, "Split Kick" and "Night in Tunisia," the cultural valence of *Orgy in Rhythm* and *Holiday for Skins* emphasizes the sacred rhythms of Santería and their cultural continuities with African "tribal" rhythms, as they were often described in the 1950s. The 6/8 clave bell pattern in Cuba, after all, is identical (except for the convention of its notation) to the 12/8 bell pattern found in several West African cultures, including the Ewe and the Yoruba.[88]

Blakey was not alone in making this musical linkage. At least three other major projects that made the connection between freedom in Africa and African America also used the 6/8 (12/8) clave bell pattern of Afro-Cuban sacred music (or a close variation) and included both African and Caribbean musicians: Max Roach's *We Insist! Freedom Now Suite* (1960), Randy Weston's *Uhuru Afrika* (1960), and Art Blakey's *African Beat* (1962). Among the Caribbean musicians not previously mentioned were

Ray Mantilla, Cándido Camero, Armando Peraza, and Montego Joe; among the African musicians were Babatunde Olatunji and Solomon Ilori.

The linkages among Africa, the Caribbean, and African America were not merely symbolic but, as Randy Weston and Max Roach have argued, also part of a larger black community in New York that included Spanish- and English-speaking people from the Caribbean living side by side with African Americans, especially in Harlem and Brooklyn. Randy Weston recalls how his own family embodied this meeting of the Caribbean, Africa, and African America.

> See, my dad's people came from Jamaica, Panama, and Costa Rica, and my mother's family is from Virginia. So I grew up in Brooklyn, New York. I was the first generation of New Yorkers, and I had the opportunity to savor and enjoy my mother's cooking and my fa- ther's cooking—different types of music. [There were] differences of accent, but I kept seeing the relationship between the two. And they were truly African people, just from different parts of the planet. But my father, he was a great lover of Marcus Garvey. And as a boy he told me when I was quite small, he said, "My son," he says, "you are an African born in America." And he said that "your people are a global people, and before you can really know yourself, you have to know the history of Africa. You have to know African civilization, before Africa was invaded.[89]

Max Roach, who grew up with Weston, also recalled Brooklyn as a place where the legacy of Marcus Garvey was strong. Garvey's interest in Africa, global black unity, and economic self-determination were among the things that inspired Roach's interest in Africa in these years: "Well, that all came about from Marcus Garvey, you know. Marcus Garvey was in the black community—and still is—one of the major heroes, even though he went to jail and all that kind of stuff. He really was very revolutionary."[90]

Garvey, who was born and raised in Jamaica, lived in London from 1912 to 1914, where he met many Africans interested Pan-Africanism and the struggle against colonialism. In 1914 he returned to Jamaica and formed the Universal Negro Improvement Association (UNIA), which he moved to Harlem in 1916. During the 1920s his spellbinding oratory, mass meetings, parades, and his newspaper (*Negro World*) earned him the re- spect and support of tens of thousands of black New Yorkers of African

American and West Indian descent, among them Duke Ellington's trombonist, Tricky Sam Nanton. Garvey's legacy is especially important for understanding the long history of linking spiritual, political, and Africanist interests in African American culture and its impact on the jazz world of the 1960s.[91]

Weston remembers Brooklyn as a vibrant community that prided itself on a strong musical cosmopolitanism:

> You know our parents, they were so advanced. I was just talking to Jackie McLean about that. Our parents were so incredible every day. I think . . . not only about my own mother and father, but that generation. Why? Because they listened only to the best music, and they listened to all kinds of music. So growing up we heard jazz, blues, calypso, Latin, European classical music, you name it, we'd have a variety of music. My dad would take me to the Apollo theater to hear Andy Kirk's band with Mary Lou Williams at the piano, or Duke Ellington. And at that time, people were not as put in boxes like today. Like, "I only like this kind of music." They always had the best music. So I was very fortunate to be able to grow up in Brooklyn, New York.[92]

Weston's father, Frank Edward Weston, owned a restaurant in Brooklyn that served as a meeting place for all kinds of music, people, and ideas. Weston worked there as he was building his career in the 1950s and fondly remembers his father cooking for ten or more musicians after hours and challenging them to justify whatever they were doing musically, spiritually, and politically.

A similarly vibrant account of musical life in Brooklyn is found in Bilal Abdurahman's *In the Key of Time,* a memoir of Bedford Stuyvesant from the 1940s to the 1960s. Abdurahman describes weekly jam sessions at the Putnam Central Club (near the intersection of Putnam and Classon avenues) that included musicians like Cecil Payne, Max Roach, Wilbur Ware, Ahmad Abdul Malik, Alex Korah, Randy Weston, and Wynton Kelly.[93] Charles Mingus participated in the running of these sessions in the summer of 1953, which led to the recording of an ensemble featuring the four trombones of J. J. Johnson, Kai Winding, Bennie Green, and Willie Dennis live at Putnam Central for Debut Records in 1953.[94] Abdurahman remembers several other Brooklyn clubs as offering a mixture of live and recorded music (on jukeboxes) that spanned the stylistic range of calypso, jazz, blues, and R&B, including the Elks Ballroom, Crawford's Ballroom, the Tip Top, and the Verona Cafe.[95]

In 1958 Abdurahman opened the African Quarter, a restaurant located near the intersection of Fulton Street and Stuyvesant Avenue in Brooklyn, which served African food, offered the sounds of jazz and "East African Music," and was visited by several African dignitaries, whose presence in New York increased as newly independent nations joined the UN. In the early 1960s Abdurahman played darbukka in some of the "East meets West" musical events organized by bassist and oud player Ahmed Abdul Malik, which also included Montego Joe on conga and bongo.[96]

Another event along these lines was titled "Oriental and Jazz" and featured Abdul-Malik, Richard Williams, and Bilal Abdurahman (figure 4.4). In the early 1960s concerts organized around the theme of Africa were held in Harlem as well, such as the African Bag concert in 1963 (featuring Ray Bryant's Quintet) (figure 4.5). Some of the culturally themed events

SUN. DEC. 11, 1960

TRUDE HELLER
PRESENTS

A MATINEE PROGRAM
OF

ORIENTAL AND JAZZ

SOUNDS OF THE MIDDLE & NEAR EAST

MUSIC
STARRING

AHMED ABDUL-MALIK

CALO SCOTT... CELLO
RICHARD WILLIAMS...TRUMPET
BILAL ABDURRAHMAN.. ALTO & DARABEKA

AT THE

VERSAILLES

9TH ST. & 6TH AVE.
RES. AL.4-8346

ADM.
$125

4-8 PM

FIGURE 4.4. "Oriental and Jazz." Rutgers Institute of Jazz Studies, Topics files: handbills, New York jazz clubs. Courtesy of Rutgers Institute of Jazz Studies.

JAZZ COMES BACK TO HARLEM
JIMMY DAVIS'

# « African Bag »

PRESENTS

The Beginning Of A New Creative Force In Jazz
Beginning      Sunday,      November 10, 1963
FROM 4 P.M. UNTIL

FEATURING

## Ray Bryant's Quintet

*Guest Stars:* Randy Weston, Joe Knight
Spaulding Givens, Majid Shabazz, Sadik Hakim
Louis Brown, Larry Willis, Big Black
Booker Irvin, Eric Dolphy, Ted Curson, Jackie Mclean
And Many Others-Projecting New Innovations In Music

At The Beautiful

## Club Sea Breeze

131st Street & Lenox Avenue
*New York City*      AU 6-7759

ADMISSION                                    $1.50
Tables Free 'Bar Service No Cover No Minimum
*Free Egyptian Perfume for the Ladies*

FIGURE 4.5. "African Bag." Rutgers Institute of Jazz Studies, Topics files: handbills, New York jazz clubs. Courtesy of Rutgers Institute of Jazz Studies.

made particular appeals to women, as did the "Fashions Set to Music" event held at the District 65 hall of the United Auto Workers on Astor Place. The clothes for this event were designed by Mildred Weston, and "original music to highlight the fashions" was provided by Randy Weston and Nadi Qamar (figure 4.6). The African Bag concert offered "Free Egyptian Perfume for the Ladies."

The linking of Africa and Asia was a prominent theme in the diasporic sensibilities of the late 1950s and 1960s, which was fostered in part by Islam and in part by an anticolonialist perspective that connected the fates of black, brown, and yellow people from around the world. In 1955 several African, Middle Eastern, and Asian nations who wished to remain neutral with respect to the Cold War organized an Afro-Asian conference, which was held in Bandung, Indonesia. Many African Americans were interested in this meeting of Africa and Asia, and Adam Clayton Powell Jr. was

An evening of **FASHIONS SET TO MUSIC**
(*Fashion Show and Dance*)

10pm to 3am **SATURDAY, OCTOBER 23, 1965**

Fashions by **MILDRED WESTON**

Original music **BY THE RANDY WESTON SEXTET**
to highlight **AND NADI QAMAR**
the fashions

Music for dancing / RANDY WESTON SEXTET

**DISTRICT 65 PENTHOUSE BALLROOM**
65 Astor Place, Manhattan*

**TICKET INFORMATION**

**ADMISSION:** { Advance purchase: $3.50
{ At the door: $4 –

**TABLE RESERVATIONS:** { for FOUR persons: $5 –
{ for TEN persons: $12 –

**PICKUP** at the following locations: MANHATTAN { Wil's Record Shop · 147 W. 125 St.
{ The Record Shack · 274 W. 125 St.
{ Jazz Record Center · 107 W. 47 St.
{ Folklore Center · 321 Sixth Av. (3RD St)
BROOKLYN:
Birdel's Record Shop · 540 Nostrand Av.

**PHONE** for reservations at either: 493-2412 or GL 2-0798

**MAIL** check or money order payable to: Mildred Weston · 182 Cornelia St. B'klyn.

*ONE BLOCK SOUTH OF 8TH ST. BETWEEN 4TH AV. AND BROADWAY;
IRT Lexington Av. local to Astor Pl. · BMT Brighton local to 8 St.

FIGURE 4.6. "Fashions Set to Music." Rutgers Institute of Jazz Studies, Topics files: handbills, New York jazz clubs. Courtesy of Rutgers Institute of Jazz Studies.

among the attendees. This landmark show of strength by people of color around the world made State Department officials sufficiently nervous that they refused Powell's request to attend as an official observer and also made it difficult for him to obtain a visa as a private citizen.[97]

The cultural linking of Africa and Asia also became a theme emphasized by the Nation of Islam, which sponsored several African-Asian unity bazaars in the early 1960s. Noting that Islam "covers the entire earth," the

Nation of Islam stated in 1961 that people of the white world were called "occidental," while the black world, consisting of black, brown, red, and yellow people, were known as "orientals."[98] The cultural theme of linking the East and the West in the jazz world of the late 1950s and early 1960s, in other words, often had a political subtext that is perhaps best contextualized by the growth of community spaces, events, and networks of individuals interested in exploring the cultural diversity of blackness and its relationship to Africa.

Muslim musicians were prominent in several of the musical projects that made links to Africa and the diaspora. The universalist message of Islam provided an alternative to Western modernism's vision of universality that would play an increasingly important role in the spiritual visions of jazz musicians in the 1960s. Although the religious practice of the Nation of Islam (NOI) connected Islam to an ideology of racial separation, Muslim jazz musicians were not necessarily members of the NOI. Art Blakey, as well as Ahmad Jamal, Yusef Lateef, and Sahib Shihab, were converted to Islam by the Ahmaddiyah movement, which did not share the NOI's vision of racial separation. Indeed, in the early 1960s Art Blakey (Abdullah Ibn Buhaina) expressed intense disdain for the Nation of Islam.[99] Other musicians such as McCoy Tyner (Sulaimon Saud) were Sunni Muslims, who also did not share the Nation of Islam's position on separation. As Art Blakey explained to his French interviewers in 1963, "Islam brought the black man what he was looking for, an escape like some found in drugs or drinking: a way of living and thinking he could choose in complete freedom. This is the reason we adopted this new religion in such numbers. It was for us, above all, a way of rebelling."[100]

## Uhuru Afrika

In November 1960 pianist Randy Weston recorded *Uhuru Afrika,* a four-movement composition celebrating the emerging independent African nations. It was recorded two months after the historic admission of sixteen sub-Saharan African nations to the United Nations, which brought thousands of delegates and dignitaries to New York, including Fidel Castro, whose delegation moved to the Theresa Hotel in Harlem after inhospitable treatment at a midtown hotel. Twelve of these nations issued a statement the day after their admission asking the Cold War powers to refrain from confronting each other on the African continent. That year had already been a dramatic one in the civil rights movement, for the entire country was riveted by the contagious spread of student lunch-counter sit-ins that were intended to bring about an end to segregated public accommodations. In October Martin Luther King had been imprisoned on trumped-up charges following a sit-in at Rich's department store in Atlanta and, in what turned out to be the gesture that swung the election, Senator John F. Kennedy called Coretta Scott King to wish her well.[101]

As Randy Weston recalls, the social atmosphere of the late 1950s was key to the genesis of *Uhuru Afrika,* which means "Freedom Africa" in Kiswahili:

Now, in the Civil Rights days it was like a tremendous spiritual energy that covered all the fields of music, art, and poetry. There was a tremendous movement for African American people to get as much freedom as possible. So the musicians were caught up into this wonderful period. I can't explain how it happened, but it happened in the late 1950s. I had already met the great arranger Melba Liston. And we wanted, I wanted, to do a work of music which would describe the global African people. . . . If you look globally we speak many different languages, we live in many different parts of the planet. We have a lot of diversity. At the same time, there's a lot of similarity in things that we do . . . and in addition to that, many of the African countries were just getting their independence. And the wonderful thing about being in New York, the United Nations was there. So I had an opportunity to meet many African diplomats. Many people from Kenya, from Nigeria, from Ghana, from Egypt, many parts of Africa. And I would always talk to them to try to understand a little bit more about the continent. As Langston Hughes always said, [Africa is] our ancestral home.[102]

In Weston's view it was especially important to do a celebratory work because the prevailing image of Africans in mainstream American culture in the 1950s had been defined by the *Story of Little Black Sambo* and Tarzan movies.[103] Recalling the awkwardness of reading the book in grade school Weston commented, "I was sitting next to a white child, and we were buddies. But when we looked at this same book, I think our lives changed at that particular moment. So I was very disturbed by the image of us as a people." The fact that in Tarzan movies Africans were presented as without language filled Weston with the desire to begin *Uhuru Afrika* with an African language. A number of African diplomats recommended Kiswahili since it was a Bantu language that was used in both the northeastern and southern regions of the continent.[104]

*Uhuru Kwanza,* the first movement, is divided into two parts. The first is a spoken invocation by Tuntemeke Sanga, a diplomat from Tanzania, who is accompanied by Cándido Camero on conga. It opens with "Freedom! Uhuru, Uhuru Kwanza. Freedom, Freedom First!" Weston explains: "That meant that many people were saying, 'Well, African countries shouldn't have their independence until they do this or until they do that.' We said no. First of all, our freedom, our independence."

Cándido Camero's conga leads the percussion section into a rolling 12/8 feel that is joined by percussionists Armando Peraza, Babatunde Olatunji, Max Roach, Charlie Persip, and G. T. Hogan. The second part of *Uhuru Kwanza* features Randy Weston on piano, who presents all twelve pitches of the chromatic scale by playing a whole-tone scale that begins on C and then modulates down a half step and returns. The melody that follows has a rhythm to which the word "Uhuru" can be sung (figure 4.7).[105]

For texts, Weston went to Langston Hughes, who had had a huge impact on Weston's life. He asked for a "freedom poem for African people" and lyrics for a song about the African woman because "its very important to recognize the power of the African woman, which are our mothers, our sisters, our daughters. . . . Langston wrote a beautiful text."

The first stanza of the poem makes the African lady a metaphor for the future of the African continent, one of the relatively few unsexualized odes to women in the jazz literature. The following year, Abbey Lincoln would record it on her album *Straight Ahead.* On *Uhuru Afrika,* the first stanza was sung by Martha Flowers.

*Night is gone—*
*I hear your song,*
*African lady.*
*The dark fades away,*
*Now it's day,*

FIGURE 4.7. Randy Weston, "Uhuru Kwanza," part 2, New York, November 1960, Roulette R 65001, transcribed by I. Monson. Composed by Randy Weston 3 1961, renewed 1989. Worldwide administration by Black Sun Music (SESAC), a div. of Mayflower Music Corp.

*A new morning breaks.*
*The birds in the sky all sing*
*For Africa awakes.*
*Bright light floods the land,*
*And tomorrow's in your hand.*
*African lady.*

Trombonist and composer/arranger Melba Liston orchestrated and arranged Weston's compositions for big band. The arrangement of "African Lady" features the flutes of Yusef Lateef and Les Spann as the birds awakening behind Flowers's vocal. Liston's writing, which ranges from lush, thick, beautifully voiced textures to harmonically tense and rhythmically assertive brass writing, is crucial to the dramatic unfolding of the second and third movements: "African Lady" and "Bantu."

Weston remembers that "Melba was writing music up to the last second of the day [before the recording]" and that the copyist, whose feet swelled up from the effort, was copying music "all over the house to get done in time to do this recording." The orchestra included a who's who of the contemporary jazz scene with Clark Terry, Benny Bailey, Richard Williams, and Freddie Hubbard on trumpets; Slide Hampton, Jimmy

Cleveland, and Quentin Jackson on trombones; Julius Watkins on French horn; a reed section that included Gigi Gryce, Sahib Shihab, Budd Johnson, Yusef Lateef, Cecil Payne, and Les Spann; and two bassists, George Duvivier and Ron Carter.

The band recorded two days in a row at New York's Bell Sound studios beginning at 9:00 A.M. "And believe it or not," Weston recalled, "not one person was late. And that's why I say it was a spiritual get-together." The work is serious but at the same time overflowing with optimism and a utopian vision of the future. "Kucheza Blues," its final movement, was intended to capture the joyfulness of freedom finally achieved. Its title is based on the Kiswahili word *kucheza,* which means "playing" or "dancing."[106] Weston explained that the song says that, on "that day when have our freedom and our independence as a people, we're going to have a big party . . . and that's 'Kucheza Blues.'"

Yet, as Weston acknowledges, *Uhuru Afrika* was not very popular at the time, in part "because the term 'African American' was sort of not quite *in,* you know. We were Negroes and colored. We have other names, we have many names. But at that particular time it wasn't very popular." The interest in African liberation and the diaspora was an intensifying presence in the aesthetic agency, musical practice, and political thinking of musicians in the 1950s, but it was a passionate interest of a relatively small group of people in the African American artistic and literary scenes. As the civil rights movement intensified in the early 1960s, many more people would come to view the link between Africa and jazz as a crucial cultural connection.

# 5

## Activism and Fund-Raising from *Freedom Now* to the Freedom Rides

O N JANUARY 15, 1961, the Congress of Racial Equality (CORE) sponsored a benefit performance of *We Insist! Max Roach's Freedom Now
Suite* at New York's Village Gate. The poster announcing the event (figure
5.1) depicted three African American men seated at a lunch-counter sit-in,
making explicit through visual means the link between the political events
of 1960 and the subject matter of the *Freedom Now Suite*.[1] It is the same
photograph that graced the album cover of the Candid recording and is
modeled on widely distributed photos of the lunch-counter sit-ins held in
Greensboro, North Carolina, and many other locations in February and
March 1960.[2]

Like Duke Ellington in "Black, Brown, and Beige," the composers of
the *Freedom Now Suite* (Max Roach and Oscar Brown Jr.) presented in
music a panoramic perspective on African American history and summed
up the contemporary hopes and demands of African Americans at the
crossroads of an intensified civil rights struggle. The *Freedom Now* benefit
was unusual in its explicitly political dramatic content and use of images
from contemporary events. In other respects, however, it was one among
dozens of events held between 1960 and 1967 in which jazz musicians
donated their services to civil rights organizations and other related causes.
Billed as all-star concerts, "cocktail sips," "steak-outs," receptions, swing
parties, variety shows, or fund-raising dinners, these events raised money
and generated a sense of political involvement among audience members

CORE *presents*

**MAX ROACH**

# FREEDOM NOW
SUITE

*featuring*

**MAX
ROACH
QUINTET**

**ABBEY
LINCOLN**

**OLATUNJI**

## WORLD PREMIER PERFORMANCE
## SUNDAY JANUARY 15th, 4-7 P M
## THE VILLAGE GATE · 185 THOMPSON STREET

CONTRIBUTION: $2 50  TICKETS AVAILABLE AT
**THE VILLAGE GATE**; ALSO **THE RECORD SHACK**,
274 WEST 125 ST.; **THE FOLKLORE CENTER**, 110
MACDOUGAL ST.; AND **CORE** OFFICE, 38 PARK ROW

FIGURE 5.1. Poster of *Freedom Now Suite* benefit concert, held January 15, 1961.
Courtesy of Art D'Lugoff.

at a time when what might be called a culture of commitment was
emerging.

Benefit concerts are among the most obvious forms of political participation by jazz musicians in the early 1960s. Ranging from small club-
hosted events to gala performances at concert halls and stadiums, these
fund-raisers benefited many different causes, including civil rights, African

independence, and black labor organizations. On many of these occasions jazz musicians appeared either alongside gospel singers and folk musicians or on the same bill with more mainstream entertainers such as Frank Sinatra and Sammy Davis Jr. Actors and writers were also among those drafted for these fund-raising events, including Sidney Poitier, Ruby Dee, Ossie Davis, Peter Lawford, Marlon Brando, and Lorraine Hansberry.

Among those who participated in fund-raising events were proponents of a full range of jazz styles, including Count Basie, Louis Armstrong, Miles Davis, Duke Ellington, Cannonball Adderley, Thelonious Monk, Dizzy Gillespie, Dave Brubeck, John Coltrane, Sarah Vaughan, Prince Lasha, Ella Fitzgerald, Paul Bley, Don Friedman, Max Roach, Abbey Lincoln, Eric Dolphy, Charles Mingus, and numerous others. For many jazz fans, the number of fund-raising concerts done by well-known jazz musicians in the early sixties, as well as the diverse jazz styles represented in them, is likely to come as a surprise. Ever since Amiri Baraka's *Blues People* and Frank Kofsky's *Black Nationalism and the Revolution in Music,* the jazz literature has typically associated free jazz with the raging politics of the sixties. The fact that an aesthetically broad range of African and non–African American musicians regularly lent their names to civil rights (and other political) organizations in the years between Greensboro and Black Power has gone relatively unnoticed.[3]

Although socially minded concerts had been a feature of the jazz landscape since at least the 1930s, when Duke Ellington, Benny Carter, and many others played for a variety of causes, including the Scottsboro Boys and the NAACP (table 5.1), a threshold was crossed on February 1, 1960, when the student lunch-counters sit-ins began in Greensboro, North Carolina.[4] The speed with which these protests spread across the South announced a new period of direct mass action whose symbolism, events, and ideologies deeply affected not only the jazz world but also American society as a whole. The image of four African American college students seated politely but insistently at a Woolworth's lunch counter portended an activism that was to permeate the entire decade.

Benefit concerts occurred in response to the major events in the civil rights movement, including the Greensboro sit-ins of 1960, the Freedom Rides of 1961, the Birmingham movement and the March on Washington in 1963, and the Mississippi voter registration projects of 1964. Although benefit concerts generated considerable amounts of money for civil rights organizations, their purpose and popularity cannot be fully explained by

TABLE 5.1. Some fund-raising concerts, 1933–1959

| Date | Location | Billed as | Benefit for/Sponsor | Participants[1] |
|---|---|---|---|---|
| 1933 | Rockland Palace, 155th and 8th Ave., New York City | | Scottsboro Boys, International Labor Defense (ILD) | Benny Carter Orchestra, Duke Ellington (solo piano), Tallulah Bankhead, Martha Raye[2] |
| 12/23/38 | Carnegie Hall | Spirituals to Swing | New Masses (Marxist periodical) | Count Basie, Jo Jones, Walter Page, Buck Clayton, Lester Young, Jimmy Rushing, Helen Humes, Hot Lips Page, Tommy Ladnier, Sidney Bechet, Dan Minor, Leonard Ware, Albert Ammons, Meade Lux Lewis, Pete Johnson, Big Joe Turner, Sister Rosetta Tharpe, Sonny Terry, Mitchell Christian Singers, Big Bill Broonzy, Ruby Smith, James P. Johnson[3] |
| 12/24/39 | Carnegie Hall | Spirituals to Swing | Theater Arts Committee | Golden Gate Quartet, Ida Cox, Benny Goodman Sextet, Buck Clayton, Count Basie, Lester Young, Charlie Christian[4] |
| 1/23/43 | Carnegie Hall | Black, Brown, and Beige | Russian war relief | Duke Ellington Orchestra[5] |
| 1943? | Golden Gate Ballroom | All-victory Rally for Ben Davis Jr. | | Teddy Wilson (organizer), Pearl Primus, Hazel Scott, Billie Holiday, Mary Lou Williams, Ella Fitzgerald[6] |
| 4/16/44 | | | birthday party for Paul Robeson | Mildred Bailey, Count Basie, Mary Lou Williams, Duke Ellington, Jimmy Durante[7] |
| 1/21/51 | Metropolitan Opera House | | NAACP Legal Defense and Educational Fund | Duke Ellington orchestra[8] |

(continued)

TABLE 5.1. (continued)

| Date | Location | Billed as | Benefit for/Sponsor | Participants[1] |
|---|---|---|---|---|
| 5/24/54 | Renaissance Casino, New York | | Salute to Paul Robeson | Thelonious Monk, Pete Seeger, Leon Bibb, Lorraine Hansberry, Alice Childress, Julian Mayfield, Karen Morely[9] |
| 5/28/54 | Eastern Parkway Arena | | Brooklyn NAACP | Ella Fitzgerald, Harry Belafonte, Steve Allen[10] |
| 5/1956 | Madison Square Garden | | In Friendship | Harry Belafonte, Duke Ellington, Coretta King[11] |
| 10/25/59 | Birdland | | NAACP | not listed[12] |

1. I provide several lists of benefit concerts in this chapter, but they are by no means comprehensive. The problem with lists of scattered events such as these is that they are never likely to be complete. I list them and my sources for each one for the benefit of other interested researchers. Another source of information about benefit concerts in this time period is Brian Ward, *Just My Soul Responding: Rhythm and Blues, Black Consciousness, and Race Relations* (Berkeley: University of California Press, 1998).

2. John Hammond, *John Hammond on Record: An Autobiography* (New York: Penguin, 1981), p. 85.

3. Ibid., pp. 199–206.

4. Ibid., pp. 231–32.

5. Mark Tucker, *The Duke Ellington Reader* (New York: Oxford University Press, 1993), p. 153.

6. Martin Bauml Duberman, *Paul Robeson* (New York: Knopf, 1988), pp. 283–84.

7. Ibid., pp. 284–85.

8. "Point and Counterpoint: Duke at the Met, *Metronome* 67 (Feb. 1951), p. 8.

9. Duberman, *Paul Robeson*, p. 425.

10. "Belafonte Plays for NAACP Show," *Pittsburgh Courier* (May 19, 1954), p. 19.

11. Taylor Branch, *Parting the Waters: America in the King Years, 1954–63*, (New York: Simon and Schuster, 1988), p. 209. In Friendship was an organization formed in the aftermath of the lynching of Emmett Till in 1955. It supported victims of racist vigilantes in Mississippi.

12. Executive board minutes, *Allegro* 34, no. 1 (Nov. 1959). p. 4.

the economic dimension alone. Many of these events offered a dramatic forum in which Northern audiences could hear directly from Southern activists about day-to-day life on the front lines of the movement. They also created social spaces in which musicians and audiences could feel as though they were *doing something* to aid the Southern struggle. Table 5.2 provides a detailed list of many such events.[5]

Participation in fund-raising events did not always indicate full endorsement of a particular organization's political ideology, however. As Clark Terry recalled, "All of the organizations—SNCC, CORE, NAACP—all of them were very very important organizations, as far as we were concerned. And we supported them all."[6] In the early 1960s Terry performed at benefits for CORE, SNCC, SCLC, and A. Philip Randolph's Negro American Labor Council (NALC). Many other musicians performed benefits for multiple political organizations, including Dizzy Gillespie (CORE, National Urban League [NUL], NALC, SCLC), Dave Brubeck (SCLC, NAACP, SNCC, CORE), and Max Roach and Abbey Lincoln (CORE, SNCC, NAACP, SCLC, Malcolm X). Musicians seemed to respond to particular events in the civil rights movement rather than show exclusive loyalty to particular organizations. This is not to suggest that musicians were without ideological preferences or were unprincipled in their activities, but rather to emphasize that practical political action often carried greater weight than ideological purity, especially in times of crisis.

After the passage of the Civil Rights Act of 1964 and the Voting Rights Act of 1965, the number of events sponsored by mainstream civil rights organizations decreased, as politically related concerts shifted to cultural nationalist arts organizations, where the explicitly political and spiritual force of black music, dance, and art was celebrated. Among the best known of these organizations was Amiri Baraka's Black Arts Repertory/School (BARTS), whose regulars in 1965 included Sun Ra, Albert Ayler, Milford Graves, and Andrew Hill.[7]

To understand the significance of benefit concerts in these years, it is important to consider them in relationship to the most visible events of the civil rights movement, the aesthetic debates emerging in jazz, and the intensified attention paid to issues of race and economics in the music industry. The following two chapters describe the political events that took place between 1960 and 1967 in sufficient detail to provide a sense of the daily news to which musicians responded and establish that many of the

TABLE 5.2. Some fund-raising concerts, January 1960–May 1961

| Date[1] | Location | Billed as | Benefit for/Sponsor | Participants |
|---|---|---|---|---|
| 1/20/60 or 1/27/60 | New York, Village Gate | Africa at the Gate | Africa Defense and Aid Fund | Leon James, Al Mims, Ellis Larkins, Leon Bibb, Josh White, Lorraine Hansberry[2] |
| 6/2/60 | Wheeler Hall, University of California–Berkeley | benefit concert for Southern Negro students | scholarship fund for students expelled from Southern schools for antidiscrimination activities | Oscar Peterson trio, Cannonball Adderley Quintet[3] |
| Summer 1960 | Jackie Robinson's home, Stamford, CT | Afternoon of Jazz | student sit-ins (CORE, SCLC) | Ella Fitzgerald, Duke Ellington, Joe Williams, Sarah Vaughan, Carmen McRae[4] |
| 8/7/60 | New York, Village Gate | sit-in for CORE | CORE | Thelonious Monk, Jimmy Giuffre, Bill Henderson, Clark Terry[5] |
| 8/27/60 | Chicago, Comiskey Park | Second Annual Chicago Urban League Jazz Festival | Urban League | Maynard Ferguson Band, the Cannonball Adderley Quintet, Dizzy Gillespie Quintet, and Lambert-Hendricks-Ross, Sammy Davis Jr., Frank Sinatra[6] |
| 8/28/60 | New York, Village Gate | | CORE | (names not available)[7] |
| Fall 1960, Sunday nights | New York, Village Gate | Cabaret for Freedom | Martin Luther King Jr. | Sidney Poitier, Sarah Vaughan, Zero Mostel, Jack Gilford, Lonnie Sattin, Abbey Lincoln, Max Roach[8] |
| 1/15/61 | New York, Village Gate | CORE Presents: Freedom Now Suite | CORE | Max Roach, Abbey Lincoln, Booker Little, Marcus Belgrave, Julian Priester, Eric Dolphy, Larry Ridgley, Maya Angelou, Ruby Dee, four conga players[9] |
| 1/27/61 | New York, Carnegie Hall | Tribute to Martin Luther King | CORE and SCLC | Frank Sinatra, Dean Martin, Sammy Davis Jr., Joey Bishop, Peter Lawford, Count Basie Orchestra, Carmen McRae, Tony Bennett, Mahalia Jackson[10] |

| Date | Location | Organization | Event | Performers |
|---|---|---|---|---|
| 4/1961 | Detroit | NAACP | Fight for Freedom | Sammy Davis Jr.[11] |
| 4/17/61 | New York, Hunter College | Africa Defense and Aid Fund | Africa Freedom Day | Dizzy Gillespie, Miriam Makeba, Herbie Mann, Tom Mboya, Kenneth Kaunda, Billy Taylor, Dinizulu Dancers, Camilla Williams, Henrique Galvao, Sen. Hubert Humphrey[12] |
| 4/17/61 | New York, Tavern on the Green | NALC (A. Philip Randolph) | dinner/dance | Art Blakey and the Messengers, Dakota Staton, Coleman Hawkins, Randy Weston, Cecil Payne[13] |
| 5/19/61 | Carnegie Hall | African Research Foundation | African Research Foundation presents Miles Davis | Miles Davis and Gil Evans[14] |

1. This list is not intended to be comprehensive.
2. Alvin Hall, " 'Africa at the Gate' Aided African Fund," *New York Amsterdam News* 50, no. 5 (Jan. 30, 1960), p. 13.
3. Marvin Rich to Ralph J. Gleason, June 2, 1960, CORE series 5, box 1, folder 8; "A Full Evening with Sinatra, Martin, Davis, Lawford, Bishop," *New York Amsterdam News* 51 (Jan. 14, 1961), p. 13.
4. David Falkner, *Great Time Coming: The Life of Jackie Robinson, from Baseball to Birmingham* (New York: Simon and Schuster, 1995), p. 274.
5. Jimmy McDonald to George Haefer, July 25, 1960, Institute of Jazz Studies topics files: race problems.
6. Don DeMichael, "Urban League 'Festival,'" *Downbeat* 27 (Oct. 13, 1960), p. 20; "Sammy Davis Jr. Brought Friends to Chicago Jazz Bash," *Pittsburgh Courier* (Sept. 10, 1960), p. 23.
7. Executive board minutes, *Allegro* 34 (Aug. 1960), p. 15.
8. " 'Cabaret for Freedom' New Theatre Movement," *New York Amsterdam News* 50 (Nov. 19, 1960), p. 18. Maya Angelou recalls that all of these performances were held in the summer of 1960; the *Amsterdam News* coverage, however, indicates that they occurred later. See Maya Angelou, *The Heart of a Woman* (New York: Bantam, 1997), p. 81.
9. CORE presents *Freedom Now Suite* (poster), Jan. 15, 1961, series 5, box 28, folder 8; "Roach Suite," *New York Amsterdam News* 51 (Jan. 7, 1961), p. 11; Taylor Branch, *Parting the Waters*, p. 574.
10. Harry Belafonte, solicitation letter, Jan. 27, 1961, CORE series 5, box 28, folder 2.
11. "Sammy Davis Jr. Sparks Record $60,000 Take for Detroit's NAACP," *Pittsburgh Courier* (Apr. 22, 1961), p. 2.
12. "Africa Freedom Day," *New York Amsterdam News* 51 (Mar. 25, 1961), p. 17.
13. "Art Blakey, Dakota at NALC Salute," *New York Amsterdam News* 51 (Apr. 15, 1961), p. 18.
14. Julian "Cannonball" Adderley, "Cannonball on the Jazz Scene," *New York Amsterdam News* 51 (May 27, 1961), p. 17; executive board minutes, *Allegro* 36 (June 1961), p. 16.

issues hotly debated in the context of the civil rights movement were largely the same kinds of issues that emerged in the jazz world.

Aesthetic issues also became highly politicized in this period. In the two and a half months prior to the Greensboro sit-ins, the jazz world buzzed over the New York debut of Ornette Coleman, whose gala opening at the Five Spot extended from the middle of November 1959 until the end of January 1960 (just days before the sit-ins began). In the United States, the debate over the value and meaning of avant-garde expression in jazz consequently began as the political drama of lunch-counter sit-ins unfolded on TV screens and radios and in newspapers. It was not until after the Freedom Rides that the debate became truly nasty.

Coleman initially enjoyed the support of many influential critics, including Martin Williams, Gunther Schuller, and John Wilson, and although there was much grumbling behind backs, few critics were initially willing to announce themselves as the new moldy figs. Over the next few years many avant-gardists claimed a direct relationship between a musical modernism free of chord changes, compulsory tonality, timbral orthodoxy, and the obligation to swing and a radical, assertive, political consciousness. An "outside" musical approach consequently came to signify for many a political critique of racial injustice.[8]

Part of the challenge of thinking through this history is to resist the temptation to rigidly map aesthetic positions and politics. Those who preferred their jazz more "inside" were not necessarily more politically conservative, although they could be. Conversely, those who championed the "New Thing" were not necessarily more activist in their orientation, although they could be. Avant-gardists ranged from the militant activism of Archie Shepp to the more spiritual consciousness of John Coltrane. Individual musicians made their way through the highly volatile landscape of the early 1960s amid deeply conflicting forces—those of the civil rights movement that demanded activism and those of the music, which demanded disciplined practicing and much hard work. Even the most artistically single-minded musicians were often not satisfied by standing on the sidelines. Participation in the movement or making music speak to the astonishing events taking place in the South were choices that some musicians felt added to the authenticity and gravitas of their music. As Abbey Lincoln explained, "I think that the artists joined the bandwagon because it makes your work valid. You have to perform, you have to sing or play about something."[9]

## Background of the Sit-Ins

The Greensboro sit-ins have attained a mythical status in the accounts of the civil rights movement. On Monday, February 1, 1960, four students from North Carolina Agricultural and Technical (A&T) College (Ezell Blair Jr., Franklin McCain, Joe McNeil, and David Richmond) sat down at the Woolworths lunch counter in Greensboro and demanded service equal to that accorded white patrons. They returned the next day with reinforcements, a phenomenon that spread like wildfire throughout the southeast. Within a two-month period the sit-in movement, as it came to be called, had spread to fifty-four cities in nine states and captured the imagination of racial progressives in the North and South. The sit-in movement, like jazz improvisation, was usually described as "spontaneous" and "contagious"—something that magically inspired the entry of black college students and youth into the civil rights movement. Their example, in turn, stimulated the participation of white students in direct-action protest, and these students later turned their protests against the war in Vietnam.

As Aldon Morris has carefully documented, however, the sudden ignition of direct-action protest in 1960 would not have been possible had the ground not been well prepared within Southern black communities by the organizational and educational efforts of various groups, including the SCLC, NAACP Youth Councils, CORE, the Highlander Folk School, the Fellowship of Reconciliation (FOR), and the Southern Conference Educational Fund (SCEF). Morris credits the SCLC, in particular, with developing the black organizational and tactical base capable of supporting expanded direct-action activities in the early 1960s.[10]

Between 1957 and 1960 members of the NAACP Youth Councils and CORE conducted sit-ins in approximately sixteen cities, including Saint Louis; East Saint Louis; Kansas City; Oklahoma City; Tulsa; Louisville, Kentucky; Miami; Durham, North Carolina; Nashville; and Atlanta. Despite the common image of the 1960s sit-ins arising spontaneously, a closer look at the historical record reveals that their rapid spread in 1960 occurred in cities and towns that had seen prior activity and where networks of formal and informal communication were already established. The swift expansion of sit-ins in the wake of Greensboro, in other words, mobilized preexisting organizational and personal networks. The Greensboro students had all been members of the NAACP Youth Council, headed by attorney Floyd McKissick. McKissick, in turn, was a veteran of a series of sit-ins in parks, hotels, and bus waiting rooms in Durham in the late 1950s. Through George Simpkins, head of the NAACP chapter in Greensboro, the students from North Carolina A&T were well aware of the Durham demonstrations. They had also attended high school together in Greensboro, where in 1958 and 1959 the NAACP Legal Defense Fund systematically challenged local efforts to maintain school segregation.[11]

The four students had carefully prepared for their actions at the Woolworth store and had a network of adult supporters in place, including George Simpkins, Eula Hudgens (a veteran of CORE's Journey of Reconciliation in 1947), and Ralph Johns, a white clothing store owner sympathetic to the NAACP. On February 1, they bought school supplies, then sat down at the lunch counter and announced their intention to return every day until they were treated the same as the white patrons. On Saturday there was a bomb scare as four hundred demonstrators gathered at the Woolworths, along with Klansmen and Confederate-flag-waving white youths who harassed the protesters. A week after the Greensboro sit-ins, demonstrations began in Durham and Winston-Salem. Charlotte and Raleigh followed in quick succession. Protests then spread to South Carolina, Virginia, and Nashville, Tennessee. In March demonstrations took place in Montgomery, Birmingham, Baton Rouge, New Orleans, Memphis, Atlanta, and Savannah, all cities that had been centers of activity during the fifties.[12]

## The Formation of SNCC

Nashville was particularly important in the subsequent development of the civil rights movement. Several leaders of the nascent SNCC emerged from Nashville, including John Lewis, Diane Nash, James Bevel, Cordell Reagon, Marion Barry, Matthew Jones, and Bernard Lafayette. In 1959, Reverend James Lawson, under the auspices of the Nashville Christian Leadership Council (NCLC), conducted workshops on nonviolence that were attended by many of the future leaders and other students in Nashville's black colleges. At the end of the year students conducted test sit-ins in Nashville's department stores; consequently, when the Greensboro sit-ins began, they were poised for action. By February 13, 1960, the student wing of the NCLC nudged their elders into beginning nonviolent demonstrations that by early May had successfully integrated downtown Nashville's lunch counters.[13]

Ella Baker, acting director of the SCLC's national office in Atlanta, facilitated the founding of SNCC by organizing a "Southwide Student Leadership Conference on Nonviolent Resistance to Segregation" at her alma mater, Shaw University in Raleigh, North Carolina. Baker, whose advocacy of a decentralized, noncharismatic approach to leadership brought her into conflict with the predominantly male and ministerial leadership of the SCLC, felt that, in order to consolidate the student movement, various leaders needed to convene to share ideas. Over the weekend of April 15–17, three hundred students gathered in Raleigh and debated whether they should affiliate with one of the existing civil rights organizations or form an independent association. Many of the students were irritated with the SCLC (the organization they were most likely to consider joining) for capitalizing on the student sit-ins in its fund-raising activities without returning much of the income generated to the students. With Baker's encouragement, the students chose to form an independent, decentralized organization with far less bureaucracy than either the SCLC or the NAACP and began developing an ideology that stressed concern for all forms of racial domination, not simply lunch counters and department stores.[14]

The emergence of a student movement led by African American college students inspired an unprecedented level of interest among not only African Americans but also white college students in the North, where advocacy of racial justice generated fewer reprisals than in the South. During the sit-ins in 1960, activists from the Students for a Democratic Society (SDS)—including Robert Haber and Tom Hayden—headed south to observe the meetings from which SNCC was organized. As Morris has emphasized, SNCC provided a tactical and organizational "protest model" for emerging white student organizations such as the SDS.[15]

## Benefit Concerts

The Congress of Racial Equality was the first nonviolent direct-action organization to attain high visibility in the New York area in the wake of the Greensboro lunch-counter sit-ins. Its visibility on the national scene, as well as in New York, was due in part to the efforts of Marvin Rich, who, as community relations director, was charged with handling public communications and special fund-raising projects. Rich had pioneered direct-mail fund-raising for CORE and sent out weekly press releases on CORE's activities and had overseen the organization of benefit concerts. He recalls that the fund-raising concerts arose in response to the public's indignation at the treatment of students at the sit-ins: "Benefits really began . . . with the huge increase in publicity after the sit-ins of 1960. . . . Then people would call us. . . . Something would happen in the newspaper. People would be indignant. They'd want to do something, and we'd do it."[16] Nat Hentoff concurred: "The atmosphere, especially in a place like New York, was very much, 'we've got to do something. We've got to have these benefits. And we've got to do whatever we can.' It was just part of the air."[17]

Among the first fund-raising events sponsored by CORE at the Village Gate was a "Sit-in for CORE" on August 7, 1960, featuring Thelonious Monk, Jimmy Giuffre, Bill Henderson, and Clark Terry.[18] "Sitting in," of course, had a long-standing meaning in the jazz world—going up on the bandstand to play a tune or two with the regular musicians, usually by invitation. The students' sit-ins offered an opportunity for a double entendre—linking the sitting in at the Village Gate to the larger moral struggle of the civil rights movement (and also to the sit-down strikes of the labor movement in the 1930s.)[19]

Union regulations required that many musicians be paid something for their performances. The American Federation of Musicians at first turned down CORE's request to allow musicians to donate their services to the benefit. Local 802 (New York) was extremely consistent in its policies regarding the approval of benefit concerts: As long as the minimum number of musicians mandated for the room were paid scale, the union would approve the use of additional musicians on a volunteer basis. If the minimum number of musicians for the room was not met, the union would deny permission. As Marvin Rich remembers, at first CORE was unaware of the procedures: "We never had any real problem, but we had to go through the rigmarole. We were beginners. We didn't know how to do it." Once the sponsors guaranteed that the required number of players would be paid minimum scale, approval was granted. In many cases, the individuals who were paid would kick back their pay to the sponsoring organization, as did the musicians who played for a SNCC fund-raising dinner in 1965.[20]

Many fund-raising events were held at the Village Gate during the latter half of 1960. Owned and run by Art and Bert D'Lugoff, the Gate had opened in 1958 as a venue primarily for folk and ethnic music. Among the artists who appeared there were Nina Simone, Odetta, Pete Seeger, and Leon Bibb, all of whom performed frequently for civil rights organizations in the early 1960s. Folksingers had long been associated with the leftist trade union movement of the thirties and forties. In the fifties, partly through the efforts of the Highlander Folk School in Monteagle, Tennessee, folksingers became increasingly associated with the struggle for civil rights. The singing of folk songs from around the world became an integral part of the cultural environment at Highlander, as well as an approach to repertory that was quite popular in folk music circles in the late fifties. Art D'Lugoff's taste for folk and ethnic music thus drew upon a cultural legacy associated with the progressive trade union movement of the thirties and forties and the folk music scene of the 1950s. Before entering the music business in the midfifties D'Lugoff had, in fact, been an organizer and a public relations person for the United Electrical Workers (a union known for its overall progressive politics).[21]

D'Lugoff describes his interest in jazz as a natural extension of his interest in folk music. Since many people were aware of his history of leftist politics and appreciated the "coffee shop" atmosphere of the club, he was often approached about hosting fund-raising events at the Gate. In this context, then, it is not surprising that D'Lugoff once booked Odetta and John Coltrane on the same bill or that African artists such Miriam Makeba and Hugh Masekela were among the artists who performed at the club.[22]

In the fall of 1960 the Gate began having a "Cabaret for Freedom" on Sunday nights, organized by Maya Angelou and Godfrey Cambridge to benefit the SCLC. Actors, musicians, and comedians, including Sarah Vaughan, Max Roach, and Abbey Lincoln, would drop by to express their views about segregation, integration, and freedom. As a writer for the *Amsterdam News* reported, the shows included everything "from Langston Hughes' poetry to Nigeria's Liberation song" and was "as topical as today's headlines."[23]

A variety-show format, for better or worse, was often used for fund-raising concerts both big and small. In August 1960 the Chicago Urban League held a huge fund-raiser at Chicago's Comiskey Park that attracted some fifteen thousand people. The aesthetics of civil rights organizers and the jazz world, not surprisingly, did not always match. Although the second annual "Chicago Urban League Festival" included four jazz acts—the Cannonball Adderley Quintet, the Dizzy Gillespie Quintet, the Maynard Ferguson Band, and Lambert, Hendricks, and Ross—Don DeMichael, reporting for *Down Beat,* lamented that "they were rushed on stage and pulled off as quickly as possible" since the main portion of this show was turned over to Sammy Davis Jr., Frank Sinatra, and Peter Lawford. "The jazz portion was cut short—way too short—for those who came to hear jazz." Nevertheless, the event raised $250,000, and Sammy Davis Jr. was presented the Urban League's Citation of Merit for his help.[24]

Civil rights organizers were guided more by their goal of maximizing the number of attendees than in presenting aesthetically unified performances. They were also inexperienced in sponsoring concerts and sometimes made major mistakes with sound systems, publicity, and other arrangements. Three hours before the Comiskey Park show, for example, the organizers decided to sell tickets in the right- and left-field stands and to place seats for large donors on the field, without giving the sound company advance warning. During Lambert, Hendricks, and Ross, audience members in the right and left fields shouted "Can't hear, can't hear," and the big donors seated on the field experienced bad sound throughout. Dizzy Gillespie performed three works, including "Swing Low, Sweet Cadillac," "The Mooche," and "A Night in Tunisia," while Cannonball Adderley left the stage after "Our Delight" and "This Here." DeMichael summed up his frustration by suggesting that, "if there is another festival, it is hoped that the social workers will consult those who know something about jazz.[25]

Sometimes celebrities overinterpreted the offer of civil rights organizations to cover their expenses. Such was the case with the "Tribute to Martin Luther King" held at Carnegie Hall on January 27, 1961, shortly after the inauguration of John F. Kennedy. The lineup included Sammy Davis Jr., Frank Sinatra, Dean Martin, Joey Bishop, and Peter Lawford, with the assistance of the Count Basie Orchestra, Carmen McRae, Tony Bennett, and Mahalia Jackson (figure 5.2). Tickets went for $25 a head (more than five times the average ticket price at the time), but, as Marvin Rich recalled about booking Frank Sinatra's entourage, "That was a disaster. We raised a lot of money and spent a fortune. These guys flew in from the West Coast first class with their entourage. They stayed in fancy hotels. They ate, they drank . . . we made a few bucks." Something similar occurred when Josephine Baker did a benefit for CORE in September 1963. The poster advertised that "Miss Baker will appear in her fabulous, newly created $250,000.00 wardrobe" but did not mention that she sent the bill for importing the costumes to CORE. A dispute over the $581 bill resulted in CORE's paying $481 of the cost.

As Val Coleman, who set up the concert, recalls, "I remember that we ended up not making any money even though we were in Carnegie Hall and the place was packed. The place was absolutely packed." In situations such as these, the economic distance between the celebrities' lives and

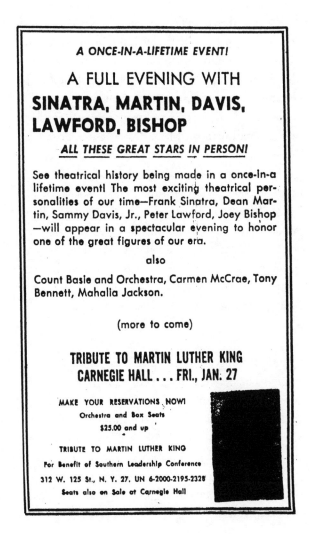

FIGURE 5.2. "Tribute to Martin Luther King." *New York Amsterdam News* 40, no. 2 (January 14, 1961), p. 13.

those of the civil rights organizers was particularly acute. At a time when SNCC field secretaries were paid between $10 and $45 per week, those who organized benefit concerts were constantly mediating between a world of frontline political action always in dire need of finances and a world of celebrity entertainers and moneyed donors who would part with their assets most readily at classy events that were costly to sponsor.[26]

## Black Nationalism in Counterpoint

As Morris has noted, the wildfire ignition of student sit-ins in 1960 depended heavily upon a mass base developed by the SCLC, NAACP Youth Councils, and CORE in the late 1950s. The leadership that increased this base was predominantly black, and in the late 1950s the primary sources of SCLC funding were the memberships of black churches.[27] In 1960 the sudden influx of white interest and money into the movement set a number of tensions in play that ultimately led the civil rights movement (and jazz, too) in the direction of black nationalism, Black Power, and cultural nationalism. The term "black nationalism"—a broad concept whose central principle is self-determination—must be distinguished from "black national separation," a more specific political position that is associated most prominently with Elijah Muhammad's Black Muslims (Nation of Islam).

The Muslim Program, published regularly in *Muhammad Speaks,* explained "What the Muslims Want" and "What the Muslims Believe" through two lists of programmatic wants and beliefs. The number one demand was "We want freedom. We want full and complete freedom." Muhammad's view of integration and national separation is presented in the ninth point of belief:

> We believe that the offer of integration is hypocritical and is made by those who are trying to deceive the black peoples into believing that their 400-year-old open enemies of freedom, justice and equality are, all of a sudden their "friends." Furthermore, we believe that such deception is intended to prevent black people from realizing that the time in history has arrived for the separation from the whites of this nation. If the white people are truthful about their professed friendship toward the so-called Negroes, they can prove it by dividing up America with their slaves.

In the Muslim program, the demand for national separation was also a demand for reparations:

> We want our people in America whose parents or grandparents were descendants from slaves, to be allowed to establish a separate state or territory of their own—either on this continent or elsewhere. We believe that our former slave masters are obligated to provide such land and that the area must be fertile and minerally rich. We believe that our former slave masters are obligated to maintain and supply our needs in this separate territory for the next 20 to 25 years—until we are able to produce and supply our own needs. Since we cannot get along with them in peace and equality, after giving them 400 years of our sweat and blood and receiving in return some of the worst treatment human beings have ever experienced, we believe our contributions to this land and the suffering forced upon us by white America justifies our demand for complete separation in a state or territory of our own.[28]

When Malcolm X announced his defection from the Nation of Islam (NOI) and his formation of the Muslim Mosque, Inc., at a press conference on March 12, 1964, he defined his political philosophy of black nationalism more broadly: "We must control the politics and the politicians of our community. They must no longer take orders from outside forces. We will organize, and sweep out of office all Negro politicians who are puppets for the outside forces."[29] The central issues in this definition are self-determination and control of community institutions rather than state formation. Malcolm X also emphasized the importance of youth in political transformation and the limited role that whites could play: "Whites can help us but they can't join us. There can be no black-white unity until there is first some black unity. There can be no worker's solidarity until there is first some racial solidarity. We cannot think of uniting with others, until after we have first united among ourselves. We cannot think of being acceptable to others until we have first proven acceptable to ourselves."

Although relatively few African Americans advocated national separation as proposed by the NOI, increasing numbers of civil rights activists were drawn to those parts of the black nationalist message that emphasized self-determination—black leadership in the struggle for racial justice, black control of organizations setting policies affecting black communities, economic self-help, and exercising the "power to define" historical and cultural representations of the African American experience.[30]

The desire to limit white participation in these organizations often grew out of the frustrations of African Americans, who had long coped with their status as a numerical minority. As Lani Guinier has observed, in a winner-takes-all form of electoral democracy, the outnumbered minority often has its policy preferences outvoted by the majority over and over again, which compromises the fundamental fairness of the system. As Michael Dawson has argued, one consistent African American response to their political, economic, and social exclusion in American society has been to emphasize black unity, autonomy, and communal obligation.[31]

The entry of white liberal and radical activists into the civil rights movement in large numbers, while critical for the eventual passage of civil rights legislation, posed a number of problems for the movement. The tendency of white leaders to take over in political organizations—practically, ideologically, or numerically—as well as the growing financial reliance of the civil rights movement on non-African American sources of income, exposed deep racial fault lines over which heated and emotional debates took place. The issue for many African American leaders was how to ensure that the vital needs and demands of black Americans were not restricted by dependence on multiracial financial support and the often different agendas of white liberals and radicals. By 1966 (in SNCC) and 1967 (in CORE) a combination of factors led to the exclusion of whites from these previously integrationist organizations: the centrality of self-determination in African American political thinking, the intensifying critique of white liberals and radicals in movement organizations, and the dissatisfaction with nonviolence as a tactic in the face of murderous white violence against the civil rights workers. With the exception of violence, to a large extent these issues were paralleled in the world of jazz.[32]

## Music and Black Pride

The symbolic centrality of African American music and of jazz in particular in the celebration of cultural pride was tied to the fact that jazz was an interracially and internationally recognized arena of black excellence—a domain of cultural leadership in which African Americans were the reigning cultural heroes. In jazz the racial hierarchy was symbolically inverted, with black excellence setting the aesthetic standards by which non–African American musicians were evaluated rather than vice versa. As I argued in chapter 3, between 1950 and 1967 this was not simply a matter of racial loyalty since white critics and audiences increasingly embraced African American musical standards of excellence and evaluated white musicians with respect to them. In many ways the alternative modernism (see chapter 3) crafted through the musical agency of jazz musicians adopted a definition of universality that placed African American musical values at the center—swing, blues, and improvisation.

If racist discourse critical of the civil rights movement often cited the ways in which African Americans did not measure up to white educational and moral standards, jazz provided an arena in which the tables were turned. In the heat of polarized aesthetic debates it was white jazz musicians who were called upon to prove their musical equality and compensate for their "culturally disadvantaged" backgrounds. For many African Americans this must have been sweet revenge.

To disentangle the charges and countercharges made at this time in both politics and music, we must move beyond an either/or conception of the political struggles in the jazz world as integration versus separatism. The desire for self-determination cut across the political spectrum and affected organizations that struggled for integration, as well as those that advocated national separation. It was not uncommon for individuals, both black and white, in the early sixties to express support for aspects of both black nationalism and integration. Moreover, emphasis on one side or the other was often *situational,* with African Americans drawing lines of racial solidarity in response to white power plays or insensitivity and whites charging reverse racism in response to the racial boundaries erected in the interests of self-determination. The larger question that interests me here is not *whether* racially essentialist positions were taken in the jazz world at this time, for they certainly were, but under what circumstances individuals and groups drew the racial boundary firmly and under which other conditions the line was more porous.

## The *Freedom Now Suite*

In many ways the story of Max Roach's *Freedom Now Suite* encapsulates the tensions between the discourses of black nationalism and the mainstream civil rights movement.[33] The *Freedom Now Suite* is perhaps the best-known jazz work with explicitly political content from the civil rights years. Written by Max Roach and Oscar Brown Jr., the work is organized as a historical progression through African American history and reveals a narrative shape similar to the one chosen by Duke Ellington for *Black, Brown, and Beige.*[34] *We Insist! Max Roach's Freedom Now Suite,* as the Candid recording is titled, moves from slavery to emancipation to the contemporary civil rights struggle and African independence in five movements: "Driva' Man"; "Freedom Day"; "Triptych: Prayer, Protest, Peace"; "All Africa"; and " Johannesburg." The liner notes begin with a thunderous quotation from A. Philip Randolph: "A revolution is unfurling—America's unfinished revolution. It is unfurling in lunch counters, buses, libraries and schools—wherever the dignity and potential of men are denied. Youth and idealism are unfurling. Masses of Negroes are marching onto the stage of history and demanding their freedom now!"[35]

Although it is best known through the recording, the *Freedom Now Suite* was performed live as a benefit concert for CORE at the Village Gate on January 15, 1961.[36] The event had been set up by Jimmy McDonald, a folksinger from CORE, whom Abbey Lincoln and Max Roach knew through a group of socially aware musicians. Billed as the "world premier performance," the *Freedom Now Suite* was presented with an ensemble that included dancers (Maya Angelou among them) and a narrator (Ruby Dee). The band, led by Max Roach, included Booker Little, Marcus Belgrave, Julian Priester, Eric Dolphy, Walter Benton, Michael Olatunji, Larry Ridley, four conga drummers, and Abbey Lincoln—a lineup somewhat different from the one that appeared on the recording, which had included Coleman Hawkins. According to Dan Morgenstern, who reviewed the performance for *Metronome,* "interaction between music and dance was perhaps not as organic as it could be at the Savoy Ballroom, but strong enough to pinpoint the continuing relationship between the two forms." Dolphy played an extended solo on bass clarinet that was "refreshingly original and moving," and Roach's drumming "paced the performance with impeccable control and surging strength." Morgenstern concluded that *Freedom Now* "consciously employs jazz as a weapon in the good fight and proves it can be a potent one."[37]

Several more performances of *Freedom Now* took place in 1961. In April the work was performed at the Jazz Gallery to mixed reviews. A reviewer for *Variety* found that the material had a "bitter mood" and described the works as "new-frontier club stuff and most likely a little too far out in uncut timber for most tastes." Reception, however, seemed to depend on the audience. During the summer of 1961 portions of the suite were performed to an enthusiastic audience at the fifty-second annual convention of the NAACP in Philadelphia. The performance took place in the grand ballroom of the Sheraton hotel and included Lincoln, Brown, and Roach. Indeed, the work was so successful at the convention that plans for a tour of the South were formulated in the fall of 1960, although Abbey Lincoln recalls that in the end the tour never actually took place.[38]

Nat Hentoff's liner notes to the recording explain that the *Freedom Now Suite* grew out of a collaboration between Max Roach and writer-singer Oscar Brown Jr. on a large choral work that was to have been performed on the hundredth anniversary of the Emancipation Proclamation (January 1, 1963), the date that since *Brown v. Board of Education* (1954) had been the NAACP's goal for the attainment of complete desegregation. The rapidly developing political events of 1960 were offered as the reason for a change in direction that ultimately led to the recording of the work in late August and early September 1960.

Although Max Roach recalls an invitation from the NAACP to write a piece for the centennial of the Emancipation Proclamation as key to the project, Brown remembers things differently.[39] According to Brown, the original plan was to write a long work titled *The Beat* that would "tell the story of the African drum from Africa up to contemporary times." "All Africa" was originally intended to begin the work, followed by "Driva' Man," depicting conditions under slavery, and "Freedom Day," celebrating the Emancipation Proclamation. Africa in this plan began rather than ended the work, suggesting a more evolutionary perspective on history than that in the *Freedom Now Suite*.[40]

Brown first met singer Abbey Lincoln when she was performing at the Black Orchid in Chicago in 1957. At her request he wrote the song "Strong Man" (recorded on October 28, 1957) for her then boyfriend, Max Roach. Lincoln introduced Brown to Roach, and the two regularly talked about music with one another. From these conversations the idea for *The Beat* gradually emerged. Brown recalls Roach using a melodica to compose. As Brown put it, "Max at the time had one of those little pianos, I forgot what you call them, but you blew in them. So he taught me those tunes, and we composed with him playing that instrument." The two of them continually argued about politics during their collaboration and finally parted ways over differences about how the work should end. As Brown recalled:

I wrote a sonnet, a Shakespearean sonnet:

> *The voice of love is lifted now in song*
> *That sends its echoes orbiting the earth*
> *Inviting all mankind to sing along*
> *In tribute to its kind for all its worth.*

So I was preaching love. Max thought that Malcolm X had a better solution than Martin Luther King. That was the end of our dispute at the time, which was a very serious one. So that whole collaboration was aborted, and at that point it was never completed—although it was pretty near completion when we fell out.[41]

Max Roach, when asked about this in my interview with him, agreed: "Oh yeah, we fought. We never could finish it. It [still] isn't finished." The problem, he suggested, is that "we don't really understand what it *really* is to be free. The last song we did, 'Freedom Day,' ended with a question mark." The question occurs at the end in the middle of the first stanza of the piece:

> *Whisper listen whisper listen*
> *Whisper say we're free*
> *Rumors flying must be lyin'*
> *Can it really be?*

Brown was irritated that he did not know about the *Freedom Now Suite* recording until he received a post card from Nat Hentoff requesting biographical material to be included in the liner notes to the album. Brown was disappointed that the music from their collaboration had been rearranged without his knowledge to serve Max Roach's political vision. Like many contemporary reviewers, Brown disliked the screaming included in the "protest" section of "Triptych," the segment of the work that proved to be most controversial. Although their collaboration was stormy, Brown stressed that he and Roach were in basic agreement over the need to dedicate one's artistic work to social justice. Their differences of opinion were over issues Brown described as "vital to the times" and about which everyone around them was debating both inside and outside of the jazz world. As Brown put it, "In fact, during that whole period we were not estranged. We were together in a sense; we were arguing. We were arguing about the screaming. We were arguing about the image he wanted Abbey to have."[42]

Although Brown's and Roach's political differences were very real, they do not divide very easily into the common associations of leftist/nationalist/separatist and liberal/accommodationist/integrationist. Brown stressed that his model for politically committed art was Paul Robeson (decidedly a leftist) and that he was proud that Robeson had spoken on his behalf during his run on the Progressive Party ticket for the Illinois state legislature in 1948. Likewise, Roach's interest in black nationalism did not prevent him from doing the world premiere performance of the *Freedom Now Suite* as a benefit for CORE or from performing a scaled-down version of the suite for the 1961 annual convention of the NAACP, held in Philadelphia shortly after the Freedom Rides. Although Roach and Brown had many differences, like many other musicians and jazz fans engaged in similar debates during the heat of the civil rights movement and Black Power, they shared a commitment to activism that sometimes outweighed ideological disagreements.

The importance of activism is clearly expressed in Max Roach's decision to make the album available to political organizations. In 1963 an article in the *New York Amsterdam News* announced that copies of the album would be available free of charge to "any fund-raising organization requesting it." That the album could be perceived as politically dangerous across international boundaries is evident in South Africa's decision to ban the sale of the *Freedom Now Suite* in 1962—a response to "Tears for Johannesburg," the piece that Max Roach dedicated to the victims of the Sharpeville massacre, the infamous slaughter of demonstrators who were nonviolently protesting apartheid pass laws.[43]

## The Music of the *Freedom Now Suite*

The politics of the *Freedom Now Suite* have received far more attention than the music. If 1960 was the year of the lunch-counter sit-ins, protests against pass laws in South Africa, and the admission of sixteen African nations to the UN, it was also the year when the debate over Ornette Coleman and free jazz rippled through the jazz community. The *Freedom Now Suite* occupies a space somewhere between mainstream jazz modernism and the New Thing. It makes use of blues form and chorus structures in some of its movements and almost always defines tonal centers, although often through ambiguous harmonic means such as parallel whole tone or quartal voicings. Aspects of the work that take from more avant-garde stylistic trends in 1960s also include its use of a pianoless ensemble texture, moments of collective improvisation, such as occur at the end of "Tears from Johannesburg," and, of course, the screaming in "Protest."

Dealing with "the music" in jazz is often confused with simply providing a structural account of the music—its keys, harmonies, rhythmic patterns, melodic styles, textures, timbres, genres, and forms. The *Freedom Now Suite* offers an opportunity to think about how these musical dimensions also carry symbolic associations that are key to generating a deeper expressive power. The questions to ask are, what musical means did Max Roach and his band choose to convey the socially engaged message they desired, and how do the structural and symbolic aspects of the music combine?

The *Freedom Now Suite* draws on both long-standing musical symbols of African American cultural identity (the blues and the spiritual) and more immediate historical contexts, such as the civil rights movement, African independence, and the Sharpeville massacre, to weave a web of musical interconnectedness. Modernism is always present, too, as Roach and his musicians strive not only to make use of the African and African American legacy but also to do so in a modern way. I would like to highlight a few musical dimensions of the *Freedom Now Suite* that are key to its expressive power.

"Driva Man," which opens the suite, is a work song based on a transformation of the blues form. Abbey Lincoln starts out a cappella in C minor, accompanying herself on the tambourine and singing lyrics that describe the brutality of slavery:

> *Get to work and root that stump*
> *Driva man'll make you jump*
> *Better make your hammer ring*
> *Driva man'll start to swing*

*Ain't but two things on my mind*
*Driva man and quittin' time*

The blues, normally in 4/4, are performed here in 5/4, with the tambourine and later the rim shot evoking the crack of the driver man's whip on beat one of every measure. The full blues progression is completed in six bars rather than twelve. When the horns enter, Coleman Hawkins's tenor saxophone plays the melody, while trumpet, trombone, and a second tenor accompany in parallel, whole-tone voicings. Although Lincoln began in Cm, when the horns enter, the bass line is in Ab. Later (3:23), when the same horn voicings return (at the same pitch), the bass line is in Cm. Here Roach plays with the tonal ambiguity of symmetrically structured chords (figure 5.3).

The legacy of the spiritual is especially strong in "Triptych," a movement that is itself divided into three parts: "Prayer," "Protest," and "Peace." "Triptych" is a duet between Abbey Lincoln and Max Roach that moves from expressive interplay between wordless voice and percussion (on "Prayer") to an eruption of screaming (on "Protest") and back to "Peace." "Prayer" is perhaps best described as a wordless spiritual or moan centering on an E minor pentatonic scale. Abbey Lincoln is at her most

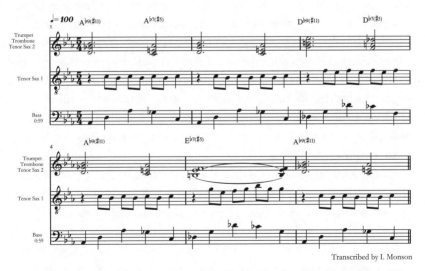

FIGURE 5.3. Max Roach, "Driva' Man," *We Insist! Freedom Now Suite*, head. *We Insist! Freedom Now Suite*, Candid CCD 9002. Used by permission of Milma Publishing.

haunting as she slowly builds from low to high in call and response with Roach's drums. A notable musical detail is Roach's tuning of the drum set to match the tonality of Lincoln's voice. Roach introduces Lincoln by playing a descending perfect fourth. Throughout the section Roach uses this interval to provide tonal support for Lincoln's singing.

"Protest," near the structural center of the suite, provides the most avant-garde moment in the work. Abbey Lincoln performs a minute and twenty seconds of stylized screaming accompanied by continuous rolling figures on the drums. Lincoln recalled that it was Max Roach's idea, not hers, to include the screaming: "It wasn't an approach to music that I would have chosen, but because I thought of him as a teacher—he preceded me—I did what I could to please him." Lincoln, whose voice throughout is the vibrant carrier of the message, took greater heat for political messages in the *Freedom Now Suite* than Roach, something that was to become apparent after the release of her album *Straight Ahead* in 1961.[44]

In comparison to the extended laments, wails, and shrieks played a few years later by artists such as Albert Ayler and John Coltrane, the avant-gardism of Lincoln's "Protest" is fairly mild. This segment of the performance nevertheless generated the most criticism, perhaps because of the explicit programmatic meaning ascribed to it. The liner notes state that " 'Protest' is a final uncontrollable unleashing of rage and anger that have been compressed in fear for so long that the only catharsis can be the extremely painful tearing out of all the accumulated fury and hurt and blinding bitterness. It is all forms of protest, certainly including violence." Here Roach and Lincoln explicitly reject the philosophy of nonviolence advocated by the Martin Luther King and the mainstream civil rights organizations despite the fact that they did not object to performing the work on behalf those very same groups. The association between sound and meaning forged here is more didactic, with the composer telling us what meaning we should take away. "Peace" also has an intended programmatic meaning—to represent the protester after she has done everything possible to assert herself. Lincoln's wordless spiritual, now more breathy and jagged, continues over a 5/4 meter played by Roach.

Appearing as it does at the beginning ("Driva' Man"), in the middle ("Peace"), and at the end ("Tears for Johannesburg"), 5/4 meter frames the large-scale shape of the *Freedom Now Suite*. Given the popularity of Dave Brubeck's "Take Five" from the *Time Out* album of 1959, it would be hard not to read Roach's metrical choice as a commentary on "Take

Five."[45] Although experiments in different meters (including Roach's own "Jazz in 3/4 Time" from 1957) had long preceded Brubeck's album, the version of 5/4 time most under discussion in jazz at the time of the *Freedom Now Suite* was surely Brubeck's.

The amount of media attention devoted to Brubeck and other prominent white West Coast musicians was a sore point among African American musicians in the fifties and early sixties. The press, in their view, overlooked more deserving African American figures such as Thelonious Monk, Sonny Rollins, Art Blakey, and Max Roach. By framing the *Freedom Now Suite* in 5/4 Roach turned the meter associated with "Take Five" on its head, using it in a more ambitious way both musically and politically. If the 5/4 in the *Freedom Now Suite* is in part a commentary on "Take Five," it would not be the first time that Roach had showed an interest in interracial one-upsmanship. He had, after all, recorded *Rich versus Roach* with Buddy Rich in early 1959.[46] This is what I meant when I said in chapter 3 that a sense of interracial competition through music is an important subtext to this period of colossal achievement in jazz.

In "All Africa" and "Tears for Johannesburg," the *Freedom Now Suite* points to Africa though the use of a percussion ensemble, rhythmic ostinatos, and open-ended modal frameworks. "All Africa" begins with Oscar Brown's ode to the beat, sung by Abbey Lincoln. Lincoln then recites the names of dozens of African ethnic groups, including the Yoruba, Mandingo (Mande), and Masai. Olatunji accompanies Lincoln on a drum and responds to her in Yorùbá by interjecting, according to the liner notes, proverbs about freedom from each group. An African diasporic sensibility is musically enacted in the extended percussion solo that follows this recitation through the use of a well-known seven-stroke bell pattern (discussed in chapter 4) found not only in West Africa but also in the sacred music of the Caribbean and Brazil.

"All Africa" leads directly into "Tears for Johannesburg," a vehicle for open blowing organized by a 5/4 ostinato in B♭ minor. Lincoln begins by wordlessly intoning the pitches of a melody that will appear most clearly articulated only at the very end of the movement. After her sustained delivery, the horns enter, adding a bit more definition to the melody but still improvising substantially around it, with Booker Little's trumpet leading the way. Open-ended solos (by Booker Little, Walter Benton, and Julian Priester) over the vamp follow. At times the ostinato is momentarily transposed down a half step to A, which provides a feeling of leading tone resolution to the otherwise stable Bb minor tonality. When the horns return (after percussion solos), their clear projection of the harmonized melody (in fourths) reveals that "Tears for Johannesburg" has inverted the usual order of melody and embellishment by presenting paraphrased versions of the composition first and the most direct statement of the melody last (figure 5.4).

Open-ended modal frameworks in the late fifties and early sixties often expressed a non-Western aesthetic interest. This is apparent in John

FIGURE 5.4. Max Roach, "Tears for Johannesburg," *We Insist! Freedom Now Suite,* Candid CCD 9002. Used by permission of Milma Publishing.

Coltrane's improvisations on "Africa" and "India" recorded in the year following the *Freedom Now Suite*. Although the Coltrane recordings are often cited as examples of a free-blowing modal approach, Max Roach's *Freedom Now Suite* (recorded before Coltrane's classic modal works) is not often credited with contributing to this emerging aesthetic. Indeed, one product of a close look at the *Freedom Now Suite* is the realization that Max Roach's contributions as a composer deserve much greater attention.

## Sonny Rollins's *Freedom Suite*

Sonny Rollins's *Freedom Suite* (1958) (with Max Roach on drums) is the closest precedent to the impulse embodied in the *Freedom Now Suite* and likely a work that ignited Roach's interest in composing an extended work with social commentary. Rollins's work is purely instrumental and also pianoless, featuring a trio with bassist Oscar Pettiford, Max Roach, and Rollins, in a nineteen-minute work that is organized like a nightclub set. There are three main tunes in the set—medium tempo, ballad, and up tempo—linked by a transition melody in 6/8 between the principal pieces. In keeping with the tendency of musicians to respond to contemporary political events, Rollins recorded this work five months after the Little Rock, Arkansas, school desegregation crisis. Since the work was wordless, Rollins included an explicit political statement on the cover: "America is deeply rooted in Negro culture: its colloquialisms, its humor, its music. How ironic that the Negro, who more than any other people can claim America's culture as his own, is being persecuted and repressed, that the Negro, who has exemplified the humanities in his very existence, is being rewarded with inhumanity."[47]

Unlike the *Freedom Now Suite,* however, *Freedom Suite* did not emerge at just the historical moment when the civil rights movement greatly accelerated. Although the Little Rock crisis deeply affected the nation, the movement had not yet generated the momentum and audacity that it did three years later. Riverside also underplayed the political content of the album, at least in comparison to Nat Hentoff's liner notes on *We Insist!* Although Rollins's statement is set off in a box, Orrin Keepnews's liner notes preferred keeping the political connection ambiguous rather than overt: "It [Freedom Suite] is not a piece about Emmett Till, or Little Rock, or Harlem, or the peculiar local election laws of Georgia or

Louisiana, no more than it is about the artistic freedom of jazz. But it is concerned with all such things, as they are observed by this musician and as they react—emotionally and intellectually—upon him."[48] Riverside, in other words, chose to present the politics of the *Freedom Suite* with greater artistic distance than the more "in your face" approach of Candid Records.

## Candid Records

*On some of those occasions I think we really felt we were making history.*
—Nat Hentoff

It is fortunate for the *Freedom Now Suite* that 1960 was not only the year of the Greensboro sit-ins but also of Nat Hentoff's brief career as a record producer for Candid Records. Several of the best-known "political" recordings of 1960 and 1961 (including *Freedom Now,* Mingus's *Original Faubus Fables,* and two albums organized by the Jazz Artists Guild) were released on Candid Records, a short-lived subsidiary of Cadence Records. During the summer of 1960 Archie Bleyer, chief A&R (artists and repertoire) man at Cadence (and conductor of the house band for Arthur Godfrey's radio show), decided that he would like to make a contribution to jazz by forming a new record label devoted solely to the genre. Since he knew little about the music, he approached Hentoff about heading up the label. Part of the deal was that Hentoff could record anyone—absolutely anyone he wanted. Hentoff named the label Candid and, during a year that seemed to him a "fantasy come to life," recorded some of the most adventurous music around.[49]

The *Freedom Now Suite* was the fruit of recording sessions that took place at Nola Penthouse studio on August 31 and September 6, 1960. Hentoff recalls having first heard portions of the suite at the Village Gate during the summer of 1960, well before the 1961 world premier benefit for CORE. Hentoff approached Max Roach about recording for Candid but expected to hear that the work was already under contract. Much to his surprise, Roach had no contract and was happy to record for the new label. Abbey Lincoln recalls Hentoff's support as crucial: "Nat came for Roach and for me. He knew we were having a hard time. And he thought the music was valid. One of our few allies at the time was Nat Hentoff."[50]

Few established recording companies would have had the nerve to issue an album like *We Insist! Max Roach's Freedom Now Suite,* especially with a cover photograph and liner notes emphasizing its political content. A year earlier Columbia Records had nixed the lyrics to Charles Mingus's "Fables of Faubus," which appeared on *Mingus Ah Um* as an instrumental. On October 20, 1960, Mingus recorded the piece with lyrics for Candid Records. The lively exchange between Mingus and drummer Dannie Richmond, which had been a part of live performances of the work since 1957, were made available to a larger public for the first time on this recording under the title "Original Faubus Fables":

*Oh Lord, don't let them shoot us,*
*Oh Lord, don't let them stab us,*
*Oh Lord, don't let them tar and feather us*
*Oh Lord, no more swastikas*

*Oh Lord, no more Ku Klux Klan*
*Name me someone who's ridiculous, Dannie:*
*"Governor Faubus"*
*Why is he so sick and ridiculous?*
*"He won't permit us in his schools"*
*Then he's a fool.*

*Boo, Nazi Fascist supremists!*
*Boo, Ku Klux Klan, with your Jim Crow plan*

*Name me a handful that's ridiculous, Dannie Richmond*
*". . . [undecipherable] Thomas, Faubus, Russell, Rockefeller,*
   *Byrd, Eisenhower"*
*Why are they so sick and ridiculous?*
*Two, four, six, eight—they brainwash and teach you hate.*
*H-E-L-L-O—Hello*[51]

Candid was not yet in business when Mingus recorded "Prayer for Passive Resistance," a remarkable blues, in Antibes in July. By starting out in two, moving to four, then walking in triplets (tripling the time as in "Wednesday Night Prayer Meeting"), Mingus created a shape of increasing rhythmic density over which Booker Ervin plaintively wailed.[52]

With the *Freedom Now Suite* and *Charles Mingus Presents Charles Mingus* under his belt, it is no wonder that Hentoff felt that his tenure at Candid "was the most satisfying and exciting part of my whole career, not only in jazz." In November he organized two sessions featuring some of the veterans of the previous summer's Newport Rebel Festival, which Mingus and Max Roach had organized. Mingus had been furious with the regular Newport Festival for its conservative programming and for grossly underpaying him in previous festivals. After rejecting George Wein's offer of $700 for the 1960 festival (to which he replied that he would not play for less then $5,000), Mingus explored the possibility of staging an alternative festival at the same time as the regular one.

Hentoff introduced Mingus to Elaine Lorillard, the wife of Louis Lorillard, a key figure in the Newport Jazz Festival. Elaine, who was going through a nasty divorce from Louis, was quite happy to aid Mingus in causing grief for her ex-husband. She contacted the owner of the Cliff Walk Manor, who agreed to allow the musicians to organize a festival on the grounds of his beachfront resort hotel. The musicians would keep all of the proceeds from the entrance fees since the owner, Nick Cannarozzi, expected to make extra profits on the bar and hotel rooms. An extraordinary lineup of musicians was assembled for the festival, including the bands of Charles Mingus, Max Roach, Ornette Coleman, Randy Weston, and Kenny Dorham. A meeting of the generations was also a by-product of the Newport Rebel Festival, as older veterans, including Coleman Hawkins, Roy Eldridge, Jo Jones, and Duke Jordan, performed there as well.[53]

There were only fifty people on hand to hear the first afternoon of the festival, but those present were treated to Charles Mingus and Ornette Coleman in alternating sets. Some of the musicians stayed in the Lorillard mansion, while others camped on its grounds. By the end of the weekend the music had succeeded in attracting crowds of up to five hundred. Meanwhile, the regular festival had been forced to close after some of its drunken guests turned violent on Saturday night.

On Sunday the Newport Rebels decided to organize the Jazz Artists Guild (JAG), whose mission was to book concerts and sponsor projects over which musicians would have both economic and artistic control. Although short lived, the JAG demonstrated that it was possible for jazz musicians to form collectives to advocate on their behalf both artistically and economically.[54] In November the JAG put together two recording sessions for Candid Records, released as *The Newport Rebels* and *The Jazz Life,* which included ensembles that comprised primarily people who had appeared at the Newport Rebel Festival. The first included Max Roach, Jo Jones, Abbey Lincoln, Eric Dolphy, Walter Benton, Cecil Payne, Booker Little, Benny Bailey, Kenny Dorham, Julian Priester, and Peck Morrison. The second featured Roy Eldridge, Jo Jones, Jimmy Knepper, Eric Dolphy, Tommy Flanagan, and Charles Mingus. The JAG also sponsored concerts drawn from Newport Rebel personnel, including a weeklong engagement at the Seventy-fourth Street Theater that was advertised in the *Amsterdam News*.[55]

## Speaking Out

In addition to benefit concerts, the Newport Rebel Festival, and the musical projects of Candid Records, the activism of the student sit-ins also inspired many musicians to speak out publicly. Just as the Montgomery bus boycott seemed to up the level of activism among musicians in its wake, so did the lunch-counter sit-ins. The pages of the *Pittsburgh Courier*, in particular, devoted much attention to musicians' reactions to the sit-ins and issues of racial equality. In April 1960 Count Basie described the lunch-counter sit-ins as a "beautiful movement" that he supported completely. "They're trying to knock us down but we get right up again."[56]

In May, Cannonball Adderley publicly criticized classical music impresario Sol Hurok for describing jazz as amoral and a curse (on British TV): "I'm sure I would have found strength to defeat each argument, categorically—especially in light of the fact that Hurok . . . has never shown any tendencies toward integration."[57] In July Duke Ellington protested the standard practice of white acts taking first billing on interracial shows when he refused to take second billing on an engagement in Los Angeles with comedian Mort Sahl. When negotiations with Sahl went nowhere, Ellington refused to appear on stage with his orchestra.[58]

In August Harry Belafonte blasted "parlor liberals" who professed support for the student sit-in movement but were too fearful to make donations or speak out publicly on their behalf: "A lot of artists I know will invite Sidney Poitier and myself to dinner, tell us of their love for their Negro maids, chauffeurs, and hairdressers. They sound off. We go home and maybe in a year or six months or a week, we call on them saying there are courageous students who need money for bail or scholarships in case they cannot return to their schools. We say that we only need $100 and that we read where they made $1,500,000 last year. They tell us they have to hear from their accountants."[59]

One of the more remarkable incidents reported by the *Courier* occurred in February 1960, not long after the sit-ins began. Lena Horne was dining at the Luau in Los Angeles when she overheard a man cursing at her after having been informed she was there. The man, one Harvey Vincent, had said, "That lousy n—. I do not like n—s. I don't care who they are. That n— b— shouldn't be here." After she requested that the man stop his insults to no avail, she threw three ashtrays at him. "I prefer fighting my battles with the NAACP and in a place like Little Rock, but when that man insulted my race, I just got boiling mad and popped him. And I have no intention of apologizing to him."[60] This is the same Lena Horne who nine years previously had counseled Roy Eldridge that putting up with some indignities was the price of racial advancement (see chapter 2).

Ray Charles appeared in the pages of the *Courier* in the spring of 1961 after students at the historically black Paine College in Augusta, Georgia, had requested that he cancel a concert that was scheduled to take place in a segregated auditorium. Although he had already arrived in Augusta before the students succeeded in contacting him, he promptly cancelled the concert and said, "I feel that it is the least that I can do to stand behind my principles and help the students in their fight for their principles."[62] Just as the Montgomery bus boycott was followed by a boost in activism among musicians, so, too, did the student lunch-counter sit-ins of the 1960s increase the willingness of musicians to speak out.

## Miles Davis

Musicians were stimulated to speak out, not only by the civil rights movement but also by the racially unjust treatment they received while working as professional musicians.[62] Miles Davis's experience at Birdland on August 26, 1959, offers an example:

"I had just finished doing an Armed Forces Day, you know, Voice of America and all that bullshit. I had just walked this pretty white girl named Judy out to get a cab. She got in the cab, and I'm standing there in front of Birdland wringing wet because it's a hot, steaming, muggy night in August. This white policeman comes up to me and tells me to move on. At the time I was doing a lot of boxing and so I thought to myself, I ought to hit this motherfucker because I knew what he was doing. But instead I said, 'Move on, for what? I'm working downstairs. That's my name up there, Miles Davis,' and I pointed up to my name on the marquee all up in lights. He said, 'I don't care where you work, I said move on! If you don't move on I'm going to arrest you.' I just looked at his face real straight and hard, and I didn't move. Then he said, 'You're under arrest!' "[63]

When Davis refused to allow Officer Gerald Kilduff to arrest him, a struggle ensued during which Miles was beaten about the head with a billy club by a detective named Donald Rolker, who had rushed to the scene to assist Kilduff. Davis was arrested, his cabaret card was confiscated, and—depending upon which newspaper account is heeded—he required between two and five stitches in his head.[64] The struggle was so noisy that members of the Hodges-Robbins Orchestra who were rehearsing across the street put their mike booms out of the window and captured on tape New York City's finest calling Miles Davis the n-word. Although *Down Beat* received a letter suggesting that Davis's attitude was to blame for the incident, in general, the jazz community, both domestic and international, was indignant.[65]

In October 1959 after a two-day trial Davis was acquitted of the disorderly conduct charge he had received. Judge Kenneth Phipps noted that taking a breath of fresh air between sets was perfectly normal behavior for musicians at nightclub engagements.[66] Davis was tried a second time on the charge of third-degree assault and was acquitted in January 1960. Although a suit against the New York City Police Department was announced, the attorney who had been retained to file the claim missed the deadline and Davis consequently lost the $500,000 in damages.[67] As Davis recounts in his *Autobiography*, "that changed my whole life and whole attitude again, made me bitter and cynical again when I was starting to feel good about the things that had changed in this country."[68]

### Benefit for the African Research Foundation

Miles Davis's activism at this stage of the Movement, however, did not take the form of a benefit for a civil rights organization. Rather, his attention turned to Africa. On May 19, 1961, Davis performed a benefit concert for the African Research Foundation at Carnegie Hall.[69] Featuring Gil Evans's orchestra and Davis's quintet with Wynton Kelly, Hank Mobley, Paul Chambers, and Jimmy Cobb, the concert is better known by its recording, *Miles Davis at Carnegie Hall*.[70]

The African Research Foundation (ARF), (now the African Medical and Research Foundation) was founded in 1957 by a group of three white doctors who were concerned about making health care services available in post-independence Africa. Known as the "flying doctors," they developed mobile units (first on trucks, then on planes) that took primary health care services to remote regions of sub-Saharan Africa.[71] By 1961 they were a multiracial organization committed to the goal of leaving black Africans in charge wherever they operated. Julius Nyerere, head of the Tanganyika African National Union (TANU) and soon to be the first president of independent Tanganyika (now Tanzania), was a frequent visitor to the African Research Foundation (ARF) office in New York, something that may have interested Miles. Nyerere supported a version of African socialism that stressed self-reliance and communalism and later influenced the cultural nationalism of Maulana Karenga.[72]

Davis became aware of the ARF through Jean Bach, a friend of founder Thomas Rees and someone who Miles dated briefly.[73] According to Ronald Moss, those most heavily involved with the organization were "all jazz nuts," regularly attending concerts and performances in New York. Davis had been reluctant to accept a concert hall engagement in New York, but his interest in the ARF apparently tipped the balance. Carnegie Hall was booked, Gil Evans' orchestra engaged and plans were made to record the concert. Joe Eula's poster for the concert (from which the album cover was taken) featured Davis's signature 'S' posture emanating from the mouth of an elephant. The concert was heavily attended (a sell-out) and raised $25,000 toward a mobile medical unit.[74]

The concert was nevertheless picketed by Max Roach and several demonstrators, who questioned the politics of the African Research Foundation. During Davis's performance of "Someday My Prince Will Come" (the opener for the second half), Roach and a companion emerged, sat down on stage, and held up placards reading "Africa or the Africans," "Freedom Now," and "Medicine without Murrow Please." Davis left the stage angered and returned only after guards had removed Roach from the stage. According to George Simon who reviewed the concert for the

*Herald Tribune,* "Davis, who till then had been playing his usual fine, cool trumpet, returned and began blowing some of the wildest, free-swinging jazz this reviewer has heard from his horn in many a moon."[75] Roach's protest, it seemed, had a beneficial effect on Davis's performance. Afterward Roach apologized for interrupting after the concert.[76]

The demonstrators accused the liberal, predominantly white ARF of having connections with CIA front groups and, consequently, of playing into the hands of colonialism. According to Ronald Moss, Roach had been misled into thinking that the ARF was a "white supremacist organization in league with South Africa" when, in fact, the organization had no contact with South Africa until after Mandela became president. Nevertheless, the ARF was a liberal rather than revolutionary organization.[77]

African nationalist sentiment, it should be remembered, was at a fever pitch in the spring of 1961 in the wake of the assassination of the Congo's Patrice Lumumba. Max Roach and Abbey Lincoln had been involved in the demonstrations at the UN that included members of the United African Nationalist Movement, the Liberation Committee for Africa, and On Guard. Other musicians, such as Dizzy Gillespie, were also interested in events in Africa. On March 3, 1961, at Carnegie Hall, Gillespie premiered a work that was dedicated to the newly independent African nations, and he participated in a celebration of African Freedom day in April of that year.[78]

The demonstration at Davis's May 19 concert was not the only source of conflict that evening. Earlier in the day Davis had angered Teo Macero by canceling the scheduled recording of the concert, despite the fact that arrangements for moving Columbia's recording equipment had already been made. Nonetheless, when Macero arrived at the hall, he asked a hall employee whether any recording equipment were available. A small monaural 1/4 track deck (a Webcor) that recorded at 7-1/2 rps, a mixing pot, and four microphones were found; Macero recorded surreptitiously and illegally from the front left of the house. After the concert Macero threw the tape at Davis, exclaiming "This could have been a great record!" A few hours later, in the middle of the night, Davis called Macero and asked him to arrange for the release of the tape. In order to secure permission from Carnegie Hall, Macero talked the shop steward into helping him comply retroactively with union rules.[79]

What should have been a stereo recording, consequently, is a mono recording made under technically challenging circumstances. The selections with the Gil Evans orchestra suffer most from the inadequate recording equipment. In addition, the subsequent deletion of several small group tunes from the original release has further obscured the strength of the quintet's performance that evening.[80] Yet, on *Walkin', Teo, Oleo, No Blues,* and *I Thought About You,* the rhythm section of Wynton Kelly, Paul Chambers, and Jimmy Cobb is truly impressive, anticipating aspects of the open, adventurous accompanimental style that Ron Carter, Herbie Hancock, and Tony Williams would perfect a few years later. Miles scoops, slides, and soars over the top.

## The Freedom Rides

The Freedom Rides, which riveted the attention of the nation from May 14 through May 25, 1961, provided the next major impetus for civil rights fund-raising events that included jazz musicians. Louis Armstrong, Cannonball Adderley, Gerry Mulligan, Oscar Brown Jr., Dizzy Gillespie, Billy Taylor, Horace Silver, and Art Blakey were among the musicians who performed for fund-raising events that took place from the end of June 1961 through early 1962 (table 5.3).

The brutality of the white resistance that this nonviolent direct-action campaign provoked distinguishes it from the comparatively peaceful lunch-counter sit-ins of 1960. Capsule summaries of the Freedom Rides, which frequently passed quickly from bus ride to beating to triumph, fail to communicate the magnitude of the danger the Freedom Riders faced, the warlike conditions that organized violence produced in Alabama, and the radicalizing effect it had on the movement. The Kennedy administration's reluctance to send federal troops to Alabama for political reasons (both domestic and international) prolonged the crisis.[81]

The Freedom Rides, a project organized by CORE, was designed to determine whether the Southern states were complying with the Supreme Court's ruling in *Boynton v. Virginia* (1960), a decision that extended the prohibition against segregation in interstate transportation to waiting rooms and other terminal services. Thirteen Freedom Riders (seven black men, three white women, and three white men) in two groups (one on Greyhound, one on Trailways) departed from Washington, D.C., on Thursday, May 4, traveling by day and participating in mass meetings in the evenings. Although three riders had been beaten at the terminal in

TABLE 5.3 Some fund-raising concerts, June 1961–1962

| Date | Location | Billed as | Benefit for/Sponsor | Participants |
|---|---|---|---|---|
| 6/28/61 | New York, Randall's Island | | CORE Freedom Riders | Louis Armstrong, Gerry Mulligan, Cannonball Adderley[1] |
| 7/7/61 | New York, Channel 13 WNTA | telethon | CORE Freedom Riders | Oscar Brown Jr., Nina Simone, Theodore Bikel, Horace Silver, Art Blakey, Orson Bean, Joey Bishop, Billy Taylor, Lena Horne, Theodore Bikel, Cal Tjader, Hi Fi's, Leon Bibb, Tarriers, Ronnie Chapman[2] |
| 7/14/61 | Philadelphia | | NAACP annual convention | Freedom Now Suite, Max Roach, Abbey Lincoln, Michael Olatunji, Sarah Vaughan, Oscar Brown Jr. |
| 8/6/61 | New York, St. Albans, home of Count Basie | | NCCJ (National Council of Churches) | Olatunji, Count Basie, and others[3] |
| 1961 | Benefit for CORE at Mrs. Wexler's residence | | | Count Basie Orchestra[4] |
| Sept. 1961 | Nashville | Salute to Freedom Riders | SCLC | Harry Belafonte, Chad Mitchell, Miriam Makeba[5] |
| Fall 1961 | San Francisco Opera House | | NAACP | Miles Davis[6] |
| 12/1/61 | New York, McMillan Theater, Columbia University | | SNCC | Maynard Ferguson and other jazz and folk artists[7] |
| 1/26/62 | Apollo Theater | | Negro American Labor Council (NALC) | Dizzy Gillespie, Modern Jazz Quartet, Jerome Richardson, Hank Mobley, Sonny Clark, Clark Terry, Oscar Brown Jr., Nina Simone. Appearances Johnny Hartman, Ruby Dee, Ossie Davis[8] |

(continued)

TABLE 5.3 (continued)

| Date | Location | Billed as | Benefit for/Sponsor | Participants |
|---|---|---|---|---|
| 2/4/62 | Village Gate New York | cocktail party | CORE | (names not available)[9] |
| 3/62 | | | SNCC | Harry Belafonte, Martin Luther King, Bob Moses Charles McDew[10] |
| 3/26/1962 | Studio of Jan Yoors, 329 E. 47th Street, champagne party | You Are Cordially Invited to Attend a Ruckus with Dizzy Gillespie (cocktail party) | CORE, Freedom Riders | Dizzy Gillespie[11] |
| 6/6/1962 | Atlanta | | CORE | Harry Belafonte Miriam Makeba[12] |
| 1962 | Seattle | | | Dizzy Gillespie[13] |

1. "Jazz Supports the Freedom Riders," *New York Amsterdam News* 51 (June 24, 1961), p. 17.
2. "Big Telethon Set to Aid Freedom Riders," *New York Amsterdam News* 51 (June 24, 1961), p. 17; Jesse H. Walker, "CORE Telethon 4½-Hour Success," *New York Amsterdam News* 51 (July 15, 1961), p. 16.
3. "Rhythm at the Pool," *New York Amsterdam News* 51 (Aug. 12, 1961), p. 14.
4. Val Coleman, interview with author, July 23, 1997. Coleman does not recall the date. Mrs. Wexler was connected to the Wexler coffee fortune.
5. Taylor Branch, *Parting the Waters*, p. 515; Belafonte fell ill and had to cancel. The SCLC lost money on the venture.
6. "Miles Davis 'Approved' for Bay Concert," *Down Beat* 28 (July 20, 1961), pp. 13–14.
7. "Jazz Show at Columbia," *New York Amsterdam News* 51 (Dec. 2, 1961), p. 18.
8. Jesse H. Walker, "Modern Jazz Show Held for Labor," *New York Amsterdam News* 41 (Feb. 3, 1962), p. 16.
9. *CORE-Respondent*, vol. 1 (Feb. 4, 1962), CORE series 5, box 17, folder 1.
10. Branch, *Parting the Waters*, pp. 578–79.
11. "You Are Cordially Invited to Attend a Ruckus with Dizzy Gillespie" (invitation), Mar. 26, 1962, Institute for Jazz Studies, topics files: race problems.
12. "Belafonte Heads Deep South," *Pittsburgh Courier* (May 26, 1962), p. 13.
13. Telegram to Marvin Rich, June 22, 1962, CORE series 5, box 28, folder 5.

Rock Hill, South Carolina, on May 9, things were relatively peaceful until they crossed into Alabama on Mother's Day, May 14.[82]

When the Greyhound bus pulled into Anniston, a white mob armed with clubs, knives, iron pipes, and bricks tried to force the Freedom Riders from the bus as two Alabama state investigators traveling undercover desperately held the bus door shut. The mob, undeterred by the police along its edge, pounded on the bus and slashed its tires. The driver backed up and drove off, chased by dozens of cars, but when the tires soon flattened, the bus was disabled outside of town. The mob smashed the bus windows and threw a firebomb into the vehicle from the rear. The bus filled with smoke and flames as the mob now tried to seal in the Freedom Riders by barricading the door. At this point, one of the undercover investigators brandished his pistol, causing the attackers to retreat and providing a window of opportunity needed to open the door. As they exited, the Freedom Riders were beaten by the mob as the bus went up in flames.[83]

When the driver of the second bus (which pulled into Anniston an hour later) heard of the attack on the Greyhound bus, he incited the white passengers to forcibly move two black students from the front seats to the back of the bus so they would be allowed to proceed. In the process the students and two of their white group members resisted and were beaten, one unconscious. The bus continued on to Birmingham, where police commissioner "Bull" Connor had made an advance agreement with the Ku Klux Klan: The police would wait fifteen minutes before interfering with their planned "welcome" for the Freedom Riders, something the FBI had known about since May 5. In that fifteen minutes there was a bloody thrashing that included not only the Freedom Riders but also members of the press. Jim Peck, a white group member, suffered head wounds that required fifty-three stitches to close, and he was turned away from the first hospital at which he sought treatment. The group scattered but reconvened at the home of Fred Shuttlesworth, head of the Alabama Christian Movement for Human Rights (ACMHR).[84]

On the following day, after a night of negotiations between Shuttlesworth, Robert Kennedy, Governor John Patterson, and Bull Connor, this first group of Freedom Riders attempted to continue the ride to Montgomery, but Greyhound could not find a driver willing to undertake the mission. They then aborted the project, decided to fly to New Orleans, and were followed by an angry mob to the airport.[85]

At this point SNCC stepped in. On May 17 Diane Nash sent a new contingent of Freedom Riders to Birmingham, but they were soon arrested by "Bull" Connor after another long scene of mob intimidation. Over the next two days a complicated series of negotiations between the Justice Department, the Alabama state government, and Shuttlesworth took place, which resulted in the Freedom Riders continuing on to Montgomery on Saturday, May 20. Although state troopers protected the bus to the city line, the Montgomery police abandoned the streets to a mob, which resulted in another brutal set of beatings, capped by a bonfire lit from the contents of the Freedom Riders' suitcases.[86]

The following day Martin Luther King Jr. and James Farmer arrived in Montgomery, and a mass meeting was held at Ralph Abernathy's "Brick-a-Day" Church. When an angry white mob surrounded the church, an all-night siege began. In the midst of the crisis, Robert Kennedy ordered six hundred federal marshals into Montgomery, but they were unable to contain the mob. Alabama's Governor Patterson declared martial law and sent in the National Guard to disperse the white segregationists, but the militia also intimidated the fifteen hundred African Americans inside the church by refusing to allow them to leave until 4:30 A.M.[87]

The Kennedy administration ultimately made a deal with the states of Alabama and Mississippi. The local authorities would be allowed to arrest the Freedom Riders in Jackson, Mississippi, provided they ensured safe passage of the bus to Jackson, Mississippi. There the Freedom Riders refused bail and elected to serve jail time rather than pay fines. The drama of these first Freedom Rides inspired a continuing flow of riders to Mississippi throughout the summer and fall of 1961. Coordinated by the Freedom Ride Coordinating Committee, these riders included members of CORE, SNCC, SCLC, and the NAACP.[88] These actions resulted in the arrests of an additional 328 people. The Freedom Rides not only succeeded in eliminating segregation in interstate transportation in a matter of months (the Kennedy administration pressed for an expedited Interstate Commerce Commission ruling, which went into effect on November 1, 1961) but also inspired many people to drop what they were doing and work full time for movement organizations.[89]

Art Blakey had been following the news. A few days after the imprisonment of the first Freedom Riders in Jackson, Blakey took time out of a recording session with his fabled quintet (with Wayne Shorter, Lee Morgan, Bobby Timmons, and Jymie Merritt) to record a drum solo he called "The Freedom Rider," which also became the title of the album on which it was released. Blakey's seven-and-a-half-minute solo makes use of many of the gestures heard in his African-diasporic-tinged drum solos of the 1950s (discussed in chapter 4). The Afro-Cuban time-keeping pattern from "Message from Kenya" (1953), the drum rolls and playing of conga patterns on the tom toms heard on "Ritual" (1957), and the use of pitch bending on the toms to give a talking-drum effect can all be heard. The new gestures here are the bashing sounds on the ride cymbal at regular intervals, which are difficult not to hear as the crashing of billy clubs on the Freedom Riders' heads, and a knocking idea followed by a descending shape on the toms. This gesture, which is prominently repeated at the beginning of the solo and alluded to later (6:16–6:27), is insistent, as if to say, "We're knocking at the door" and are not going away.

Nat Hentoff's liner notes describe the atmosphere at the time of the recording:

> At the time of this recording . . . the battle of the bus terminals had not been won, and there was a feeling of impregnable determination among civil rights actionists to send Freedom Riders into the South until all the jails were filled—if that were necessary to end segregation of interstate travelers. In his absorbing, deeply personal solo, Art Blakey conjures up the whirlpool of emotions at that time—the winds of change sweeping the country, the resistance to that change, and the pervasive conviction of the Freedom Riders that "We Shall Not Be Moved."[90]

Donations began flowing into CORE headquarters in New York soon after the initial Freedom Rides. During the summer of 1961 alone CORE raised more than $228,000, as much as during the entire previous fiscal year. Even so, the organization was overwhelmed by legal and bail expenses related to the imprisonment of Freedom Riders in Mississippi. State officials doubled jail terms and tripled fines, which added to the expenses that CORE and the other movement organizations incurred. Because it frequently owed tens of thousands of dollars more than it could pay out, CORE expanded its fund-raising efforts in New York (and elsewhere) in 1961 and 1962 and increased the number of its chapters in the metropolitan area from three to nine.[91]

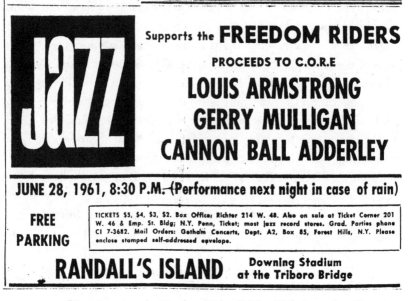

FIGURE 5.5. "Jazz Supports the Freedom Riders." *New York Amsterdam News* 40, no. 25 (June 24, 1961), p. 17. Used by permission.

On June 28 CORE sponsored a major fund-raising concert on New York's Randall's Island, at which the bands of Louis Armstrong, Gerry Mulligan, and Cannonball Adderley performed. Billed as "Jazz Supports the Freedom Riders," it was a strictly jazz event, unlike the joint tribute to Martin Luther King at Carnegie Hall in January (figure 5.5). A few weeks later CORE organized a four-and-a-half-hour telethon for the Freedom Riders that was broadcast on New York's WNTA, channel 13. Writer Louis Lomax and Betty Frank, a radio personality, hosted the show, which featured appearances by Billy Taylor, Lena Horne, Cal Tjader, Art Blakey, Oscar Brown Jr., and Horace Silver. James Farmer, who had been released from jail that very day, was interviewed by Mike Wallace toward the end of the telethon, adding the vividness and authenticity of a firsthand voice. The event generated $36,000 in pledges and nearly $30,000 in actual revenues.[92]

On a smaller scale, many people sponsored fund-raising parties in their homes, at which an entrance fee was charged and donated to CORE. On Monday, March 26,1962, Dizzy Gillespie played at an upscale version held

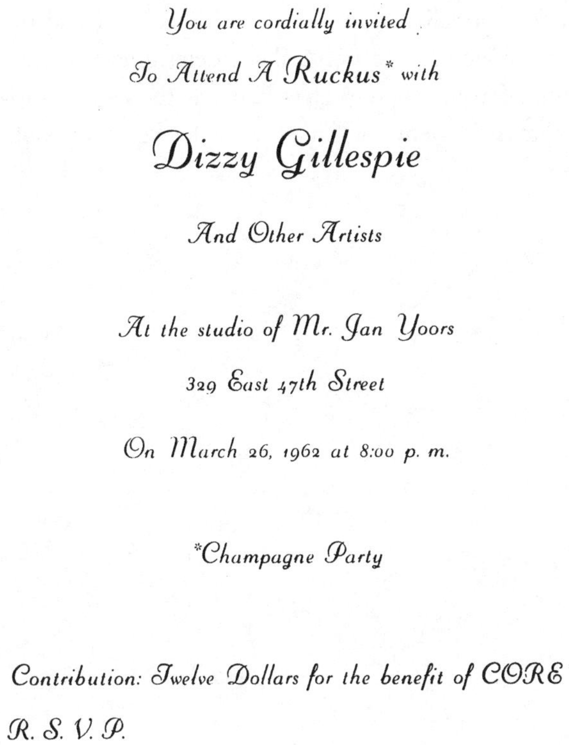

*You are cordially invited*

*To Attend A Ruckus\* with*

# Dizzy Gillespie

*And Other Artists*

*At the studio of Mr. Jan Yoors*

*329 East 47th Street*

*On March 26, 1962 at 8:00 p. m.*

*\*Champagne Party*

*Contribution: Twelve Dollars for the benefit of CORE*

*R. S. V. P.*

FIGURE 5.6. A Ruckus for CORE. Rutgers Institute of Jazz Studies. Topics files: race problems, 1962. Courtesy of Rutgers Institute of Jazz Studies.

at the midtown studio of Jan Yoors. An engraved invitation advertising "A Ruckus with Dizzy Gillespie and Other Artists" was geared to an elite audience (figure 5.6). The $12 admission was nearly five times the $2.50 donation that was expected a year earlier at the benefit performance of the *Freedom Now Suite*. Virtually all of the civil rights organizations cultivated wealthy donors by holding "class appropriate" fund-raising events with elite appeal, often catering to bourgeois tastes that were disdained by activists on the front lines of the movement. Because jazz was popular with the liberal moneyed intelligentsia, name attractions in jazz such as Dizzy Gillespie, Count Basie, Miles Davis, Thelonious Monk, and Dave Brubeck helped draw them to these events.

The fundraising events in 1960 and 1961 responded to an intensification of the civil rights movement in the wake of the Student Sit-Ins and reveal a strong interest among jazz musicians in the civil rights struggle. For the most part, these performances benefited mainstream civil rights organizations, although the black nationalist issues raised by Malcolm X and the Nation of Islam (such as economic and political self-determination) simmered in the background. During the next few years, as the violent suppression of the civil rights movement continued, these background issues came to the foreground.

# 6

# Activism and Fund-Raising from Birmingham to Black Power

IN THE SUMMER of 1962, when SNCC was facing enormous expenses from the conduct of mass protests against segregation in Albany, Georgia, the organization decided to develop an independent network of financial support by opening offices in Chicago, Detroit, New York, Washington, Philadelphia, and Cleveland. James Forman and other members of SNCC's leadership encouraged Northern supporters to create "Friends of SNCC" groups to organize fund-raising parties, rallies, and concerts at which SNCC workers in the South would speak to audiences and inspire them to donate much-needed money to the organization. Between June 1962 and December 1963, combined Friends of SNCC activities raised some $359,000, which enabled SNCC to establish new voter registration projects in a dozen Mississippi communities, as well as some in Georgia, Alabama, and Virginia.[1] New York Friends of SNCC reported raising $34,000 in 1963, and in 1964 and 1965 New York was consistently the largest single contributor to SNCC's national effort, averaging $16,000/ month in 1965.

## Thelonious Monk

To celebrate the third anniversary of the Greensboro lunch-counter sit-ins, SNCC sponsored "A Salute to Southern Students" at Carnegie Hall on February 1, 1963.[2] Several jazz artists appeared on the bill, including

Thelonious Monk, Charles Mingus, Herbie Mann, and Tony Bennett, as well as the SNCC Freedom Singers. The list of sponsors on the invitation also included several other representatives from the jazz world—Cannonball Adderley, Dave Brubeck, Art and Bert D'Lugoff, Nat Hentoff, and Gerry Mulligan. Although it is not certain exactly how much money the February 1 Carnegie Hall concert generated, a Dave Brubeck concert later in 1963 generated $5,200, and a single cocktail party in December generated $12,000. Since the Carnegie Hall event was the first major SNCC fund-raiser in the North and the single most gala event of the New York chapter's 1963 activities, chances are that a considerable portion of the remaining $16,800 was earned by the February 1 event.[3]

Organization for the Carnegie hall concert began during the fall of 1962, when Bill Mahoney, a former Howard University student who had become an organizer for SNCC, sent letters to many entertainers and celebrities soliciting either their participation as performers or the use of their names as sponsors of the February 1 event. The list of performers was still not finalized in early January, when Ella Baker, one of the founding figures of SNCC, sent a letter to Miles Davis requesting that he perform at the Carnegie Hall fund-raiser. Baker's plea mentioned only Charles Mingus and Tony Bennett as performers who had already agreed to the February 1 performance. Miles Davis declined, but on Lincoln's birthday a year later he performed a combined benefit for SNCC, CORE, and NAACP efforts in Mississippi. Sometime in late January 1963 Thelonious Monk apparently agreed to perform.[4]

At the Carnegie Hall event, the audience and performers heard SNCC speakers explain the organization's current activities in Mississippi's Sunflower and LeFlore counties, two of the more conservative in the state. Sunflower County was the home of segregationist Senator James Eastland, and LeFlore was the county in which Emmett Till had been lynched in 1955. In late 1962 Mississippi authorities, in retaliation for SNCC's voter registration campaign, had cut off the distribution of federal surplus foodstuffs to the counties' many indigent residents. The SNCC speakers consequently appealed to the Carnegie Hall audience for emergency food relief.[5]

Through the event Thelonious Monk came face to face with the SNCC Freedom Singers, who, like all SNCC workers in 1963, were earning ten dollars a week for services to the organization. Bernice Reagon, a member of the Freedom Singers, recalls having dinner with Monk after the Carnegie Hall concert.

> I remember Thelonious Monk after the Carnegie Hall concert. We went out to this restaurant. Thelonious Monk is this big brooding sort of [man]. And there's a darkness around him if you're close to him. . . . I was sitting in front of him, and I was sort of scared of him. And he said, "that stuff, it's not gonna work. That stuff you all are talking about—it's not gonna [work]. I mean, it's important and I'm here." And it was the nonviolence, the "redeeming your enemy through love" kind of part. He was like basically saying, "You all are gonna get yourselves killed walkin' out here in these streets in front of these crazy white people, your local crazy white people, who've got guns." He just shook his head at that. It felt like, "I will support, in any way, my people coming together and organizing, but you all are committing some kind of suicide, walking out here in front of these crazy white people."[6]

Since Thelonious Monk is usually thought of as one of the more apolitical jazz musicians, Reagon's recollections are especially interesting. It seems that, contrary to this image, Monk *did* have definite opinions about the civil rights struggle, including questions about the viability of nonviolence as a strategy. In this regard it is important to note that many of the names appearing at fund-raising events for civil rights organizations were not considered to be particularly political. Although it is not surprising to see the names of Max Roach, Abbey Lincoln, Charles Mingus, or Archie Shepp associated with political activities, many of the musicians who appeared several times at the fund-raising events listed so far are not usually considered among the politically outspoken, including Clark Terry, Thelonious Monk, Dizzy Gillespie, Dave Brubeck, Count Basie, and Tony Bennett[7] (table 6.1).

The surprise that many jazz aficionados express upon learning of the activities of these musicians has three interlocking components. The first is the tendency to equate political militance with free jazz, a position that has been disseminated most prominently in the writings of Amiri Baraka and Frank Kofsky. The second is the active cultivation of the image of the apolitical artist by jazz musicians themselves. The third is the failure to

TABLE 6.1. Some fund-raising concerts, 1963

| Date | Location | Billed as | Benefit for/Sponsor | Participants[1] |
|---|---|---|---|---|
| 2/1/1963 | Carnegie Hall | A Salute to Southern Students | SNCC | Tony Bennett, Ossie Davis, Ruby Dee, Herbie Mann Sextet, Charlie Mingus, Thelonious Monk, plus SNCC Freedom Singers[2] |
| 5/26/1963 | McCormick Place, Chicago | | SCLC | Dinah Washington, Aretha Franklin, Mahalia Jackson[3] |
| 6/23/1963 | Jackie Robinson's home, Stamford, CT | | SCLC | forty-two musicians including Dizzy Gillespie, Dave Brubeck, Cannonball Adderley, Clark Terry, Zoot Sims, Ben Webster, Carol Sloane, Joya Sherrill, Randy Weston, and Jimmy Rushing[4] |
| July 1963 | San Francisco, ILWU Auditorium | | | Vince Guaraldi Trio, John Handy Quartet, Red Rodney Quartet, Carmen McRae Group, Ahmad Jamal Trio[5] |
| 8/5/1963 | Birmingham, AL, Miles College | AGVA's Salute to Freedom '63 | SCLC, CORE, NAACP, NUL, SNCC, NALC | Billy Taylor, Ray Charles, Johnny Mathis, Nina Simone[6] |
| 8/8/1963 | Los Angeles | | NAACP, SNCC, CORE, SCLC | Nat King Cole[7] |
| 8/20/1963 | Atlanta | Stars for Freedom | SCLC | Lena Horne, Mercer Ellington Orchestra, Billy Taylor, Lambert, Hendricks, and Bavan[8] |
| 8/23/1963 | Apollo Theater | Emancipation March on Washington for Jobs and Freedom | NALC, A. Philip Randolph | A. Philip Randolph, Tony Bennett, Cozy Cole, the Golden Chords, Coleman Hawkins, Quincy Jones, Herbie Mann, Charlie Shavers, Thelonious Monk, Art Blakey and the Jazz Messengers, Billy Eckstine, Johnny Hartman, Ahmad Jamal, Stevie Wonder, Terri Thornton, Carmen McRae, Dave "Alleycat" Thorne, Lambert, Hendriks & Bavan[9] |
| 8/24/1963 | Baltimore | Steak-out for the Cause | | Jimmy McGriff, Madhatters, Freda Payne[10] |
| 8/25/1963 | New York, polo grounds | Giant 12-Hour Civil Rights Rally | CORE, NAACP, SNCC, SCLA, NALC, NUL | Abbey Lincoln, Max Roach, Frankie Lyman, Billy Taylor, Gospel Singers, Nat King Cole, Johnny Mathis, Leslie Uggams, Duke Ellington, Miriam Makeba, Sammy Davis, Frank Sinatra. Speakers: Wyatt Walker, Whitney Young, A. Philip Randolph, James Farmer, Adam Clayton Powell[11] |

| Date | Venue | Event | Organization | Performers |
|---|---|---|---|---|
| 9/7/1963 | New York, Town Hall | | Angolan Refugee Rescue Committee | Max Roach, Abbey Lincoln[12] |
| 9/8/1964 | Jackie Robinson's home, Stamford CT | | SCLC, NAACP, CORE | Gerry Mulligan, Quincy Jones, Erroll Garner, Horace Silver, Herbie man, Sal Salvador, Billy Taylor, Wes Montgomery, Clark Terry, Tyree Glenn, Joe Williams[13] |
| 9/8/1964 | Town Hall | The Muslims Present | Nation of Islam | Abbey Lincoln, Max Roach, Clifford Jordan, Eddie Khan, Lonnie Smith, Coleridge Perkinson (director), Walter Davis Jr. trio[14] |
| 10/13/1963 | East Menlo Park, CA | | CORE | Dizzy Gillespie, James Moody, Jon Hendricks, Wynton Kelly, Paul Chambers, Jimmy Cobb, Amanda Ambrose, Teddy Edwards, Gildo Mahones, Kenny Baron[15] |
| 10/12/1963 | New York | | CORE, NAACP, SNCC, SCLC | Josephine Baker[16] |
| 10/20/1963 | Five Spot | Sit-in for Freedom at the Five Spot | CORE | Billy Taylor, Don Heckman, Ted Curson, tp; Bill Baron, as; Dick Berk, d; Ronnie Boykins, b; Kenny Burrell, gt; Ray Draper, tba; Ben Webster, ts; Billy Taylor, Joe Newman, tp; Horace Parlan, p; Frankie Dunlop (comedy), Edgar Bateman, d; Dick Kniss, b; Don Friedman, p; Helen Merrill, v; Ben Reilly, d; Dick Katz, p; Thad Jones, tp; Tommy Williams, b; Roy Haynes, d; Frank Strozier, as[17] |
| 10/27/1963 | Five Spot | Sit-in for Freedom at the Five Spot | | Bill Evans, Gary Peacock, Ira Gitler, Alan Grant, Paul Motian, Al Cohn, Zoot Sims, Sal Mosca, Dick Scott, Hal Dodson, Sheila Jordan, Jack Reilly, Dave Sibley, Prince Lasha, Paul Bley, J. R. Monterose, Eric Dolphy, Bobby Hutchinson, Joe Chambers, Ron Carter, Freddie Redd, Booker Ervin, Henry Grimes |
| 11/17/1963 | Goodson's Town Cabaret 754 E. 169th St. | Bronx CORE Cocktail Sip | CORE–Birmingham victims | Thelonious Monk, Marie Simmons, Hamilton Sisters, Chamber Jazz Quartet, Joseph Gula, Karl Martin, William 88 Keys & Orchestra, Lloyd Davis[18] |

*(continued)*

TABLE 6.1. (*continued*)

| Date | Location | Billed as | Benefit for/Sponsor | Participants[1] |
|---|---|---|---|---|
| 11/23/1963 | Carnegie Hall | All-star Concert | SNCC | Clark Terry; Bob Brookmeyer; Dave Brubeck; Lambert, Hendricks, and Bavan[19] |
| 12/6/1963 | Santa Monica Civic Auditorium | Stars for Freedom | SCLC | (names not available)[20] |

1. These lists of benefit concerts are not comprehensive.
2. A Salute to Southern Students (invitation), Feb. 1, 1963, SNCC papers, 1959–1972 (microfilm), subgroup B, series I, reel 45, frame 1097.
3. Taylor Branch, *Parting the Waters*, pp. 804–806.
4. "Jazzmen Raise Funds at Jackie Robinson's Home," *Down Beat* 30 (Aug. 1, 1963), p. 13; Leonard Feather, "On the Racial Front," *Down Beat's Music '64*, pp. 20–22.
5. Russ Wilson, "Caught in the Act: Civil Rights Concert," *Down Beat* 30 (Aug. 1, 1963), p. 37. The article gives neither the exact date of the performance nor the sponsoring organizations.
6. Feather, "On the Racial Front," p. 21; Louis Calta, "'Freedom' Shows in South Planned," *New York Times* (July 11, 1963), p. 21.
7. Nat King Cole to James Farmer, June 26, 1963, CORE records, 1941–1967, State Historical Society of Wisconsin, series 5, box 28, folder 8.
8. SCLC, pt. 3, reel 2, frame 360.
9. Emancipation March on Washington for Jobs and Freedom (poster), Aug. 23, 1963, CORE records, 1941–1967, State Historical Society of Wisconsin, series 5, box 28, folder 8; Brian Ward, *Just My Soul Responding: Rhythm and Blues, Black Consciousness, and Race Relations* (Berkeley: University of California Press, 1998), p. 269.
10. Jean McCall to Val Coleman, Aug. 24, 1963, CORE records, 1941–1967, State Historical Society of Wisconsin, series 5, box 28, folder 8.
11. "Giant 12-Hour Civil Rights Rally," *New York Amsterdam News* 42 (Aug. 24, 1963), p. 14.
12. "Freedom Album May Be Loaned," *New York Amsterdam News* 42 (Aug. 24, 1963), p. 14.
13. Feather, "On the Racial Front," pp. 20–22.
14. Abbey Lincoln, interview with author, June 13, 1995, New York; "Freedom Album May Be Loaned," p. 14.
15. Ralph J. Gleason, "Dizzy's Day in Kelly Park" (clipping from *San Francisco Examiner or Chronicle*), ca. Oct. 14, 1963, CORE series 5, box 17, folder 1; Gillespie, *To Be or Not to Bop*, p. 455.
16. Howard C. Burney to Val Coleman, Nov. 25, 1963, CORE series 5, box 28, folder 8.
17. CORE Benefit at the Five Spot Cafe (list), Oct. 20, 1963, ibid. Instrument abbreviations: tp-trumpet, as-alto sax, ts-tenor sax, p-piano, g-guitar, b-bass, tba-tuba, d-drums, v-vocal
18. Bronx CORE Cocktail Sip, Nov. 17, 1963, ibid.; "Josephine Baker" (poster) Oct. 12, 1963, ibid.
19. All-Star Concert (poster), Nov. 23, 1963. SNCC subgroup B, series I, reel 45, frame 1063.
20. SCLC, pt. 2, reel 16, frame 874.

recognize the cross-generational relationship of jazz as a whole to the culture of commitment that characterized the 1960s.

Although Amiri Baraka, as an influential theoretician of the jazz avant-garde, embraced the joining of politics and music, many musicians and critics took the position that true art was above politics and consequently was demeaned by crudely political purposes. Since art was a concept through which jazz musicians could demand entrance to the prestigious world of high culture, musicians had every reason to cloak themselves in the various guises of the artist: the eccentric, the single-minded artist detached from worldly concerns, the professional, the visionary, and the genius who is above ordinary social rules.

Thelonious Monk at many points in his career actively disdained politics. In a well-known interview with Valerie Wilmer, Monk said that he "hardly knew anything" about racial politics: "I never was interested in those Muslims. If you want to know you should ask Art Blakey. I didn't have to change my name—it's always been weird enough! I haven't done one of these 'freedom' suites and I don't intend to. I mean, I don't see the point. I'm not thinking that race thing now; it's not on my mind. Everybody's trying to get me to think it, though, but it doesn't bother me. It only bugs the people who're trying to get me to think it."[8] Monk is even reported to have said, "My music is not a social comment on discrimination or poverty or the like. I would have written the same way even if I had not been a Negro."[9]

Monk nevertheless chose to participate in the Carnegie Hall benefit for SNCC and in two other civil rights benefits later that year. In August he appeared at the Apollo Theater in a huge concert organized by A. Philip Randolph's Negro American Labor Council (NALC), which benefited the March on Washington (MOW). Other participants included Cozy Cole, Art Blakey, Carmen McRae, Billy Eckstine, Johnny Hartman, and Ahmad Jamal. In November he participated in a small CORE fund-raising event held in the Bronx for the families of the four young girls killed in the Birmingham bombings in September.

Monk's interest in politics seems to have been situational. In 1954 he appeared at a Salute to Paul Robeson concert that was part of an international campaign to pressure the State Department to reinstate Robeson's passport, which had been rescinded in 1950 after Robeson had publicly protested Truman's military policies in Korea—pointedly suggesting that "the place for the Negro people to fight for their freedom is here at home."[10] Monk, whose cabaret card had been revoked in 1951 and would not be returned until 1957, no doubt identified with Robeson's plight regardless of whether he fully agreed with his politics. If in 1958 he denied that his own music had any political significance, perhaps at this time he wished to emphasize his image as a true artist. But in 1963, Monk and many other jazz artists seem to have been greatly affected by the events in Birmingham. The lesson in the political participation of so many musicians in fund-raising concerts is *not* that jazz musicians were secretly much more political than has generally been thought but rather that the sheer force of the civil rights movement compelled even those who might ordinarily stand on the sidelines to contribute *something* to the cause.

## Birmingham 1963

Historians generally take the events in Birmingham in 1963 as a major turning point in the civil rights movement. After the disappointing failure to desegregate public facilities in Albany, Georgia, in 1962, the leadership of SCLC began planning a major campaign in Birmingham for 1963. In "Project C" (for "confrontation") the organizers sought to divide Birmingham's white power structure by combining carefully planned demonstrations with an effective economic boycott. The movement was to build in intensity over three phases. During the first phase the economic boycott would begin, coupled with small demonstrations and sit-ins. The second phase would involve mass marches on city hall, and during the third phase high school and college students would begin going to jail in massive numbers.

The primary architects of the plan were Martin Luther King, Wyatt Walker, James Bevel, and Andrew Young, and they had specific goals for the campaign: (1) desegregating lunch counters in downtown Birmingham, (2) establishing hiring procedures to ensure that blacks were allowed to compete fairly for nonmenial jobs, (3) reopening parks and playgrounds that the city had closed to avoid complying with a federal integration order, (4) eliminating charges against any demonstrators who might be arrested, and (5) appointing a biracial commission to plan an orderly timetable for the desegregation of the public schools.[11]

The boycott began on April 3, 1963, and the SCLC emphasized getting the word out to the black community through mass meetings and the cooperation of the city's clergymen. During the course of the project, song-filled mass meetings were held for sixty-five nights in a row and served to disseminate information about breaking events, generate support for the boycott and protests, bolster the courage of those who were too afraid to protest, and celebrate the courage of those who had survived the consequences of direct action. The marches to city hall began on April 6, and by Good Friday (April 12) Martin Luther King Jr. and Ralph Abernathy had been arrested for violating a state injunction against demonstrations.[12]

During this stay King wrote his famous "letter from Birmingham" justifying the moral necessity of the Birmingham project despite criticism from many corners (including the Kennedy administration, the press, and the liberal white clergy) that the demonstrations were ill timed and of questionable utility. Breaking out of his usual role as conciliator, King offered a stinging rebuke to white liberals who opposed the demonstrations: "I have almost reached the regrettable conclusion that the Negro's great stumbling block is not the White Citizen's Counciler [sic] or the Ku Klux Klanner, but the white moderate who is more devoted to 'order' than to justice, who prefers a negative peace which is the absence of tension to a positive peace which is the presence of justice, who constantly says 'I agree with you in the goal you seek, but I can't agree with your methods of direct action,' who paternalistically believes that he can set the timetable for another man's freedom."[13]

By the time King and Abernathy bailed out of jail on April 27 (on money raised by Harry Belafonte), nearly a million copies of the letter had been distributed thanks to the help of the American Friends Service Committee. In the meantime James Bevel had been conducting nonviolent workshops among Birmingham's elementary, high school, and college students, and many more were arrested in continuing demonstrations, including singer Al Hibbler.[14]

Fred Shuttlesworth petitioned the city's two governments (the result of a disputed mayoral election) for permission to hold a demonstration on May 2. The request was denied by both the Connor and Boutwell administrations.[15] The leadership of the campaign decided to go ahead with the demonstration anyway—as a children's march that comprised many of the students who had been participating in Bevel's workshops. The children gathered in the Sixteenth Street Baptist Church and emerged in waves, and by day's end nearly a thousand young people (mostly teenagers, though some were as young as six) were in the Birmingham jail.

The following day, with the city's jails filled to overflowing, "Bull" Connor's police turned fire hoses (mounted on tripods to increase their pressure) on the students, rolling an African American child down the street with the powerful torrent of water. The crowd responded by throwing rocks and bricks, as hundreds of young marchers continued to emerge from the church. The police then sent in dogs to disperse the crowd, resulting in a famous photograph of a German shepherd sinking its teeth into Walter Gadsden's abdomen. The resulting photographs and film footage, transmitted around the world, generated international outrage over the conditions in Birmingham. Celebrities including Joan Baez, Jackie Robinson, and Dick Gregory arrived in the city. On Friday, May 10, after an intensive week of news coverage and stalled negotiations, an agreement to desegregate public accommodations in Birmingham was achieved. Sitting rooms would be integrated by Monday; a biracial committee was convened in fifteen days; integrated washrooms and fountains were achieved after thirty days; and integrated lunch counters commenced in sixty days.[16]

Birmingham's success set off a summer-long contagion of protest for civil rights and a corresponding backlash. A few days after the agreement was reached, two bombs went off at the home of Reverend A. D. King, Martin Luther King's brother, and severely damaged the parsonage. Black demonstrators threw rocks and bricks despite A. D. King's appeal for nonviolence. Governor George Wallace sent in state troopers, who beat the demonstrators savagely, setting off a night of rioting. The crisis prompted President John Kennedy to announce his support of the Birmingham agreement and the federal government's unwillingness to allow extremists to sabotage it. Less than a month later NAACP leader Medgar Evers was assassinated after having launched a Birmingham-style campaign in Jackson, Mississippi. In the ten weeks after the Birmingham settlement there were some 758 demonstrations and 14,733 arrests in 186 American cities.[17]

Just as the Freedom Rides generated donations to CORE and other civil rights organizations, the SCLC was able to raise an enormous amount of money after Birmingham when King and other Birmingham veterans went on speaking tours. In Hollywood, prominent celebrities, including Burt Lancaster, Paul Newman, John Forsythe, Lloyd Bridges, Marlon Brando, and Sammy Davis Jr., made large donations at a reception, which in combination with proceeds from a rally attended by fifty thousand people, generated $75,000 for the SCLC. King then traveled to Chicago,

where, on May 26, Dinah Washington, Mahalia Jackson, and Aretha Franklin sang at an SCLC rally that generated $40,000 for the organization. In late June Jackie Robinson's "Afternoon of Jazz" featured Dizzy Gillespie, Dave Brubeck, Clark Terry, Zoot Sims, Ben Webster, and Jimmy Rushing performing in benefit for the SCLC.[18]

## The March on Washington and the Birmingham Bombing

In the wake of Birmingham, King and other movement leaders sought to pressure the federal government to pass, once and for all, federal civil rights legislation. The March on Washington was planned to publicly pressure Congress to enact such legislation. It was Birmingham and the fear that many more Birminghams might occur that caused President Kennedy to announce on June 12 that he would introduce federal civil rights legislation, as movement leaders had long been advocating. "A great change is at hand," he concluded, "and our task, our obligation, is to make that revolution, that change, peaceful and constructive for all."[19]

The Kennedy administration was opposed to the march, but the civil rights leaders persisted. So worried about violence was the administration that President Kennedy and Attorney General Robert Kennedy placed thousands of military troops on alert. Taylor Branch has called the MOW, which took place on August 28, "the first—and essentially the last—mass meeting to reach the national airwaves." The march itself featured classical, folk, and gospel performers: Marian Anderson, Mahalia Jackson, the SNCC Freedom Singers, Joan Baez, Odetta, Bob Dylan, and Mahalia Jackson. Many jazz musicians, however, played at one of the two major benefit concerts held in New York a few days prior to the march: one at the Apollo Theater on August 23, including Thelonious Monk, Coleman Hawkins, Art Blakey, Billy Eckstine, Ahmad Jamal, Quincy Jones, and Charlie Shavers, and another at the New York polo grounds on August 25, at which Abbey Lincoln, Max Roach, Duke Ellington, Billy Taylor, Nat Cole, Sammy Davis, and Frank Sinatra performed (figure 6.1). Clark Terry and Milt Hinton were unable to attend the march, but they paid for a bus so that others could attend. Although Malcolm X dismissed the march as "Farce on Washington," a mere Kennedy pep rally, he was there.[20]

Two and a half weeks after the march, Birmingham's Sixteenth Street Baptist Church was bombed on a Sunday morning (September 15), killing

FIGURE 6.1. "Giant 12-Hour Civil Rights Rally." *New York Amsterdam News* 42, no. 34 (August 24, 1963), p. 14.

four young girls, escalating the nation's fears of racial warfare, and generating worldwide indignation. The New York jazz world responded with a flurry of benefits. In October CORE held two "sit-ins for freedom" on consecutive Sundays at the Five Spot, in which more than forty musicians participated, including Ron Carter, Eric Dolphy, Billy Taylor, Don Friedman, Ben Reilly, Roy Haynes, Frank Strozier, Gary Peacock, Paul Bley, J. C. Monterose, and Zoot Sims. Thelonious Monk appeared for the Bronx CORE at a benefit for the Birmingham victims on November 17, and Clark Terry, Bob Brookmeyer, Dave Brubeck, and Lambert, Hendricks, and Bavan appeared at Carnegie Hall for SNCC on the day after John F. Kennedy's assassination (see table 6.1). On November 18 John Coltrane recorded five takes of "Alabama," a composition named for the four young women killed in Birmingham and perhaps the most moving composition dedicated specifically to a civil rights event.[21]

## Miles Davis

The most aesthetically celebrated concert of any in the fund-raising genre is undoubtedly Miles Davis's Lincoln's birthday concert (held on February 12, 1964) for Mississippi and Louisiana voter registration, which benefited SNCC, CORE, and the NAACP Legal Defense fund (table 6.2). We probably owe the live recording of the concert to a dispute Davis had with producer Teo Macero over the release of *Quiet Nights* in 1963. Davis was so angry about the premature release of this unfinished work with Gil Evans that he refused to record in Columbia's studios for most of 1963 and all of 1964. In order to keep up its catalog, Columbia was forced to make live recordings.[22]

The coalition of civil rights organizations that benefited from the concert, while ostensibly a sign of unity, was actually a condition forced on the groups by Steven Currier, the principal financier of the Voter Education Project (VEP). Currier's Taconic Foundation had been instrumental in launching the VEP after the Freedom Rides in 1961. After the March on Washington, which required considerable compromise on the part of individual organizations, a great deal of emphasis was placed on movement unity, and Currier was behind efforts at joint fund-raising. As Marvin Rich recalled, "None of the groups liked it, but we couldn't quite say no to him because he had big bucks which he would give to each of us."[23]

TABLE 6.2. Some fund-raising concerts, 1964–1967

| Date | Location | Billed as | Benefit for/Sponsor | Participants |
|---|---|---|---|---|
| 2/10/1964 | Upsala College, East Orange, NJ | | CORE | Dave Brubeck[1] |
| 2/12/1964 | Philharmonic Hall | Abraham Lincoln's birthday concert | voter registration, SNCC, CORE, NAACP Legal Defense Fund | Miles Davis Quintet[2] |
| 3/8/1964 | New York | | Local 1199 | Olatunji, Ruby Dee[3] |
| 3/24–30/64 | San Jose, Sacramento, Bakersfield, Fresno, San Diego, Los Angeles, San Francisco | | NAACP and CORE seven-day tour | Count Basie Orchestra with Joe Williams, Mahalia Jackson, June Christy, Dick Gregory, Rene Bloch, Jack Costanza, Lorez Alexander[4] |
| 4/9, 11, 18, 25/1964 | Five Spot | | CORE | (names not available)[5] |
| 4/4/1964 | Savoy Manor Ballroom, Bronx, NY | second annual dance | SNCC and CORE | Tainy Hill and Orchestra[6] |
| 5/14/1964 | closed-circuit television network | Freedom Spectacular for tenth anniversary of *Brown v. Board of Education* | NAACP | Duke Ellington, Lena Horne, Nat King Cole, Mahalia Jackson, Cannonball Adderley, Carolyn Jones, Dorothy, Dandridge, Della Reese, Tony Bennett, Harry Belafonte; co-chairs Lena Horne, Steve Allen, Sammy Davis Jr., Ed Sullivan[7] |
| 6/19/1964 | Central Plaza Ballroom, New York | Freedom and All That Jazz | CORE | Johnny Richards, Eddie Barefield[8] |
| 8/19/1964 | Shelley's Manne-Hole, Los Angeles | | COFO | Shelly Manne Quartet[9] |

| Date | Location | Event | Organization | Performers |
|---|---|---|---|---|
| 9/14/1964 | Masonic Auditorium, San Francisco | Jazz at the Masonic | CORE | John Handy and the Freedom Band, Dizzy Gillespie, Bill Cosby[10] |
| 9/17/1964 | Shelley's Manne-Hole, Los Angeles | | CORE, Chaney, Schwerner, Goodman | Philly Joe Jones, Leroy Vinnegar, Jack Wilson, Steve Allen, Paul Horn, Leonard Burns, Al "Stevo" Stevenson, John Goodman, Curtis Amy, Shelly Manne, Jack Nimitz[11] |
| 9/20/1964 | The Scene, 301 W. 46th Street, New York City | Come Sunday | CORE, 7 Arts Chapter | Benny Powell, Frank Foster, Tobi Reynolds, Quentin Jackson, Dotty and Jerry Dodgion, Thad Jones Quintet with Pepper Adams[12] |
| 12/27/64 | Village Gate | Holiday Benefit for Freedomways | Freedomways[13] | John Coltrane, Abbey Lincoln, Max Roach, Bill Dixon, Len Chandler, Dick Gregory[14] |
| Winter 1965 | Boston | | Boston Friends of SNCC | Max Roach, Abbey Lincoln, Freedom Now Suite[15] |
| 4/22/1965 | Americana Hotel, New York City | Salute to Paul Robeson on the occasion of his 67th birthday | Freedomways | individual sponsors: James Baldwin, Ossie Davis, Earl Dickerson, Dizzy Gillespie, John Coltrane, Paule Marshall, Linus Pauling, Earl Robinson, Pete Seeger, I. F. Stone; performers: Olatunji; Billy Taylor[16] |
| 4/25/1965 | New York Hilton, fund-raising dinner | Sunday Evening with SNCC | SNCC | Harry Belafonte, Marlon Brando, Diahann Carroll, Sammy Davis Jr., Barbara Streisand, Sonny Terry and Brownie McGhee, Tito Puente and his orchestra[17] |
| 5/17/1965 | Chicago, McCormick Auditorium | Freedom Rally | NAACP | Nancy Wilson |
| 5/23/1965 | private apartment in Greenwich Village | | CORE | Randy Weston Sextet, James Farmer, speaking on the U.S. civil rights struggle and his recent trip to Africa[18] |

*(continued)*

TABLE 6.2. (continued)

| Date | Location | Billed as | Benefit for/Sponsor | Participants |
|---|---|---|---|---|
| 5/30/1965 | Los Angeles sports arena | Freedom Now benefits and awards ceremony | Community Relations Educational Foundation (CREF) | Bill Cosby, Peter Lawford, Bill Cosby, Marlon Brando, Robert Culp, H. B. Barnum, Georgia Carr, Sam Fletcher, Ketty Lester, UN Children's Choir, Calvin Jackson and orchestra, the Mills Brothers, Aaron & Freddie, Martin Luther King[19] |
| 6/4/1965 | Dooto Music Center, Compton, CA | Core-A-Go-Go | CORE | Mary Love, The Superbs, Jessie Hill, the Datons, Z. Z. Hill[20] |
| 7/25/1965 | Shelley's Manne-Hole, Los Angeles | | CORE | Steve Allen, Curtis Amy, George Braith, Buddy Collette, Teddy Edwards, Freedom Jazz Quintet, Chick Freeman, Terry Gibbs, Hampton Hawes, Stan Gilbert, Horace Silver, Louis Smith, Milt Turner, Leroy Vinnegar, Jack Wilson[21] |
| 9/18/1965 | The Wexlers, 127 W. 12 Street, New York | Swing for SNCC Party | SNCC | (names not available)[22] |
| Mar. 1965 | | | SNCC | Paul Robeson[23] |
| Dec. 1966 | Village Theater, New York | | SNCC | Jackie McLean, Marion Brown, Archie Shepp, Stokely Carmichael[24] |
| 4/23/1967 | Olatunji's Center of African Culture | Roots of Africa | Center of African Culture Scholarship Fund | John Coltrane, Pharoah Sanders, Alice Coltrane, Jimmy Garrison, Rashied Ali, Algie De Witt, Juma, Billy Taylor (announcer)[25] |
| 3/29/1967 | | | | Randy Weston[26] |
| 1967 | Newark, NJ | | bail fund for Newark demonstrators | McLean and Higgins[27] |

1. Val Coleman to Jim Peck, Feb. 10, 1964, CORE series 5, box 28, folder 8.

2. "Miles Davis in Benefit," *New York Amsterdam News* 53 (Feb. 8, 1964), p. 16; Marvin Rich to Miles Davis, Mar. 13, 1964, CORE series 5, box 28, folder 8.

3. Leon J. Davis (solicitation letter), Feb. 28, 1964; SNCC subgroup B, series I, reel 45, frame 152.

4. "All-star Troupe on the Road for NAACP and CORE," *Down Beat* 31 (Apr. 9, 1964), p. 13; "Mahalia to Star at Freedom Rally," *Los Angeles Sentinel* (Mar. 26, 1964), p. A1-2.

5. Executive board minutes, *Allegro* 42 (May 1964), p. 3.

6. Second annual dance (ticket), Apr. 4, 1964, SNCC subgroup B, series I, reel 45, frame 169.

7. Klaus Stratemann, *Duke Ellington, Day by Day and Film by Film* (Copenhagen: JazzMedia, 1992), p. 484. The Ellington segment from Madison Square Garden was called "Let Freedom Ring." The occasion was the tenth anniversary of *Brown v. Board of Education*. The segment from the sports arena in Los Angeles was called "Some People." That program beamed to fifty theaters and auditoriums in the United States, although there were technical problems. "Nat Cole, Gleason Set Freedom Show," *Los Angeles Sentinel* (Apr. 23, 1964). p. G11.

8. Freedom and All That Jazz (handbill), June 9, 1964, CORE series 5, box 17, folder 1.

9. "Civil Rights Benefit to Be Held in Los Angeles," *Down Beat* 31 (Aug. 27, 1964), p. 9.

10. Brian Ward, *Just My Soul Responding*, p. 305.

11. "Hollywood Benefit Raises $1,354 for Civil-rights Campaign," *Down Beat* 31 (Nov. 5, 1964), p. 9; "Mississippi Benefit Sunday at Manne-Hole," *Los Angeles Sentinel* (Sept. 17, 1964), p. B8.

12. "Come Sunday, an Evening of Jazz for the Benefit of the Folks in Mississippi," Sept. 20, 1964, Institute of Jazz Studies, topics files: handbills, New York jazz clubs.

13. *Freedomways* was an African American literary and political quarterly started in 1961. It was edited by Shirley Graham, and advised by W.E.B. Du Bois.

14. A Holiday Benefit for Freedomways (poster), Dec. 27, 1964, Institute of Jazz Studies topics files: handbills, New York jazz clubs; "Gregory in Benefit at Village Gate," *New York Amsterdam News* 43 (Dec. 26, 1964), p. 16.

15. Ward, *Just My Soul Responding*, p. 306.

16. Duberman, *Paul Robeson*, p. 528.

17. Sunday Evening with SNCC (invitation), Apr. 25, 1965, SNCC subgroup B, series I, reel 46, frame 1226.

18. "James Farmer Speaking on His Recent African Trip and the U.S. Civil Rights Struggle" (poster), May 23, 1965, Institute of Jazz Studies topics files: handbills, New York jazz clubs.

19. "Freedom Now" (ad), *Los Angeles Sentinel* (May 27, 1965), p. B12.

20. "CORE-A-Go-Go" (ad), *Los Angeles Sentinel* (June 3, 1965), p. B8.

21. "L. A. Bash Raises $1,462 for San Fernando CORE," *Down Beat* 32, no.19 (Sept. 9, 1965), p. 11.

22. Swing for SNCC Party (invitation), Sept. 18, 1965, SNCC subgroup B, series I, reel 46, frame 1256.

23. Duberman, *Paul Robeson*, p. 540.

24. Frank Kofsky, *Black Nationalism and the Revolution in Music*, pp. 84-85; Jackie McLean, "Miles Davis, the Civil Rights and Jazz," May 4, 1997, video recording.

25. Yasuhiro Fujioka, with Lewis Porter and Yoh-Ichi Hamada, *John Coltrane: A Discography and Musical Biography*, pp. 298-99.

26. Statement of Account—Benefit Concert by the Randy Weston Sextet, Mar. 29, 1967, CU subseries I box 31, folder 24, "Weston, Randy (American Jazz in Africa) (2 of 4)."

27. Billy Higgins and Jackie McLean, "Miles Davis, the Civil Rights Movement, and Jazz," May 4, 1997, video recording.

Voter registration would be the principal focus of 1964 and 1965, and an appeal letter on "Miles Davis" letterhead, which advertised the concert, succinctly explained the movement's current focus: "The civil rights movement is launching an all-out drive to register Negro citizens in Mississippi and Louisiana. Hundreds of field workers are pouring into these states at this moment, setting up registration clinics, preparing potential voters for registration tests, transporting citizens to the registrars offices. All of this costs money—and the most urgent need is for cars—durable automobiles that can transport our people into and out of the widespread rural areas of both states."[24]

A handwritten note explained: "This is the so-called 'rich folks letter,' so titled and written by Val Coleman. We're typing individual copies for people we hope will buy—like Nelson Rockefeller, etc. We're using this stationery rather than CORE, SNCC, or NAACP paper hoping it will catch their attention as something different."[25]

Although the benefit had been a long time in the planning, Davis apparently did not tell his band that they would all be waiving their customary fees until the night of the performance. Since the band had not worked for six months, some of the sidemen were not happy about Davis's having committed their earnings without their consent. Ron Carter was particularly annoyed; he wanted to be paid and to decide how much he wanted to give and to which organization. Although Davis's autobiography creates the impression that Carter (who is not named) was unreasonable, Carter had only a few months before donated his services to a CORE benefit at the Five Spot (see table 6.1). The band argued back and forth, but Davis insisted that they waive their fees as a group. Consequently, as he told the story in his autobiography, "When we came out to play everybody was madder than a motherfucker with each other and so I think that anger created a fire, a tension that got into everybody's playing."[26]

Two albums were issued from the performance, *My Funny Valentine,* which includes most of the slower tunes, and *Four & More,* which includes the up-tempo pieces. The former album has been described as "one of the very greatest recordings of a live concert." Subsequent generations of jazz musicians and scholars have closely studied the inspired playing of the entire quintet, with the subtle metric transformations and innovative sound of one of the most revered rhythm sections in jazz. Davis's recording of "Stella by Starlight" has long been one of the pieces that his fans cite to refute charges that his technical command of the trumpet is substandard. Unlike many benefit concerts, the Philharmonic Hall concert did not include speeches and direct testimony from veterans of the movement's front lines. Davis did not play any pieces that were specifically dedicated to civil rights events; rather, he played his usual repertory with inspired excellence and allowed the music to speak for itself.[27]

Although the music from this concert has become canonic to the generations that have followed, on the night of the concert the band members were not so sure. Herbie Hancock remembers that "We all felt dejected and disappointed. We thought we had really bombed! ... But then we listened to the record—it sounded fantastic!" The concert generated approximately $6,000 in proceeds, but according to Raymond Robinson from the *Amsterdam News* the house was only a quarter full. Perhaps there had not been enough publicity or the ticket prices were too steep (they ranged from $3 to $50, which was considerable at the time). A few weeks later Davis received a letter reporting that CORE had been able to send a thousand dollars to the voter registration efforts in Iberville, Louisiana, and the same amount to help rebuild the Plymouth Rock Baptist Church in Plaquemine.[28]

## So What?

What do these benefit concerts reveal about jazz in the early 1960s? Why should we be interested in concerts and small club gatherings that, with a few notable exceptions, were not likely among the most aesthetically successful performances of the day? The role of benefit concerts in the lives of most individual musicians was marginal—sandwiched between more professionally demanding events like headlining engagements at major clubs, making recordings, negotiating future bookings, and touring domestically and internationally. Yet, when looked at collectively, fund-raising events leave a remarkable trail of musicians interacting as best they could with the civil rights movement blazing around them.

One of the principal ways in which the civil rights movement affected people in the world of jazz was in its persistent demand that people take a stand and put their bodies on the line for their convictions. Heated arguments took place both within movement organizations and between different groups about not only political principles and ideologies but also putting them into practice. Whether musicians translated movement values into radical aesthetics or fund-raising concerts, those who "talked big" but were not available for action could expect to have their hypocrisy confronted. The civil rights movement, after all, was a moral movement just as much as it was a political one. Its fundamental message played on the glaring hypocrisy of racial segregation. How could a country that claimed to be the leader of the free world and whose Declaration of Independence declared that "all men are created equal" defend racial segregation? How could anyone doubt that this was unjust? How could the United States ignore the fact that black Americans were being denied the most basic democratic right—the right to vote?

The moral challenges that the movement placed on its supporters—to put up or shut up and to lay down one's body for justice—cast a long shadow. Local civil rights marches were often directed to reluctant and (justifiably) terrified members of the black community, who initially "sat on their porches" as activists marched by. Shaming people into action was thus a frequent component of the movement's moral challenges. Charles Neblett, one of the SNCC Freedom Singers, describes the way in which Malcolm X was shamed into coming to Selma, Alabama, in January 1965:

> He [Malcolm X] walked up to us and invited us to his mosque. We went there, and he sat there, and he looked at us. He said, "You're very brave, but you're very foolish." I think they really had a love-hate relationship with us. They really admired the people using nonviolence on the line. So we told them, say, "Look, you guys up here doin' all the talkin'—why don't you go down there and do something?" And you know, Malcolm came... yeah, he went to Selma. We challenged him, say, "Okay, you talkin' all bad up North. Now why don't you come on down to Mississippi where we're at? We'll find out who's bad!"[29]

Bernice Reagon amplified Neblett's point by explaining how Nina Simone was pressured into going down South:

> We really understood that there was a lot of rhetoric. And rhetoric is very important. But we also thought that there was something else happening, where there were hundreds and thousands of people saying "I will walk this space in my town, and you will either *move* or kill me this day." And that's a different kind of witness. It takes a

different kind of step. I think that's one of the challenges we made. I can remember Cordell [Reagon, founder of the SNCC Freedom Singers]—it was so embarrassing. Nina Simone was trying to say her contribution was through her music. And Cordell said, "But if you come down to the struggle, you will be involved *beyond* singing. Singing is all right, but you need to put your body on the line." And she came.[30]

It is not hard to see how intimidating the moral challenges of front-line organizers could be. As Fred Shuttlesworth once remarked, "There's two kinds of people. People who are committed to the movement and people who get committed by the movement." Many Northerners felt quite small when confronted with the extraordinary bravery of the civil rights activists. In what might be called a "culture of commitment" that pervaded the early 1960s, an enormous amount of peer pressure was placed on people, including musicians, to show where they stood. As Clark Terry remembers, "Everybody was involved. Nobody was content to sit back and allow crap to be poured all over his head. We all felt like it was our duty to get involved in one form or another."[31]

Although jazz musicians were among the most active supporters of civil rights causes and were substantially more outspoken than R&B musicians in the early 1960s, they were nevertheless notably absent from the front lines of the Southern grassroots civil rights campaigns. Folk, gospel, or popular singers such as Odetta, Mahalia Jackson, Nina Simone, Bob Dylan, Joan Baez, Josh White, and Pete Seeger were more likely to be seen below the Mason-Dixon line.[32] One exception to this trend was Billy Taylor's participation in "Salute to Freedom '63" in Birmingham, Alabama, in August 1963. The concert, which featured Ray Charles, Johnny Mathis, Billy Taylor, and Nina Simone, drew some fifteen thousand people to benefit the SCLC, SNCC, NAACP, CORE, NUL, and NALC. The city of Birmingham had originally promised the American Guild of Variety Artists (AGVA), which had organized the show, that the event could be held in the Birmingham City Auditorium with integrated seating. But three weeks before the concert, the city reneged by claiming that the auditorium had to be painted before August 10 and consequently was unavailable. The event was held instead on the football field of Miles College, a historically black institution. Another exception was singer Al Hibbler, who was arrested in a demonstration during the Birmingham campaign in the spring of 1963. Even though many jazz musicians attended the March on Washington, the *New York Amsterdam News* wondered aloud why Duke Ellington, Louis Armstrong, or Billy Eckstine had not performed at the march.[33]

In many ways, benefit concerts offered a relatively easy form of activism. Musicians could contribute to the cause by allowing the civil rights movement to capitalize on the cultural prestige of their music. Fundraising concerts also provided a means to give public witness to their social values without having to step outside the communicative medium in which they were most comfortable. Music, moreover, was a medium that many musicians felt to be political in and of itself. By sponsoring the concerts, civil rights organizations conversely gained desperately needed finances and a public forum in which to expand their Northern audience.

Marvin Rich, who led fund-raising efforts for CORE, found that benefit events were as important in generating a sense of "ownership and participation" as they were in generating funds. When a well-known musician did a fund-raiser, "then the next step becomes easier." After Jackie Robinson sponsored his "Afternoon of Jazz" benefits, CORE found it less difficult to ask him to cochair a committee developing a community center in honor of Chaney, Schwerner, and Goodman, the three voter rights organizers who were killed in Meridian, Mississippi, in June 1964. Once a performer had done one benefit, it was less challenging to convince that person to do another.[34]

The Northern fund-raising event mediated between the front lines of the movement and a community of supporters who longed for a way to demonstrate with their bodies and their pockets that they stood for racial justice. There are many ironies in this relationship. As SNCC organizers in the South battled beatings, bullets, and fear, the celebrity dinner committee of the New York Friends of SNCC put on hundred-dollar-a-plate, black-tie fund-raisers. In April 1965, SNCC's "Sunday Evening with SNCC" with Harry Belafonte, Marlon Brando, Sammy Davis Jr., Barbara Streisand, Tito Puente, and Sonny Terry grossed $82,019.49 in one evening (figure 6.2). The financial report from the event indicates that the musicians returned their checks to SNCC in two ways: by direct return and by donating to the Artists Civil Rights Assistance Fund (ACRAF), an organization founded by Chad Mitchell and Mary Travers to make it easier for musicians to donate to civil rights organizations. Dizzy Gillespie, Quincy Jones, and Ralph Gleason served on the board of directors.

The flyer in the figure reads:

YOU ARE
CORDIALLY INVITED
TO ATTEND

# Sunday Evening with SNCC

...endered to Grant

...young Negroes sat down
...ter in Greensboro,
... historic movement
...rdinating Committee — SNCC).
...ow, in terms of equal
...ote, is an eloquent
...ull emancipation left
...ys.

...hiladelphia, Mississippi
...ctors of the South,
...C field workers daily
...nd even death itself
...eality.

...ca's greatest artists in
...NCC", you are providing
...our mutual objective:
...ook at his neighbor and

...ainters and graphic artists,
...y by in mankind's struggle
...cifically
...nt.

featuring

Harry Belafonte   Barbra Streisand
Marlon Brando     Sonny Terry
Diahann Carroll   and
Sammy Davis, Jr.   Brownie McGhee

Produced and Directed by Himan Brown
Lighting by Ralph Alswang
Choreography by Walter Nicks
Script by Walter Bernstein
Music Conducted by Maurice Levine

Tito Puente and His Orchestra

SUNDAY, APRIL 25, 1965
New York Hilton, Grand Ballroom
Reception: 6:00 P.M.    Dinner: 7:30 P.M.
Subscription: $100 per person / Black Tie

FIGURE 6.2. Sunday Evening with SNCC. SNCC papers, 1959–1972 (microfilm), 1965.

The success of SNCC's black-tie affair indicates just how mainstream and fashionable donating to civil rights organizations had become by 1965.[35]

## Complex Motivations

*I look back at that time and I think well I'm not sorry for anything. I did what was in my heart, and I was right too. I'm disappointed though, that for many people it was only another opportunity to be seen and heard.*

—Abbey Lincoln

Not surprisingly, musicians and activists brought a wide range of human motivation to political engagement. As the testimony of Reagon and Neblett shows, activists on the front lines were harsh critics of human weakness and deployed the moral righteousness of the cause to both inspire and shame people into action. Some participated in the movement to avoid humiliation; some for the righteousness of the cause; and some for the chance to lead and be important. In most people a mixture of motivations from altruism to selfishness lived simultaneously. One could, after all, "do the right thing" and also have one's needs for power and prestige gratified. Part of the satisfaction of the hard work of movement organizing was, indeed, the exercise of power—*forcing* the government to take a stand. Val Coleman of CORE recalled proudly that "There was a time in '3, '64, and briefly in '61 during the Freedom Ride when we sort of owned the world.... Presidents shook." One could be utterly dedicated to the principles of the movement but also greatly enjoy the awe, respect, and cachet that militance conferred. One could selflessly subject oneself to beatings and death threats but also make sure to be first in front of the camera when the reporters arrived. Where does dedication end and posturing begin? There is no simple dividing line.[36]

Certain names appear again and again in connection with fund-raising concerts: Max Roach, Abbey Lincoln, Cannonball Adderley, Dizzy Gillespie, Count Basie, Clark Terry, Tony Bennett, Billy Taylor, and Dave Brubeck. Val Coleman recalled that Cannonball Adderley was one of the first musicians to do events for CORE: "Let me tell you who was the first and most important supporter of CORE, long before anybody else in the jazz community... Cannonball Adderley. Cannonball did stuff for us when people didn't know who the hell we were." Cannonball, as Coleman remembers, even attended the founding meeting of the Seven Arts chapter of CORE.[37]

Other musicians preferred to maintain a separation between the bandstand and their political views and activities. However, proponents of this position were not necessarily unconcerned with the world around them. Ron Carter explains:

> I certainly never used the regular bandstand to make my views heard. Those bands that did, I admired them for doing it, but I thought that the bandstand was a place for a different kind of routine, a different arena.... I would tell somebody off the bandstand what I felt. I would go to a meeting without taking my bass. I never took my bass. At that time music was still very prominent in most of my associates' minds. While they were aware of all of the social inequities in the states, as we had all suffered through them by and large, the bandstand was not where they expressed those feelings. They would just decide not to go to a certain club [that treated musicians badly]. They might decide this record label was being outrageous with their royalties stuff. Most of us would not record for them.[38]

Economic conditions in the music industry and the aims of the civil rights movement were often intertwined in the minds of musicians, and many ultimately acted upon their political concerns in the economic domain. Ron Carter's view of the relationship between art and politics also cultivates the stage as a hard-won *professional* arena for jazz musicians, something political in and of itself. During the peak years of the civil rights movement the principled separation between art and politics was placed under siege by the dramatic force and moral power of the civil rights movement. While the documentation of fund-raising concerts for civil rights organizations provides one lens on the relationship of musicians to civil rights events, one should not presume that those whose names are absent from these lists were blithely unconcerned about the world around them.

The price of extensive outspokenness, after all, could be very high. Abbey Lincoln and Max Roach, for example, found recording contracts difficult to obtain in the late 1960s. Being branded as "difficult" by record companies, club owners, critics, or major contractors could lead to a noticeable decline in economic well-being. It is not surprising, then, that as protest became more acceptable, a greater number of musicians were willing to publicly associate their names with the civil rights movement. At some point (certainly by the time of the March on Washington) it even became fashionable to participate. When protest developed an aesthetic imperative of its own, perhaps there the temptation to posture was the greatest.

## Summer 1964 to 1967

In 1964 and 1965 the popularity of fund-raising concerts for the principal civil rights organizations waned. A number of reasons account for this, including a public that was saturated with benefit events, increasing racial tensions within the civil rights movement, the signing of the Civil Rights Act of 1964 and the Voting Rights Act of 1965, and the escalation of U.S. military involvement in Vietnam. A cogent coincidence illustrates the interpenetration of civil rights and Vietnam beginning in 1964: The very day that the bodies of James Chaney, Michael Schwerner, and Andrew Goodman were found in Neshoba County, Mississippi, was also the day that President Johnson ordered air strikes against North Vietnam in retaliation for attacks against the U.S. destroyer *Maddox* in the Gulf of

Tonkin. As early as April 1965 SNCC leader Bob Moses had spoken out against military escalation in Vietnam, and in 1966 both SNCC and CORE took firmly antiwar positions.[39]

By 1964, deeper issues of race, politics, class, and separatism were beginning to absorb the attention of those interested in racial justice in both jazz and the civil rights movement. The 1964 summer voter registration project in Mississippi, which brought hundreds of Northern white students to the South, crystallized many tensions that had long been incubating. The Summer Project, as it was known, had been organized by the Council of Federated Organizations (COFO), a coalition of civil rights associations engaged in voter registration and education efforts in Mississippi. Since the federal government refused to act except under conditions of extreme crisis, activists planned a summer of confrontation featuring hundreds of white students from the North. The strategy, in part, attempted to use societal racism to the movement's end. Although state and federal authorities easily ignored atrocities committed against black civil rights workers, national sentiment, they reasoned, would not tolerate the same treatment of white college students from prestigious schools. Students also brought access to corridors of power and publicity through their families' business and social connections.[40]

From the beginning, African American organizers were ambivalent about bringing white students to the front lines. The tendency of well-educated whites to "gravitate to command posts" caused resentment from veterans of the front lines, and some of them suggested placing restrictions on the role of the white volunteers. Despite the strategic reasons for inviting the students, some felt that such a strategy reinforced an unhealthy dependence on whites. Others thought that whites should direct their organizing efforts toward the Southern white community, but the students, who longed for interracial communion, resisted. In any case, the Northern students encountered an ambivalent reception and quickly learned that the realities of the Southern struggle and everyday Southern black life were something quite different from what they had imagined.[41]

After the signing of the Voting Rights Act on August 6, 1965, the movement suffered from what August Meier called "a crisis of victory." Now that federal legislation had been accomplished, what next? The brutal intensity of the battle required to achieve these elementary democratic rights, moreover, left many weary, cynical, and feeling that the struggle against racism had only just begun. Meier noted with some irony that "White support for the movement was greater than ever before, yet activists were growing increasingly hostile toward white liberals, suspicious of white participants, and more separatist in their outlook....At the very time that nonviolent direct action had become most fashionable—with thousands of Americans, black and white, converging on Selma, Alabama, during March 1965, in support of King's campaign there...people in the most militant sectors of the movement considered the technique essentially obsolete."[42]

As activism became mainstreamed, in other words, the leaders of the movement turned to conceptualizing more fundamental changes in American society. Many African Americans felt that white liberal strategies were simply insufficient to address the problems of black poverty, education, and police brutality in black communities. As the direct action organizations moved increasingly in the direction of Black Power issues (including black-controlled political parties, economic development, cultural pride, and a deeper understanding of Africa), many began to state explicitly what had long been an undertone among movement radicals—whites were increasingly unwelcome in SNCC and CORE. African Americans needed to lead their own organizations and determine their own direction without the interference of whites, who resisted more radical solutions for ameliorating the conditions of the black poor. Radical whites, they reasoned, should understand that now was the time to relinquish their leadership positions in CORE. Some accepted this analysis and left voluntarily; others left in protest, but, in either case, by the end of 1966 only a few remained in CORE and SNCC. Those who stayed accepted a redefinition of their role: They would organize white people, and blacks would organize black people. Stokely Carmichael remained willing to form alliances with radical whites but emphasized the need for all-black organizations. He compared Black Power to the concerted political efforts of European ethnic groups, such as the Irish and Jews, to gain political power.[43] Nevertheless, after intense debate, SNCC voted to formally exclude whites at its national conference in December 1966. Although it took until 1968 for CORE to exclude whites completely, the two major themes of debate in both SNCC and CORE from 1964 to 1967 were African American leadership and control and whether or not whites should be excluded from leadership positions.[44]

## Black Power

The slogan "Black Power" became a focus of public debate during the summer of 1966, after Stokely Carmichael popularized it in a June 16 rally in Greenwood, Mississippi, in which he appeared with Martin Luther King and Floyd McKissick of CORE. The three civil rights leaders had united to finish James Meredith's walk across Mississippi, which had been intended to demonstrate that African Americans could exercise their newly won voting rights without fear. Instead, Meredith was wounded by three shotgun blasts in the mob violence, and the resulting atmosphere in Mississippi was so tense that both McKissick and King agreed to let the Deacons of Defense, an armed group, provide protection for the march. At the rally in Greenwood, Stokely Carmichael, who took up a slogan coined by Willie Ricks, stirred the crowd by arguing that the demand that day must be for black power, not simply civil rights.[45]

Black Power meant different things to different constituencies. For some African Americans, Black Power was simply exercising "control over our lives, politically, economically, and psychically"; for others its aims included the destruction of capitalism and a revolutionary transition to socialism. Still others viewed its call for economic self-determination as a mandate for black capitalism. Harold Cruse argued that "Black Power is nothing but the economic and political philosophy of Booker T. Washington given a 1960s' militant shot in the arm and brought up to date."[46]

The slogan "Black Power" arose from extended debate between 1964 and 1967 among militant civil rights activists in SNCC and CORE who had faced murderous violence and intimidation in their organizing efforts. This contrasts with the black nationalism of the Nation of Islam, which had discouraged participation in the marches and demonstrations of the civil rights movement, a position that ultimately drove Malcolm X to leave the organization. Historians have seen the emergence of Black Power as resulting from both Malcolm X's influence on the grassroots organizers and the growing emphasis on economic and political empowerment in the post–civil rights and voting rights movements.

Ultimately the political landscape of the black nationalism of the late 1960s divided into two principal tendencies—cultural nationalism and revolutionary nationalism. The latter called for black self-determination and empowerment within the frame of a Marxist analysis of class, race, and capitalism. Cultural nationalism, on the other hand, rejected Marxism as white and instead favored an African socialism that stressed self-determination, cooperative economics, black unity, and cultural celebration. It emphasized the development of autonomous black political organizations and the creation of a strong black cultural identity. The Black Panther Party of Huey Newton and Bobby Seale has often been used to exemplify revolutionary nationalism, while the US organization led by Maulana Karenga has generally been viewed as the principal example of cultural nationalism.[47]

One of the hallmarks of cultural nationalism was its celebration of Africa as a cultural and spiritual model for creating a new, positive, black identity, something that had also been a strong emphasis in Elijah Muhammad's Nation of Islam. In the early 1960s the Nation of Islam sponsored several African Asian "unity bazaars," which featured arts, crafts, speeches, and live music. They were generally twelve-hour events that were designed to promote black businesses, disseminate the message of the Nation of Islam, and build a global sense of black unity. These Muslim bazaars, as they were often called, took place in New York, Chicago, Washington, DC, Boston, and Newark (table 6.3). Although these were not fund-raising concerts in the same sense as those put on by SNCC, CORE, SCLC, and the NAACP, they dramatized the renaissance in clothing, food, music, religion, and art that celebrated a cultural vision of African American self-transformation. Dinizulu and his African dancers were often the featured stars of the African Asian bazaars (figure 6.3). Founded by Nana Dinizulu and Alice Dinizulu in the 1950s, the Dinizulu Dancers performed a variety of traditional African dances. In 1965 Nana Dinizulu was initiated into the Akan religion in Ghana and later founded an Akan religious community in the United States.[48]

Michael Babatunde Olatunji is familiar to jazz audiences as the person who introduced many jazz musicians of the late 1950s and 1960s to African music in general and Nigerian music in particular. Olatunji came to the United States in 1950 on a scholarship to attend Morehouse College in Atlanta. In Nigeria he had drummed with the theatrical troupe of Hubert Ogunde, whose work combined music, dance, and theater with a message of African nationalism. Alarmed at the ignorance of Africa displayed by his fellow students and Americans in general, Olatunji started a musical troupe among the students at Morehouse. In 1954 he moved to New York to attend New York University and begin doctoral studies in public administration, which he abandoned four years later when he could not

TABLE 6.3. Some Nation of Islam events, 1962–1967

| Date | Location | Billed as | Participants[1] |
|---|---|---|---|
| Sept. 1962 | New York | | Olatunji[1] |
| 11/10/1962 | New York | African Asian bazaar[2] | |
| 6/15/1963 | New York, 369th Armory | African bazaar | Dinizulu and His African Dancers; speaker Malcolm X[3] |
| July 1963 | Washington, DC, Muhammad's Mosque No. 4 | benefit concert | Babatunde Olatunji, Calvin X, Stacey X, Ralph Dawson[4] |
| 8/17/1963 | Boston, Boston Arena (238 St. Botolph) | African Asian bazaar | Dinizulu and His African Dancers; speaker Malcolm X[5] |
| 9/13/1963 | Chicago, Trianon (62nd and Cottage) | African Asian bazaar[6] | |
| 9/8/1964 | New York, town hall (123 W. 43rd St.) | The Muslims Present an Evening with Max Roach and Abbey Lincoln | Max Roach, Abbey Lincoln, Clifford Jordan, Lonnie Smith, Coleridge Perkinson, plus Walter Davis Jr. Trio[7] |
| 4/4/1964 | Chicago, Trianon (62nd and Cottage) | African Asian unity bazaar | |
| 5/4/1964 | New York, Rockland Palace (155th and 8th Ave.) | African Asian bazaar[8] | Walter Dickerson Quartet, Walter Davis Trio, George Price and the Islanders Steel Band, speaker Minister James 3X[9] |
| 6/23/1964 | Newark, NJ, King Hiram Lodge (105 Broad St.) | African Asian unity bazaar | Samuel 8X and His Jazz Specialists, George Price and the Islanders Steel Band[10] |
| 10/27/1964 | Chicago, Trianon | African Asian unity bazaar[11] | |
| 5/4/1965 | Springfield, MA, Rialto Skating Rink (82 Walnut St.) | unity bazaar | Red Bruce's Jazz Trio; speaker Louis X[12] |

| Date | Location | Event | Performers |
|---|---|---|---|
| 10/26/1965 | Chicago, Trianon (62nd and Cottage) | benefit show | Julian Priester Quintette + 2, Quartette Très Bien[13] |
| 10/26/1965 | New York, 369th Armory (142nd and 5th Ave.) | gigantic unity bazaar | Walter Dickerson, Dinzulu, Blue Mitchell, Roy Haynes, George Price and the Islanders Steel Band, speaker Louis Farrakhan[14] |
| 5/31/1966 | Washington, DC, Radio Music Hall (815 V St. NW) | unity bazaar | Jiver's Jazz Combo, speaker Lonnie Shabazz[15] |
| Apr. 1967 | New York | unity bazaar | Quartet Shahid, Cecil Payne and group, George Price and the Islanders Steel Band[16] |

1. "Of Drums and Drummers," *Muhammad Speaks* 1, no. 14 (Sept. 15, 1962), p. 4.
2. "African Asian Bazaar," *Muhammad Speaks* 2, no. 3 (Oct. 31, 1962), p. 24.
3. "African Bazaar" (ad), *Muhammad Speaks* 2, no. 20 (June 21, 1963), p. 18.
4. "African Drummer Entertains Washington Mosque," *Muhammad Speaks* 2, no. 22 (July 19, 1963), p. 14.
5. "African Asian Bazaar" (ad), *Muhammad Speaks* 2, no. 22 (July 19, 1963), p. 14.
6. "African Asian Bazaar" (ad), *Muhammad Speaks* 2, no. 26 (Sept. 13, 1963), p. 19. The advertisement appeared a week late.
7. "The Muslims Present an Evening with Max Roach and Abbey Lincoln," *Muhammad Speaks* 3, no. 25 (Aug. 28, 1964), p. 14.
8. "Another Great African Asian Bazaar" (ad), *Muhammad Speaks* 3, no. 16 (Apr. 24, 1964), p. 17.
9. "Unity Bazaar" (ad), *Muhammad Speaks* 3, no. 17 (May 8, 1964), p. 15.
10. "African Asian Unity Bazaar" (ad), *Muhammad Speaks* 3, no. 19 (June 5, 1964), p. 20.
11. "African Asian Unity Bazaar," *Muhammad Speaks* 4, no. 2 (Oct. 9, 1964), p. 21.
12. "Unity Bazaar," *Muhammad Speaks* 4 (Apr. 30, 1965), p. 20.
13. "Benefit Show and Dinner," *Muhammad Speaks* 5 (Oct. 22, 1965), p. 4.
14. "The Muslims Present a Gigantic Unity Bazaar" (ad), *Muhammad Speaks* 5 (Oct. 15, 1965), p. 6.
15. "Unity Bazaar" (ad), *Muhammad Speaks* 6 (Nov. 11, 1966), p. 18.
16. "Record Unity Bazaar Throng Treated to Outstanding Musical Entertainment," *Muhammad Speaks* 7 (Apr. 21, 1967), p. 18.

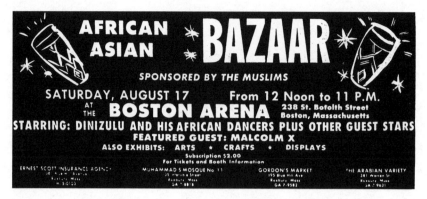

FIGURE 6.3. African Asian bazaar, "African Asian Bazaar" (ad). *Muhammad Speaks* (July 19, 1963), p. 14.

obtain funding to do research in Nigeria. He recorded *Drums of Passion* for Columbia in 1959, which proved to be an enormous success. Although it sold at least two hundred thousand copies, Olatunji had signed a contract that denied him royalties. He often appeared on double bills with first-rank jazz musicians, such as Charles Mingus (figure 6.4).[49]

Olatunji appeared at several African Asian bazaars sponsored by the Muslims and also at other NOI events. In 1963 he performed at a special fund-raising event for Washington's Mosque No. 4, at which he lectured about African music, commented on the racial situation in the United States, and performed with his troupe to an audience that included Sister Clara Muhammad, wife of Elijah Muhammad. He also attended a "unity party" in Chicago for Muhammad's University of Islam. The Nation of Islam's interest in African liberation movements and the cultural connection between African Americans, as well as its emphasis on economic self-determination, made it a strong forerunner of the themes taken up by cultural nationalists later in the decade. Several jazz musicians appeared at the African Asian bazaars and other Muslim events, including Walter Dickerson, Walter Davis Jr., Max Roach, Abbey Lincoln, Clifford Jordan, Julian Priester, Lonnie Smith, Blue Mitchell, and Roy Haynes (figures 6.5–6.7).

In December 1964 John Coltrane, Abbey Lincoln, Max Roach, and Bill Dixon performed a benefit for *Freedomways,* an influential journal devoted to politics, arts, and culture whose first editor was Shirley Graham Du Bois, wife of W.E.B. Du Bois (figure 6.8). The journal attracted contributions from across the political and artistic spectrum of the civil

FIGURE 6.4. "Olatunji and His Drums of Passion/the Charlie Mingus Quintet,"
Rutgers Institute of Jazz Studies, Topics files: handbills, New York jazz clubs, 1963.
Courtesy of Rutgers Institute of Jazz Studies.

FIGURE 6.5. The Muslims present Max Roach and Abbey Lincoln. *Muhammad
Speaks* (August 28, 1964), p. 14.

FIGURE 6.6. Gigantic unity bazaar. *Muhammad Speaks* (October 15, 1965), p. 6.

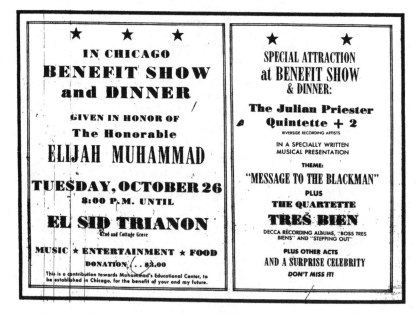

FIGURE 6.7. "Benefit Show and Dinner Given in Honor of the Honorable Elijah Muhammad." *Muhammad Speaks* (October 8, 1965), p. 16.

FIGURE 6.8. A holiday benefit for *Freedomways*. Rutgers Institute of Jazz Studies. Topics files: handbills, New York jazz clubs, 1964. Courtesy of Rutgers Institute of Jazz Studies.

rights and African liberation movements, including Martin Luther King, Ossie Davis, Paul Robeson, Kwame Nkrumah, Julius Nyerere, Julian Bond, Max Roach, Abbey Lincoln, and Harry Belafonte. Coltrane also appeared at a salute to Paul Robeson sponsored by *Freedomways* on April 22, 1965, on a roster that included Dizzy Gillespie, Olatunji, and Billy Taylor. Two years later Coltrane performed at Olatunji's Center of African Culture a few months before his death in 1967. Events such as these have not left a paper trail as deep as those for the principal civil rights organizations, but as Roswell Rudd recalls about his tours with Archie Shepp, it seemed like "every concert was a benefit."[50]

Jackie McLean, Archie Shepp, and Marion Brown appeared with Stokely Carmichael in a benefit for SNCC in December 1966 at the

Village Theater in New York. McLean recalls that A. B. Spellman appealed for his help: "A. B. Spellman came to my house one day and said 'Jackie, SNCC is in trouble. They're trying to raise some money. Do you think you can come to this theater?' . . . Anyway it was a big theater, and I called Billy [Higgins] up again, and the same band, Scottie Holt and Lamont Johnson. And we went to that theater that day, and Stokely came. And we played. And Archie played that day."[51]

McLean also recalls going to Brooklyn with Billy Higgins and Lee Morgan to play benefit concerts for the Black Panthers: "Billy and I, we were in the trenches. We used to go to Brooklyn and raise money for the Panthers. We used to go to Jersey for the Panthers. Go to Philadelphia. . . . Lee Morgan was another one. We used to go to Brooklyn and raise money for the Panthers. And we never got anything for that. We didn't expect anything. That was part of what we were supposed to do."[52]

It should no longer be surpising that McLean, with his roots in bebop, and Morgan, with his leading role in hard bop, were among those who played for the Black Panthers, but for those who equated only free jazz with black nationalism, McLean's and Morgan's participation was unexpected. Frank Kofsky, for example, found McLean's participation "so much the more notable" for this reason. "After all," he explained, "no one would have been particularly surprised had the benefit been planned by Archie Shepp or Cecil Taylor or Marion Brown or Bill Dixon, but *Jackie McLean?*" [emphasis in original].[53]


### Newark

McLean's commitment to using music in service of the African American community was no fluke. When the Newark rebellion erupted in July 1967, McLean mobilized his band again:

> The Newark riots took place on one day, the next day I got up and called Billy. The lawyer called me, a lady, I can't think of her name. Sister what always wore a hat. She's a famous lawyer. She called me and said "Jackie we need you to come to Newark. The fires are still burning, but we want you to come into a church and play so we can raise money to bail the people that got arrested yesterday in the riots and get them out." So I said, okay let me get on the phone.

So I called up my band. I called Billy, I said, "Billy it's no money in this, man, and we gonna work hard today. We're gonna play from noon until maybe six, almost straight to raise money to get these people out of jail." So it was Billy Higgins, Scottie Holt, and Lamont Johnson, and myself. We went over to Newark. We played from about twelve in the afternoon. Guys were coming in with bandages on their heads and arms broken. And everybody that they bailed out they brought to this place where we were playing and stood them up on the stage. We played all day.[54]

Newark was so *close* to New York. As protests spread across the nation's black communities between 1964 and 1967—with riots in Philadelphia, Watts, Chicago, Cleveland, Houston, Cincinnati, Nashville, Detroit, and Newark and across northern New Jersey—issues of racism could no longer be distanced as a Southern problem.

Newark had been a tinderbox throughout the spring and early summer. Activists were angry when Mayor Hugh Addonizio proposed using 150 acres of the predominantly black central wards as a site for a new medical school. They viewed the plan as a thinly veiled ploy to move African Americans out of the neighborhood and dilute their political power. When the secretary of the Board of Education retired, community activists proposed the city's budget director—an African American with a master's degree in accounting—for the position. The mayor, however, clung to his candidate—a white man with a high school education.

Since the Newark school system was seventy percent black, the community viewed this as a glaring affront. Even though in the end neither candidate was appointed (the incumbent decided to remain for another year), African American residents were furious over the mayor's refusal to appoint a highly qualified African American candidate. They were also angry that the mayor declined to create a police review board to investigate incidents of police brutality. The mayor instead transferred complaints to the FBI, which never seemed to follow through with the investigations. In May and June activists attended and sometimes disrupted city meetings to register their dissatisfaction with the city's policies and plans.

When John Smith, a black cab driver was arrested and beaten by the police on the evening of July 12, residents were not very reassured by Mayor Addonizio's promise that the incident would be thoroughly investigated. After a rally against police brutality on July 13, angry protesters threw rocks and bottles at the police station, many calling for "Black Power." After the police dispersed them, protesters began breaking into stores, particularly white-owned businesses along Springfield Avenue. The National Guard was called in on Friday, July 14, and over the next few days twenty-three people were killed in the rebellion (twenty-one black, two white) as Guardsmen and police shot looters. Several innocent bystanders were killed by stray bullets, including an elderly man, six women, and two children.

Throughout the rioting the police and Guardsmen claimed that they shot after being subjected to sniper fire. The U.S. Commission on Civil Disorders later found that, due to poor communications between the local police and the Guardsmen (they operated on different radio frequencies), much of what was presumed to be sniper fire in the midst of the rioting was actually Guardsmen mistaking police shots for sniper bullets and vice versa. The atmosphere of racial animosity was severe. As protesters targeted white-owned businesses they believed exploited their community, Guardsmen shot into stores displaying "soul brother" signs indicating that they were black owned.[55] Less than a week later the first of three annual Black Power Conferences was held in Newark, which led to a strong alliance between Maulana Karenga and Amiri Baraka, that ultimately led to the election of an African American mayor in Newark in 1970.[56]

Amiri Baraka's Spirit House was later singled out by the Commission on Civil Disorders as a locus of "Black Nationalists, Black Power advocates, and militants of every hue." Baraka was arrested and severely beaten at a police roadblock during the rioting for allegedly shooting at the police (even though there were no weapons in the car). He was forced to pay a $25,000 bond in order to be released, an amount that at that time was among the highest ever demanded for a similar offense. Friends of his mother put up their houses as collateral. Of the events in Newark he observed, "It was no riot, it was a rebellion."[57]

Baraka founded Spirit House (located at 33 Stirling Street) in 1966. It sponsored music, poetry readings, and intense debate on issues of Black Power and black nationalism. Baraka recalls that he had a "deep anti-white feeling" at the time and that the founding of Spirit House was in part to make up for the guilt he felt for his "long-term residence in and worship of the white elitist culture and aesthetic" (in Greenwich Village). The first major project of the center was the Afro-American Arts Festival, an idea inspired by the World Festival of Negro Arts sponsored by Leopold Senghor in Dakar, Senegal, in 1966. Stokely Carmichael, Harold Cruse, and Baba Oserjeman and his Yoruba Temple Dancers and Drummers were among the participants. Spirit House also published a literary magazine called *Afro-American Festival of the Arts,* which featured works by Larry Neal, Ben Caldwell, Sonia Sánchez, and others. In all of these endeavors, African American music was given the highest artistic and cultural significance.[58] As Baraka put it, "The fact of music was the black poet's basis for creation. And those of us in the Black Arts movement were drenched in black music and wanted our poetry to be black music."[59]

Black music, like Black Power, took on multivalent meanings as artists and audiences claimed the symbolic power of jazz for their particular purposes. Within the jazz world the debate over integration and Black Power was played out in tandem with the aesthetic debate over free jazz. Both revolutionary and cultural nationalists claimed the New Thing as a musical symbol of the transformation of African American consciousness and the ascendancy of Black Power. Yet, as this chapter has demonstrated, the political activism of jazz musicians during the civil rights and Black Power years took a wide variety of forms and included musicians that ranged from the most eminent, straight-ahead players to the prophets of jazz experimentalism.

# 7

# The Debate Within

## White Backlash, the New Thing, and Economics

A S THE LAST two chapters have shown, between 1960 and 1967 there was a regular rhythm between events in the political world and activism in various forms on the part of jazz musicians. At the same time, jazz musicians struggled and debated vociferously among themselves about the politics of race within the jazz world, the economic racism of the music industry, and the newly emerging aesthetics of what has variously been called free jazz, the New Thing, avant-garde jazz, freedom music, serious music, Great Black Music, and experimentalism.[1]

Although Frank Kofsky charged *Down Beat* magazine with censoring political debate in its pages, one of the most notable differences between the *Down Beat* of the 1950s and that of the 1960s is the amount of space devoted to public forums that aired intense and racially polarized debates on these themes.[2] Although these events frequently climaxed with deep divides between black and white participants, secondary splits often occurred as well—between older and younger musicians, between white advocates of color blindness and white leftists sympathetic to black nationalism, and between those for whom merit was measured in relationship to musical standards of mainstream jazz and those who advocated the unbounded experimentalism of the New Thing. This chapter analyzes two of these panel discussions—"Racial Prejudice in Jazz" (*Down Beat*, March 1962) and "Point of Contact" *(Down Beat Music '66)*—not only for what they reveal about the racial discourse of the 1960s but also for their on-going relevance to debates about music and race in the twenty-first century. I am not the only one to have analyzed theses debates, and I urge readers to also read the excellent accounts of Eric Porter and Farah Griffin.[3]

## Straight Ahead and Racial Prejudice in Jazz

On February 22, 1961, Abbey Lincoln took the lion's share of the *Freedom Now Suite* band into the studio to record an album under her own name titled *Straight Ahead*.[4] The album featured compositions and arrangements by Mal Waldron, Max Roach, Oscar Brown, Thelonious Monk, Randy Weston, and Julian Priester combining thick five-part horn voicings, poignant improvised solos, and shifting textures, with Lincoln's expressive voice and lyrics. The musical effect was modern, dramatic, and explicitly political through both song lyrics and Nat Hentoff's liner notes, which stress Lincoln's self-awareness as an African American as central to her artistic voice. Often celebrated in jazz writing today, the album was blasted in the pages of *Down Beat* in November 1961 by critic Ira Gitler, who accused Lincoln of "becoming a professional Negro," poor intonation, "banal" lyrics, excluding whites from the direct address of her album, and mistaking propaganda for art.

Gitler also passed judgment on her participation in an organization called the Cultural Association for Women of African Heritage (CAWAH) by suggesting that she was "misguided and naïve" in her interest in African Nationalism: "She is involved in African nationalism without realizing that the African Negro doesn't give a fig for the American Negro, especially if they are not blackly authentic. I would advise her to read *A Reporter at Large* in the May 13, 1961, issue of the *New Yorker* or talk to a Negro jazzman of my acquaintance who felt a strong draft on meeting African Negroes in Paris. Pride in one's heritage is one thing, but we don't need the Elijah Muhammed [*sic*] type of thinking in jazz."[5]

Although Gitler praised two of the seven compositions on the album—"Blue Monk" and "When Malindy Sings"—he found the album "subpar" and could not resist slamming the singer one more time at the close: "Now that Abbey Lincoln has found herself as a Negro, I hope she can find herself as a militant but less one-sided *American* Negro. It could help her performance."[6]

Although Gitler was known to be a feisty critic and had already generated several irate letters to the editor with his negative reviews of Dave Brubeck's *Time Out* and Cannonball Adderley's *Cannonball Adderley Quartet in San Francisco,* the review of *Straight Ahead* went far beyond his usual commentary.[7] According to the editors, *Down Beat* received three or four letters like the one from Clyde Taylor published on January 4, 1962, which argued that Gitler's review seemed "indelibly tinged with white supremacist convictions." In response to Gitler's put-down of *Straight Ahead* Taylor fired back:

> As the review proceeds, Gitler gets whiter and whiter, and the smug condescension thicker and thicker. His last statement that Abbey should stick to being an *"American* Negro" has so many malodorous connotations that it is only possible here to point out one: "Come off it, Abbey honey, and be a sweet little colored girl like the kind we taught you to be and expect you to be. We want you to be *our* little colored girl." If he knew anything about people, Gitler would be able to see that it is just this kind of basic disrespect that prompts Abbey Lincoln, and thousands of others like her, to look elsewhere for a point of view that will allow them a broader humanity.[8]

But the publication of this letter did not end the controversy, and so editor Don DeMichael organized a panel discussion at the *Down Beat* offices to explore the problem of racial prejudice in jazz. Two consecutive issues of *Down Beat* were devoted to an edited transcript of the discussion, which included several performers and critics—Abbey Lincoln, Max Roach, Ira Gitler, Nat Hentoff, Lalo Schifrin, Don Ellis, Bill Coss, and Don DeMichael.[9] The issues that dominated the discussion are all mainstays of interracial American conversations about race and music: (1) whether Abbey Lincoln was "exploiting" her blackness to further her career, (2) social versus biological explanations of cultural and musical difference, (3) the musical quality of *Straight Ahead* versus its political content, (4) whether reverse racism or "Crow Jim" existed in the jazz world, (5) who was entitled to evaluate or speak about jazz and the black experience, and (6) whether integration was an unproblematic social goal.

## "Professional Negro"?

Despite his obvious discomfort with Abbey Lincoln's politics, early in the panel discussion Gitler claimed that his two-star (out of a possible five-star) rating was based on the music alone. Lincoln disagreed: "You didn't rate it for the music alone. You couldn't have, because in the whole article you talked about me as a human being and about my attitudes which you can't possibly even know about, Ira. How can you?... What makes you come to all the conclusions that you came to? The Muhammed-type thinking. And you said I was a professional Negro, which is really funny. It is impossible for me to be a professional Negro because I *am* a black woman."[10]

After Gitler explained that he thought Lincoln was using the fact that she was Negro to "exploit a career," Max Roach asked, "Who knows more about the Negro than the Negro? If anybody has the right to exploit the Negro, it's the Negro. Everybody else up until this point has been exploiting the Negro. And the minute the Negro begins to exploit himself, even if this was so, here comes somebody who says they shouldn't exploit themselves. But who *should* exploit the Negro? Here's the point: she has a perfect right to exploit the Negro" (pp. 21–22).

Nat Hentoff agreed with Max Roach and told Gitler that his use of the term "professional Negro" was "really the worst kind of epithet because it immediately implies falseness, dishonesty" (p. 23). Later Abbey Lincoln referred to her earlier career as a supper club singer: "You know, when I *was* a professional Negro nobody seemed to mind.... There was a time when I was *really* a professional Negro. I was capitalizing on the fact that I was a Negro, and I looked the way Western people expect you to look. I wore ridiculous dresses, and I sang the songs that were expected. I was a professional Negro. I was not an artist. I had nothing to say. I used inane, stupid material on the stage. And as soon as I said, 'I don't want to do this anymore; I want to give the best that I have to the public,' they came down on me with all four feet" (p. 24).

## "Crow Jim"

The positions Lincoln and Roach took in the *Down Beat* panel were sharpened against the implicit and explicit charges made by critics Gitler and Don DeMichael that white musicians were discriminated against in the new political climate. Lincoln and Roach were called upon repeatedly to prove that they were not racist against whites, and, in response, they defended their right to speak from a privileged position by reason of their *social experience* as blacks. The central concern for many of the white participants was their belief that white musicians were not being hired by black musicians because of their race. "We might as well use the term Crow Jim," argued Don DeMichael. "To me, a lot of the Negro jazzmen have limited the people that they say swing—the people they will hire—to Negroes. They will say white guys don't swing, don't play jazz, and they have stolen our music." Lincoln added, "And they have," while DeMichael responded, "They haven't. I don't agree with you there" (p. 25). In the discussion that followed, Roach argued that the topic of African American hiring of other African Americans had been misunderstood: "They think the guys are shutting them out, but if a guy wants a *good* jazz player, nine times out of 10 he stands a better chance of getting him from the black population than from the white population because of exposure" (p. 25). Roach took great care to mention a black musician who immersed himself in classical music, had a doctorate in music, but could not swing because of insufficient exposure to jazz.

However, DeMichael was not satisfied: "You're saying we are a product of our social environment; therefore jazz is learned. Why would a Negro boy learn jazz better than a white boy?" Roach answered, "My son—he listens to records all day. From before he was born—in his mother's belly—that's all he's been hearing." DeMichael responded, "So has my son," and Roach affirmed his commitment to a social explanation by saying, "All right. Then he stands a chance" (p. 25).

The ability of Gitler and DeMichael to construct the white jazz musician in a "one down" position relative to black musicians, despite the structural economic advantages that white musicians had in the music industry (see chapter 2), as well as Max Roach's confidence that the better jazz musician would usually be the African American musician, emanates from the atypical social position of black music in American society. As Burton Peretti has noted, while the cultural practices of white Americans have been treated as the mainstream of U.S. history, in music "white jazz history is an appendix to an African-American mainstream."[11]

As the listening preferences of both African and non–African Americans of the 1950s and 1960s indicate, African American musicians increasingly set the aesthetic standards for the genre as a whole, served as heroes and idols to the vast majority of jazz listeners, and consequently tended to command the greatest cultural prestige and symbolic value (see chapter 3). When Max Roach suggested that the better jazz musician would usually be the African American musician, he inverted the usual race/merit associations in U.S. society and mobilized the cultural prestige of the music and racial associations to defend the hiring practices of his fellow musicians. But the suggestion that, by standards of merit alone, African American musicians might be justified in hiring predominantly black musicians was met by charges of reverse discrimination. Most of the white participants, including Gitler, agreed with Roach that excellent white jazz musicians existed, but they were the exception rather than the rule (pp. 25, 26).

Since the charge of reverse racism and the debate about ethnic particularity versus color blindness are two of the key discursive impasses in interracial conversations about race, jazz, and merit, it may be helpful to see how the conversation unfolded at this moment in 1962. Early in the conversation Roach suggested that Gitler did not write his review as if he "even understood what [experiences] a Negro goes through." Gitler replied that "I haven't experienced them because I'm not a Negro, but I understand some of them" and later added that his understanding came from having "been close to a lot of Negroes." Roach took the position that "you cannot understand it like I can."

Roach and Lincoln both sought some kind of acknowledgement from their interlocutors that there was something *special* about their relationship to African American music and American racism by virtue of their social experience as African Americans. Roach argued his case by offering an example from another ethnic group (to which Gitler and Hentoff belonged): "I would have to spend a lifetime as a person who didn't come up under Judaism in studying it to get remotely close to what you really fell like when millions get murdered or something. I didn't feel the same way you do. And you can't feel something that happened in the South the way I feel it" (p. 22).

Lalo Schifrin interjected that there was a "human level" beyond ethnic affiliation and that "there are basic feelings of human beings that could happen in any kind of race" (p. 22). Don DeMichael, who had written a rapturous review of Lincoln's previous album, *Abbey Is Blue,* two years earlier, sought affirmation from Lincoln about a previous conversation they had had: "But when we talked in Chicago, you remember our talking about not the struggle for just one man but for all men?" Lincoln replied: "I'm for that. Yet my struggle first is for my people" (p. 22). Max Roach distinguished between the ideal of universalism in the future and the practical realities of the day: "That's a socialist dream, Don. . . . But this is not a dream. We're not dreaming. What you're talking about is a dream. We all would hope for something like that, but in the meantime we have to go on the street. We have to react."

Nat Hentoff supported Lincoln and Roach and added that a "period of catharsis" was to be expected:

> I don't think it's realistic to expect the American Negro right now to expend any energy, or any significant amount of energy, toward working for "all of mankind." There's just so much that has to be done right now. If the kids in the South—and I speak especially of the ones I know in the Student Nonviolent Co-ordinating Committee, who are to the left of Martin Luther King in terms of direct action right now . . . They've thought it out. And sure, they're for unilateral disarmament and other kinds of supranational concerns, but right now they're in the South because that's the area of focus for a Negro, and I think if I were a Negro, I'd feel the same way. And it seems to me that another aspect of this that no one's brought out is that it's also unrealistic not to expect a period of catharsis for the American Negro—a period where all the rage and bitterness and anger and torment has to get out. I think it's very healthy that it gets out in the music and in writing and in all those areas. (p. 23)[12]

Gitler voiced agreement with Hentoff's statement, but then went on to say, "I felt she was leaning too much on her Negritude in this album" (p. 23). Lincoln asked, "How did you come to that conclusion? What did the material say? Randy Weston's "African Lady," that said anything about being black. The rest of the tunes—it all depends on how you listen to them—were about social conditions. 'Straight Ahead' [the album's title track] would apply to anybody" (p. 23).

It turns out that it was Nat Hentoff's liner notes rather than the lyrics to the songs underlay Gitler's reasons for his political commentary. The liner notes emphasized Lincoln's new consciousness as an African American woman and interest in African nationalism:

What particularly struck me...were the power and emotional range of Abbey's singing and her vividly personal timbre and phrasing. There is also a deeper capacity to become totally part of a song. When the material calls for scraping harshness or even growling (at the close of "African Lady"), there is no attempt to compromise and try to keep at least a partly "pretty" sound. Similarly when the song speaks of sensuality, that's all there too—not coyly, but with the impact of remembered hunger. This is a *woman* singing, and more specifically, it is a Negro woman, because part of the striking liberation of Abbey's singing has come from a renewed and urgent pride in herself as a Negro. Like Max Roach, who has been a vital force in her musical development, Abbey is intensely involved in the movement for equality here and is also absorbed in the whirlpool of African nationalism. She is, in fact, president of the Cultural Association for Women of African Heritage. A few nights after this album was completed, I went to the Carnegie Endowment International Center to hear James Baldwin and several African nationalists speak. I was not surprised to see Abbey and Max in the audience.[13]

What delighted and interested Nat Hentoff, however, set off alarm bells for Ira Gitler, who belittled Lincoln's interest in African nationalism as "misguided and naïve" (probably not words he would have used to describe Roach or Mingus) and equated it with "Elijah Muhammad–type thinking" (which perhaps illustrated his own misguidedness and naivety about the relationship between the two).

The Cultural Association for Women of African Heritage was a short-lived organization that Abbey Lincoln formed in the early 1960s. As Lincoln recalled, "It's an organization that I formed, and one of the stipulations was that the women would wear African hairstyles and we would we would explore our culture, our African ancestors."[14]

Among the members were Maya Angelou and Rosa Guy. Their most widely publicized event was the silent protest held in the UN general assembly on February 15, 1961, to protest the assassination of Patrice Lumumba of the Congo. During Adlai Stevenson's remarks in support of Dag Hammarskjöld (whom many held responsible for Lumumba's death) a contingent of women in mourning veils and men with black armbands stood silently to protest. A struggle occurred when security guards attempted to remove them from the gallery, and the incident was described as a "riot" on the front page of the *New York Times* the following day. Meanwhile, what had been planned as a small symbolic event had been transformed into an enormous demonstration in the streets outside the UN. Much to the surprise of the women of the Cultural Association for Women of African Heritage, their appearance at Oscar Micheaux's bookstore in Harlem the night before had inspired an enormous number of people to head downtown to protest the killing of Lumumba and the UN's role in the Congo.[15]

The *New York Times* described the event as "the most violent demonstration inside United Nations headquarters in the world organization's history" and seemed determine to cast the demonstrators as African nationalist separatists who turned away would-be white picketers. The demonstrators marched westward along Forty-second Street and were charged by mounted policemen as they approached Times Square. Lincoln recalls that the NBC television news program with Chet Huntley falsely reported that the demonstrators inside the UN carried bicycle chains and brass knuckles.[16]

## Exclusion

The biggest fear expressed by the white participants in the *Down Beat* panel discussion was that of being excluded by African Americans, musicians in particular. At one point Abbey Lincoln was asked point-blank by Bill Coss whether she believed in separatism: "First, I'd like to qualify this by saying, Bill, this is a very personal thing—whether I do or whether I don't—it's like your religion, but I would like to say it just does not happen to be true. I'm not that idiotic that I'd dislike people because of the color of their skin. I dislike what white people have done to my people. Intensely" (p. 24).

At a broader level of social analysis, the white fear of exclusion (by the excluded) is quite ironic, but at another it speaks to the exceptional cultural place of African American music in U.S. culture. For despite the phenomenon of white ownership of record companies and magazines, the cultural, moral, and musical capital in the jazz world was increasingly defined by its African American heroes. Many of the white participants in the panel discussion—Don DeMichael and Bill Coss in particular—seemed to long for Lincoln and Roach to validate their participation in jazz and did so by trying to get them to affirm a universalist "above and beyond" race perspective. However, the more the non–African Americans insisted on a rhetoric of color blindness, the more Roach and Lincoln (and often their ally, Nat Hentoff) insisted on a rhetoric of autonomy.[17]

Indeed, as things became even more polarized in the debate, Max Roach seemed to confirm their worst fears. After having pointed out that the bitterness of African Americans toward white Americans was "a natural thing," Max Roach imagined a hypothetical race war: "Look, the revolution starts between black and white, say if it got that bad. . . . We've all got guns against each other. No matter how I feel about you, I'm going to have to shoot because white guys over there are going to shoot everything black, and black guys are going to shoot everything white. Where am I going to go, man? . . . The best way would be to be with your people if there's a black and white war" (p. 25). At that point the transcript of the panel discussion stops and is replaced by the word "HUBBUB."

After the discussion resumed, they tried to talk about integration. Of the white participants, only Nat Hentoff seemed to be unthreatened by the most provocative statements made by Lincoln and Roach and, like other young white radicals of his generation, articulated a leftist class analysis in arguing for a more thoroughgoing transformation of U.S. society. "If Negroes equate with the whites in accepting the economic system as it is, in accepting the political system as it is, then I don't think integration will have done Negroes enough good" (p. 25). Although the panel discussion ended on a note of unity, Hentoff described the atmosphere at the event as "tense, tense, tense."[18]


## Some Larger Points

As I mentioned in chapter 5, I am less interested in whether racially essentialist positions were taken in these debates than in the situational circumstances that made the racial divide at times rigid and uncrossable and at others more porous and tolerant. African Americans often reacted to cultural insensitivity or white power plays by drawing the racial boundary more firmly, while whites frequently charged reverse racism in response to African Americans' emphasis on self-determination and black cultural identity. The insistence of many of the white participants in the panel discussion on racial prejudice in jazz that Lincoln and Roach embrace a universal interracial vision of the future only succeeded in provoking Lincoln and Roach to draw the line between black and white more deeply. Lincoln and Roach wanted the panel members to recognize that being black mattered and gave them a special vantage point on the experience of racism. They also wanted them to support the validity of expressing that viewpoint on *Straight Ahead.* Instead they were accused of being exclusionary and reverse racists:

> LINCOLN: Why is it that because I love my people and I want human dignity, must I be a racist? Why is that I say to you, Don, Dizzy Gillespie is a great musician. Does that mean that you are inferior? This is the whole thing. Because I say my people are worthwhile and should be free, does this mean I hate the white man?
> BILL COSS: No, Abbey, it only means that if you say *only* my people can be.
> LINCOLN: Only? That's true. But have I ever said this? (p. 23)

The crucial issue in exchanges like this, it seems to me, is that the denial of black difference is experienced as a white power play that does not acknowledge the larger structural and economic situation in the music industry. In an article written a few months later for *Muhammad Speaks,* Max Roach explained the economic history underlying his disbelief in the charge of reverse discrimination and his advocacy of black economic self-determination: "How can those who charge 'crow jim' explain the very 'healthy' living and fame gained through jazz by (to name a few) Dave Brubeck, Stan Kenton, Gerry Mulligan, Shelly Manne, Stan Getz, Gene Krupa, Anita O'Day, Al Hirt, Benny Goodman, [Buddy] Rich, Jack Teagarden, and June Christy? How can they explain that so few Negroes (of a great majority of fine artists) can boast the same kind of money the white artists are privileged to make? In what other society can an artist be so flagrantly plagiarized, ignored, and deprived and still be cast as the 'heavy'?"[19]

During the panel discussion Roach tried to articulate a two-tiered social analysis of racial difference during a consideration of the musical differences between black and white. He, on the one hand, expressed his belief that there were no inherent racial differences but, on the other, argued that the social system created differences that were very real and had to be acknowledged:

But actually, I believe that there is no difference. But because of society . . . Do you know what the social system is? The black man is here, and the white man is there. So we get a chance to operate at one level to our fullest capacity, and you get a chance to operate at another. So we both contribute different things because we are not together. . . . But society today makes it different—not because you're black or he's white—given the same tools, we'd all be straight. But society puts you over here, puts him over there, so, consequently, your contribution is in very different degrees. You do best what you have to work with here, and he does best with what he has to work with over there.[20]

This is similar to what I have been arguing throughout *Freedom Sounds,* namely that (1) in a racially stratified society, structural differences remain even though musical aesthetics have spread beyond their original borders, (2) through musical and social practice people mobilize the resources and discourses available to them in order to cope with the situation, and (3) acknowledging these differences is key to developing a more productive interracial conversation about race, power, music, and social vision in the twenty-first century.

For years I have taught courses in African American music and watched my students fall into disputes that reproduce many of the arguments voiced in the 1962 debate on racial prejudice in jazz. Perhaps the most common conflict that continually reemerges is the one set off by white students (and/or other non–African Americans) when they insist that music is colorblind and that African American claims of a *special* relationship to the music by virtue of being African American is exclusionary or essentialist. In trying to explain to the white students why this is such an irritating question for many African Americans, I ask them whether they can think of any other ethnic group that is asked so regularly to deny their ethnic particularity? Are Italians decried as essentialist if they express a feeling of special relationship to Italian opera and the various Italian cultural values and practices in which it is historically embedded? Are women asked not to feel a special relationship to menstruation, childbirth, and the experience of sexism by virtue of being women? Are Irish Americans asked not to feel a special relationship to Saint Patrick's Day even though it has long since become a generalized American event? So when white students in my courses feel excluded when their African American classmates express a special connection to the history and culture of African American music, are they being fair?

I don't think so. To many non–African Americans, the African American claim of a special relationship to the music feels like a guilt trip in which they are made to feel personally responsible for the entire history of racism in the United States. Hence many white students would like to deny that race matters or focus on their own feelings of injury when their African American classmates insist that they have a privileged relationship to African American music. In moving past this logjam it is imperative for non–African Americans to think more analytically and less personally about their relationships to African American music and the way they are embedded in larger structural and discursive histories.

One issue to think about is the rather circumscribed set of interests that non–African Americans often have in African American culture. To put it bluntly, white Americans since the 1960s seem to have been interested primarily in the *fun* parts of African American culture: music, dance, sports, fashion, and that elusive quality of hipness. There seems to be no parallel desire among non–African Americans to share the experience of attending a bad inner-city school, getting racially profiled on the New Jersey Turnpike, having a greater chance of being (or having a relative) incarcerated, or having one's home appreciate less because it is located in a black neighborhood. This is simply to say that it is only respectful to acknowledge real social differences and the historical circumstances that have produced them, as well as the different individual needs—psychological, cultural, political, and social—that various constituencies bring to the musical table. It is easier to acknowledge shared ground when power differences are not ignored and easier to avoid making a fetish of difference when the complexity of discourses and social practices that people use to *break out* of the socially imposed limits of their categories are kept in mind.

One discursive weapon that some African Americans have used to defend their ground in interracially conflictual conversations is to assert that white Americans' relationships to the music are not real in the way they are for African Americans and that that white players and audiences can therefore succeed only in being imitators. Yet, since it is virtually impossible for an American to grow up in the United States without hearing African American music (on TV, radio, Internet, or live) and consequently without developing a relationship to it, how can non–African American aficionados of jazz and other African American types of music be expected to view themselves as simply outsiders? It is quite possible, after all, for whites, Asians, Latinos, and members of any other constituency to have *real* relationships to the repertory and their own extensions of them without having to assert that those relationships are exactly the *same* as those of African Americans. Yet what frequently provokes the denunciation of whites as mere imitators is precisely white refusal to allow African Americans the right to celebrate their special contribution to this repertory and history and to find solace in this cultural legacy.

## Gender

One of the ironies of the fact that a review of *Straight Ahead* occasioned this outpouring of racial angst is that it is a far less explicitly political album than Max Roach's *We Insist! Freedom Now Suite*. In order for the refrain on the tune "Straight Ahead" to be heard as a commentary on race ("For some this road is smooth and easy/Travelin' high without a care/But if you got to use the back roads/Straight ahead can lead nowhere"), it is the listener who must supply the social context. The same is true for "Retribution," whose chorus ("Just let the retribution/Match the contribution, baby"), follows the verse "Don't want no silver spoon/Ain't askin' for the moon/Give me nothing/Don't want no favors done." These are for the most part indirect political commentaries even though "Miss Lucy," from James Weldon Johnson's text, is said to make only "noise," in comparison to the "notes a-flyin' " in "When Malindy Sings," and the lyrics to "African Lady" speak portentously of the awakening of the African continent.

Yet, it is not accidental that Ira Gitler found himself unloading his anxiety about black militancy in jazz on this album. As a singer and a woman, Lincoln was a far more vulnerable target for musical and political criticism than Max Roach or Charles Mingus, whose politically outspoken work he did not demean.[21] Neither singers nor women have enjoyed the same prestige as their instrumentalist male colleagues, and Lincoln was not widely known at the time despite having previously recorded four albums under her own name.[22] Gitler had been particularly harsh about Lincoln's pitch stability: "Her bad intonation could be excused if it led toward the achievement of something positive," read the review.[23]

Lincoln is far from the only jazz musician to have been accused of "bad intonation": Billie Holiday, Betty Carter, Ornette Coleman, and many others have also received this criticism. Since pitch shading is an important expressive resource in blues and jazz, the notion of a pure standard of intonation against which musicians should be judged is itself problematic, for the Western tempered scale is a compromise with the overtone series to begin with.[24] When the question of whether Lincoln sang out of tune on the album emerged in the debate, Roach defended her: "She didn't sing out of tune on any of the tunes" (p. 23). Yet there are moments in several of the pieces when she *is* vulnerable to the charge of poor intonation despite the fact that the overall dramatic power of Lincoln's delivery against the haunting timbral colors of the band more than compensates. The most striking examples are the second line of "In the Red" ("Can't raise a dime"), when she never seems to fully center on the sustained pitch on the final word (0:27–0:30), and her shaky initial entrance on "Straight Ahead," which is done with bass alone as accompaniment.

However, these were very difficult and unusual arrangements for a singer. As Lincoln recalled in 1995, "It was just difficult to sing the album. It wasn't fun to sing because there was so much in the arrangements. And a lot of it was discordant."[25] Take the opening two phrases of "In the Red," which required Lincoln to enter on the #9 of an A7#9b13 chord, descend chromatically, and then leap a tritone to a sustained pitch on the ninth of the chord (figure 7.1).[26]

Although Lincoln is quite flat on the final G# the first time the melody appear, when it reappears later in the piece (2:47), it is in tune.[27] Booker Little's arrangement of this piece, which used extended harmonies throughout and often voiced the altered parts of the harmonies above the vocal line, were not exactly singer friendly. Indeed, Little seems to have wanted

FIGURE 7.1. "In the Red," opening phrase, Abbey Lincoln, *Straight Ahead,* New York, February 22, 1961, Candid CD 79015. Used by permission of Milma Publishing.

FIGURE 7.2. "Straight Ahead," first entrance of Abbey Lincoln, *Straight Ahead,* New York, February 22, 1961, Candid CD 79015. Used by permission of Milma Publishing.

to make the arrangement challenging. Lincoln recalled that "Booker said to me after we recorded it, 'I didn't think you could sing it.' And I thought, 'I wonder why he would write something he didn't think I could sing?' He was like that."[28]

In "Straight Ahead," Lincoln's first entrance is a bit tentative, but then Art Davis's bass line, which created a tritone between the voice and the bass on syllable "head," did not provide much tonal support (figure 7.2). However, the second time around (0:55), when the accompaniment is fuller and the bass line more tonally supportive, her pitch is strong and stable.

Lincoln does not view *Straight Ahead* or the *Freedom Now Suite* as her best work and in 1995 looked back at the 1960s as a time when she was not in full control of the artistic process. "I picked the songs, but I had nothing to do with the arrangements, but things have really changed now because I wouldn't let anybody do that to me again!" When asked whether the intervening years had taught her how to take better control, she said, "Defend myself. Yeah, because that's what you have to do. For the most part it's a man's music. The men bring you into it. And sometimes they will help you. They will gather and help you to get through. So I always had a lot of encouragement from Thelonious Monk, people like that. John Coltrane, Charles Mingus, and especially from Roach, who gave me the impression that he knew that I had great talent. But, I don't know, when I look back and think about some things, it turns me off a little."[29]

## Aftermath

The careers of both Abbey Lincoln and Max Roach suffered in the aftermath of the Racial Prejudice in Jazz panel discussion. Lincoln did not record another album under her leadership until 1973, and Roach, who had recorded twenty-one albums under his own name between 1953 and 1960, recorded only eleven between 1961 and 1971.[30] It is clearly Abbey Lincoln's career that took the biggest hit. Although the jazz industry in general declined in the same period, no doubt their outspokenness coded both of them as "difficult" in the music industry. Ira Gitler was denounced at a meeting of the Jazz Artists Guild (the group that had grown out of the Newport Rebel Festival), and they discussed sending a letter to *Down Beat* asking for his removal, but nothing ever came of it. He does not feel that his participation in the panel discussion or the original review adversely affected his journalistic career.[31]

One of the most enjoyable parts of my research for this book was the opportunity to interview several of people involved in the Racial Prejudice in Jazz discussion, including Abbey Lincoln, Max Roach, Nat Hentoff, and Ira Gitler. They all offered reflections on the dialogue and looked back on those years in different ways. Toward the end of my interview with Max Roach, I gave him a photocopy of the panel discussion transcript, and he took a moment to read parts of it. He laughed and said, "Sounds just like you, Roach" and added that he and Gitler were still friends even though he thought Gitler continued to believe that music and politics were separate: "Ira could never take it seriously. 'Max, [he would say], 'what has politics got to do with music?' What has breathing got to do with life? Living, you know, what's happening.'"[32]

A few moments later his eyes spotted a photograph of Abbey Lincoln glaring at Ira Gitler that had been taken the night of the debate. He laughed again and said, "She's like, now what the hell is he talking about? Does he know what he's saying? Does he know what he's saying? I don't remember who set it up [the panel discussion], but it was a great idea. And that argument still prevails.... [He reads some more] Wow, no wonder she jumped down his throat. She's looking at him so strange. He ends the article by saying, 'Now that Abbey Lincoln has found herself as a Negro, I hope she can find herself as a militant but less one-sided American Negro. It could help her performance!'"

Roach seemed very nostalgic about Lincoln even though it had been some thirty years since their divorce. Recalling the duos they had done together he was rapturous: "When she opens her mouth to sing...it's perhaps my imagination, [but] I literally have at times seen the sound that comes from her body. I see the sound. I'd not only hear it but see it. She's phenomenal.... She to me is in the realities of life."

He also admired her ability to come up with a clever response in racial situations and told a story about an interview in Canada in which Lincoln had been talking about herself as a black woman. The interviewer had asked her why she kept referring to herself as black when she was not really black (and held up a black object for comparison). Lincoln had responded in a flash, "Well, I call myself black for the same reason you call yourself white, [and] you're not really white." Mr. Roach laughed and said, "She knocks me out. She's fast as greased lightning" and added that she was an "awfully gifted woman" and very serious.

Nat Hentoff was not particularly interested in commenting on the debate itself and focused instead on the making of the recordings and Candid records (see chapter 5).[33] Ira Gitler was clearly a bit sheepish about the panel and regrets using words like "exploit" and "Negritude" but held to his musical opinion of the album. He says he does not believe that music and politics are separate but thinks that any project has to be "musically valid first": "Now, Mingus was able to be very political, but the music was powerful, and it worked. When it's just for the purpose of [politics], then it doesn't work. I don't think they can be separate. . . . There are people who are apolitical, but, you know, being black in America, I don't think you can avoid it. So I think they intertwine, but the end result is in the music, if you want to know. That's my attitude."[34]

Since Gitler liked the music of the *Freedom Now Suite* and did not object to its politics, he thought the conflagration over his review of *Straight Ahead* was less about the racial attitudes than his criticism of Lincoln's singing: "I still say that the crux of that anger . . . I could understand her being angry, you know, the 'professional Negro' phrase and my criticisms, but I think the crux of it was I criticized her singing. . . . Naturally, if you're an artist and somebody gives you a bad review, you don't like it."

When I asked him whether he would take back anything that he said during the discussion, he answered, "No, I was just trying to be honest and just trying to say the way I felt. . . . I said, 'You can't feel it in the same way, but you can certainly understand it because it's being done to human beings.' I wouldn't take back any of the things I said in the dialogue. It's just that at the beginning especially I felt like really put upon and felt I had to defend myself."

The degree to which some of his comments in the panel discussion were racially offensive and might warrant an apology was not part of his way of thinking about it. In the end, by virtue of his long track record of writing liner notes and jazz journalism that advocated and celebrated the contributions of many African American musicians, he did not view himself as somebody who "oppressed black people." He pointed out that, even after the Racial Prejudice in Jazz discussion, Max Roach had agreed to be interviewed for Gitler's book *Jazz Masters of the Forties* and that he had been invited to Lincoln and Roach's wedding.[35] The fact that his position within the jazz world as a journalist and critic may have made it in Lincoln and Roach's best interest to maintain cordial relations was not part of his analysis. Yet it is also true that, because they all had mutual stakes in the music industry and had longer track records with one another, some of the tension could be diffused over time. Gitler put it this way: "But, see, the jazz world may be a microcosm of the greater world, but this is one of the places where for years there was genuine give and take between blacks and whites as people. It wasn't perfect, and there was prejudice there on both sides but not to the extent of our greater society. Because, you know the old saw, when you get to know someone, you can't hate them. What you don't know you can hate."

## Abbey Lincoln Looks Back

Abbey Lincoln's recollections of the 1960s were the most complicated. When I formally interviewed her in 1995, I was surprised both by her unwillingness to claim the role of heroine and by the deep criticism she expressed toward political activists of the 1960s, especially those who had failed to live up to the movement's ideals. I had expected a more triumphant narrative (such as I heard from several men), which would seem to better fit the image of the woman who sang about "All Africa" in the *Freedom Now Suite*, asked for "Retribution" on *Straight Ahead*, and played the female lead in Michael Roemer's power film about the South, *Nothing but a Man.* Her critique was at times searing: "I look back at that time, and I think, well, I'm not sorry for anything. I did what was in my heart. And I was right, too. I'm disappointed, though, that for many people it was only another opportunity to be seen and heard. . . . That's why there's not a mumbling word anymore. You don't hear anybody saying anything. They all want some money. . . . When I think of putting my career on the line for this mentality, it makes me angry sometimes."[36]

Her criticism was directed not toward the political ideals of the civil rights movement or black pride but rather toward those who did not live up to their communal obligations, those who later made it economically but failed to give anything back to the black community, and those whose vulgar or stereotyped performances "cursed their ancestors" for nothing but material gain. "Nothing for the children. This is the outcome of all these things that people did and died [for]. I mean, people died and went through hell." In her opinion this materialist mentality disgraces the memory of those who sacrificed their lives for the movement, including people like Martin Luther King and Malcolm X.

Lincoln's hard-edged look back at her own passage through the civil rights years is from the vantage point of someone who prefers her later years: "So I like my later years, these years, my mature years. They're the most peaceful and introspective and rewarding of all my life. I don't suffer from the fears that I had as young woman."

Although she had been willing to discuss her early career in considerable detail when I interviewed her in 1995 (and what she told me parallels what she has told other interviewers),[37] when she was celebrated at a conference at Columbia University in December 2001, she adamantly preferred to be known only for her present-day career: "Don't treat me like I'm already dead. Talk about what I'm doing today!"[38] This, of course, puts a person who is writing a historical work in a difficult situation.

Even though in 2001 Lincoln bridled at the mention of the *Freedom Now Suite* and *Straight Ahead* and did not consider them to be her best work, from a historical point of view there is no denying the impact and power of these albums and the role of her voice in making them so. But she does not want them presented as defining moments in her career and or in who she is today. As she said in 1995, "I don't scream anymore. I sing about my life. The songs I sing are about the life I've had. So I was just practicing then. . . . I feel accomplished [now] too, because I've learned to be a writer. I sing the songs that I write. I don't sing anybody else's material for the most part except for some old standards every once in a while. And I've become a composer as well. And I feel sufficient to myself as far as the music is concerned. And I'm glad those days are behind me."

One of Lincoln's main reasons for not wanting to revisit the 1960s is her ex-husband Max Roach. She emphasizes that she had a successful career both before and after her marriage in part to counter the tendency of some to portray her as the *creation* of Max Roach.[39] As many women in jazz have discovered, it can be hard to get credit for being a whole person and making one's own aesthetic choices even when one pays the political and economic consequences more deeply than the men. In 2001 Lincoln was adamant about emphasizing how oppressive men were to her the 1960s and did not want that truth buried in a "same-old" retelling of the glories of civil rights and Black Power years: "When I discovered God was also female, I freed myself, you know. That's when I found my freedom. I said to my mother once, 'Momma . . . if God is everything, it would have to be at least he and she, wouldn't it? If there is any such thing as God, it is male and female.' And when I took my power, I have had a better life ever since."

However reluctant Lincoln may have been to revisit the 1960s, from the vantage point of history it would be criminal not to draw attention to the contribution of her voice to political consciousness in jazz during that era. For a time, after all, Lincoln's voice virtually embodied the sound of the new black woman, the new black person in America: strong proud, assertive, honest, and creative. Her turn toward a more outspoken repertory occurred before Nina Simone's, and she was virtually alone in her generation of jazz singers in taking up the political gauntlet.[40] In addition, the panel discussion in *Down Beat* brought into the open a whole host of interracial tensions that needed airing in the worst way. Over the next four years, several more panel discussions were held on the issues of race, jazz, and economics. Dialogues like these are rare today. Lincoln's willingness to confront what she felt to be an unfair review and allow the panel discussion to be published in *Down Beat* was a remarkably brave thing to do in 1962. As she has said, "I'm an outspoken person, and I've discovered over the years that most people are not. They think things but never say them because they have ambitions. They're afraid that their ambitions will be wrecked if they come clean and tell you what's in their heart."[41]

One of the most powerful things about Abbey Lincoln is the way she presses you to think more profoundly and more honestly than you did before you encountered her. Whether one encounters her on the stage, on a recording, or in conversation, her deep presence and intensity can knock you right off your feet. Nat Hentoff once put it like this: "Abbey has an integrity that can cut your head off."[42] Some forty years after the civil rights movement, as later generations long for an uncomplicated narrative of heroism and triumph and many writers are tempted to deliver it, Lincoln asks us to dig deeper in the search for the truth and meaning of those years. Though many of us in younger generations would like her to claim the mantle of revolutionary African American heroine—which I emphasize is our need, not hers—she has made it very clear that she will not stand for it.

## The Cultural Vanguard

Three years after the Racial Prejudice in Jazz debate, *Down Beat* sponsored an even more rancorous discussion among several musicians (Cecil Taylor, Cannonball Adderley, Archie Shepp, Sonny Murray, and Roland Kirk) and the owner of the Village Gate, Art D'Lugoff. Dan Morgenstern, an associate editor of the magazine, moderated the session and asked the participants to discuss the ostensibly innocuous question of "the jazz scene today." What ensued was an intense debate over the New Thing, why it was not being booked in jazz clubs, economics and race, divisions within the new black music, and the racial composition of its audience. Cecil Taylor set the tone by beginning his remarks with a call for a boycott: "I propose that there should be a boycott by Negro musicians of all jazz clubs in the United States. I also propose that there should be a boycott by Negro jazz musicians of all the record companies. I also propose that all Negro jazz musicians boycott all trade papers and journals dealing with music. And I also propose that all Negro musicians resign from every federated union in this country that has anything to do with music."[43]

Archie Shepp agreed with Cecil Taylor's position and went on to critique jazz impresarios for knowing nothing about the music, exploiting the artists who have made the clubs possible, and failing to hire the leading representatives of the jazz avant-garde. As the discussion unfolded it became apparent that both Taylor and Shepp viewed themselves as part of an artistic vanguard whose mission was to inspire the audience, critics, and club owners to rise to their level. The skillful combination of the discourses of avant-garde modernism, black self-determination, anticommercialism, and anticapitalism was at once brash, demanding, and vulnerable to charges of inconsistency and being self-serving.

Amiri Baraka was a key theorist of the revolutionary potential of the new black music, but so were several musicians, including Cecil Taylor, Archie Shepp, and Bill Dixon. For Baraka, the music of Ornette Coleman, Cecil Taylor, and others represented the fruit of "the Negro's fluency with some of the canons of formal Western nonconformity, which was an easy emotional analogy to the three hundred years of unintentional nonconformity his color constantly reaffirmed." Baraka argued that, through this engagement with European concepts of art and bohemianism, African American jazz musicians had been able to reject the "shoddy cornucopia of American popular culture" and make of their alienation high art.[44]

Yet the fundamental idea that modern musical abstraction, with its dissonance and atonality, is radical or revolutionary shared a great deal with European and Marxist presumptions about the relationship between art, politics, and form. Georgina Born argues that the association of an avant-garde with a leftist social revolution has its origins in the French socialism of the nineteenth century and that it was amplified by the suppression of modernist art in Nazi Germany and Stalinist Russia. After World War II, the abstract musical modernism of the serialism in Europe was widely viewed as antifascist and antitotalitarian.[45]

Theodor Adorno, who provided many of the legitimizing philosophical arguments for this position, saw abstraction and disruption as essential aspects of the modern social life: "Scars of damage and disruption are the modern's seal of authenticity; by their means, art desperately negates the closed confines of the ever-same; explosion is one of its invariants." The social contractions of contemporary social life furthermore manifested themselves in formal musical expression: "The unsolved antagonisms of reality return in artworks as immanent problems of form."[46] The new jazz vanguard of the early 1960s seemed to accept this presumption about the relationship between structures of musical expression and politics. The idea that a radical break from the mainstream jazz conventions of chord changes, timbral color, chorus structures, and the playing of standards symbolized a radical political or racial consciousness, circulated widely in the jazz world of the early 1960s.

In many ways European discourses of art, bohemianism, and revolution were especially useful in providing a way for advocates of the new music to position themselves above the "white middle-brow" tastes of jazz critics and other white jazz fans.[47] By using European critiques of mainstream America's lack of artistic sensibility, Baraka attacked those who failed to see the deeper implications of this musical revolution and intellectually one-upped white jazz critics and other representatives of the capitalist music business. That the advocates of serious music viewed the combination of African America and European concepts of art as beneficial to American music in general is apparent in this comment by Jeanne Phillips: "The music says what's really happening here. And now that the Negro has become more educated and the Negro musician has learned all the techniques of European classical music, then it's the Negro musician who keeps the culture of America alive. Because America doesn't have any other culture of its own, except what the Negro gave it and what it borrowed from Europe, and I think Europe is dead."[48]

Through the wielding of discursive weapons such as these, Baraka, Shepp, Taylor, and other members of this young jazz intelligentsia used modernism both to defy racially imposed limitations on what an African American artist could be and to demand the development of a new, more revolutionary black consciousness. As Bill Dixon remarked in the film *Imagine the Sound,* in the 1960s the advocates of the serious new music "lectured" and confronted the audience with the demand that African Americans accept the new music as *their* music.[49]

There have been many debates over what to call this music. In an essay written in 1961 Amiri Baraka actively embraced the term *avant-garde* to describe the new trend in the music.[50] Nevertheless, by the time of the *Point of Contact* debate in 1965, many musicians viewed the term as being too white—that is, too closely linked to the Western intellectual heritage to be useful in describing a music through which many sought to define a new kind of self-determined African American artistic community. The New Thing, the New Music, and the New Black Music were other terms that were used at the time to describe the work of musicians such as Ornette Coleman, Cecil Taylor, Bill Dixon, and Albert Ayler. After the recording of Ornette Coleman's album *Free Jazz* in 1961, "free jazz" became a favored term since it seemed to point directly to the connection between the music and the politics of the freedom struggle.

As George Lewis has argued, however, the use of "free jazz" to describe the music fails to do justice to the compositional interests of many artists and the collective organizations they founded to nurture their creative activities, such as Chicago's Association for the Advancement of Creative Musicians (AACM). The AACM (whose one hard-and-fast rule for its members was that "all music presented had to be original products of the musicians giving the event") developed the term "Great Black Music, Ancient to the Future" to describe its creative vision. Another term often used is "experimentalism." Indeed, the rehearsal band (from which the AACM emerged) led by Muhal Richard Abrams was called the Experimental

Band.[51] By the time that A. B. Spellman's *Four Lives in the Bebop Business* was published in 1966, the term "serious music" seems to have taken hold among many musicians.

In their work, artists such as Sun Ra and John Coltrane, on the other hand, distanced themselves from the modern Western intellectual heritage of the avant-garde by emphasizing spirituality and religion (especially non-Western spirituality) as the ethical center of the new music. Here the relationship between the music and the higher power of a creator was more important in creating the progressive, self-determined community of the future than a Western-conceived, anticapitalist revolution. To me, what seems to unite the Marxist and European avant-garde imaginings of revolution with the spiritually rooted visions of cultural rebirth, however, is their vanguardist stance. Whether spiritual or political/economic reasoning underlay the claim, the artist was viewed as being of advanced consciousness and endowed with a special ability to help audiences more richly imagine their liberation. Whether viewed as a prophet or revolutionary leader, in other words, the artist had a vanguard role to play.

If history has shown that African American audiences ultimately failed to widely accept this music as an emblem of identity and empowerment, the deft juggling of Western conceptions of art, revolution, and anticapitalism, as well as non-Western conceptions of art, spirituality, and transcendence by artists as diverse as Sun Ra, Archie Shepp, Cecil Taylor, and John Coltrane, nevertheless cannot be relegated to the status of a cultural sideshow. Here the melding of European ideas of an artistic vanguard and Pan-African and Pan-Asian religious ideas helped to define a conception of music as a sphere in which radical redefinitions of the self could take place—redefinitions that helped many musicians and their devoted audiences to break out of the socially imposed niche that U.S. society had defined for black music. Since the accepted role for black music was popular commercial entertainment, it is not surprising that young African American musicians found the European discourse of avant-garde modernism so useful in breaking out of their stereotyped place in the American imagination.

For champions of free jazz, their aesthetic opponents were reactionaries—the moldy figs and Uncle Toms of their generation. This judgmental stance was similar to the moral censure used by the civil right activists to goad Southern African Americans into joining the civil rights movement or, in the musical sphere, to shame prominent musicians who continued to play for segregated audiences in the South in the 1950s (see chapter 2). Nevertheless, this rather simplistic mapping of musical aesthetics and politics was full of contradictions. For one thing, the elitism embedded in the modernist disdain of the popular was at odds with the mass-based grassroots politics of the civil rights movement. Avant-garde jazz improvisations, after all, were not freedom songs that could be sung in jail.

As the music became harsher and more dissonant, many African American listeners were drawn to the more accessible pleasures of hard bop and R&B. Much to the embarrassment of those vanguardists who were deeply committed to combining musical experimentation with a celebration of black pride and autonomy, as the decade wore on, according to many observers, the audiences for the New Thing became white and whiter. Here a black radical intelligentsia often encountered its white radical counterpart, clamoring for admission to a tension-filled racial dialogue. It is not surprising that radical whites found the new serious music quite appealing, for the discourse of the avant-garde rupture promised them a means of redefining the self as well—in this case, imagining a new kind of radical whiteness that rejected the racial status quo and found common cause with the revolutionary aspirations of their radical African American counterparts.

Writing during the summer of the Freedom Rides, Baraka argued that the New Thing was not a matter of imitating white European classical music but of using modernism to explore black roots, especially blues and bebop. "Ornette Coleman has to live with the attitudes responsible for Anton Webern's music whether he knows that music or not." It was only fitting, therefore, that jazz musicians should draw on modern aesthetics to articulate their contemporary visions of blues and bebop, genres Baraka maintained were autonomous in the sense that they were "beginnings," defining the various kinds of Afro-American music coming after them. The brilliance of the young vanguardists, in Baraka's view, was their extension of the melodic and rhythmic profundity of these genres to say something new: "Ornette Coleman uses Parker only as a hypothesis; his . . . conclusions are quite separate and unique." The avant-garde, then, took black roots music and the modern circumstances of the world ("if an atomic bomb is dropped on Manhattan, moldy figs will die as well as modernists") to articulate a socially relevant and aware new black music.[52]

Those writing for the Nation of Islam's *Muhammad Speaks* did not buy it. After attending a performance of John Coltrane's classic quintet (with Eric Dolphy, Elvin Jones, Jimmy Garrison, and McCoy Tyner) on

Chicago's south side in early 1963, their reviewer found that "these men are deliberate dealers in discord and dissonance that has no plan and goes nowhere." Sounding much like *Down Beat* critic John Tynan, who dismissed the music of Coltrane as "anti-jazz," the reviewer lamented that there was "no apparent attempt to play what is recognized in most places as 'jazz' as most fans know and love it," the *Muhammad Speaks* reviewer saw Coltrane's popularity as a white phenomenon: "The fact that Coltrane has a large white following is a clue to the conclusion that his music, in the main, hits only that portion of the American populace that does not really know and understand jazz, but follows the fingers of the white critics."[53] Since Coltrane's playing in early 1963 was generally quite "accessible" by later standards, one can only imagine what *Muhammad Speaks* would have written about Cecil Taylor or Albert Ayler.

Singled out for praise, on the other hand, was hard bopper Eddie "Lockjaw" Davis. Noting in the headline that "Cool Scholars Scarce as 'Lockjaw' Blows His Horn," the reviewer for *Muhammad Speaks* praised Davis's "full-toned tenor" as "the reflection of those sometimes forgotten years before jazz took off in diverse directions." Here *Muhammad Speaks* chose to publish a perspective that took a position the exact opposite of Baraka's at a time when the debate over the New Thing was beginning to consume the emerging younger generation of jazz musicians.[54] Yet four years later, shortly after Coltrane's death, the publication apparently changed its mind:

> Trane moved more souls than their Beethovens or Bachs or Wagners and so do his black compatriots who live and die little heralded in the unlocked confines of their regions, most dying even before their greatest songs are unleashed from their throats. So MUHAMMAD SPEAKS presents this simple eulogy to this Black Colossus and his widow and the four small children he left behind; their father fulfilled the potentials of his genes and spread the germs of immortality he had inherited from black ancestors in Africa into rivers deeper than his imitators dared to tread; and his phenomenal performances opened special spheres for untold millions in this world and in the worlds to come.[55]

The shift in the editorial policy at *Muhammad Speaks* was something more than a change in aesthetic position, however. If free jazz seemed deeply indebted to Western European notions of artistic rebellion in its early years, by mid-decade the work of Sun Ra, Albert Ayler, and John Coltrane had infused its musical experimentations with a transcendent spirituality that was deployed by some as a means of emphasizing universality across cultural lines and by others as a means of defining the boundary between black and white even more starkly. In Coltrane's music, spirituality functioned primarily to emphasize an ethnically inclusive universalism, but to the Nation of Islam and also Maulana Karenga's US Organization (to which Baraka and many others were drawn in the late sixties), the spiritual community envisioned was a decidedly black one. In a variation of Leopold Senghor's view of the "African personality" as inherently more spiritual and communal, whites were viewed as less capable of tuning in to the universal energy and as an active obstacle to the formation of a truly self-aware blackness. Although the Black Panther Party's (BPP) more Marxist approach saw a role for progressive alliances with white leftists, Karenga's US organization was deeply suspicious of any such relations with whites.[56]

As Scot Brown has argued, the positive value assigned to religion and spirituality was a key difference between a Marxist view of socialism and the African socialism proposed by Senghor. For Senghor and several other African intellectuals, such as Julius Nyerere, Sekou Toure, and Kwame Nkrumah, African traditional culture—with its emphasis on communalism, egalitarianism and collectivity—would be the basis for a genuine post-colonial African identity. Julius Nyerere, who had been elected president of Tanzania in 1962, attempted to implement an African socialist program that he called *Ujamaa*, the Kiswahili word meaning "familyhood." This became one of Karenga's Seven Principles of Blackness *(Nguzo Saba)*, which serve as the basis for the Kwanzaa holiday celebration that he first established in 1966. In the context of an African socialism, spirituality provided a foundation for socialist revolution that was not only different from the European-based Marxist tradition but also arguably more ancient and hence more authentic. The spiritual turn in cultural nationalism in many ways provided an unambiguously African basis for social revolution that avoided the uncomfortable dependence on the European heritage of Marxism. Karenga's thinking, nevertheless, also drew on the theme of the interconnectedness of Africa and Asia that had been such a prominent theme in the Nation of Islam. Karenga's third principle of blackness, *Ujima,* which emphasized collective work and responsibility, was inspired by Sukarno's Indonesian concept of "let's pull together." Sukarno had been president of Indonesia at the time of the Bandung conference of 1955.[57]

## Point of Contact

Don DeMichael and Dan Morgenstern, at this time the national and New York editors, respectively, of *Down Beat* magazine organized the Point of Contact debate. According to Morgenstern, DeMichael "was one of the most fair-minded people I've ever seen in that position. And he really was concerned about giving equal time and equal space to all that. Also because he felt—and all of us felt—that from an aesthetic standpoint and from a strictly musical standpoint, some of the things that were happening not only were debatable but had to be debated because they dealt with very basic things about the art form."[58]

A year earlier the *Down Beat* yearbook had published a panel discussion about the pros and cons of the jazz avant-garde among an all-white group of jazz critics that included Dan Morgenstern, Ira Gitler, Don Heckman, Don Schlitten, and Martin Williams. In some ways the Point of Contact debate was a predominantly black answer to that more apolitical conversation. The African American participants included Cannonball Adderley, Cecil Taylor, Archie Shepp, Sonny Murray, and Roland Kirk, while the white participants included club owner Art D'Lugoff and moderator Dan Morgenstern. The plan had been to include representatives of the New Thing (Taylor, Shepp, and Murray), a bridge figure who was involved in both inside and outside styles (Roland Kirk), and somebody whose work was primarily not involved with the avant-garde (Cannonball Adderley). From the outset Adderley was viewed as a potential de facto mediator because Morgenstern did not believe that, as a white person and representative of the leading jazz magazine, he stood much chance of effectively holding the fort. In fact, Rahsaan Roland Kirk did most of the informal moderating: "Rahsaan was the one that I remember. He was the one who let some semblance of order into this thing because he had this big, wonderful cane, which was sort of like a tree trunk. He would bang that on the table and say '*Let the man talk!* Let him finish!' You know, because he was blind and because he had this big stick. He managed to get some attention. The whole thing was like a free-for-all."[59]

In the Point of Contact debate, the main practical issues underlying the heated exchanges between Archie Shepp and Cecil Taylor on the one hand and Art D'Lugoff on the other were economic. For Shepp, the fact that D'Lugoff had booked singer Carmen McRae, activist and comedian Dick Gregory, and John Coltrane on the same bill indicated the insensitivity of club owners to the fact that Coltrane's artistry required more than the thirty-five-minute set allotted to him:

> I think that's indicative of something. I think it's indicative of the level of mentality of most club owners. I don't say that personally toward Art D'Lugoff; I don't mean to make it a personal dialog. I do say that those impresarios who control jazz are, on the whole, the dregs of impresarios. Jazz is singularly unique in that the people who control it are thoroughly ignorant of it, know nothing about it. I know something about club owners. I don't claim to know more than anyone else, but I know about them from the worm's eye view. (p. 20)

Shepp and Taylor both criticized the particular booking practices of clubs in which they had worked, including the Village Gate, Jazz Gallery, and the Village Vanguard, but also protested the racial structure of the music industry. Archie Shepp held the club owners responsible for his inability to work full time in jazz: "I must say that I have never been treated well by club owners. I've been in this music for 15 years and I've never worked a solid week in this country. I've never made my living playing jazz. I now work as a merchandiser at Abraham & Strauss. I do that, I think, at the default of the club owners. The club owners are only the lower echelon of a higher power structure which has never tolerated from Negroes the belief we have in ourselves that we are people, that we are men, that we are women, that we are human beings" (p. 29).

Throughout the panel discussion D'Lugoff tried to defend his booking practices by explaining the economics of running a jazz club:

> I think there's a problem not only in jazz clubs but in all clubs. I think artists who work in clubs, historically, under most systems, have been exploited, are being exploited. However, I would also say that it's getting harder and harder to make a living with a club. Part of this is due to automation—TV, records. ... There is also the

question of audience—how the audience reacts, whether it comes, whether it pays. Remember the audience not only pays my salary and those of the waiters but also the artists' salaries. If we do not make enough money to cover that, we have to close. (p. 20)

Citing the closings of Birdland, the Jazz Gallery, and the Blue Angel, he questioned the assertions of Shepp and Taylor that the club owners were living high off the hog while the artists suffered.[60] If the club owners were getting rich at the artists' expense, why, he asked, had so many clubs closed? "When Archie talks about a bonanza, I think he's mistaken and inaccurate. . . . I don't claim to be an artist—I am a businessman. And I would like to remind all artists—whether they be jazz or ballet or classical— that they're also business people. They've got to make a living and take care of their families" (p. 20).

Yet Cecil Taylor knew it was possible to work under better conditions since he had been very well treated in Europe: "I worked in conditions that I can't work in here. Every major city I went to in Europe, I had a radio show, a television show, and lectures, as well as working in clubs. And they paid me even for the lectures" (p. 25).

Shepp's and Taylor's critiques of the jazz business, however, implied that the music had moved beyond the conceptual confines of the nightclub and required a more radical economic restructuring of the jazz business. Unlike their more entrepreneurial hip-hop counterparts of the 1980s and 1990s, the experimentalist musicians of the 1960s envisioned an anticapitalist or European-style social welfare state solution for the economic viability of jazz as an art music. In their view cooperative communal organizations run by the musicians themselves, as well as an increase in funding for governmental arts programs to support them, would be the wave of the future. These organizations would provide a home base for aesthetic activism and allow musicians to nurture the future of Great Black Music without outside interference.[61]

As Dan Morgenstern recalled, the major practical matter underlying the Point of Contact dialogue was that Taylor and Shepp wanted D'Lugoff to give them a gig. Shepp even began a financial negotiation in the middle of the panel discussion, asking D'Lugoff for $850 a week.[62] Shepp and Taylor implied that a failure to support the New Thing in general and them in particular was racist. D'Lugoff argued that eighty percent of the people he hired were black and that he simply could not afford to hire musicians who did not draw an audience large enough to pay for the salaries of the band members and the club's operating expenses.

The assertion that the experimental music did not draw an audience, however, was very much disputed by Cecil Taylor, Bill Dixon, and Amiri Baraka. In *Four Lives in the Bebop Business*, A. B. Spellman argued that, far from damaging business, Cecil Taylor's appearances at the Five Spot in 1956 had helped to transform the club from an "ordinary Bowery bar" into a mecca for "uptown Bohemia." Advocates of the new music pointed to the structural inequalities that enabled non–African Americans such as Joe Termini, Max Gordon, and Art D'Lugoff to more easily become entrepreneurs at a time when credit markets blatantly discriminated against black borrowers. To Spellman, after the Five Spot failed, Termini had nevertheless been able to sell the club and recoup enough to open a new one that catered to more commercial tastes and consequently had accumulated his capital on the back of jazz: "Before Cecil, Termini could not have thought of opening a discothèque. He now has a shiny new room at a better location which is suitable for live or recorded popular music. It is typical of the jazz experience that modern jazz has brought him to this."[63]

From Art D'Lugoff's point of view, however, he had invested in a rundown building in an undesirable neighborhood in the mid-1950s, worked hard to build it into a uniquely integrated venue (the Village Gate), donated its space to benefit concerts for civil rights organizations and other political causes, and was less interested in becoming as rich as possible than in keeping the club economically afloat in a time when popular music and R&B were more of a draw than jazz. Earlier in 1965 he had participated in a discussion that centered on Amiri Baraka's famous denunciation of club owners as "hip bartenders" who knew nothing "except the sound of the falling coin."[64]

D'Lugoff protested that it was the club owners who actually put their money where their mouth was and that his reluctance to book some of the experimentalists was simple: "Three years ago, against my better judgment and instincts, I played one of Jones' favorites at a price I considered outrageous at the time. I lost my shirt. Now, that very same artist approaches me through his manager and requests a return gig at almost double the money. How crazy can you get?"[65] D'Lugoff perhaps had reason to be indignant since, just two weeks before this exchange appeared in *Down Beat*, he had made the Village Gate available for a Sunday afternoon benefit concert for Baraka's Black Arts Repertory Theater and School that was recorded live by Impulse! and released as *The New Wave in Jazz.*[66] In many ways his club had been more open to the new music than other major jazz clubs. D'Lugoff challenged Amiri Baraka (then Jones) to open a club himself: "If LeRoi Jones thinks that the owning, running, and booking of a club is so simple and so lucrative, he's welcome to get on board and try his hand (the way Charlie Mingus and the Jazz Artists Guild did a few years ago). There are a lot of empty stores—in fact, come to think of it, the Jazz Gallery is still empty and beckoning. How about it, Mr. Jones? Want to give it a whirl?"[67]

## An Underground

This was precisely the point, however: Given economic racial discrimination, African Americans were less likely to be able to open clubs, especially in white neighborhoods. Although it perhaps seems quixotic from the vantage point of the post–Cold War, adamantly entrepreneurial twenty-first century, the interest of the young jazz intellectuals in cooperative organizations and government support was actually a practical approach for those interested in creating more power and economic options for the new generation of jazz musicians.

In Amiri Baraka's view, if New York jazz clubs were failing to support the new music, "the music will have to be heard underground." By 1963 several coffee shops, including the White Whale, Take 3, the Playhouse Coffee Shop, Café Avital, and Café Metro, in Greenwich Village and the Lower East Side had begun to feature what Baraka called "good jazz by younger musicians." Musicians were beginning to play concerts in the lofts, which had previously been used primarily for rehearsals. The typical advertising campaign for such concerts consisted of a small ad in the *Village Voice* and some hand-lettered posters that were informally hung around downtown neighborhoods. According to Baraka, "there are almost always very enthusiastic and empathetic, if not crushingly huge, audiences who respond. And they are usually treated to very exciting jazz, a kind of jazz that is getting increasingly more difficult to find in any regular jazz club in New York."[68]

Perhaps the best way to understand the burning passion that people had for the New Thing is to think of it as an *underground* that rejoiced not only in the excitement of creating new sounds that were experimental and visionary but also in alternative imaginings of the performance space, economics, and the nature of the musical community itself. In this day of aging jazz audiences, it is perhaps difficult to remember that this was in many ways a youth movement whose fans were mostly in their twenties or thirties and saw their appreciation of the music as a sign of exceptional musical awareness. To these avid musicians and aficionados of experimental jazz, the music symbolized something bold, revolutionary, and personally transformative. The new performance spaces provided a novel sort of atmosphere for hearing jazz, one that enabled extended uninterrupted sets, a more intimate relationship between the artists and the audience, and an opportunity to explore a more theatrical and political performance sensibility.

One of the more ambitious underground projects was the October Revolution, a series of concerts organized by trumpeter Bill Dixon and Cecil Taylor, which attracted an audience of seven hundred over four consecutive days.[69] Held at the Cellar Café near Ninety-first and Broadway, the musical sets started at 4 P.M. and finished at midnight, after which panel discussions about the new music and its future ran until the wee hours. Out of these concerts and discussions grew the Jazz Composer's Guild, whose members included Cecil Taylor, Archie Shepp, Roswell Rudd, Sun Ra, John Tchicai, Mike Mantler, Burton Greene, Paul Bley, and Carla Bley. The idea behind the guild was that musicians needed an organization that was better than the American Federation of Musicians in representing their interests. As Bill Dixon put it, the purpose of the Jazz Composers Guild was "to establish the music to its rightful place in society; to awaken the musical conscience of the masses of people to that music which is essential to their lives; to protect musicians and composers from the existing forces of exploitation; to provide an opportunity for the audience to hear the music; to provide facilities for the proper creation, rehearsal, performance, and dissemination of the music."[70]

Some of the practical goals were to produce their own concerts and negotiate contracts for nightclub and concert appearances for all of the members. Long-term plans included forming a record company and acquiring a building that would serve as a center for concerts, workshops, educational activities, and practice space. None of the members was working regularly at the time the guild was formed.

In December the Jazz Composers Guild put on its first series of concerts, which was billed as "Four Days in December," at Judson Hall. Two groups were featured each evening—the Cecil Taylor Unit and the Bill Dixon Sextet on December 28, the Paul Bley Quintet and the Jazz Composers Guild Orchestra on December 29, the Archie Shepp Quartet and the Free Form Improvisation Ensemble on December 30, and the Le Sun-Ra Arkestra and the Roswell Rudd–John Tchicai Quartet on December 31 (figure 7.3). The first night pulled a standing-room-only crowd of 300, while the remaining nights drew about 150 each. In any case, the success of these two concert series served as a basis for optimism about the possibilities of alternative means of organizing musical events. The guild was soon holding weekly discussions among its members, sponsoring weekly concerts, and had headquartered itself in the Contemporary Center, a small loft space located at 180 Seventh Avenue, two floors above the Village Vanguard.[71]

Nevertheless, almost as soon as it had formed, the members of the group betrayed their commitment to conduct recording and performing negotiations only through the guild. Archie Shepp began negotiations with Impulse! without telling the guild, which infuriated the other members when they found out, but also indicated the difficulty of sticking to collective negotiations in a performance economy that rewarded individuals. According to Cecil Taylor, this "scabbing on the part of its musicians, both white and black," is what led to the breakup of the organization.

There were also considerable racial tensions in the group. Bill Dixon reported that some of the white members felt threatened by the fact "that a black man . . . myself, Cecil . . . could conceive and execute an idea that would be intelligent and beneficial to all." Moreover, because of the structural racism in the music industry, the white members had more opportunities in musical fields beyond jazz and thus were viewed as being less in need of support. As Dixon put it, "It must be remembered that white men *elect* to play jazz; their musical horizons are not bound by an enforced social tradition that relegates them to one area of musical expression." In other words, the white members were in some respects held personally responsible for the collective structural advantages of white privilege. Sun Ra added sexism to the field of tension by opposing Carla Bley's membership in the group. According to Valerie Wilmer, Sun Ra regaled the members "with the old seamen's legend which says that taking a woman on a voyage will sink the ship. As a consequence he maintained it was bad luck for Carla Bley to be on board their particular vessel."[72]

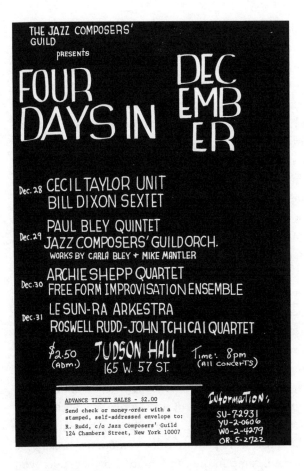

FIGURE 7.3. The Jazz Composers Guild presents "Four Days in December." Topics files: hand-bills, New York jazz clubs, Courtesy of Rutgers Institute of Jazz Studies.

## Is It Black Enough?

The Achilles heel of the new music as the ultimate revolutionary *black* music was its ambivalent reception among African Americans themselves. In *Four Lives in the Bebop Business,* A. B. Spellman recounts the difficulties Cecil Taylor faced when he performed at the Coronet, a white-owned club in Brooklyn's Bedford Stuyvesant, with a predominantly African American clientele. The white owner had invited Taylor's group to play, but the African American manager, "who seemed to feel that this music was not good enough for the Coronet," fired Taylor after the first set. According to Spellman, "Cecil was very hurt, very dragged," and the crowd was digging it, but a competitiveness existed "between musicians who are not involved in the new music with those who are" that accounted for the hostile reception.

In Spellman's analysis, the "old-style funk of the 1950s"—that is, hard bop—dominated the club. "The Coronet funk players had taken on some of the more progressive aspects of the music of Coltrane and others, but they had not gone so far as to absorb the new developments of musicians such as Cecil Taylor." It could not be that the manager and some of the audience simply had different aesthetic ideas about what was excellent black music; they simply had not yet opened themselves to the new black vanguard. In some ways this could be viewed as a variant of an older racial uplift ideology: The audience was backward and needed to be raised to a new level by the more advanced. When Cecil's band defied the firing and Sonny Murray sat down at his drums to begin a second set, one of the manager's friends threatened him with a knife. The next night Jackie McLean played in an outside style with Tony Williams and was punched in the mouth.

Although countervailing stories appear, such as the one told about Milford Graves's successful appearance at the Storefront Museum in Queens a few years later, it was very difficult for the African American leaders of the new experimental music to admit that their music was a tough sell to many segments of the African American audience.[73] Taylor explained his failure at the Cornet like this: "My experience up in Brooklyn, in a ghetto community, was not the result of the fact that the music wasn't getting to them, but that the night manager was a black man who had an interest in keeping the music from getting to the community because he was committed to a certain camp in the community. The bartender, you know how bartenders are, he worked on those people." Spellman concluded that Taylor and other musicians on the experimental scene found themselves "alienated from both the white and black communities" and faced an economic predicament that made it difficult "to develop their music to its fullest potential."[74]

Given the sensitivity of the topic, it is not surprising that the moments in the Point of Contact debate that provoked the most acrimonious exchanges occurred when Art D'Lugoff asserted that the audience that came to hear Taylor and Shepp was "white, not black" and questioned whether their music was synonymous with black music. "What's black music? Your music?" he asked. Shepp began his definition with bluesman Lightning Hopkins, and D'Lugoff immediately replied, "He's played at the Village Gate," which he repeated when the examples of Archie Shepp and Cecil Taylor were offered. Shepp replied, "For pay?"

The discussion then began to center on the structural aspects of racism in the music industry. The exchange between Shepp and D'Lugoff illustrates a common type of impasse in interracial dialogues of the period:

SHEPP: When every major club in this country is owned by white men, and I defy you to tell me where there's a major black club...

D'LUGOFF: Let's face it. White people own most of the country, and you're so right. We're not arguing about that. That's a fact. That does not make it right.

SHEPP: Are you planning to give your club to a black man?

D'LUGOFF: Why should I?

SHEPP: What are you talking about?

D'LUGOFF: What are *you* talking about? What you're saying is a very obvious thing...

TAYLOR: The point is there is no longer any discussion that can be had. That's why I've made the proposals. That we boycott these clubs. (pp. 24–25)

Cecil Taylor went on to summarize the nature of the impasse and propose that the only solution to getting beyond it was for African American musicians to unite and talk among themselves about social change:

There is not going to be any discussion, because they're not going to listen. He's going to tell us about finances, and I'm going to talk about music and what it means. I'm saying that the failure of even the so-called avant-garde critics has been that even with their hipped-up knowledge of social dynamics in this structure, they have not been able to force the power structure to alter its policies. So I'm saying now that it has always been about *us.* Don't worry about what they say about us. We're no longer reflecting or vibrating to the white energy principle. The point is: we know who we are. We have a whole history of music in this country. We don't have to talk to Art D'Lugoff about what is black music. That's irrelevant. We *know* what black music is. The point is: let us black musicians get together and talk about social change. (p. 25)

This is the same man who a few moments earlier had said, "When I say Negro musicians, I don't mean to exclude those white musicians with social consciousness" (p. 21). Taylor drew the racial line only after being provoked by a white person on the sensitive topic of how black the new music was. It was one thing to encounter an African American audience in Brooklyn that questioned the music's racial bona fides, but to encounter a similar argument from a white person seemed to provoke Taylor into drawing his racial line in the sand.

Yet the need to justify avant-garde jazz as authentic black music was caught up in the same problem that we saw at work in the racial sound stereotypes of the 1950s (see chapter 3). If jazz—and African American music more generally—has always been the result of a complex synthesizing of multiple aesthetics (African, European, Caribbean, folk music, blues, popular music), why should the existence of the European elements in avant-garde (its vanguardism, its bohemianism, its investment in a concept of art that is above and beyond the popular, its anticommercialism) necessarily undermine its claim to blackness? If aesthetics have been more mobile and pluralistic than social structures, as I have argued, and what musicians do with particular aesthetics in their musical practice is more important than the racial origins of a particular gesture, why has the idea that "the New Thing is less black" become a refrain in many recent portrayals of jazz history?[75] Taylor's own view of his relationship to European influence was not so different from the discourse-structure-practice framework I have been proposing: "Everything I've lived, I am. I am not afraid of European influences. The point is to use them—as Ellington did—as part of my life as an American Negro."[76]

However, in the late 1960s the celebration of "doubleness" or "inbetweenness" was hardly in vogue. Although fluency in the modernist "canons of formal Western nonconformity" that Baraka wrote about in *Blues People* may have been an extremely useful discourse in one-upping hip white people in the jazz world, as a means of proving ethnic authenticity to the militant segments of the African American political community, the avant-gardism of the new music was harder to justify. In this historical context, the discourse of cultural nationalism, with its celebration of an African basis for socialism and communal transformation, provided many musicians with a stronger foundation for working on their African American identities, both individual and communal.

One reason for the growth of exclusionary or antiwhite commentary in the rhetoric of African American members of the new black music at this point was, as Eric Porter has suggested, the need for African Americans to demonstrate to one another their racial righteousness.[77] One of the principal reasons that Malcolm X supported the exclusion of white people from the Bandung Conference of 1955 was that their presence undermined the development of black unity: "The number-one thing that was not allowed to attend the Bandung conference was the white man. He couldn't come. Once they excluded the white man, they found that they could get together. Once they kept him out, everybody else fell right in and fell in line."[78]

Freezing out the white people and drawing the racial line was seen as crucial to the promotion of unity against a common enemy. As Malcolm X put it, "Whites can help us, but they can't join us. There can be no black-white unity until there is first some black unity." And it was this goal of black unity that animated so many of the music collectives of the late 1960s and 1970s, including the Association for the Advancement of Creative Musicians, the Union of God's Musicians and Artists Ascension, the Collective Black Artists, and the Black Artists Group.[79] That achieving black unity was difficult is apparent in the racial disunity that erupted during the Point of Contact debate.

## Racial (Dis)Unity

The vanguardism of Cecil Taylor and Archie Shepp was characterized by a self-appointed quality that left them open to the criticism of other musicians. The fly in the ointment throughout the Point of Contact debate was multi-instrumentalist Rahsaan Roland Kirk, who early on in the discussion complained about the hierarchies among African American musicians in the New York jazz scene. Kirk told Cecil Taylor that when he lived in Columbus, Ohio, he had dreamed of playing with Taylor but, after arriving in New York, found that Taylor had brushed him off. Arguing against separating the New Thing from straight ahead, Kirk took this position: "We're doing what the white man wants us to do—separating ourselves from the music. Instead of all of us getting together and playing and accepting each other, we're getting farther away. I would like to play with Cannonball, and I'd like to play with Cecil. But if I come to Cecil he would say, 'You don't know my arrangements' " (p. 21). Taylor tried to sound a note of black unity, but Kirk insisted that Taylor had mistreated him on several occasions:

KIRK: I've asked you to play a couple of times.
TAYLOR: No, you haven't.
KIRK: Yes, I have.
TAYLOR: This is the first time I've met you.
KIRK: Met me? You don't remember . . . meeting me one night in front of the Five Spot when we talked about sending a petition to Washington?
TAYLOR: Yes, but this is the first time we've actually sat down . . .
KIRK: I saw you at the Vanguard, and I asked you to play with me when you were down there with Sonny Rollins.
TAYLOR: No, I don't remember that. . . .
KIRK: That's the kind of thing I've been going through since I've been in New York. Either you don't remember or you have arrangements. I'm saying that music is not like that. I feel that I can play in any type of music and that's what I've always dreamt of doing when I was in the Midwest to get myself together to come here and play. (p. 21)

Differences between Cannonball Adderley and Taylor also emerged when Adderley questioned the wisdom of his call for a boycott of the clubs and the jazz press. Adderley argued that it was difficult enough to play in the clubs as it was: "I'm trying to tell you there's damn near a boycott now. Or else he's boycotting me. You know what I mean?" (p. 26). Taylor responded that the music had outgrown the system and that musicians ought to "bring a consciousness of the people for their stake in the music." Arguing that the jazz press was important in making a broader public and perhaps resentful of Taylor's monopolization of the conversation, Adderley pointed to the way in which Taylor had benefited from the support of white writers: "I think you're very fortunate, Mr. Taylor, in having had someone so literate as Mr. Hentoff to praise your virtues, to the detriment of those who might have gone before or people who are your contemporaries" (p. 26).

In response, Taylor questioned Adderley's racial self-awareness: "You have fallen into a very unfortunate trap. . . . You mean you don't understand my relation to you because of what Nat Hentoff says? What? Then you're blinded by the white man. That's all I can say to you" (p. 26).

Adderley protested Taylor's inference that he had "been brainwashed by the white man" and reached the boiling point when Taylor asked him why he had not heard of him without the benefit of the jazz press. "You were lucky because you were up north," responded Adderley. "I was a southern boy scuffling, trying to get by the *real* white man." Things went from bad to worse as Adderley testified to conditions in Fort Lauderdale, Florida, that included his having seen a lynching victim on the court-house lawn in 1934: "What I'm trying to tell you, Cecil Taylor, is that you're a Johnny-come-lately to this. I've known this all my life. You're just becoming acquainted with this because you've been getting educated" (p. 28).

A rupture in the conversation occurred after this that appears in the transcript as "indecipherable argument." Dan Morgenstern recalls that things got out of hand at the panel discussions partly because "the first thing that happened when people started coming in for the discussion was that—I forget who it was—says, 'What've you got to drink here? There's nothing to drink.' So we had a bottle of scotch and something else, so by the time we got started some people had already had a few under their belt."[80]

When the debate resumed, Archie Shepp provided a class analysis to the mix by arguing that for too long African Americans had allowed class difference to divide them economically, socially, and educationally. Roland Kirk accused them all of talking like white men. Archie Shepp criticized Dan Morgenstern for not moderating the conversation more aggressively, and Taylor expressed embarrassment at this irruption of racial disunity: "I think Don DeMichael in Chicago [editor of *Down Beat*] and his other cohorts are laughing at this ugly division that happened between Cannon-ball and myself and the tricks that language can play." (p. 31).

Taylor expressed skepticism that anything he had said would actually appear in *Down Beat*, citing its record of having buried various African American artists in favor of white artists in the 1950s (p. 31). However, the publication of the extended transcript in the *Down Beat Yearbook* indi-cated one of the big transformations in the jazz press of the 1960s. *Down Beat* did, in fact, open its pages to extremely frank and divisive discussion of racial issues and greatly expanded its coverage of African American musicians.

However uncomfortable the racial debates may have made white audiences, many were also attracted to them like moths to a flame. Many longed to hear the *truth* about racial oppression and took the new revolutionary black musicians as a window into the justifiable anger of black Americans. They too wanted to distance themselves from the Uncle Toms of moderation, as well as from other white people, through their embrace of radicalism and black nationalism. Frank Kofsky, who offered a Marxist analysis of jazz and black nationalism, provides the most prominent example.

If some white liberals and radicals were perhaps masochistic in their acceptance of the racial putdowns of angry black nationalists, others may also have noticed that the insults hurled at whites were not much worse than those that African Americans hurled at each other. It is as if the tactics of moral exhortation and shaming deployed by civil rights activists and black nationalists to motivate the complacent had been transferred to the musical world. No one was safe from personal attack or moral judgment.

## Rhetoric and Practice: Structure Personalized

Although essentialist discourses were often used to draw the line between black and white in the heat of argument, the raising of the racial boundary was frequently circumstantial and compensated for by practical personal relationships and much longer histories of knowing one another within the jazz world. These debates were in some ways public rituals of racial catharsis in which the white representatives were made to stand symbolically for the whole history of white racism and the African American representatives were made to exemplify the entire history of racial injustice. During heated arguments the distinction between the personal and the sociological, the micro and the macro frequently collapsed as the structural became personal.

Dan Morgenstern recalls that, after the Point of Contact debate, Cecil Taylor asked Art D'Lugoff for a ride downtown and that Archie Shepp asked to borrow a few bucks from him. The ritual of catharsis had dissipated some of the anger, in other words, and people went on with more practical relationships and interconnections. Morgenstern remembers an even more intense political debate in that occurred at the Newport Jazz Festival, New York in 1973. The panel was called "The Drum" and was sponsored jointly by the Institute of Jazz Studies and the Institute of Pan-African Culture at the University of Massachusetts, Amherst. Morgenstern was the only white person and on a panel that included Max Roach, Jo Jones, Archie Shepp, John Bracey, Bill Hasan, Dr. John Lovell Jr., and Fred Tillis. The previous year, Max Roach had confronted a similar panel on the " Jazz and Sociology" at the New York Newport festival because it had included only white participants, so the inclusion of several African Americans on various panels in 1973 seems to have been in response.[81] At that time Morgenstern was the national editor of *Down Beat,* and consequently served as a representative of the white power structure. "They really raked me over the coals," he recalled:

> And after it was over I walked outside, and several people came up and expressed their sympathy and disassociated themselves, I mean black people. And then finally Max came out, and of course Max had known me for many many years. But Max gave me a big hug, and then he said, "You gotta understand, Dan," he said, "You gotta understand that this is nothing personal. This is a stage that we have to go through." In other words, I was the symbol of power or whatever in my [ironic tone] tremendously powerful position as editor of this magazine.[82]

The venting of anger toward individual white people in the jazz community, of course, displaced a great deal of structural anger on a particular individual. At these moments the structural was personalized and embodied in the figure of someone who could be only partially responsible. Yet the challenging of white authority was certainly a healthy and necessary impulse, even if at its most extreme a logic of payback dominated. These debates forced non–African Americans to think about racial issues in jazz whether they liked it or not. Many of the white people who went through these uncomfortable events without sinking into a reactive discourse of reverse racism emerged on the other side with stronger individual relationships to the African Americans in the jazz community and an even deeper commitment to whatever sense of togetherness the jazz world offered. Morgenstern did not cite his experience in 1973 as some kind of exceptional event but rather as something that was typical: "Even at its most heated . . . there still was an undercurrent of a kind of thing that in the jazz world—to an extent at least—there was a kind of—like a fraternity. I mean, Max's response to me there was typical of that—that was the thing."

The racial rhetoric in the jazz community of the early to mid-1960s, as these panel discussions show, was intense, divisive, ideological, and personal. And it was not particularly fair. But it was also deeply engaged and passionate in a way that infused the practice of the music with a depth that so often eludes present-day efforts. It is no accident, in my view, that the musical flowering that took place between 1956 and 1967 happened against the backdrop of this socially and politically noisy background. The sense that a great deal was at stake led to an intense musical practice that to this day forms the core of what it is to be a jazz musician.

# 8

# Aesthetic Agency, Self-Determination, and the Spiritual Quest

THE MUSICIANS OF jazz in the 1950s and 1960s engaged just as intensively in music itself as they did in the political debates that raged around them. If the comfortable narratives of jazz heroism, triumph, and celebration have sometimes flattened the political and social struggles that musicians faced in pursuing their craft, so too have the jazz pedagogy books of the last three decades flattened the intense interplay between musical theory and practice that is one of the hallmarks of this golden age of modern jazz.

Today's students who are enrolled in the jazz programs of places such as the Berklee College of Music, the New England Conservatory, the University of North Texas, the New School, the Manhattan School of Music, Eastman, and—the latecomer to it all—the Juilliard School have at their disposal dozens of jazz theory texts that codify in various ways the musical thinking and improvisational practice of this intensely creative period. Musicians of the 1950s and 1960s had no standard curriculum to follow in achieving proficiency in improvisation but rather had to develop their own modes of theorizing and practicing that included, among other things, studying harmony, listening to the advice and guidance of other musicians, participating in jam sessions, learning solos from recordings, practicing melodic licks, and, for some, reading "how to" columns in publications such as *Down Beat*.

The commitment to an intellectual engagement with the materials of music, that is, to theorizing improvisation, seems to have been a central preoccupation of many of the key innovators in jazz. There is no more central figure in this quest than George Russell, whose *Lydian Chromatic Concept of Tonal Organization* placed the relationship of chords to scales at the center of the way that jazz musicians talk about harmony and melody. Although Russell's system for thinking about modes and scales is far broader than the style that has become known as "modal jazz," he was nevertheless a central figure enabling its emergence. In this chapter I first examine Russell's quest for a comprehensive musical system as an example of the intersection between musical theoretical understanding and a search for spiritual depth that so animated the aesthetics and practice of musicians such as John Coltrane and Sun Ra. I also consider how an expanded understanding of modal jazz as a link between mainstream and experimental jazz might encapsulate the many themes explored in this volume.

## Theory and Self-Determination

To talk about music theory and jazz is to raise the specter of that old debate about whether jazz is primarily an intuitive or intellectual art and with it the racialized chain of associations (like soulful versus abstract, warm versus cold, genuine versus contrived) that tend to position black-ness as intuitive and spontaneous and whiteness as cold and rational. In the heated racial exchanges of the mid-1960s cultural nationalists and advo-cates of Black Power often upheld this distinction by celebrating the nat-ural soulfulness and emotional depth that lie at the heart of black music. However useful this rhetorical strategy may have been in demarcating a line of cultural ownership that the invading army of liberal and radical whites could not cross, it also had effect of "deauthenticating" a long his-tory of African American intellectual engagement with music by associat-ing the abstract and intellectual with whiteness.

When critic Gunther Schuller suggested that Cecil Taylor's album *Jazz Advance* "lets us in on the workings of his mind, but not his soul," A. B. Spellman noted that he "exposed a particularly sensitive nerve and ground a lighted cigarette in it." In response, Taylor emphasized that he consid-ered himself to be a blues improviser and that to underscore the technical and classical side of his music "was like giving the tractor more credit for the crop than the earth."[1]

If Taylor sought to distance himself from his conservatory training by stressing the blackness of the blues and intuition, in the early 1960s Ornette Coleman took a somewhat different discursive stance by linking his spontaneous and intuitive approach with a Western discourse of unfettered emotional expression—the abstract expressionism of painters such as Jackson Pollock, whose painting *White Light* adorned the cover Coleman's *Free Jazz* album. At the time, Coleman expressed an aesthetic ideal of unmediated emotional expression: "When our group plays, before we start out to play, we do not have any idea what the end result will be. Each player is free to contribute what he feels in the music at any given moment. We do not begin with a preconceived notion as to what kind of effect we will achieve." Like his painter friends, he found that some people were confused by his music: "Many people apparently don't trust their reactions to art or to music unless there is a verbal *explanation* for it. In music, the only thing that matters is whether you *feel* it or not. You can't intellectualize music; to reduce it analytically often is to reduce it to nothing very important. It is only in terms of emotional response that I can judge whether what we are doing is successful or not."[2]

As Ted Gioia has argued, statements like these enabled some white critics to view Ornette Coleman as a kind of primitive whose appeal and authenticity resided in classic racial fantasies of the other.[3] But Coleman's emphasis on unmediated intuitive emotional expression also had its links to Sartre's existentialism (with its emphasis on trusting the instincts as a guide to existentialist action) and German romantic ideas of genius—that intuitive originality for which no rational rule can be given. For Kant, genius was an unexplainable gift of nature, rather than something that could be acquired by study alone.[4] Ambivalence about the intellect as a path to artistic creation, in other words, is shared by the Western and African American aesthetic traditions.

Jazz musicians have been particularly suspicious of institutionalized approaches to musical understanding. As Max Roach argued, being outside of the mainstream institutional channels was a good thing for the creativity of jazz: "We wouldn't have the Duke Ellingtons and the Charlie Parkers if we had gone to the universities and got doctorates because our minds would have been locked into something else." In his view, academia is "okay if you want to get a job and be like everybody else. But if you want to go outside and above all that and be like Charlie Parker, Bud Powell, Chick Webb, and these people, academia can't touch you."[5]

Rather, a self-actuated quest for knowledge and understanding was very much respected in jazz circles of the 1950s and 1960s. As musicians explored various ways of thinking about harmony, rhythm, melody, and sound (timbre), they both applied ideas acquired through the study of Western music to improvisational practice and developed their own distinctive harmonic conceptions and practice devised to fit the demands of an improvising musician. In the 1950s and 1960s some of the most notable developments by jazz musicians were the conception of harmony rooted in modes and scales, the "rootless" piano voicings, complex approaches to chord substitution, modal jazz (which included quartal harmony, vamp-based open-ended forms, pedal points, and decreased harmonic density), new approaches to collective improvisation, and the incorporation of timbres and aesthetic principles derived from non-Western forms of music.[6] In the absence of a formalized jazz pedagogy, all jazz musicians in some ways had to become their own music theorist, devising harmonic approaches and individualized practice routines that enabled them to maximize their aesthetic agency and creative success on the bandstand. As Paul Berliner's *Thinking in Jazz* has so thoroughly documented, musicians have devised a seemingly limitless number of ways of thinking about improvisation that they deploy in an "eternal cycle" of "improvisation and precomposition."[7]

To become one's own theorist—to have one's own concept that in turn leads to the expression of one's own voice—was among the highest aesthetic ideals of the art form. To become an improviser at this high level was to become aesthetically self-determining in a world in which other forms of self-determination or agency were more easily frustrated. This was an existential rather than a social self-determination, in other words. It is not surprising that Sartre found in jazz improvisation an attractive analogy for his philosophy. Existentialism, after all, emphasized the idea that "existence precedes essence" and that "there is no reality except in action." Consequently, human beings are defined by their actions and choices rather than a predetermined nature. However, Sartre's existentialism was also extremely individualistic and ultimately resonated very strongly with masculinist understandings of human action. By stating that the ultimate definition of masculinity for Charles Mingus was the "will to self-determination," Nichole Rustin very perceptively drew a link between masculinity and self-determination that helps to explain the tenacity of male dominance in jazz. If self-determination is an ultimately masculine quality, what could be more frightening and unattractive than a woman who is as self-determining as a Charlie Parker, a John Coltrane, or a Miles Davis?[8]

For African American musicians, to seize hold of the reins of musical thinking was in many ways to shatter the idea that their special gift was simply talent rather than intelligence. In this sense the positive value placed on the intellectual exploration of music during the late 1940s and 1950s was anything but a capitulation to whiteness. If musicians at first seemed overly concerned about proving their understanding of harmony as a prestige discourse, they ultimately developed an improvisational musical practice, harmonic inventiveness, body of compositions, and cultivation of aural skill that far surpassed any debt to classical music.

## George Russell: *The Lydian Chromatic Concept of Tonal Organization*

George Russell (1923– ) grew up in Cincinnati, Ohio, where he spent his youth playing in a Boy Scout drum and bugle corps, absorbing the music of the African American church, and admiring the arranging achievements of his next-door neighbor, Jimmy Mundy, a famous arranger for Earl Hines, Benny Goodman, and Count Basie. While a student at Withrow High School, Russell played drums in a local nightclub and later received a scholarship to play with the Wilberforce University jazz ensemble. He soon moved to Chicago, where he first encountered the music of Thelonious Monk and received his first public recognition as a composer of music for a nightclub called El Grotto. After selling his big-band arrangement of *New World* to Benny Carter, he moved to New York. A relapse of tuberculosis soon left him hospitalized for fifteen months at Saint Joseph's hospital in the Bronx (143rd and Brook Avenue) from 1946 to 1947. While confined to his bed, he began music theoretical investigations that later culminated in the *Lydian Chromatic Concept of Tonal Organization* (LCC).

Russell recalls thinking intensively about two issues. The first was a statement made by Miles Davis that his highest musical goal was to "learn all the changes"; the second was his observation that many bebop musicians ended their tunes on a raised fourth. As Russell told it:

Miles sort of took a liking to me when he was playing with Bird along the street. And he used to invite me up to his house. We'd sit down and play chords. He liked my sense of harmony. And I loved his sense, so we'd try to kill each other with chords. He'd say, "Check this out." And I'd say, "Wow." And I'd say, "Listen to this . . ." I asked him one day on one of these sessions, "What's your highest aim?—musical aim?" and he said, "To learn all the changes." That's all he said [laughs]. At the time I thought he *was* playing the changes, you know. That he was relating to each chord and arpeggiating or using certain notes and extending the chord and all that. The more I thought about that, the more I felt there was a system begging to be brought into the world. And that system was based on chord scale unity, which traditional music had absolutely ignored. The whole aspect of a chord having a scale that was really its birthplace.[9]

In the *Lydian Chromatic Concept* Russell argued that the C Lydian mode—c, d, e, f♯, g, a, b—comes closest to expressing the harmonic (vertical) sonority of a C major triad and consequently was its parent scale.[10] The argument is based on two ideas from Western musical theory: the importance of the circle of fifths (and its implications of the fifth as a tonic defining interval) and the ability of linear tetrachords to imply a tonic. From this perspective the Lydian mode expresses a C major tonality more perfectly than the major scale for two reasons. First, the Lydian mode is generated by linearizing the first seven fifths in the circle of fifths (C, G, D, A, E, B, F♯). Second, if the Lydian scale is partitioned into two disjunct tetrachords, the first tetrachord resolves to G, and the second resolves to C (by virtue of the half steps between F♯ and G and B and C). The tonal centers generated by these linear segments form the interval of a perfect fifth. By the same procedure, the major scale forms the interval of a perfect fourth by producing tonal centers on F and C (figure 8.1).

Citing composer Paul Hindemith, Russell argued that the root of a perfect fifth is the bottom note and the root of a perfect fourth is the upper note. By this reasoning, the linear structure of the C Lydian mode reinforces C as a tonal center, while the linear structure of the C major mode reinforces F as a tonal center. Consequently, the Lydian mode is more vertically aligned with a C major triad than the major scale, which requires a IV-V-I progression to resolve (pp. i–iv). Russell summarized his case for the importance of the Lydian mode as follows: "The major scale *resolves* to its tonic major chord. The Lydian scale *is* the sound of its tonic major scale" (p. iv.)

FIGURE 8.1. George Russell: Lydian mode versus major mode. Concept Publishing © 1958, 1964, 2001. Used by permission.

Having established his case for the Lydian mode as the parent scale of the C major triad, Russell worked out the appropriate parent scales for every other chord quality. In so doing he constructed a family of six Lydian (vertical) scales that, when combined, produce the twelve tones of the Lydian chromatic scale (figure 8.2).[11]

Russell systematized the harmonic implications of the Lydian scales in a tonal gravity chart that lists chord qualities and the Lydian scales that produce them. To these he added two horizontal scales (the major scale and the blues scale) and the nine-tone scale, a composite scale produced by combining the Lydian scale, the Lydian augmented, and the Lydian diminished scales. His interest lay not only in locating a parent scale for every chord type but also in helping the improviser identify a series of possible scales arranged in order of their increasing distance from the parent scale. When Russell speaks of "vertical polymodality," he is referring not only to a parent scale but also to a group of scales, a family of possibilities for the musician to explore.

One of the most intuitively appealing aspects of the concept to improvising musicians has been Russell's notion of three types of "tonal gravity": vertical, horizontal, and supravertical. The improviser, in Russell's view, can choose to relate to tonality in three general ways: (1) allow each chord as it passes to determine the choice of scales (vertical tonal gravity; pp. 22–27); (2) impose a single scale on a sequence of chords that resolve to a tonic (horizontal tonal gravity; pp. 28–35); or (3) improvise the chromatic melody in relationship to the overall tonic of the entire piece (supravertical tonal gravity; p. xviii).[12] Examples of music embodying these principles include

FIGURE 8.2. The six Lydian scales. George Russell, *The Lydian Chromatic Concept of Tonal Organization* (New York: Concept, 1964), transposed from pp. 4–5. Concept Publishing © 1958, 1964, 2001. Used by permission.

John Coltrane's "Giant Steps" (1959; vertical), Lester Young's solo on "Dickie's Dream" (Basie 1939; horizontal), and Ornette Coleman's "Lonely Woman" (1959; supravertical). Freedom is ultimately what Russell is after, but one fully aware of all tonal possibilities. With the concept Russell argues: "*You are free to do anything your taste may dictate,* for you can resolve the most 'far out' melody since you always know where home is (the parent member scale within the parent Lydian Chromatic Scale)" (p. 27).

The various editions of the Lydian concept have offered slightly different sets of scales. The 1953 version included four Lydian scales (Lydian, Lydian augmented, Lydian diminished, and the 9 tone, plus two auxiliary scales—auxiliary augmented and auxiliary diminished) but left out the auxiliary diminished blues scale (diminished scale beginning with a half step). The nine-note scale included the pitches C, D, Eb, E, F♯, G, G♯, A, B, and C (the chromatic starting on a C scale minus C♯, F, and B♭). Rather than conceiving the Lydian system as coterminous with the twelve-tone chromatic scale, the 1953 version instead produced the eleven-tone scale (by combining the six scales of his system.) This left the augmented prime (C♯) out of the chromatic collection.

Another principal difference between the 1953 and the 1959 versions of the concept is the inclusion of two "tonality extender charts" in the former, which suggests that the student either superimpose (in the ascending direction) or subimpose (in the descending direction) tonal centers—depending on whether a vertical or horizontal effect is desired—by various systematic paths through the circle of fifths (by one fifth, by two fifths [i.e., by step], or by three fifths [i.e., by minor third]).[13] Later versions leave the pathways to more distantly related tonal centers more open ended. The 2001 edition includes seven Lydian and four horizontal scales.[14]

The practical result of Russell's recalibration of the harmonic system with the Lydian mode as home base was the generation of scale choices for realizing harmonic progressions that sounded more modern than those typically used in bebop. This is because the Lydian-based scales included more altered pitches (such as the b5) in their structure. Russell's example melodies in the 1959 and 1964 editions, which harmonize the same progression with each of the Lydian scales, dramatically illustrate the melodic variety made possible by applying a progressively outgoing sequence of scales to the chord progression.[15]

Russell's own compositions represent the most impressive use of his system. After completing the *Lydian Concept of Tonal Organization* in 1953, Russell began to compose extensively and by 1956 had recorded an influential body of work, including "Ye Hypocrite, Ye Beelzebub," "The Day John Brown Was Hanged," "Fellow Delegates," and "The Ballad of Hix Blewitt." Among the members of this ensemble were trumpeter Art Farmer, pianist Bill Evans, and bassist Milt Hinton. Russell also taught many musicians the principles of the LCC formally or informally, among them Art Farmer, Bill Evans, Carla Bley, Eric Dolphy, Miles Davis, and David Baker. In 1958 Miles Davis cited George Russell, Bill Evans, and Gil Evans as the three people who knew the most about the harmonic implications of scales and his primary inspirations for beginning to write tunes with few chord changes. Although the term "modal jazz" is usually associated with Davis's "Milestones" from 1958 and *Kind of Blue* (1959), it is clear that systematic thinking about chords and scales was something for which George Russell was already widely known and that other leading musicians were exploring.

Russell's decision to calibrate his harmonic system relative to the Lydian rather than major scale has contributed to the lack of acknowledgement he has received for pioneering a systematic approach to the relationship of chords and scales. The chord/scale approach to jazz pedagogy has become the standard way of teaching jazz improvisation, but in a form that is measured relative to the major scale. In 1959 John Mehegan published a chord/scale approach to jazz harmony that restricted itself to sixty seventh chords—five chord qualities (major, dominant, minor, half diminished, and diminished) on each of the twelve pitches of the chromatic scale. Russell's student David Baker later published a series of improvisation books beginning in 1969 that became the models for a more widespread chord/scale method (also calibrated from the major scale) of teaching jazz improvisation.[16]

Why then has Russell been so insistent about the priority of the Lydian scale? For Russell, the Lydian chromatic concept of tonal organization has never been simply a theory of music. Indeed, he has consistently viewed it as a life-giving philosophy that mingles elements of religion, science, and non-Western spirituality. For Russell, working on this concept was literally life giving, in the sense that his quest enabled him to endure the lengthy hospitalization that was central to his recovery from tuberculosis. As with John Coltrane and Sun Ra, Russell's relationship to music theory, systematicity, and unity is perhaps better placed in the context of a pan-denominational spirituality merging elements of religion, science, self-knowledge, and mysticism. Russell stressed the intuitive quest for knowledge that the concept represents: "This is intuitive intelligence. It's intelligence that comes from putting the question to your intuitive center and having faith, you know, that you're intuitive center will answer. And it does. I had gone through a number of religious experiences as a child. I was sort of forced into it. My mother was very religious. Searching for something desperately."

Russell grew up with what he calls "deep black church music" and credits this music with allowing him to experience not only notes and beauty but also the life in it. "It opened a door to a life that wasn't stagnant and that was exploratory and that was an open door to the universe" (Russell, interview, 1995). Indeed, Russell recoils from the idea that his theory is academic.

See, a lot of people feel that it's academic, [especially] if they have an academic feeling. I'm not really an academic. It just made perfect sense for me to educate myself, but once I educated myself I didn't mean to stumble on something that I had to make a complete commitment to—absolute commitment.

The quest for deeper knowledge and inner exploration, for Russell, is linked to his interest in a variety of religious and spiritual beliefs, including those of G. I. Gurdjieff. Russell acknowledges that there is "a lot of correlation" between the Lydian chromatic concept and the thinking of Gurdjieff. A number of the terms that Russell employs can be found in Gurdjieff's series of books titled *All and Everything.*[17] Russell, for example, refers to the concept as the "all and everything of tonality" and the "all and everything of music." Indeed, Gurdjieff's talks about gravity, harmoniousness, space travel, the planet Saturn, unity, and the idea of spiritual essence seem to have provided a fertile means for Russell to combine his interests in tonality, philosophy, modernity, the non-Western world, and self-awareness.[18] Gurdjieff, an Armenian, traveled to Egypt, Saudi Arabia, Turkey, Tibet, and India in the early twentieth century in his search for knowledge of ancient metaphysical traditions. He synthesized elements of Hindu, Buddhist, Sufi, and Christian religious ideas into a body of teachings, including music and dance, which gained adherents in France, Germany, and the United States.[19] Russell's identification with international spiritual ideas underlies his assertion that the concept is "the first theory to unite the music of the East and the West and be applicable to both of them."

Like Max Roach, Russell is suspicious of formal education: "I always dreaded the small life, the small mind, which I sensed controlled the educational system.... The streets would be my school and food for my art." The rebelliousness of formulating a musical philosophy that inverts traditional understandings of harmony by placing the "devil's interval" (the tritone) at the center of musical understanding is also of significance. Given the choice of pursuing a traditional understanding of musical structures or of inventing his own system, Russell chose the path of self-determination and with it a link to what Cornel West has called the prophetic: "Prophetic Theology cuts much deeper than the intellect; Prophetic Theology forces us to exemplify in our own lives what we espouse in our rhetoric. It raises questions of integrity, questions of character, and, most importantly, questions of risk and sacrifice."[20]

## John Coltrane and Theory

George Russell was not alone in seeking a simultaneously theoretical and spiritual understanding of music. When he recorded an arrangement of Rodgers and Hart's "Manhattan," he recalls John Coltrane puzzling over Russell's reharmonization of the piece for more than an hour in an attempt to reharmonize Russell's chord changes. Russell tells the story not to claim an influence on Coltrane but to emphasize that Trane "had a highly developed theoretical system [of his own], and he was just trying to work it into this arrangement for the purposes of his solo."

Many studies of Coltrane's harmonic principles have paid particular attention to the genesis of the *Giant Steps* chord progression that divides the octave in three and tonicizes each division as new key area. As Lewis Porter and David Dempsey have argued, the progressions seem to have harmonized a symmetrical pattern drawn from Nicolas Slonimsky's *Thesaurus of Scales and Melodic Patterns* and applied it initially as a substitute for the ubiquitous ii-V-I pattern. In more recent work, Jeff Bair has identified several other Slonimsky patterns that Coltrane used as part of his melodic vocabulary in improvisations from the mid-1960s. This is not to suggest that Coltrane simply copied Slonimsky but instead to argue that one of the hallmarks of a creative theoretical mind is the ability to see implications in readily available materials that far surpass their original purpose. The patterns in Slonimsky's book are melodic, not harmonic, yet for Coltrane they provided insight into far-reaching new directions for his harmonic, as well as melodic, language. Although countless students of improvisation have explored Slonimsky's book, it seems safe to say that no one has surpassed Coltrane in aesthetic use.[21]

Throughout his life Coltrane was fascinated by symmetry in not only melody and harmonic progression but also compositional form. Porter's classic study of *A Love Supreme* identifies a symmetrical tonal plan for the four-movement work, Coltrane's use of symmetrical interval patterns, and the way that the final movement uses Coltrane's spiritual text as the basis of melody. Saxophonist Dave Liebman has offered a similarly penetrating analysis of *Meditations* that also links the exploration of symmetry with Coltrane's passionate quest for the spiritual. Coltrane's interest in symmetry as a sign of the divine also led him to cross-cultural spiritual explorations of music that included Indian and Chinese modes of musical understanding.[22]

Although symmetry has long been of interest to Western classical composers as well, the use of symmetrical patterns by improvising musicians requires a level of practical conceptual mastery that is far beyond what is required of the classical performer. Coltrane, as is widely known, was a compulsive practicer who was known to have spent his breaks with his horn continually in his mouth. Playing and inventing materials that were then practiced in twelve keys and throughout all registers of the horn turned intellectual knowledge into embodied knowledge, which in turn fed the discovery of new ideas both mental and physical. It is through a continual process of dialogue among the senses, intellect, and body that the great jazz improvisers of the 1950s and 1960s were able to play intuitively and passionately with materials of great complexity that they had themselves devised.

Much mystification remains about improvisation as an unmediated expression of emotion or spiritual energy, in part because the very act of performance so effectively disguises the preparation and education of musical intuition that is so much a part of a musician's life. This is what that obsessive-compulsive activity known as practicing tends to do: both excite the performers with the joy of hearing and drive them through endless cycles of repetition and discovery. The embodied knowledge so cultivated becomes the basis of the ability to perform intuitively and responsively without the conscious overintrusion of intellectual interventions during performance.

The racial coding of the intuitive, natural, and spiritual as black and the intellectual and unemotional as white is to me one of the worst discursive legacies of the 1950s and 1960s. In the quest to prevent non–African Americans from erasing the centrality of African American culture in the history of the music, activists both black and white often resorted to various versions of Senghor's concept of the African personality, which took the classic racist stereotypes of the West and turned them into essentialized, naturalized virtues. If many African Americans deployed the idea of "It's a black thing; you wouldn't understand" to justifiably assert the right to cultural self-determination, and if many liberal and radical whites used essentialized ideas of blackness to support their own agendas of cultural rebellion, the fact remains that this enduring stereotype is ill suited to describe the constant quest for knowledge and its humane expression that underlay the flowering of Afro-modernism in jazz in this period.

As George Russell remarked, "I think the driving force for bebop coming out of swing was the dissatisfaction of black intellectuals and especially after the return from WWII. They felt they were coming back to the same old thing, and they were. And this whole feeling of blacks as an inferior intellect, you know. . . . I think it was a very muscular drive that bebop represented. To convince—to try again to convince—small-minded people that, if you have any kind of sensitivity at all, you can see that this music does not come from someone who lacks complexity."[23]

## Modal Jazz

In many ways John Coltrane is the ultimate bridge figure in jazz history. His musical explorations mastered the discipline of vertically oriented harmonic improvisation, convened a band that most deeply explored the implications of modal jazz, and became arguably the most influential exponent of the experimental in jazz. He is fervently admired by advocates of each of these stylistic tendencies and remains the only jazz musician to have had a church founded in his name.[24]

As a scholar, I tend to view the stylistic movement known as modal jazz in a similar light—as a stylistic tendency that bridged that overrated divide between the mainstream and the experimental with creativity and passion that continues to inspire generations later. As George Russell's Lydian Chromatic Concept of Tonal Organization illustrates, scales and modes are conceptually much broader than the style known as modal jazz, and many scholars and critics have recognized the need to reframe its history.

Although the introduction to George Russell's "Cubana Be" (1947) is among the first modally conceived compositions in jazz, most jazz history books prefer to define modal jazz very narrowly and take either Miles Davis's *Milestones* (1958) or "So What" (1959) as the first examples of the style.[25] The composition "So What" has indeed become the most canonical example of a modal jazz. The A sections of this thirty-two-bar AABA form present a theme in d Dorian, and the B section transposes the same idea up a half step to eb Dorian. There are no functional harmonic cadences. Lead sheets represent the harmonic structure of the composition as two chords—dm7 for the A sections and ebm7 for the B section. In the 1959 recording of "So What," pianist Bill Evans realized the sonority as a stack of three fourths and a major third (D, G, C, F, A), a voicing that has come to be called a "so what" voicing. Improvising soloists were not restricted to the notes of the Dorian mode. While the improvisations of Davis and Bill Evans remain close to the mode, John Coltrane and Cannonball Adderley play more freely over the tonally stable background.[26]

The term "modal jazz" has come to be associated with these two musical characteristics: fewer chords (than jazz standards or bebop compositions) and (consequently) greater freedom of note (and scale) selection over a relatively more stable tonal background. The rhythmic implications of tonally open frameworks have received less attention. Freed from the necessity of delineating frequently changing harmonies, bassists expanded their use of pedal points, pianists accompanied long sections with intricate vamps and riffs, and drummers played with greater rhythmic density and cross-rhythms than had been customary in early styles. Among the most spectacular realizations of the rhythmic, as well as tonal, implications of modal structures are those found in the recordings of the John Coltrane Quartet between 1960 and 1964 and those of the Miles Davis Quintet between 1963 and 1968. These ensembles featured two of the most revered rhythm sections in jazz: McCoy Tyner, Jimmy Garrison, and Elvin Jones of the former group and Herbie Hancock, Ron Carter, and Tony Williams of the latter.

The traditional definition of modal jazz is based on the so-called church modes of Western music. These are scales built on a particular rotation of the major scale (Dorian is the major scale beginning on the second degree, Phrygian on the third degree, etc.). It would be misleading to restrict the term "mode" to this sense since the scales that jazz musicians have used in more open-ended compositions include many more than these. Although jazz musicians tend to use the word "mode" as synonymous with "scale" (that is, a particular collection of pitches arranged from low to high), when viewed from a cross-cultural perspective, mode is a more complicated idea. As Harold Powers has stated, while mode in the West has tended to imply a scale and its intervallic structure, in the improvisational traditions of the Middle East and India, the idea of mode specifies particular pathways through a pitch collection, as well as melodic gestures. A raga or makam, in other words, is something more specific than a scale and less specific than a complete melody. Melodic gestures in jazz are most often studied as "patterns" or "licks" that are characteristic of a particular style (blues licks, John Coltrane licks, or pentatonic licks, for example), but many of them are rooted in particular scales.

I use the term "modal" in an expanded sense to imply five interrelated musical phenomena: (1) compositions featuring a lower density of chords (than jazz standards that emerged from Tin Pan Alley or Broadway musicals) or whose harmonic frame is specified in scales; (2) extended horizontally conceived solos that use scales and their segments to connect harmonies; (3) the use of vamps and pedal points to create open-ended frameworks for improvisation; (4) the development of nontriadic vertical sonorities that can nevertheless imply one or more traditional harmonies; and (5) an expanded vocabulary of rhythmic feels and melodic gestures that actively draw from non-European and North American sources (especially African and Caribbean). Of these, only the first two have been considered essential to defining the style known as modal jazz. The last three, however, seem critical in the identification of modal tendencies in the playing and reharmonization of more typical jazz repertory and an appreciation of how the melodic language was expanded in the more outgoing tonal directions (to use George Russell's terminology) of free jazz. To these musical traits must be added something more ineffable: a joy in exploring ambiguities in musical means—from piano voicings that can imply several chord functions to phrasing that disguises rather than delineates the formal boundaries

### Miles Davis: "My Funny Valentine"

Some music theorists would exclude from the concept of modal jazz any scale that uses a leading tone or pieces that include V7-I (dominant to tonic) cadences. In their view the melodic resolution of a leading tone or the harmonic resolution of the tritone in a dominant seventh chord locates a musical gesture within the realm of functional tonality.[27] I suggest that modal playing would usefully be defined by taking George Russell's concept of horizontal tonal gravity as a point of departure. Although Miles Davis's solo on "My Funny Valentine" from 1956 cannot be said to be modal in the sense of four of the five preceding criteria, Davis once commented while explaining his interest in modal approaches: "You know, we play 'My Funny Valentine' like with a scale all the way through."[28] The scale in question is C minor, which Davis presents in various guises throughout the solo. This makes sense, of course, since C minor 7 is the tonic chord of the piece. In bars 5–12 (0:30– 0:56) the scale is played twice, first beginning on C and then on G (figure 8.3).

FIGURE 8.3. Miles Davis, "My Funny Valentine," New York, October 26, 1956, Prestige (LP) 7166. Words by Lorenz Hart Music by Richard Rodgers © 1937 (Renewed) Chappel & Co. Rights for extended renewal term in U.S. controlled by WB Music Corp. o/b/o The Estate of Lorenz Hart and The Family Trust U/W Richard Rodgers and The Family Trust U/W Dorothy F. Rodgers (administered by Williamson Music). All rights reserved. Used by permission.

Rather than articulate the individual harmonies as they go by, Davis relies on a melodic cell from the melody of the tune and the ability of different segments of the scale to imply the underlying harmonies. When he arrives at the bridge, where the key shifts to the relative major (Eb), Davis exploits the tonal ambiguity that is possible in a modal approach by playing an opening gesture that neither confirms nor denies an Eb major tonality, but ends emphatically in a gesture commonly played to articulate c minor. This is a classic descending gesture that lands on the ninth of the cm7 chord (figure 8.4). In other words, Davis's improvised melody plays on the ambiguity between c minor and Eb major. Davis's ballad playing, so often celebrated for its lyricism and simplicity, often moves in a horizontal direction in these years by refraining from meeting the obvious deadlines of the chords, yet exquisitely implying the overall tonal framework. This joy in the ambiguities of tonality seems to me to be one of the hallmarks of the improvisational language of this period.

FIGURE 8.4. Miles Davis, "My Funny Valentine," New York, October 26, 1956, Prestige (LP) 7166. Words by Lorenz Hart Music by Richard Rodgers © 1937 (Renewed) Chappel & Co. Rights for extended renewal term in U.S. controlled by WB Music Corp. o/b/o The Estate of Lorenz Hart and The Family Trust U/W Richard Rodgers and The Family Trust U/W Dorothy F. Rodgers (administered by Williamson Music). All rights reserved. Used by permission.

## Vamps and Pedal Points

There are perhaps no more compelling vamps and pedal points in all of jazz than the those of John Coltrane's quartet with McCoy Tyner, Elvin Jones, and Jimmy Garrison. Yet the magic began before Jimmy Garrison joined the band, as Coltrane's 1960 recording of "Body and Soul" illustrates. The way in which the use of modal devices can breath life into old standards is particularly apparent here.

McCoy Tyner's quasi-clave two-bar vamp on an Eb minor chord, accompanied by Steve Davis's Ab pedal point in the bass line, creates a feel that is almost Latin, except for Elvin Jones's swing ride-cymbal. Tyner continues with the vamp once Coltrane has entered with the melody, transposing and varying it according to the changes, while Davis continues with the pedal point throughout the A section. The B section begins with an apparently more conventional approach to the changes that is wonderfully interrupted by the sounding of *Giant Steps* changes in the last four bars of the bridge (1:15). This alternation between sections anchored by vamps and pedal points and more traditional feels had by the time of these recording sessions (which produced the albums *Coltrane's Sound, My Favorite Things,* and *Coltrane Plays the Blues*) become a distinctive quality of the group.

The use of these modal devices on a decidedly nonmodal composition illustrates the way in which these harmonic and rhythmic devices reframed the entire aesthetic feeling of the piece. Although McCoy Tyner is particularly known for his use of quartal voicings and pentatonics, many of his vamps in his early work with the Coltrane quartet also do very creative things with tertian harmonies. For today's musicians, the ability to rearrange and recompose standards by using vamps and pedal points has simply become part of the jazz language.[29]

Coltrane's interest in spiritual ideas from around the world was accompanied by listening to the music of India, the Middle East, and Africa. Coltrane even studied North Indian music for a brief time with sitarist Ravi Shankar, and members of Coltrane's group, according to band member McCoy Tyner, were also quite interested in Indian music. It is surely no surprise that jazz musicians who were already interested in open-ended improvisations over vamps would recognize kindred musical spirits in the melodically rich improvisational music of India and the Middle East. Jazz musicians who listened to Indian classical music could see in the drone a device that could unify long stretches of melodically elaborate improvisation and in tala a cyclical time structure to support it. John Coltrane's lengthy solos over drones, often in intensive duet with drummer Elvin Jones, as Nisenson has observed, had obvious parallels with the interplay between soloist and tabla in North Indian classical music.[30]

George Russell would describe the tonal gravity of North Indian classical improvisation as supravertical—improvisation with respect to the overall tonality of a piece. In the early 1960s performance of modal jazz pieces, whether Coltrane's extended versions of "My Favorite Things" and "Africa" or the Miles Davis quintet's lengthy explorations of tunes such as "Milestones" and "So What" (Davis 1964) became increasingly supravertical and dronelike in orientation. In Russell's terms, as performers expanded the boundaries of modal tunes, a move took place from horizontal to supravertical tonal organization. To frame this as a cross-cultural change, as musicians began improvising over fewer chord changes, jazz improvisation came to more closely resemble the open-ended linguisticity of Indian and Middle Eastern music that Harold Powers has described. Indeed, Coltrane's solos, which after 1961 frequently lasted an hour or longer, became comparable in length to North Indian performances, much to the distress of some critics.[31]

I have been drawn again and again to Coltrane's improvisation on "Wise One," which is based on a twelve-bar progression that features cadences in two key areas a minor third apart. The progression includes a ii-V-I in gm and a V-I in e minor, and the two are inalterably linked by a modal shift in the last two bars to E dominant 7, which leads smoothly back to the beginning. Throughout the piece Elvin Jones plays variations on a mambo ride-cymbal pattern, and Jimmy Garrison play a variation on tumbao rhythm in the bass. McCoy Tyner does not vamp here but dances in and out with syncopated voicings. What is remarkable about the solo is not only its motivic development and slowly paced development but also the way in which his expressivity is as smooth, fluid and free as if he were playing on one chord. The first and second choruses follow a stepwise ascent in long tones that both illustrates the voice-leading possibilities in the progression and creates a feeling like that evoked by the opening of a North Indian alap (figure 8.5, boxes).[32]

Chorus three begins to release some of the pent-up energy by unleashing rapidly descending lines from still rising target pitches (figure 8.6, small boxes). Chorus four begins with the first appearance of a rhythmic motive (two sixteenths and a quarter) that reappear much later in the solo (figure 8.6, large boxes).

FIGURE 8.5. John Coltrane, choruses 1–2, "Wise One," *Crescent,* Englewood Cliffs, NJ, April 27, 1964, Impulse! IMPD-200. © 1977. Renewed 2005, Jowcol Music. Used by permission.

This is jazz meets Afro-Cuba meets India meets the blues while simultaneously moving beyond them all. Yet this is not another call to enshrine John Coltrane as the ultimate universal musician—for so often that discursive move becomes just another revival of the discourse of color-blindness, which tends to erase cultural differences and the systemic power imbalances that continue to underlie it. This is rather a call to celebrate Coltrane's deeply personal musical synthesis, which simultaneously embraced his cultural identity as an African American and refused to be contained by it. For this is one of the deepest lessons of Afro-Modernism—that it is possible both to be honest about one's origins and to cultivate the knowledge and expressive means to become something more than the sum of one's social categories.

Although it has become fashionable to critique Frank Kofsky's attempts to portray Coltrane as a revolutionary black nationalist at the expense of neglecting his spiritual interests, a number of events at which John Coltrane appeared during the 1960s complicate this picture.[33] It is true that he recorded a composition in honor of Martin Luther King Jr. (titled "Reverend King"), but Coltrane's name is noticeably absent from benefit events for mainstream civil rights organizations such as the SCLC, CORE, SNCC, or the NAACP.

FIGURE 8.6. John Coltrane, choruses 3–4, "Wise One," *Crescent,* Englewood Cliffs, NJ, April 27, 1964, Impulse! IMPD-200. © 1977. Renewed 2005, Jowcol Music. Used by permission.

However, his name *does* appear at three events that suggest possible interests in Marxism, the black arts movement, and African nationalism. An interest in Marxism is suggested by his appearances at benefits for the journal *Freedomways* and Paul Robeson in late 1964 and early 1965 (see chapter 6). Coltrane's participation at a benefit concert for Amiri Baraka's Black Arts Repertory Theatre/School at the Village Gate on March 28, 1965, which was recorded and released as *The New Wave in Jazz,* suggests his interest in supporting the creation of African American arts institutions in the black community. His last public appearance was at a benefit concert for Olatunji's Center of African Culture, an organization that was intended to awaken the interest of the Harlem community in learning about Africa. Indeed, at the very end of his life Coltrane had planned to do several self-produced concerts with Olatunji and intended to travel to Africa for further musical explorations. Olatunji had a long-standing interest in black nationalism and the Nation of Islam (see chapter 6).

I do not mention these events to rehabilitate Kofsky's view of Coltrane as a revolutionary black nationalist but to emphasize that Coltrane's universalism and a positive embrace of African American strategies of self-determination are not necessarily contradictory impulses.[34] That cultural nationalists, Marxists, proponents of color blindness, spiritual explorers, and aesthetic modernists have all claimed his legacy is hardly surprising.[35] Each hears in his music an analogy for their own experience, their own passions, and their own desires for self-transformation.

It is perhaps the deeply personal quality of jazz improvisation that has made its modernism so strikingly different from the post–World War II modernism of experimental classical art music, which has often sought to underplay the expression of individual voice (through chance operations or indeterminacy, for example) in favor of formal achievement or the structuring of randomly occurring sonic events.[36] The modernism of jazz has retained an investment in the romantic quality of the artist and the sovereignty of the individual voice, a quality that renders it (pace Derrida) potentially anachronistic in the eyes of many postmodern observers. Yet the idea that the agency of musicians can change the world, that the abstract play of pitches, rhythms, and timbres can inspire people to act, and that the distinctiveness of an individual voice can be utterly transformative continues to grip the imaginations of those drawn to the sounds of jazz. However fragmented, in other words, may be the contemporary postmodern, mass-mediated, globalized, spectacularized, and corporatized economy, the unfettered improvisatory explorations of musicians still seem to hold out the possibility of a utopian communal wholeness and redemptive individual freedom.

## Utopian Visions

In the case of John Coltrane and George Russell, reflections on harmony and symmetry did not lead to satisfaction with a structural understanding of music as the ultimate goal. Rather, each one found in music a pathway to religious and spiritual experience and, with it, utopian imaginings of a better world. Although some writers have described the deep presence of the religious in African American aesthetics, as well as the desire to reclaim a mythic African past as "anti-modern,"[37] I suggest that this persistent link between music, the divine, and politics highlights the complexity of African America's "counterculture of modernity," as Paul Gilroy has put it.[38] The coexistence in African American thought of religious longing, an interest in ancient history, and the modern values of progress and self-determination are hardly unusual.

Cornel West has drawn attention to the linking of the religious and modernity in African American history and culture through the idea of "prophetic pragmatism." By this he means a philosophy that "promotes the possibility of human progress *and* the human impossibility of paradise." For West the idea of *imago dei*—that humans are made in God's image—contains a radical egalitarianism that is of particular urgency to people who are denied humane treatment due to various structures of oppression, including race and class.[39] Indeed, from this perspective, the religious impulse has been necessary to sustain a sense of hope and optimism in the face of the odds against success in political struggles for justice. As could be said about the deep commitment of Southern activists in the civil rights movement, "you have to have deep, deep religious faith to stay in the struggle for a long time."[40]

Questions of identity, in West's perspective, also lead to religious, as well as the political, concerns. If identity is about the human need for belonging and protection, as well as comfort in the face of death and uncertainty, it is not far from "that deep existential level where religion resides."[41] To admit this is to call into question the Enlightenment's focus on reason alone as the ruling spirit of the modern subject. Humanism, in the African American tradition, West seems to argue, has emphasized a combination of modern subjectivity and a religious sensibility.

The belief of many musicians in the ethical, spiritual, and moral qualities of music (its deeper level) and simultaneously in modernity's values of progress, individual rights, and self-determination seems to be particularly tied to black music's view of what it is to be human. As West has observed, "This rich tradition of black music is not only an artistic response to the psychic wounds and social scars of a despised people; more importantly, it enacts in dramatic forms the creativity, dignity, grace and elegance of African-Americans without wallowing in self-pity or wading in white put-down. The black musical tradition is unique in this country because it assumes without question the full humanity of Americans of African descent and thereby allows blacks and others to revel in it."[42]

*This vision is something more than music as resistance.* Rather, this is where music becomes an ethical and moral stance that affirms the human dignity (or soul) of not only the individual performer but also the entire community. No matter how great the personal sins of the individual (from drugs to alcohol to sexual excess), music so envisioned offers a path of redemption and enactment—for imagining and creating a freer, more ideal community.

Like Cornel West, Robin D. G. Kelley finds that the linking of the modern and the spiritual is central to African Americans' visions of freedom. Kelley has argued passionately that in considering the historical impact of black radical thought in the twentieth century, intellectuals must focus not only on its protest and anger but also on its vision for the future. In what he admits is a utopian perspective, he argues that imagining a new world is something poetic: "We must remember that the conditions and the very existence of social movements enable participants to imagine something different, to realize that things need not always be this way. It is *that* imagination, that effort to see the future in the present, that I shall call 'poetry' or 'poetic knowledge.' "[43]

Kelley takes his inspiration from Aimé Césaire and Suzanne Césaire, who combined a critique of colonialism with an interest in surrealism. By surrealism, the Césaires meant a revolution of the mind that both looks toward the future and embraces the power of experience beyond the rational. As Kelley argues, "In many ways surrealism has real affinities with aspects of Afrodiasporic vernacular culture, including an embrace of magic, spirituality, and the ecstatic—elements Marxism has never been able to deal with effectively."[44]

In Suzanne Césaire's view, surrealism from an African diasporic viewpoint had potentially transcendent implications: "Our surrealism will supply this rising people with a punch from its very depths. Our surrealism will enable us to finally transcend the sordid antimonies of the present: whites/Blacks, Europeans/Africans, civilized/savages—at last rediscovering the magic power of the mahoulis, drawn directly from living sources."[45]

This universalistic aspiration of black nationalist thought—in its various instantiations from revolutionary nationalism to cultural nationalism, as well as Senghor and the Césaires' conception of Negritude—gave it ambitions well beyond simply creating a utopian social order for people of African descent alone. This new social order would also be crucial in saving the soul of whites, who had degraded themselves by the brutal acts they had committed in the course of practicing slavery, colonization, and racism. Expressed differently, this utopian, transcendent vision of a world without racism and oppression effectively inverts the universalist aspirations of the Western Enlightenment. If reason alone could not produce a humane social order, it suggests that perhaps combining reason with an African diasporic or pan-spiritual vision (that draws from the religious perspectives of all of the formerly colonized) can.

## Sonic Explorations

The cultivation of utopian visions in music has been particularly associated with musicians of the avant-garde, whose sonic explorations longed to give musical expression to these ideals. Every musical parameter—melody, rhythm, timbre, instrumentation, harmony, counterpoint—was opened to exploration. Many musicians wanted to move beyond traditional chromatic harmony and the chorus structures they articulated as the principal means of organizing improvisation. Modal jazz, which had already undermined the hegemony of the chorus structure by decreasing harmonic density and opening up the possibility of improvisation over extended vamps, had already expanded the conception of improvisation.

Like modernist European composers of the early twentieth century, the experimentalists seemed to equate a break with tonality with revolution. In the context of the civil rights movement and black nationalism, the abstract cries and shrieks of the New Thing were often taken as anger rather than as the spiritual exploration they were to many of its practitioners, such as John Coltrane, Sun Ra, and Albert Ayler.

As Richard Abrams, one of the founding members of Chicago's Association for the Advancement of Creative Musicians (AACM), saw it, the spiritual plane was best approached through the abstract, not the concrete, and he associated the concrete with harmony. Abrams and Roscoe Mitchell viewed melody, rhythm, and timbral exploration as the primary musical means of achieving spiritual transcendence, which they defined as a place where intuition and intellect meet through collaborative action.[46]

This deep spiritual quality would be among the most important aesthetic qualities desired in the Great Black Music that the AACM wanted to foster. As Ronald Radano has observed, "According to Abrams and Mitchell, then, harmony stood as an aesthetic barrier that restrained black musicians in their search for spiritual unity. As the principal component of European-based music, it became a metaphor for white cultural dominance and oppression: harmony was a sonic reconstruction of the chains that had bridled blacks, of the rationalism that had stifled African spiritualism."[47]

This rejection of harmony nevertheless had much in common with Schoenberg's "emancipation of dissonance," in which the break with tonality was viewed as progressive and potentially emancipatory. As Baraka's *Blues People* suggests, the abstraction of the New Thing indicated that African American artists were conversant in the Western traditions of nonconformity.[48] A shared metaphor operates in both discourses (dissonance = rebellion) but is put into practice in drastically different ways. Similarly, the association of the musical and the spiritual has a long tradition in German, as well as African, diasporic aesthetic thinking. Adorno's definition of art, for example, includes the idea that true art is transcendent and hence spiritual: "Only in the achievement of this transcendence, not foremost and indeed probably never through meanings, are artworks spiritual. Their transcendence is their eloquence, their script, but it is a script without meaning, or, more precisely, a script with broken or veiled meaning.... Art fails its concept when it does not achieve this transcendence; it loses its quality of being art."[49]

For Adorno this transcendence was imminent in the sound itself and in the artwork's striving to exceed itself. These convergences between the abstract music of jazz's experimental wing and the aesthetic perspectives of contemporary Western art music have caused some observers, most famously Wynton Marsalis, to dismiss the musical outpourings of experimentalists such as Cecil Taylor, Ornette Coleman, and the Art Ensemble of Chicago as too imitative of white aesthetics. Nevertheless, unlike the classical explorations of groups such as the Modern Jazz Quartet in the 1950s, which sought to prove the legitimacy of jazz in the eyes of lovers of Western classical music, the AACM did not seek mainstream acceptance. Rather, it designated itself as a community organization dedicated to serving its Chicago southside constituency.

The AACM's founding principles articulated a collective vision, and this is one of key ways in which the utopian visions of the jazz experimentalists diverged from the individualistic concept of freedom that undergirds the European aesthetic tradition. Adorno viewed collectivity with extreme suspicion in part because he associated it with fascism.[50] The AACM's vision of community was much more akin to a West African conception of the relationship between the individual and community as described by John Chernoff: "But in an African context, such as a musical event, individuality is related to participation, and in the complex relationships of an African community context, character is understood as a sense of one's relationships with others, as a continuing style of involvement and making do, and hence as a focus for moral judgments."[51]

That AACM's collective ideal is summarized in its nine goals, which have remained constant since the organization's founding in 1965. Among these are creating "an atmosphere conducive to artistic endeavors for the artistically inclined," conducting "free training for disadvantaged city youth," "encouraging sources of employment for musicians," setting "an example of high moral standards for musicians," upholding "the tradition of cultured musicians handed down from the past," stimulating "spiritual growth in musicians," and assisting other "complementary charitable organizations."[52] The AACM, which has produced several prominent groups of experimentalists (including the Art Ensemble of Chicago, Air, Eight Bold Souls, and the Ethnic Heritage Ensemble) enacted a community-minded form of self-determination that has successfully sustained itself in its home community for more than forty years.

One of the most important imperatives for AACM members is the rule that "all music presented had to be original products of the musicians giving the event." According to George Lewis, through this ideal the AACM built a community of composers, not only improvisers.[53] The creative environment of the AACM and its school thus offered a space for the cultivation of a composerly perspective among musicians in a world where the mainstream tended to presume that the creativity of African American musicians was exclusively improvisational.

Sun Ra's musical explorations were also both composerly and deeply informed by a broad spectrum of spiritual and Afrocentric thought—from the Baptist Church to Gurdjieff, from ancient Egypt to outer space. His spiritual interests and utopian vision of blackness have been insightfully documented by both John Szwed and Graham Lock.[54] What interests me here is the delight in sonic experimentation that Sun Ra's vision of the Arkestra as a spiritual community produced. In Sun Ra's view, the musical techniques he developed were not from human sources. Rather, Sun Ra viewed himself as a spiritual agent of God whose mission was to make art for the sake of the creator.[55] If God was space, as Sun Ra believed, the ultimate goal of the music was space travel. As Szwed has noted, Sun Ra's theatrical/magical/musical universe was a form of "black science fiction" that was saturated with themes of freedom, apocalypse, and survival.[56] Trumpeter Fred Adams explained the connection between sound and space travel: "Just playing the right note or the right chord can transfer you into space, and also those who are listening. If they are listening carefully and are sincere enough, they can feel the energy that is being projected, and can travel along with you."[57]

Unlike the AACM, whose organization was participatory and egalitarian, Sun Ra viewed himself as a spiritual leader chosen by the Creator and consequently expected the members of his Arkestra to respect his absolute authority. As John Szwed recounts, Sun Ra often punished musicians who disobeyed by removing them from publicity posters, cutting their solos from recordings, or failing to announce their names during concerts. In this respect, Sun Ra functioned more like an authoritarian patriarch than a radical egalitarian. Indeed, according to Szwed, Sun Ra viewed the rhetoric of freedom as a trick. What was needed instead were strong leaders who commanded the respect of their followers.[58]

Sun Ra took great pride in the fact that his music had been created without the sponsorship of any white person. Although much of his music after 1965 was abstract, he did not take a principled position against harmony. Indeed, one of the remarkable things about the Arkestra was its ability to play a broad range of music—from swing arrangements of standards (as on *Holiday for Soul Dance*) to the vamp-based *Space Is the Place*, with its sing-along chorus, to the extroverted abstract blowing of "Cosmic Chaos" from *Heliocentric Worlds*, vols. 1–2, and the static timbral explorations of "Spectrum" from *The Solar Myth Approach.*[59]

To listen to Sun Ra and the Arkestra is to hear the music of someone in love with sonic possibility in all of its forms. As it was for Duke Ellington, the large orchestra was Sun Ra's instrument. He called his pedal-point-based sections "space keys," demanded that every note a musician played be a "living note," and rehearsed reactions to particular musical cues rather than arrangements per se.[60] In other words, he devised a kind of improvised but directed contrapuntal call and response that allowed musicians improvisational freedom but allowed him to control the overall shape of the performance.

## Back on Earth

As the examples of the AACM and Sun Ra illustrate, the utopian visions of the jazz experimentalists could be (but were not necessarily) egalitarian in philosophy. Consequently, they could be (but were not necessarily) inclusive of men and women, black, white, and brown. Like all visions of a better world, any attempt to place ideals into practice seem destined, upon close examination, to disappoint. Spiritual in the context of the black arts movement was often a code word for blackness. It was something that white people were not and people of African descent were. It was a quality that could be used to draw a boundary around African American cultural space at a time when the cultivation of self-help and self-love was essential in creating a sense of black pride and autonomy. Just as women in the nascent feminist movement felt the need to form consciousness-raising groups in order to air their frustrations with sexism and heal their self-hate without the presence of men, so did many African Americans feel the need to talk about race and culture among themselves.

Yet, both the AACM and Sun Ra had ultimately to contend with the realization that some of their most passionate supporters were also liberal and radical whites, to whom the utopian blackness articulated in the music became in some respects their vision as well. It is as if, despite their realization that they were not black and were welcome only some of the time, they understood both that universality need not be white and that the apparent racial boundaries drawn in the process of aesthetic and cultural self-determination were not always strictly observed.

In the end, the metaphor of self-determination—and music as a path to its realization—was an idea many non–African Americans could transpose to their own social and personal circumstances. If non–African Americans often failed to realize that the responsibility to become self-determining was not simply an individual matter for African Americans, they *did* appreciate the magnitude of their heroes' musical achievements. If what they saw was a musical enactment of freedom in a world that still kept African Americans in psychic chains, they wanted to taste the feeling and participate—not simply on behalf of the oppressed but also on their own behalf.

# 9

## Coda

THE PRIMARY GOAL of *Freedom Sounds* has been to explore the interplay between music and politics in jazz during the years of the civil
rights movement and African independence. The narrative has moved
among the economic and structural dimensions of racism in the music
industry, the discourses used by musicians to justify and legitimate their
political and aesthetic perspectives (among them colorblindness, modernism, black nationalism, and self-determination), and the often more complicated and contradictory everyday practices of musicians that sometimes
drew the boundary between African and non–African American starkly
and other times not. During these years, musicians from multiple aesthetic
persuasions valued political activism of various kinds and channeled an
enormous amount of creative energy into aesthetic innovation. The music
became a symbol of social progress, self-determination, freedom, excellence, and spirituality.

I hope to have provided enough historical examples drawn from the
economic history of the music to have persuaded my readers that systemic
racial practices in the music industry created enormous differences in the
lives of black and white musicians that could not help but feed the chronic
racial disputes and resentments that erupted regularly within the world of
jazz. I hope to have illuminated the contradictory and complicated role
that the discourses of modernism and modernity played in both justifying
rebellion against the racial status quo and falling short of supporting African American efforts to find a means of self-determination in a society in
which they were (and continue to be) outnumbered.

The crucial issue at the center of this historical analysis has been the recognition that the aesthetic streams contributing to jazz have proved to be far more mobile and hybrid than the sociological and economic status of the various demographic groups who have drawn upon them in the processes of aesthetic agency that produced this golden era of modern jazz. Put another way, the musical language of jazz has been far more pluralistic, democratic, and cosmopolitan than the racially stratified society that produced it.

It is possible to draw a diagram of this larger picture that illustrates the key point I wish to make. In figure 9.1 the top row of circles represents the free-flowing aesthetic mix that has characterized jazz and American popular music. The bottom row of circles represents the partially overlapping but more rigidly bounded social and demographic categories in the United States. Although any musicians whose roots are in one of these social or demographic categories can deploy their musical agency in a way that draws from multiple musical aesthetics, the social categories to which individuals are assigned (perceptually or legally) have been far more rigid. Although the hope of the mainstream civil rights movement was to ensure that future generations would be judged by the "content of their character" rather than the color of their skin, recent work in sociology, economics, and political science has shown that African Americans some fifty years after the start of the civil rights movement remain disadvantaged relative to every other American demographic group, including recent immigrants. Although far more people are now claiming multiracial identities than during the civil rights and Black Power years, in everyday life individuals are often perceived to belong primarily to one of these categories on the basis of how they look and are treated according to stereotypes of that category.

Throughout the twentieth century African and non–African Americans alike have wanted to break free from the rigidities of sociological categories through music, yet it is non–African Americans who have had more freedom in crossing these racial boundaries in society. Welcomed into the black and tan clubs on Chicago's south side and Harlem's dance halls, many young white musicians such as Jack Teagarden, Bix Beiderbecke, Mezz Mezzrow, Benny Goodman, and Artie Shaw found themselves musically and personally transformed by their encounters with African American music.

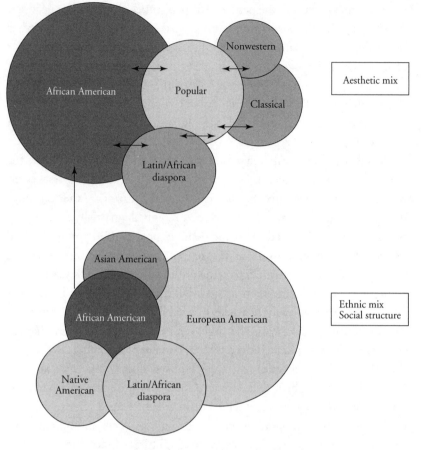

FIGURE 9.1. Aesthetic mix versus sociological mix.

The structural advantages of being white in the music industry (in the 1930s and 1940s) led to the popularization of big band swing music in the 1940s by major white bands such as Benny Goodman's, whose first hits included several arrangements composed by African American Fletcher Henderson. The economic success of the white swing bands and the American public's mistaken assumption that Goodman had originated the style led to a greater cultural protectiveness on the part of African American musicians. The discourse about white musicians as primarily imitators who profited excessively from the creativity of African American musicians grew well in this soil. As chapter 2 has shown, segregated practices in the American Federation of Music and the nature of copyright law created a market that did not compensate African American musicians in proportion to their contributions to musical style. Under these circumstances, it is not surprising that African American musicians in the 1950s seemed to grow more reluctant to acknowledge the musical skills of their white competitors.

In chapter 3 I proposed a framework for moving beyond the familiar discursive standoff between jazz as black music and jazz as a colorblind music. Making the distinction between the free flow of several aesthetic streams and the relative immobility of race-based social hierarchies (as depicted in figure 9.1) was key to my contention that musicians can share many features of musical style but at the same time have different (and unequal) social relationships within the music industry, within racial hierarchies off the bandstand, and within other more impersonal aspects of society. However powerfully experienced the feelings of universality and boundless community may be in the act of musical performance, music alone has never had the power to transform the underlying social structure.

The primary reason for African Americans' dissatisfaction with the discourse of colorblindness as a description of the aesthetic mix in American popular music is that it does not give African American musicians credit for their substantial influence on the aesthetics of this music or recognize how underpaid they were for their contributions. To put it another way, not only does the ideology of color blindness fail to acknowledge the size of African Americans' aesthetic contributions (greater than the demographic size of the African American population), but it also fails to draw attention to the fact that the racially structured music industry of the mid-twentieth century did not ultimately compensate African American artists in proportion to their cultural influence. From this point of view, the deployment of colorblindness ideology to minimize the recognition of African American leadership in music such as jazz simply is not fair. Moreover, to describe the feelings of cultural protectiveness that this situation has created as reverse racism baldly mischaracterizes the social dynamics that often provoke the drawing of the essentialist line.[1]

Is there a way to move beyond this impasse—one that does not rely on guilt tripping or finger pointing but rather takes as a point of departure ethical reflection on the rather complicated processes of cultural exchange that music so clearly demonstrates? I have argued in chapter 3 that the process of cultural exchange among African Americans, European Americans, and other ethnic or social streams is not so much reciprocal as recursive. By this I meant to draw attention to processes of exchange, whereby something borrowed is introduced into a new context, where it is repeatedly drawn upon in a new social framework—that is, internalized in a musician's musical practice—to generate a new musical style (in that context).

Of course, what may be evaluated as a "new sound" in one social context may or may not earn that aesthetic evaluation in another. Dave Brubeck's sound, for example, was certainly something new—not simply a rote imitation of existing styles—but was nevertheless more popular in non–African American than African American circles (which is not to say that his music did not have African American fans.) Also documented in chapter 3 is the growing embrace in the 1950s and 1960s of African American performers by non–African Americans. A growing number of white Americans showed less race loyalty to white jazz performers than seemed to be the case in the 1940s. This is another way of saying that a growing segment of non–African Americans began to embrace aspects of black musical style as their own, which perhaps explains why feelings of rejection can be so strong when Africa Americans raise an ethnic boundary around cultural ownership.

As I have pointed out in chapter 7, one of the classic arguments white Americans have made in response to black assertions of cultural ownership of the music has been to demand that African Americans give up the claim that they have a privileged relationship to the music by virtue of being black. Yet, as I hope this historical investigation has helped to clarify, what seems most urgent in creating a better interracial dialogue about African American music is for non–African Americans to think through the *particularity* of their own needs and expectations of it. No one's relationship to the music, after all, is universal; everyone comes to it from particular places on the social and historical map. To acknowledge this is the first step in learning to respect each other's differences.

African Americans' claims of a special relationship to black music by virtue of sharing the deeply personal social experience of racial discrimination do not invalidate the fact that the ubiquitousness of black music in American culture has also created a history of non–African American relationships to the music that is no less real or authentic. It is much easier for African Americans to acknowledge the musical strengths of white performers if advocacy for white performers is decoupled from an ideology whose agenda is minimizing the significance of African American leadership in the history of the music of this period. For many white American lovers of black music, this means simply acknowledging that they begin from a different sociological and symbolic relationship to that fundamentally hybrid thing called black music, which was bequeathed by a long social history beyond their immediate control.

Would it not be better for the souls of white folks if we were able to acknowledge—with no strings attached—that jazz and African American aesthetics were for twentieth-century American music something like what spirituals were for the nineteenth century? As W.E.B Du Bois said of the spirituals, perhaps they were "the most beautiful expression of human experience born this side of the seas . . . and the greatest gift of the Negro people."[2] Has the narrative of reverse discrimination so poisoned our souls, that those of us who are white cannot acknowledge the influence of African American music on our hearts and minds, without resentment or colorblind conditions?

This is emphatically not a message of social determination, for, in the end, the enduring effect of modernism in jazz has always been the deeper presumption that through one's musical and artistic practice it is possible to break beyond the limits of any given pregiven category. This has also been one of the deepest spiritual messages of the music. What should ultimately matter is not where the journey began so much as what is done along the way. This delicate balance between who we are as members of larger collectivities and as individual voices is something that the history of jazz makes plain in ways that, in my opinion, have a significance far beyond music history. These are some of the central ethical issues that face our increasingly pluralistic and global world, and our future will be defined by the success with which we engage them.

But is there anything inherently moral, ethical, progressive, rebellious, or visionary about improvisation per se? It may surprise my readers to learn that I do not think so. This, despite the fact that I have just spent eight chapters tracing the impact of the civil rights movement, African nationalism, and the Black Power movement on debates over aesthetics, politics, economics, and race in the jazz world. If ever jazz was involved in shaping a social and political vision, as well as an ethical and spiritual sense of community and accountability, this was it. To argue that improvisation itself—that is, the manipulation of sounds, timbres, rhythms, pitches, and composition in real time—does not guarantee ethical virtue, however, is not to say that jazz improvisers did not play an active role in articulating a social and political vision, but that that vision is located in *people* and what they do rather than in the formal properties of improvisation itself. Improvisation, after all, is one of the near universals of music. Virtually all known musical cultures engage in some form of improvisation (yes, even Western classical music), even if some social groups or cultures do not value it very highly. Variation, embellishment, repetition, elaboration, departure, and return can all be illustrated through musical examples drawn from all over the globe.

The particular resonance of music and politics in jazz history and its progressive ethos comes not from its privileged articulation of freedom in musical form, as a thinker such as Adorno might argue,[3] but from the way musicians and their audiences have responded to the juncture of music and larger historical and social forces. How a musician such as John Coltrane, Dave Brubeck, or Max Roach connected them is a matter of both aesthetic agency and historical moment. The musical process of improvisation models the possibility of that engagement but cannot bequeath it alone. The association of freedom and the sounds of jazz is part of a historical process, not only a musical one.

The historical span explored in *Freedom Sounds* is one in which an enormous grassroots political movement dedicated to the dismantling of Jim Crow segregation developed from the audacity of daring activists whose strategic defiance of the rules of segregation ultimately inspired (and exhorted) others to take up the torch. Like African American music, the message of civil rights organizers resonated broadly within and beyond African American communities and set off a series of divisive political and social debates that had implications for not only American society but the globe as well. These debates were larger than any single individual (or group, for that matter) and became part of the ethical fabric of daily life, part of the set of issues that defined what it was to be an American citizen.

By aesthetic agency I mean the choices musicians make in crafting their musical voice—choices made necessarily against the backdrop of living in particular places at particular moments in time and from the vantage point of occupying a specific configuration of social positions (age, race, gender, class, and so on ). For developing a musical voice is fundamentally a process of synthesis that results from practicing, performing, discovering, and being moved by the experience of playing and hearing music. It comes from being inspired, challenged, and prepared to take the risk of beginning a musical engagement that could end in either joy or humiliation. It comes not only from interacting with other musicians on the bandstand but also from living in the world.

The historical events of the civil rights movement and African independence produced an unusually intense level of political and aesthetic debate in the jazz world and also some of the most exquisitely beautiful music in the entire history of the art form. The debates over racial sound stereotypes, economics, integration, self-determination, ownership and control, and authenticity have not died out in American culture in the post–civil rights years, but the centrality of jazz in articulating them has declined dramatically as hip hop has taken up the legacy of these debates. Was the social relevance of jazz a flash in the pan? Was it a historical anomaly that temporarily conferred upon the elitism of art a social relevance it could not sustain? Or was it, as John Coltrane's example suggests, a life-giving quest for knowledge and excellence that still has much to teach us?

As the audience for jazz has shrunk in the United States, many theories have circulated as to the cause for its lackluster showing in commercial markets. Some observers blame the avant-garde for driving away the traditional African American base of the music. Others blame the institutionalization of a jazz pedagogy that is far more comfortable addressing the technical qualities of the music rather than its historical and social meanings. Another explanation for the relative invisibility of jazz in its home culture is the lack of state support for broadcasting and arts performance similar to that available in Western Europe.[4]

Although the cultivation of the status of art in a post–World War II world that was content to keep jazz in the comfortable space of entertainment music seems to have been the right thing to emphasize at the time, it appears that a striving toward the status of art cannot be the only goal. There has been a high price paid for the success of jazz as a modern art music—among them, the shrinking of the market for jazz to the size of the market for classical music and the loss of a considerable portion of its African American audience. Today the music that is most powerfully articulating social and political concerns—at least in the eyes of the post–civil rights generations—is hip hop.

I write my closing thoughts more than a year after Hurricane Katrina destroyed New Orleans and laid bare the continuing depth of racial disparity in the United States. The mobilization of musicians on behalf of New Orleans has made me reflect on all of the benefit concerts that took place during the civil rights years. During the 1960s the civil rights and Black Power movements were so strong that they demanded that musicians and entertainers take a stand. The efforts for New Orleans have taken place in a political climate in which the right wing of the political spectrum is far more activist than the left. On September 17, 2005, I watched the television broadcast of Marsalis's Higher Ground live benefit concert and was filled with emotion as the sounds of the New Orleans style were drastically recontextualized and infused with new relevance and poignancy by the tragic breaking of the levees and the destruction of the neighborhoods that birthed jazz.

In the intervening time, musicians from multiple genres have done benefit concerts or made CDs, the Center for Jazz Studies at Columbia University has sponsored a major conference titled "New Orleans: Rebuilding the Musical City," and organizations such the Jazz Foundation, Tipitina's Foundation, Save Nola Music, New Orleans radio station WWOZ, and many others have raised funds and established networks for aiding New Orleans musicians and other hurricane survivors. Nevertheless, this nascent movement for New Orleans has not captured the attention of the national media, in part because of the urgency of the war in Iraq; thus, the prospects of rebuilding a vibrant neighborhood-based musical culture such as existed before seem depressingly remote.

The sudden destruction of New Orleans and the displacement of its vibrant African American–centered culture seem to me a metaphor for American culture of the most haunting kind. American popular culture has drawn much sustenance, joy, and pleasure from all of the African American music in its presence, and all of the hybrid fruit its followers have borne. It has easily absorbed and assimilated that musical feeling, its slang, and its visual style but is often indifferent to the continuing race-based suffering of it poorest citizens. Will the sudden devastation of New Orleans result in a rebuilding plan that celebrates the black and hybrid African American heritage of New Orleans, or, now that American culture has so thoroughly consumed and incorporated its aesthetic (as it does any other product), will it once again turn its back and claim that race no longer matters? Twenty years from now will jazz, like rock, become thought of as white music in the American context? Will it be considered a primarily European music, as critics like Stuart Nicholson contend?[5]

It is my hope that thinking through the complex interaction of race, politics, and music in the years of the civil rights movement and African independence has helped to make unmistakably clear the striving for freedom and dignity that is central to the ethos of this music. I hope also that these pages have attuned readers to the historical contexts that shaped these associations. That the ethical dimensions of this music history happen to coexist with the pure pleasure and beauty of the musical sounds themselves is one of the deepest gifts of the music.

# Appendix A: Abbreviations and Acronyms

| | |
|---|---|
| AAAR | African Academy of Arts and Research |
| AFM | American Federation of Musicians |
| ANTA | American National Theatre and Academy |
| CAA | Council on African Affairs |
| COFO | Council of Federated Organizations |
| CORE | Congress of Racial Equality |
| CPP | U.S. Department of State, Cultural Presentations Program |
| CU | Bureau of Educational and Cultural Affairs Historical Collection, U.S. Department of State, Cultural Presentations Program. |
| ICC | Interstate Commerce Commission |
| ICES | International Cultural Exchange Service |
| IEP | International Exchange Program |
| JAG | Jazz Artists Guild |
| JATP | Jazz at the Philharmonic |
| NAACP | National Association for the Advancement of Colored People |
| NALC | Negro American Labor Council |
| NCLC | Nashville Christian Leadership Council |
| NOI | Nation of Islam |
| NUL | National Urban League |
| SCLC | Southern Christian Leadership Conference |
| SNCC | Student Nonviolent Coordinating Committee |

# Appendix B: Interviews, Archival Sources, and Recordings

## Interviews

Brown, Oscar, Jr., interview with author by telephone, June 20, 1998.
Carter, Ron, conversation with author, April 23, 1995, New York, NY.
———, interview with author, July 31, 1995, New York, NY.
Coleman, Val, interview with author by telephone, July 23, 1997.
D'Lugoff, Art, interview with author, January 5, 1997, New York, NY.
Gitler, Ira, interview with author, October 21, 2000, New York, NY.
Hentoff, Nat, interview with author, January 2, 1997, New York, NY.
Keepnews, Orrin, interview with author by telephone, July 15, 2004.
Lincoln, Abbey, interview with author, June 13, 1995, New York, NY.
———, telephone conversation, December 4, 2001.
Macero, Teo, interview with author, March 15, 1995, New York, NY.
Morgenstern, Dan, interview with author, June 20, 1995, Newark, NJ.
Moss, Ronald. Interview with author by telephone, April 21, 1995.
Rich, Marvin, interview with author, January 3, 1997, New York, NY.
Roach, Max, interview with author, April 3, 1999, Cambridge, MA.
Rudd, Roswell, interview with author, June 28, 1998.
Russell, George, interview with author, August 7, 1995, Jamaica Plain, MA.
Terry, Clark, interview with author, March 27, 1997, St. Louis, MO.
Weston, Randy, conversation with author, April 13, 1999, Cambridge, MA.

## Archival Sources

American Federation of Musicians. Local 802. Minutes of the Trial Board (microfilm). New York University, Tamiment Library.

Bureau of Educational and Cultural Affairs Historical Collection (CU). U.S. Department of State. Cultural Presentations Program. Special Collections Division. University of Arkansas Library, Fayetteville, AR. The collection uses the abbreviation CU. The records are organized into subseries, boxes, and folders. Since the collection was being cataloged at the time they were consulted, some of the box and folder numbers may have changed.

Congress of Racial Equality Records (CORE), 1941–1967. State Historical Society of Wisconsin, Madison, WI. Records are organized into series, boxes, and folders.

Institute of Jazz Studies (IJS). Rutgers University, Newark, NJ. Records are organized into topic files and file names.

Records of the Southern Christian Leadership Conference, 1954–1970 (microfilm). Records are organized into parts, reels, and frames.

Student Nonviolent Coordinating Committee Papers, 1959–1972 (microfilm). Records are organized into subgroups, series, reels, and frames. The original records are housed at the Martin Luther King Library and Archives, Atlanta, GA.


## Recordings

Abdul-Malik, Ahmed. *Jazz Sounds of Africa,* Englewood Cliffs, NJ, May 23, 1961, and August 22, 1962, Prestige PRCD-24279–2.

Adderley, Cannonball. "This Here," *Greatest Hits: The Riverside Years,* San Francisco, October 20, 1958, Milestone Records MCD-9275–2.

Armstrong, Louis. *Satchmo the Great,* recorded various locations, 1956, Columbia CK 53580.

Basie, Count. "Sent for You Yesterday," *Big Band Jazz,* New York, February 16, 1938, Smithsonian RD 030-2.

———. "Tickle Toe," *The Essential Count Basie,* vol. 2, New York, March 19, 1940, Columbia CK 40835.

Blakey, Art. "Art Blakey's Comments on Ritual," *Ritual,* New York, February 11, 1957, Blue Note CDP 7 46858 2.

———. "Dinga," *Holiday for Skins,* vol. 2, New York, November 9, 1958, Blue Note BST-84005.

———. *Drum Suite,* New York, February 22, 1957, Columbia CL 1002.

———. "The Freedom Rider," *The Freedom Rider,* Englewood Cliffs, NJ, February 12, 18, and May 27, 1961, Blue Note CDP 7243 8 21287 2 4.

Brown, Joe Washington, and Austin Coleman. "Run, Old Jeremiah," *Afro-American Spirituals, Work Songs, and Ballads,* Jennings, LA 1934, Rounder Records CD 1510.

Brubeck, Dave. "Pennies from Heaven," *Brubeck Time,* New York, October 14, 1954, Columbia CK 65724.

———. "Take Five," *Time Out,* New York, July 1, 1959, Columbia CK 65122.

Charles, Ray. "Hard Times," *Ray Charles: The Birth of Soul, 1954–1957,* Atlantic 7 82310–2.

Cole, Nat King. "Sweet Lorraine," *The Complete after Midnight Sessions,* Hollywood, 1946, Capitol CDP 7 48328 2.

Coleman, Ornette. "Blues Connotation," *This Is Our Music,* New York, August 1960, Atlantic 7567-80767-2.

———. *Change of the Century,.* New York, October 8–9, 1959, Atlantic SD 1327.

Coltrane, John. *A Love Supreme,* New York, December 9, 1964, Impulse! GRD 155.

———. *Ascension,* Englewood Cliffs, NJ, June 28, 1965, Impulse! 314 543 413 2.

———. "Wise One," *Crescent,* Englewood Cliffs, NJ, April 27, 1964, Impulse! IMPD-200.

———, Grachan Moncur, Archie Shepp, and Charles Tolliver. *The New Wave in Jazz,* New York, March 28, 1965, Impulse! GRD-137.

Cooke, Sam. "Any Day Now," *Sam Cooke with the Soul Stirrers,* Specialty SPCD-7009-2.

Crosby, Bing. "Pennies from Heaven," *Best of Bing Crosby,* 1936, MCA Records MCAD-11942.

Davis, Miles. *Birth of the Cool,* New York, 1949, 1950, Capitol CDP 7 92862 2.

———. *The Complete Concert 1964: My Funny Valentine + Four & More,* New York, February 12, 1964, Columbia CK 40609.

———. *Miles Davis at Carnegie Hall,* New York, May 19, 1961, Columbia C2K 65027.

———. "My Funny Valentine," *Cookin',* New York, October 26, 1956, Prestige LP 7166.

*Debut Records Story, The.* Berkeley, Calif., 1977, Debut 4DCD-4420-2.

Eckstine, Billy. "Blue Moon," *Everything I Have Is Yours: The Best of the M-G-M Years,* 1948, Verve 819 442-2.

Ellington, Duke. *Reminiscing in Tempo,* New York, September 12, 1935, Columbia CK 48654.

Farmer, Art, and Benny Golson. "Killer Joe," *Meet the Jazztet,* Chicago, February 1960, Chess CHD-91550.

Georgia Sea Island Singers. "Sign of the Judgment," *Georgia Sea Islands: Southern Journey,* vol. 12, 1960, Rounder CD 1712.

Getz, Stan. "On the Alamo," *The Roost Quartets,* New York, May 17, 1950, Roulette CDP 7 96052 2.

————, and Dizzy Gillespie. "Dark Eyes," *For Musicians Only,* Los Angeles, October 16, 1956, Verve 837 435-2.

Gillespie, Dizzy. *Afro,* New York, May 21 and June 3, 1954, Norgran Records 314 517 052-2.

————. *The Complete RCA Victor Recordings,* New York, December 22, 1947, Bluebird (RCA) 07863 66528-2.

Hodges, Johnny. "Day Dream," *The Great Ellington Units,* Chicago, November 2, 1940, Bluebird (RCA) 6751-2-RB.

Jazz at the Philharmonic. *The Exciting Battle: JATP, Stockholm '55,* Stockholm, Sweden, 1955, Pablo 2310713.

*Jazz Life, The,* New York, November 1 and 11, 1960, Candid 9019.

Lincoln, Abbey. *Straight Ahead,* New York, February 22, 1961, Candid CCD 79015.

Machito. *Afro-Cuban Jazz,* New York, 1947, 1950, 1957, 1958, Saludos Amigos CD 62015.

————. *Kenya,* New York, 1958, Palladium PCD-104.

Marsalis, Wynton. *Blood on the Fields*, New York, January 22–25, 1995, Columbia CXK 57694.

Mingus, Charles. *Complete Candid Recordings of Charles Mingus: Newport Rebels–Jazz Artists Guild,* New York, November 1 and 11, 1960, Candid 9022.

————. "Original Faubus Fables," *Charles Mingus Presents Charles Mingus,* New York, October 20, 1960, Candid BR-5012.

————. "Prayer for Passive Resistance," *Mingus at Antibes,* Juan-les Pins, France, July 13, 1960, Atlantic SD 2-3001.

Modern Jazz Quartet. *Concorde,* New York, July 2, 1955, Prestige PRCD-7005-2.

————. *Django,* New York, June 25, 1953, Prestige VDJ-1515E.

———. "Vendome," *MJQ*, New York, December 22, 1952, Prestige PRLP 7059/OJC-125.

Monk, Thelonious. "Thelonious," *Genius of Modern Music*, vol. 2, New York, October 15, 1947, Blue Note 81511.

Morgan, Lee. *The Sidewinder*, Englewood Cliffs, NJ, December 21, 1963, Blue Note BST-84157.

*Norman Granz's Jazz at the Philharmonic, Hartford, 1953.* Hartford, CT, May 1953, Pablo 2308240.

Olatunji, Babatunde. *Drums of Passion*, New York, NY, 1959, Columbia, CK 66011.

Parker, Charlie. "Parker's Mood," *Yardbird Suite: The Ultimate Charlie Parker Collection*, New York, September 18, 1948, Rhino R2 72260.

Puente, Tito. *Puente in Percussion*, New York, 1955, Fania TRLP-1011.

———. *Top Percussion*, New York, July 19, 1957, RCA 3264-2-RL.

Rich, Buddy, and Max Roach. *Rich versus Roach*, New York, Spring 1959, Mercury 826 987-2.

Roach, Max. *We Insist! Freedom Now Suite*, New York, August 31 and September 6, 1960, Candid CCD 9002.

Shearing, George. *Latin Lace/Latin Affair*, Capitol 7243 4 494993 2 4.

Shorter, Wayne. "Ping Pong," *The Complete Blue Note Recordings of Art Blakey's 1960 Jazz Messengers*, Englewood Cliffs, NJ, February 12, 1961, Mosaic MD6-141.

Silver, Horace. "Ecaroh," *Horace Silver Trio*, New York, October 9, 1952, Blue Note CDP 7 81520 2.

———. "Horoscope," *Horace Silver Trio*, New York, October 9, 1952, Blue Note CDP 7 81520 2.

———. "Message from Kenya," *Horace Silver Trio*, New York, November 23, 1953, Blue Note CDP 7 81520 2.

———. "Safari," *Horace Silver Trio*, New York, October 9, 1952, Blue Note CDP 7 81520 2.

Sinatra, Frank. "Songs for Swingin' Lovers!" 1956, Capitol CDP 7 46570 2.

Smith, Jimmy. "Prayer Meetin,' " *Prayer Meetin,'* February 8, 1963, Blue Note CDP 7 84164 2.

Sun Ra. *Heliocentric Worlds*, vol. 1, New York, April 20, 1965, ESP-1014.

——— *The Heliocentric Worlds of Sun Ra*, vol. 2, New York, November 16, 1965, Get Back 1005.

———. *Holiday for Soul Dance*, 1968–1969, Evidence ECD 22011-2, Arkestra.

———. *Space Is the Place*, Chicago, October 19–20, 1972, Impulse! IMPD-249.

———. *Solar Myth Approach*, New York: 1970–1971, Affinity CD AFF 760.

Tristano, Lennie, and Warne Marsh. "Wow," *Intuition*, New York: March 4, 1949, Capitol Jazz CDP 7243 8 52771 2 2.

Waters, Muddy. "Walkin' Blues," *The Real Folk Blues*, 1950, MCA Records/Chess 088 112 822-2.

Weston, Randy. *Uhuru Africa*, New York, November 1960, Roulette CDP 7945102.

# Notes

CHAPTER I

1. "Satch Blast Echoed by Top Performers: Nixes Tour, Raps Ike and Faubus," *Chicago Defender* 53 (Sept. 28, 1957), pp. 1–2.

2. " 'Satchmo' Tells Off Ike," *Pittsburgh Courier* 48, no. 39 (Sept. 28, 1957), p. 3; "Satch Blast Echoed," p. 2. Armstrong's interview with the reporter from Grand Forks took place on Sept. 18, 1957; U.S. Army troops were deployed in Little Rock on Sept. 25; see also James Lincoln Collier, *Louis Armstrong: An American Genius* (New York: Oxford University Press, 1983), p. 317. Armstrong later toured Africa (1960), the United Arab Republic (1961), and Chile (1962) for the U.S. State Department, "Tours Completed from Beginning of Program in 1954 through June 1968 (FY1955–68)," CU subseries 1, general and historical files, box 3, folder 10. For general coverage of the Little Rock crisis see Taylor Branch, *Parting the Waters: America in the King Years 1954–63* (New York: Simon and Schuster, 1988), pp. 222–24.

3. On Armstrong's accomodationist image see Dizzy Gillespie with Al Fraser, *To Be or Not to Bop: Memoirs of Dizzy Gillespie* (New York: Da Capo, 1979), pp. 295–96; Miles Davis with Quincy Troupe, *Miles: The Autobiography* (New York: Simon and Schuster, 1989), p. 313. On performers playing for segregated audiences, see William G. Nunn Sr., "Stay Out of Dixie!" *Pittsburgh Courier* 48, no. 11 (Mar. 16, 1957), p. 6; George E. Pitts, "Segregated Audiences Should Be Abolished!" *Pittsburgh Courier* 48, no. 9 (Mar. 2, 1957), p. 22. The latter article singles out Armstrong.

4. In contemporary accounts, this film was also referred to as the *Saga of Satchmo*.

5. Max Jones and John Chilton, *Louis: The Louis Armstrong Story 1900–1971* (New York: Da Capo, 1988), pp. 31–33; "Scream 'We Want Satchmo' as the 'Saga of Armstrong' Hits Ghana," *Chicago Defender* 52, no. 46 (Mar. 16, 1957), p. 8.

6. The State Department Cultural Presentations Program had been explicitly formulated to counter the damage that racial relations caused to U.S. foreign policy. The tours are more extensively covered in chapter 4.

7. This theme is prominent in David W. Stowe, *Swing Changes: Big Band Jazz in New Deal America* (Cambridge, MA: Harvard University Press, 1994); Ken Burns, *Jazz*, a production of Florentine Films and WETA (Washington, DC, PBS Home Video, 2000); and Lewis A. Erenberg, *Swingin' the Dream: Big Band Jazz and the Rebirth of American Culture*

(Chicago: University of Chicago Press, 1998.) The theme of jazz and democracy was particularly emphasized during World War II.

8. Amiri Baraka, *Blues People: Negro Music in White America* (New York: Morrow, 1963); Frank Kofsky, *Black Nationalism and the Revolution in Music* (New York: Pathfinder, 1970); Eric Lott, "Double V, Double-Time: Bebop's Politics of Style," *Callaloo* 11, no. 3 (1988), pp. 597–605; Albert Murray, *Stomping the Blues* (New York: Da Capo, 1976); Samuel A. Floyd Jr., *The Power of Black Music: Interpreting Its History from Africa to the United States* (New York: Oxford University Press, 1995); Burton Peretti, *The Creation of Jazz: Music, Race, and Culture in Urban America* (Urbana: University of Illinois Press, 1992); Guthrie P. Ramsey, *Race Music: Black Cultures from Bebop to Hip-Hop* (Berkeley: University of California Press, 2003), pp. 96–130.

9. Peretti, *The Creation of Jazz*; Scott DeVeaux, *The Birth of Bebop: A Social and Musical History* (Berkeley: University of California Press, 1997); Stowe, *Swing Changes*; William H. Kenney, *Chicago Jazz: A Cultural History, 1904–1930* (New York: Oxford University Press, 1993); Ronald M. Radano, *New Musical Figurations: Anthony Braxton's Cultural Critique* (Chicago: University of Chicago Press, 1993); Samuel A. Floyd Jr., *The Power of Black Music*; Erenberg, *Swingin' the Dream*.

10. The best-known examples include Gunther Schuller, *Early Jazz: Its Roots and Musical Development* (New York: Oxford University Press, 1968); André Hodeir, *Jazz: Its Evolution and Essence* (New York: Grove, 1956); Ralph Ellison, *Shadow and Act* (New York: Vintage, 1964); Ian Carr, *Miles Davis: A Biography* (New York: Morrow, 1982), Leonard G. Feather, *The Encyclopedia of Jazz in the Sixties* (New York: Horizon, 1966); Yasuhiro Fujioka with Lewis Porter and Yoh-Ichi Hamada, *John Coltrane: A Discography and Musical Biography* (Metuchen, NJ: Scarecrow, 1995); John F. Szwed, *Space Is the Place: The Life and Times of Sun Ra* (New York: Pantheon, 1997); Gillespie, *To Be or Not to Bop*; Davis, *Miles: The Autobiography*; Charles Mingus, *Beneath the Underdog: His World as Composed by Charles Mingus,* ed. Nel King (New York: Knopf, 1971).

11. John Coltrane, *A Love Supreme,* New York, Dec. 9, 1964, Impulse! GRD 155; Sun Ra, *Heliocentric Worlds,* vol. 1, New York, Apr. 20, 1965, ESP-1014; Paul Gilroy, *The Black Atlantic: Modernity and Double Consciousness* (Cambridge, Mass.: Harvard University Press, 1993); Miles Davis, *The Complete Concert 1964: My Funny Valentine + Four & More,* New York, Feb. 12, 1964, Columbia CK 40609.

12. F. James Davis, *Who Is Black? One Nation's Definition* (University Park: Pennsylvania State University Press, 1991), pp. 5, 8–11.

13. A. Leon Higginbotham and Barbara K. Kopytoff, "Racial Purity and Interracial Sex in the Law of Colonial and Antebellum Virginia," in *Interracialism: Black-White Intermarriage in American History, Literature, and Law,* ed. Werner Sollors, pp. 131–32 (New York: Oxford University Press, 2000).

14. George Schuyler, cited in Sollors, ed., *Interracialism,* p. 6. The U.S. Supreme Court did not overturn laws against interracial marriage until *Loving v. Commonwealth of Virginia* in 1967; see ibid., pp. 4, 132–35.

15. See Jack D. Forbes, *Africans and Native Americans: The Language of Race and the Evolution of Red-Black Peoples*, 2d ed. (Urbana: University of Illinois Press, 1993), pp. 192–95. Some mixtures were tripartite rather than bipartite (e.g., African/Native American/European).

16. The social construction of whiteness has been the subject of a large literature, including David R. Roediger, *The Wages of Whiteness: Race and the Making of the American Working Class* (New York: Verso, 1991); Noel Ignatiev, *How the Irish Became White* (New York: Routledge, 1995); Richard Delgado and Jean Stefancic, eds., *Critical White Studies: Looking behind the Mirror* (Philadelphia: Temple University Press, 1997); Karen Brodkin, *How Jews Became White Folks and What That Says about Race in America* (New Brunswick, NJ: Rutgers University Press, 1998); Matthew Frye Jacobson, *Whiteness of a Different Color: European Immigrants and the Alchemy of Race* (Cambridge, Mass.: Harvard University Press, 1998); George Lipsitz, *The Possessive Investment in Whiteness: How White People Profit from Identity Politics* (Philadelphia: Temple University Press, 1998).

17. Sherrie Tucker, *Swing Shift: "All-Girl" Bands of the Forties* (Durham: Duke University Press, 2000), pp. 154–58; 221–24; "Jim Crow Stuff Still Spreading! Girl Trumpeter Tastes Southern Chivalry and Color Ousts Mab's Men," *Down Beat* 13, no. 16 (July 29, 1946), p. 1.

18. Naomi Pabst, "Blackness/Mixedness: Contestations over Crossing Signs," *Cultural Critique* 54, no. 1 (2003): 199, 208. I thank Sherrie Tucker for alerting me to this article.

19. Amiri Baraka (LeRoi Jones), "The Changing Same (R&B and New Black Music)," in *Black Music* (New York: Quill, 1967), pp. 180–211.

20. My thinking is also informed on this point by Anthony Giddens, *The Constitution of Society: Outline of the Theory of Structuration* (Cambridge, UK: Polity, 1984).

21. I am articulating a practice theory–based conception of culture that is discussed more fully from a theoretical point of view later in this chapter.

22. Michael C. Dawson, *Black Visions: The Roots of Contemporary African-American Political Ideologies* (Chicago: University of Chicago Press, 2001), pp. 11–13, 242, 254–55. See also Lani Guinier, *The Tyranny of the Majority: Fundamental Fairness in Representative Democracy* (New York: Free Press, 1994), pp. 1–20.

23. Ibid., pp. 21, 91–101. See also Robin D. G. Kelley, *Freedom Dreams: The Black Radical Imagination* (Boston: Beacon, 2002).

24. Terry Teachout, "The Color of Jazz," *Commentary* 100 (Sept. 1995), pp. 50–53.

25. Richard M. Sudhalter, *Lost Chords: White Musicians and Their Contribution to Jazz, 1915–1945* (New York: Oxford University Press, 1999), pp. xviii–xix.

26. For more on the relationship of early twentieth-century composers to jazz see Carol J. Oja, *Making Music Modern: New York in the 1920s* (New York: Oxford University Press, 2000), pp. 313–17.

27. The characteristics of post–WW II modernism are adapted from Georgina Born, *Rationalizing Culture: IRCAM, Boulez, and the Institutionalization of the Musical Avant-Garde* (Berkeley: University of California Press, 1995), pp. 41–44.

28. See ibid., pp. 40–45, for a longer discussion of aesthetic modernism in the twentieth century.

29. Gilroy, *The Black Atlantic*, p. 44.

30. Ibid., pp. 36, 48.

31. James C. Hall, *Mercy, Mercy Me: African-American Culture and the American Sixties* (New York: Oxford University Press, 2001, p. 10; Kelley, *Freedom Dreams*, pp. 1–35).

32. Columbia University's Jazz Study Group, under the direction of Robert O'Meally, has been the leading force in this development. See Robert G. O'Meally, Brent Hayes Edwards, and Farah Jasmine Griffin, *Uptown Conversation: The New Jazz Studies* (New York: Columbia University Press, 2004).

33. Mae Henderson, "Where, by the Way, Is This Train Going? A Case for Black (Cultural) Studies," *Callaloo* 19, no. 1 (1996), pp. 60–67; Wahneema Lubiano, "Mapping the Interstices between Afro-American Cultural Discourse and Cultural Studies: A Prolegomenon," ibid., pp. 68–77.

34. For an overview of African American contributions to anthropology see Ira E. Harrison and Faye V. Harrison, *African-American Pioneers in Anthropology* (Urbana: University of Illinois Press, 1999).

35. Mary Ann Romano, ed., "Lost Sociologists Rediscovered: Jane Addams, Walter Benjamin, W.E.B. Du Bois, Harriet Martineau, Pitirim A. Sorokin, Flora Tristan, George E. Vincent, and Beatrice Webb," in *Mellen Studies in Sociology*, vol. 36 (Lewiston, NY: Edwin Mellen Press, 2002). For the definitive biography of W.E.B. Du Bois, see David L. Lewis, *W.E.B. Du Bois: Biography of a Race, 1868–1919*, vol. 1 (New York: Holt, 1993); David L. Lewis, W.E.B. Du Bois: *The Fight for Equality and the American Century, 1919–1963*, vol. 2 (New York: Holt, 2000). On Du Bois as a historian see vol. 2, pp. 350, 367.

36. On the relevance of Du Bois to contemporary debates in poststructuralism see Nahum Chandler, "Originary Displacement," *Boundary* 2 27, no. 3 (2000), pp. 249–86.

37. A better name for ethnomusicology would be the anthropology of music. Despite its anachronistic name, ethnomusicology has been the most important academic discipline in developing an anthropological approach to the study of music.

38. As critics have pointed out, Herskovits overemphasized Dahomey and Yorubaland and left out the many cultural continuities from the BaKongo and Mande cultural areas that more recent scholarship has brought to light. For a critical assessment of Herskovits's concept of syncretism see Andrew Apter, "Herkovits's Heritage: Rethinking Syncretism in the African Diaspora," *Diaspora* 1, no. 3 (1991): 235–60.

39. Baraka, *Blues People*, pp. 9, 42.

40. Ibid., p. ix.

41. Ingrid Monson, "Blues People: Amiri Baraka as a Social Theorist," paper presented at "Blues People: 40 Years Later," symposium at Sarah Lawrence College, Bronxville, NY, Feb. 6–7, 2004.

42. Some influential works in cultural studies and postcolonialism include Gilroy, *Black Atlantic;* Stuart Hall, "What Is This 'Black' in Black Popular Culture?" in *Black*

*Popular Culture: A Project by Michele Wallace,* Gina Dent, ed., pp. 21–33 (Seattle: Bay Press, 1992); Henry Louis Gates Jr., *The Signifying Monkey: A Theory of African-American Literary Criticism* (New York: Oxford University Press, 1988); Gayatri Chakravorty Spivak, "Can the Subaltern Speak?" in *Marxist Interpretations of Literature and Culture: Limits, Frontiers, Boundaries,* ed. Cary Nelson and Lawrence Grossberg, pp. 271–313 (Urbana: University of Illinois Press, 1988); Homi K. Bhabha, *The Location of Culture* (London: Routledge, 1994); and Arjun Appadurai, "Global Ethnoscapes: Notes and Queries for a Transnational Anthropology," in *Recapturing Anthropology: Writing in the Present,* ed. Richard G. Fox, pp. 191–210 (Santa Fe: School of American Research Press, 1991).

43. Eric Porter, *What Is This Thing Called Jazz? African American Musicians as Artists, Critics, and Activists* (Berkeley: University of California Press, 2002).

44. Michel Foucault, *The Archaeology of Knowledge and the Discourse on Language* (New York: Pantheon, 1972); Giddens, *The Constitution of Society;* Pierre Bourdieu, *Outline of a Theory of Practice,* trans. Richard Nice (New York: Cambridge University Press, 1977); Jean Comaroff and John L. Comaroff, *Of Revelation and Revolution: Christianity, Colonialism, and Consciousness in South Africa,* vol. 1 (Chicago: University of Chicago Press, 1991); John L. Comaroff and Jean Comaroff, *Of Revelation and Revolution: The Dialectics of Modernity on a South African Frontier,* vol. 2 (Chicago: University of Chicago Press, 1997); Sherry B. Ortner, *Making Gender: The Politics and Erotics of Culture* (Boston: Beacon, 1996); Sherry B. Ortner, ed., *The Fate of "Culture": Geertz and Beyond* (Berkeley: University of California Press, 1999).

45. Foucault, *Archaeology of Knowledge,* pp. 31–49. My understanding of Foucault is also informed by Herbert L. Dreyfus and Paul Rabinow, *Michel Foucault: Beyond Structuralism and Hermeneutics,* 2d ed. (Chicago: University of Chicago Press, 1983).

46. I do not mean to suggest that African American music had not previously made use of these discourses, only that there was an intensified historical emphasis in the 1950s and 1960s.

47. My use of Foucault is similar to that of Bernard Gendron in Bernard Gendron, "Moldy Figs and Modernists: Jazz at War (1942–1946)," in *Jazz among the Discourses,* ed. Krin Gabbard, pp. 31–56 (Durham: Duke University Press, 1995).

48. This builds on the argument I made in Ingrid Monson, *Saying Something: Jazz Improvisation and Interaction* (Chicago: University of Chicago Press, 1996), pp. 192–215.

49. My understanding of Giddens draws primarily from Giddens, *Constitution of Society,* and William H. Sewell Jr., "A Theory of Structure: Duality, Agency, and Transformation," *American Journal of Sociology* 98, no. 1 (1992). The Giddens quotation is cited in the latter, p. 4.

50. Sewell, "Theory of Structure," p. 21.

51. Bourdieu, *Outline of a Theory,* pp. 87–88.

52. For the most complete account of how jazz musicians practice, see Paul F. Berliner, *Thinking in Jazz: The Infinite Art of Improvisation* (Chicago: University of Chicago Press, 1994). See also Travis A. Jackson, "Jazz as Musical Practice," in *The Cambridge Companion*

*to Jazz,* ed. Mervyn Cooke and David Horn, pp. 83–95 (New York: Cambridge University Press, 2002).

53. Ortner, *Fate of "Culture."* Broader work in anthropology has moved practice theory far from Bourdieu's original usage, which has been criticized for its determinism on the homogeneous concept of culture, among other things. See Craig Calhoun, Edward LiPuma, and Moishe Postone, eds., *Bourdieu: Critical Perspectives* (Chicago: University Chicago Press, 1993).

54. Among these are Veit Erlmann, *Nightsong: Performance, Power, and Practice in South Africa* (Chicago: University of Chicago Press, 1996); Steven Feld, "Aesthetics as Iconicity of Style, or 'Lift-Up-over Sounding': Getting into the Kaluli Groove," *Yearbook for Traditional Music* 20 (1988), pp. 74–113; Christopher A. Waterman, *Jùjú: A Social History and Ethnography of an African Popular Music* (Chicago: University of Chicago Press, 1990); Charles Keil and Steven Feld, *Music Grooves: Essays and Dialogues* (Chicago: University of Chicago Press, 1994); Harris M. Berger, *Metal, Rock, and Jazz: Perception and the Phenomenology of Musical Experience* (Hanover, N.H.: University Press of New England, 1999).

55. Timothy D. Taylor, *Global Pop: World Music, World Markets* (New York: Routledge, 1997); Timothy D. Taylor, *Strange Sounds: Music, Technology, and Culture* (New York: Routledge, 2001).

56. Monson, *Saying Something;* Ingrid Monson, "Riffs, Repetition, and Theories of Globalization," *Ethnomusicology* 43, no. 1 (Winter 1999): 31–65.

57. Travis A. Jackson, "Performance and Musical Meaning: Analyzing 'Jazz' on the New York Scene," PhD diss., Columbia University, 1998; Travis A. Jackson, "Jazz as Musical Practice," in *The Cambridge Companion to Jazz,* ed. Mervyn Cooke and David Horn, pp. 83–95 (New York: Cambridge University Press, 2002).

58. Guthrie P. Ramsey, *Race Music: Black Cultures from Bebop to Hip-Hop* (Berkeley: University of California Press, 2003), pp. 4, 35–38.

59. Nichole T. Rustin, "Mingus Fingers: Charles Mingus, Black Masculinity, and Postwar Jazz Culture," PhD diss., New York University, 1999, pp. 24–25, 41–42.

60. Ibid., p. 37. Porter's *What Is This Thing Called Jazz?* also devotes considerable attention to the issues of gender, race, and masculinity.


CHAPTER 2

1. To clarify, mechanical royalties are those paid by the record company to the publisher of the song, who then divides this amount (usually 50/50) with the songwriter. Artist royalties (or performance royalties) are those paid to the performing artist. For a quick introduction to music royalties see Lee Ann Obringer, "How Music Royalties Work," http://entertainment.howstuffworks.com/music-royalties6.htm (accessed Feb. 26, 2007).

2. The 1976 Copyright Act became effective on Jan. 1, 1978. Its sound recording provisions apply to recordings made on or after Feb. 15, 1972. Recordings published before

1972 are protected by state laws until Feb. 15, 2047, when they will fall into the public domain. Sidney Shemel and M. William Krasilovsky, *This Business of Music* (New York: Billboard Books, 1990), pp. 39–48, 133–60.

3. Charles Mingus, "Atlantic Record Corporation Royalty Statement, February 15, 1960," *Charles Mingus Collection*, box 55/11, Library of Congress, Washington, DC. His artist royalty rate was five percent.

4. New York's Local 802 and Detroit's Local 5 were the only exceptions to segregated locals. See Jonathan Zvi Sard Pollack, "Race, Recordings, and Rock 'n' Roll: The American Federation of Musicians and the Popular Music Challenge, 1940–1970," PhD diss., University of Wisconsin–Madison, 1999, pp. 34–35.

5. In 1938 the AFM signed licensing agreements with Victor, Decca, and Columbia that required all recording sessions to be registered with the AFM. By 1946 the AFM had signed licensing agreements with an additional 207 recording companies. See Russell Sanjek and David Sanjek, *American Popular Music Business in the 20th Century* (New York: Oxford University Press, 1991), pp. 81–82.

6. "Amalgamation" rather than "integration" is the term most frequently used in contemporary reports.

7. Pollack, "Race, Recordings, and Rock 'n' Roll," p. 61; Scott DeVeaux, *The Birth of Bebop: A Social and Musical History* (Berkeley: University of California Press, 1997), pp. 147–50; David W. Stowe, *Swing Changes: Big Band Jazz in New Deal America* (Cambridge, MA: Harvard University Press, 1994), p. 234; Margaret Howze, "Nat 'King' Cole the Pianist," Jazz Profiles from National Public Radio, 2004, http://www.npr.org/programs/jazzprofiles/archive/cole_natpianist.html (accessed Mar. 9, 2007).

8. DeVeaux, *Birth of Bebop*, p. 150; Stowe, *Swing Changes*, pp. 125–26. Liberia's President Tubman got a taste of such resentment when he traveled to Atlanta in a luxurious executive car in 1954: Indignant white railroad workers damaged its couplings, causing the car to roll away from the train in the middle of the night. Brenda Gayle Plummer, *Rising Wind: Black Americans and U.S. Foreign Affairs, 1935–1960* (Chapel Hill: University of North Carolina Press, 1996), pp. 269–70.

9. For further examples see "Jim Crow Issue Grows in Kaycee," *Down Beat* 13, no. 2 (Jan. 14, 1946), p. 15; "Eckstine, Band, Lose Job after Brawl in Boston," *Down Beat* 14, no. 2 (Jan. 15, 1947), p. 4; "Jo Baker, Ed Hall Figure in NYC Bias Cases: Jo Complains of Rude Treatment at the Stork Club," *Down Beat* 18, no. 24 (Nov. 30, 1951), p. 1; Leonard Feather, "No More White Bands for Me, Says Little Jazz," *Down Beat* 18, no. 10 (May 18, 1951), pp. 1, 13; John Tynan, "Jim Crow Shadow Hovers over Vegas Jazz Efforts," *Down Beat* 23, no. 18 (Sept. 5, 1956), p. 11; "Jazz Festival May Be Test of Vegas Integration," *Down Beat* 29 (July 19, 1962), p. 15; Pollack, "Race, Recordings, and Rock 'n' Roll," p. 209.

10. "An Ugly Story," *Metronome* 60, no. 7 (Nov. 1943), p. 4. *Metronome*'s editors at the time were Barry Ulanov and Leonard Feather. For an excellent account of the effect of Jim Crow on musicians during WWII see DeVeaux, *Birth of Bebop*, pp. 236–69.

11. "Kansas City Court Makes Just Ruling," *Down Beat* 13, no. 2 (Jan. 14, 1946), p. 10. *Down Beat*'s editorial staff included Mike Levin, Don Haynes, Jorn Doran, John Lucas, Sharon Pease, and George Hoefer.

12. "Sarah Vaughan Beaten Up by Gang," *Down Beat* 13, no. 18 (Aug. 26, 1946), p. 2. Michael Levin, "Beating of Powell by Police Becomes New Cause Celebre," *Down Beat* 13, no. 16 (July 29, 1946), p. 1.

13. Sherrie Tucker, *Swing Shift: "All-Girl" Bands of the Forties* (Durham: Duke University Press, 2000), pp. 221–24.

14. "Jim Crow Stuff Still Spreading! Girl Trumpeter Tastes Southern Chivalry and Color Ousts Mab's Men," *Down Beat* 13, no. 16 (July 29, 1946), p. 1; "Movies Fix Merit by Color of Skin!" ibid., p. 10; See also Tucker, *Swing Shift*, pp. 154–58, 221–24.

15. Goodman had recorded with Teddy Wilson in 1935. Although John Hammond is often credited with convincing Goodman to present a mixed trio, it was actually Helen Oakley who persuaded Goodman. James Lincoln Collier, *Benny Goodman and the Swing Era* (New York: Oxford University Press, 1989), pp. 138–39, 171–73; Arthur Knight, "Jammin' the Blues, or the Sight of Jazz, 1944," in *Representing Jazz*, ed. Krin Gabbard, pp. 16–21 (Durham: Duke University Press, 1995).

16. However, there are countervailing examples. Goodman presented a jam session as part of his 1938 Carnegie Hall concert, which included six members of Count Basie's band (including Basie himself and Lester Young) and a member of Ellington's band. During this segment of the show, black musicians temporarily outnumbered white performers in a mixed setting. Fletcher Henderson was among those black bands that hired several white players in the early forties. See Knight, *Jammin' the Blues*, pp. 19–21.

17. Leonard Feather, "No More White Bands for Me, Says Little Jazz," *Down Beat* 18, no. 10 (May 18, 1951), pp. 1, 13.

18. Ibid., p. 13.

19. "Can't Solve Problems by Running, Lena Tells Roy," *Down Beat* 18, no. 12 (June 15, 1951), p. 1.

20. Frank Holzfeind, "Roy Wasn't on Soap Box, Says Club Op," *Down Beat* 18, no. 14 (July 13, 1951), p. 7.

21. "Granz and the Jazz Philharmonic," *Crisis* 54, no. 5 (May 1947), pp. 143–44.

22. Ibid., p. 143; Stowe, *Swing Changes*, p. 237; Martin Bauml Duberman, *Paul Robeson* (New York: Knopf, 1988), pp. 288, 667n18.

23. Duberman, *Paul Robeson*, pp. 283, 284–85; Dizzy Gillespie with Al Fraser, *To Be or Not to Bop: Memoirs of Dizzy Gillespie* (New York: Da Capo, 1979), p. 288.

24. Zoot suits, which used an enormous amount of material, had been banned by the War Production Board in its effort to ration cloth for the production of military uniforms. Riots set off by violations of the ban occurred in the summer of 1943 in Los Angeles, Detroit, and New York. See Stuart Cosgrove, "The Zoot Suit and Style Warfare," in *Zoot Suits and Second-hand Dresses: An Anthology of Fashion and Music,* ed. Angela McRobbie, pp. 3–21 (Boston: Unwin Hyman, 1988); and Chester B. Himes, "Zoot Riots Are Race

Riots," *Crisis* 50, no. 7 (July 1943): 200–201. DeVeaux reports that Granz later admitted knowing very little about what came to be known as the "Sleepy Lagoon" case. DeVeaux, *Birth of Bebop,* p. 387.

25. "Granz and the Jazz Philharmonic," p. 144; Lillian Scott, "Producer Explains 'Crusade' on Music Jim Crow: Norman Granz Makes Appeal on Race Issue," *Chicago Defender* 52, no. 47 (Mar. 8, 1947), p. 11.

26. Singers were members of the American Federation of Radio Artists (AFRA) or later the American Federation of Television and Radio Artists (AFTRA). As Lara Pellegrinelli has observed, the fact that singers were not eligible for membership in the American Federation of Musicians illustrates that only instrumentalists were considered to be true musicians. Lara V. Pellegrinelli, "The Song Is Who? Locating Singers on the Jazz Scene," PhD diss., Harvard University, 2005, pp. 467–86.

27. My view of the American Federation of Musicians is indebted to a long and very helpful telephone conversation with Orrin Keepnews (July 15, 2004); the trial board minutes of New York's Local 802 (New York University, Tamiment Library); the executive board minutes of Local 802, published in *Allegro* (the journal of Local 802); and the following publications: Pollack, "Race, Recordings, and Rock 'n' Roll"; George Seltzer, *Music Matters: The Performer and the American Federation of Musicians* (Metuchen, NJ: Scarecrow, 1989).

28. In the early 1950s five percent of the payroll was contributed to the union welfare fund.

29. "Tootlers Get Pay Hike for Work in Cafes," *Billboard* 62 (Nov. 4, 1950), pp. 47, 49. Virtually all union documents refer to "sidemen" even when an occasional woman might appear as an instrumentalist. The fact that singers were not eligible for membership in the AFM exacerbated the gender divide among jazz musicians.

30. Prominent artists such as Miles Davis challenged the four-set nightclub format in the 1950s. By the early 1960s the minimum scale for clubs was based on a three-set format. "Adjusted Scales for Single Engagement Club Jobs," *Allegro* 34, no. 4 (Feb. 1960), p. 23.

31. The median income for black families in 1950 was $1,869. U.S. Department of Commerce, Bureau of the Census, Current Population Reports, Series P-60, *Money Income of Families and Persons in the United States,* nos. 105 and 157; available at http://nces.ed .gov/pubs98/yi/yi16.pdf (accessed Mar. 9, 2007).

32. "Scale in Los Angeles Gets 20 Percent Hike," *Down Beat* 18, no. 3 (Feb. 9, 1951), p. 1.

33. "Record Sidemen Get a Raise but It Won't Show Up in Pay," *Down Beat* 21, no. 3 (Feb. 10, 1954), p. 3; "Increase in Recording Scales," *Allegro* 34, no. 5 (Mar. 1960), p. 28. The fee for overtime was $17.17 per unit (a half hour or less).

34. Keepnews, phone conversation, July 15, 2004.

35. American Federation of Musicians, Local 802, Minutes of the Trial Board, New York University, Tamiment Library, microfilm reel 5327, pp. 935–36.

36. Ibid., reel 5327, p. 167; reel 5328, pp. 507, 675–76.

37. Ibid., reel 5328, pp. 63, 756.

38. Ibid., reel 5327, pp. 545, 792; "Executive Board Minutes," *Allegro* 38, no. 6 (June 1962), pp. 4–5; "Executive Board Minutes," *Allegro* 36, no. 11 (Oct. 1961), pp. 9–12; "Executive Board Minutes," *Allegro* 40, no. 3 (Mar. 1963), pp. 11–12.

39. Clark Terry, interview with author, Mar. 27, 1997, St. Louis, MO.

40. Ibid.

41. I have not been able to confirm the spelling of Aaron Vee's surname.

42. Terry, interview.

43. Ibid.

44. Nat Hentoff described the opposition of Local 802 President Al Manuti to Jim Crow but also his reluctance to make demands on AFM signatories to change their hiring policies. Nat Hentoff, "Meet Al Manuti," *Down Beat* 24, no. 7 (Apr. 4, 1959), p. 16.

45. Pollack, "Race, Recordings, and Rock 'n' Roll," p. 33–34. Most histories report Chicago's Local 208 as the first black local. Nevertheless, Pollack's research indicates that at the time of the founding of St. Louis Local 2 on Nov. 19, 1896, the AFM granted a separate charter to the Great Western Union (later Local 197), which represented African American musicians.

46. George Seltzer, *Music Matters: The Performer and the American Federation of Musicians* (Metuchen, NJ: Scarecrow, 1989), pp. 108–109.

47. "See Soaring Local 47 $$," *Billboard* 18 (Mar. 31, 1951), p. 16; "Coast Tootler $$ Up Sharply Due to Video," *Billboard* 64 (Apr. 12, 1952), p. 18; "Musicians Get 1955 Figures; Earn $3.8 Mil," *Billboard* 68 (June 9, 1956), pp. 16, 20.

48. Clora Bryant, Buddy Collette, William Green, Steven Isoardi, Jack Kelson, Horace Tapscott, Gerald Wilson, and Marl Young, eds., *Central Avenue Sounds* (Berkeley: University of California Press, 1998), pp. 131–32, 154, 279. The oral history materials included provide the best published account of the amalgamation of locals 767 and 47. A dissertation by Dwight Dickerson also provides firsthand recollections of the amalgamation process; see Dwight Lowell Dickerson, "Central Avenue Meets Hollywood: The Amalgamation of the Black and White Musicians' Unions in Los Angeles," PhD diss., University of California–Los Angeles, 1998.

49. Bryant et al., *Central Avenue Sounds,* p. 71.

50. Ibid., pp. 71–72, 279.

51. Charles Emge, "Move Grows to Scrap L.A.'s Jim Crow Union," *Down Beat* 18, no. 12 (June 15, 1951), pp. 1, 19.

52. Bryant et al., *Central Avenue Sounds,* p. 192.

53. Ibid., pp. 191–92, 387–88, 154.

54. Morroe Berger, Edward Berger, and James Patrick, *Benny Carter: A Life in American Music* (Lanham, MD: Scarecrow, 2001), p. 263.

55. Bryant et al., *Central Avenue Sounds,* pp. 155–56, 159–61, 251. See also Buddy Collette and Steven Isoardi, *Jazz Generations: A Life in American Music and Society*

(New York: Continuum, 2000), pp. 111–131, and Dickerson, "Central Avenue Meets Hollywood," pp. 216–20.

56. Bryant et al., *Central Avenue Sounds,* pp.156–57; Charles Emge, "Action Looms in Move to Merge L.A.'s AFM Locals," *Down Beat* 18, no. 24 (Nov. 30, 1951), p. 9. The call for a special meeting was a part of the strategy of the pro-amalgamation members.

57. "Anti–Jim Crow Candidates Win in Local 767 Election," *Down Beat* 19, no. 2 (Jan. 25, 1952), p. 1; Bryant et al., *Central Avenue Sounds,* p. 388; "L.A. Locals Nearer Union," *Down Beat* 19, no. 4 (Feb. 22, 1952), p. 18.

58. "47, 767 Merger Snags Eliminated, Says Carter," *Down Beat* 19, no. 9 (May 7, 1952), p. 5.

59. Bryant et al., *Central Avenue Sounds,* pp. 389–93, 387.

60. "47, 767 Merger Snags"; Benny Carter, "Benny Carter Sifts LA Union Issues as Interracial Merger Meets Delays," *Down Beat* 19, no. 17 (Aug. 27, 1952), p. 14.

61. Carter, "Benny Carter Sifts LA Union Issues," p. 14.

62. Ibid.

63. As Dickerson notes, the amalgamation forces requested and received help from the Los Angeles NAACP chapter in publicizing the amalgamation struggle. It was covered primarily in African American newspapers and music industry publications (such as *Down Beat*), but Estelle Edison was also able to get the election results broadcast on radio by slipping a piece of paper into the hands of Chet Huntley (then a KABC newsman) shortly before he went on the air. Dickerson, "Central Avenue Meets Hollywood," pp. 205–208.

64. Bryant et al., *Central Avenue Sounds,* pp. 393–97.

65. Dickerson, "Central Avenue Meets Hollywood," pp. 242–43.

66. A full historical study of the jazz musicians and studio, TV, and film work remains to be done. For a general account of the history of Los Angeles studio musicians, see Robert Lloyd, "Time of the Session," *LA Weekly* (Apr. 9–15, 2004).

67. Ibid. Drummer Lee Young is often mentioned as the first African American staff musician in the motion picture industry, but Buddy Collette mentions pianist Calvin Jackson. Young was initially hired to teach drums to actors (such as Mickey Rooney) who needed to play in on-camera roles. See Bryant et al., *Central Avenue Sounds,* pp. 67–70; Collette and Isoardi, *Jazz Generations,* pp. 149–55.

68. Collette and Isoardi, *Jazz Generations,* pp. 142–43.

69. In Los Angeles, Asian Americans were members of Local 47. The placement of Asians and others outside the black/white binary varied from local to local.

70. "White Local 6 in San Francisco Kills Move to Integrate," *Down Beat* 24, no. 2 (Jan. 23, 1957), p. 11; "End of a Friction," *Down Beat* 27, no. 7 (Mar. 31, 1960), p. 16.

71. "Jim Crow and the AFM," *Down Beat* 24, no. 13 (June 27, 1957), pp. 10–11; "The Line Holds," *Down Beat* 24, no. 15 (July 25, 1957), p. 9; "Official Proceedings of the 1957 Convention," *International Musician* 56, no. 5 (Nov. 1957), pp. 42–43; Clark Halker, "A

History of Local 208 and the Struggle for Racial Equality in the American Federation of Musicians," *Black Music Research Journal* 8, no. 2 (1988), pp. 207–22.

72. "A Reminder to Petrillo," *Down Beat* 24, no. 23 (Nov. 14, 1957), pp. 12–13. These were essentially the same demands contained in Resolution No. 34, which Petrillo had deferred at the 1957 convention; "Official Proceedings," pp. 42–43.

73. "Headaches for Caesar," *Down Beat* 25, no. 2 (Jan. 23, 1958), pp. 8–9.

74. Seltzer, *Music Matters,* pp. 54–66, 77–82; Bill Steif, "Calif. Atty. Gen.'s 'Reasonable Time' Stance on White-Negro AFM Merger," *Variety* 217 (Dec. 2, 1959), pp. 57–58.

75. Ralph J. Gleason, "A Blow to Jim Crow," *Down Beat* 26, no. 25 (Dec. 10, 1959), pp. 14–15; "End of a Friction," *Down Beat* 27, no. 7 (Mar. 31, 1960), p. 16.

76. Halker, "A History of Local 208," pp. 217–19.

77. Michael C. Dawson, *Black Visions : The Roots of Contemporary African-American Political Ideologies* (Chicago: University of Chicago Press, 2001).

78. John Egerton, *Speak Now against the Day: The Generation before the Civil Rights Movement* (New York: Knopf, 1994), pp. 592–59, 600–601. The trial date of *Briggs v. Elliot,* the first of the cases, was May 1951. For a full account of the *Brown* decision, see Richard Kluger, *Simple Justice* (New York: Vintage, 1975).

79. Egerton, *Speak Now,* pp. 602, 606–609; Charles M. Payne, *I've Got the Light of Freedom: The Organizing Tradition and the Mississippi Freedom Struggle* (Berkeley: University of California Press, 1995), pp. 34–35.

80. Aldon D. Morris, *The Origins of the Civil Rights Movement: Black Communities Organizing for Change* (New York: Free Press, 1984), pp. 25–35; Branch, *Parting the Waters,* pp. 186–87.

81. My account of the Montgomery bus boycott is based on those in Morris, *The Origins of the Civil Rights Movement,* and Branch, *Parting the Waters,* pp. 143–205.

82. Taylor Branch, *Parting the Waters: America in the King Years 1954–63* (New York: Simon and Schuster, 1988), p. 150.

83. Bernice Reagon, speaking at "Miles Davis, the Civil Rights Movement, and Jazz," a conference held at Washington University, St. Louis, MO, May 3–4, 1997, video recording.

84. On the strategy of the Birmingham campaign see Morris, *Origins of the Civil Rights Movement,* pp. 250–74.

85. Reagon, Washington University, May 3, 1997.

86. Charles Neblett, speaking at "Miles Davis, the Civil Rights Movement, and Jazz," a conference held at Washington University, St. Louis, MO, May 3, 1997.

87. Bernice Johnson Reagon. " 'Oh Freedom': Music of the Movement," in *A Circle of Trust: Remembering SNCC,* ed. Cheryl Lynn Greenberg (New Brunswick: Rutgers University Press, 1998), p. 117.

88. "Promoters Holding to Southern Bookings, Despite Cole Incident," *Billboard* 68, no. 16 (Apr. 21, 1956), p. 29; "A King Is Uncrowned," *New York Amsterdam News* 47, no. 16 (Apr. 21, 1956), pp. 1, 3; Brian Ward, *Just My Soul Responding: Rhythm and Blues,*

*Black Consciousness, and Race Relations* (Berkeley: University of California Press, 1998), pp. 95–96.

89. "A King Is Uncrowned," p. 3; "Cole Leaves Us Cold!: His Discs Face Huge Sales Drop," *New York Amsterdam News* 47, no. 16 (Apr. 21, 1956), p. 1.

90. "A King Is Uncrowned," p. 3.

91. Ibid.; "Cole Leaves Us Cold!"

92. These events occurred before the landmark premiere of his fifteen-minute TV show in November 1956.

93. Cole, like Benny Carter and the Mills Brothers, had faced eviction suits filed under restrictive covenants—agreements signed by homeowners promising not to sell their property to non-Caucasians.

94. Leonard Feather, "Feather's Nest," *Down Beat* 23, no. 11 (May 30, 1956), p. 33.

95. Nat Hentoff, "Counterpoint," *Down Beat* 23, no. 11 (May 30, 1956), p. 25.

96. Nat Cole, "Chords and Discords: Letter to the Editor," *Down Beat* 23, no. 11 (May 30, 1956), p. 4.

97. "Duke Flays NAACP for Halting Richmond Concert," *Down Beat* 18, no. 5 (Mar. 9, 1951), p. 1. Ellington reported having made $9,000 for the NAACP. The figure $16,000 was reported in "Proceeds from l'Affaire Duke Go to NAACP," *Down Beat* 18, no. 4 (February 23, 1951), p 1.

98. John Tynan, "Jim Crow Shadow Hovers over Vegas Jazz Efforts," *Down Beat* 23, no. 18 (Sept. 5, 1956), p. 11; Nat Hentoff, "Counterpoint," *Down Beat* 22, no. 18 (Sept. 7, 1955), p. 16. Hentoff could not recall exactly which trio he had been referring to; interview with author, Jan. 2, 1997.

99. Ralph J. Gleason, "An Appeal from Dave Brubeck," *Down Beat* 27, no. 4 (Feb. 18, 1960), pp. 12–13.

100. Ibid.

101. Norman Granz, "The Brubeck Stand: Divergent View by Norman Granz," *Down Beat* 27, no. 15 (July 21, 1960), p. 24.


CHAPTER 3

1. Amiri Baraka, *Blues People: Negro Music in White America* (New York: William Morrow, 1963), pp. 175–76, 181–82. The *Down Beat* readers' poll was published annually in the last December issue. The *Metronome* poll appeared annually in the January or February issue.

2. Although Dan Burley, an associate editor of *Jet,* and George Pitts of the *Pittsburgh Courier* were occasionally included, as *Down Beat* expanded the number of critics polled, it looked primarily to Europe. While in 1953 it advertised the participation of the "country's leading critics," by 1955 it was claiming to have polled the "world's leading critics." In 1956 the poll's lasting name first appeared as the editors announced the "Fourth Annual International Jazz Critics Poll." This was in keeping with a long-standing American tradition

of looking toward Europe for validation of American art, as well as acknowledging Europe as the seat of modernist sensibility. Burley was included in the 1954 poll, and Pitts in the 1956 poll. Burley later wrote for *Muhammad Speaks,* the newspaper of the Nation of Islam. The critics' poll appeared annually in August, sometimes the first, sometimes the last issue. For the polls mentioned here see Jack Tracy, "Ellington, Brubeck, Winners in Critics' Jazz Poll," *Down Beat* 20, no. 17 (Aug. 26, 1953), pp. 1, 7; "Basie Romps to Victory in Jazz Critics' Poll," *Down Beat* 21, no. 17 (Aug. 25, 1954), pp. 1, 7; "The Critics' Choices," *Down Beat* 22, no. 17 (Aug. 24, 1955), pp. 9–10; "It's Basie and the MJQ Again," *Down Beat* 23, no. 16 (Aug. 8, 1956), pp. 11–12.

3. I was inspired by Dan Morgnstern to investigate the magazine covers during his presentation at "Miles Davis, the Civil Rights Movement, and Jazz," a conference I organized with Gerald Early at Washington University in Saint Louis, May 3–4, 1997.

4. Richard M. Sudhalter, *Lost Chords: White Musicians and Their Contribution to Jazz, 1915–1945* (New York: Oxford University Press, 1999); Terry Teachout, "The Color of Jazz," *Commentary* 100 (Sept. 1995): 50–53.

5. Among the many writings articulating these positions are Gene Lees, *Cats of Any Color: Jazz Black and White* (New York: Oxford University Press, 1995); Richard M. Sudhalter, *Lost Chords;* Baraka, *Blues People;* and Jon Panish, *The Color of Jazz: Race and Representation in Postwar Jazz* (Jackson: University Press of Mississippi, 1997).

6. I know that Basie's emergence on the national scene came after Benny Goodman's, but he and a sizeable segment of the Basie band were swinging in the Blue Devils and Moten's band long before Goodman. On shared terms of the debate see Bernard Gendron, "Moldy Figs and Modernists: Jazz at War (1942–1946)," in *Jazz among the Discourses,* ed. Krin Gabbard, pp. 31–56 (Durham: Duke University Press, 1995).

7. Rev. Samuel Davies, quoted in Mechal Sobel, *The World They Made Together: Black and White Values in Eighteenth-century Virginia* (Princeton, NJ: Princeton University Press, 1987), p. 184.

8. Dena J. Epstein, "A White Origin for the Black Spiritual? An Invalid Theory and How It Grew," *American Music* 1, no. 2 (1983), pp. 53–59.

9. On Afro-modernism see Houston A. Baker Jr., *Modernism and the Harlem Renaissance* (Chicago: University of Chicago Press, 1987); Guthrie P. Ramsey, *Race Music: Black Cultures from Bebop to Hip-hop* (Berkeley: University of California Press, 2003), pp. 44–75, 96–130; Craig Werner, *A Change Is Gonna Come* (New York: Plume, 1999); Craig Werner, *Playing the Changes: From Afro-modernism to the Jazz Impulse* (Urbana: University of Illinois Press, 1994).

10. Johnny Hodges, "Day Dream," *The Great Ellington Units,* Chicago, Nov. 2, 1940, RCA/Bluebird 6751-2-RB; John Coltrane, *Ascension,* Englewood Cliffs, NJ, June 28, 1965, Impulse! 314 543 413-2; Charlie Parker, "Parker's Mood," *Yardbird Suite: The Ultimate Charlie Parker Collection,* New York, Sept. 18, 1948, Rhino R2 72260; Duke Ellington, *Reminiscing in Tempo,* New York, Sept. 12, 1935, Columbia CK 48654.

11. Paul Gilroy, *The Black Atlantic: Modernity and Double Consciousness* (Cambridge, Mass.: Harvard University Press, 1993), p. 35; Amiri Baraka (LeRoi Jones), *Black Music* (New York: Quill, 1967), p. 70.

12. Lennie Tristano and Warne Marsh, "Wow," *Intuition,* New York, Mar. 4, 1949, Capitol Jazz CDP 7243 8 52771 2 2; Stan Getz and Dizzy Gillespie, "Dark Eyes," *For Musicians Only,* Los Angeles, Oct. 16, 1956, Verve 837 435-2.

13. For a comprehensive introduction to African American music in all of its forms see Mellonee V. Burnim and Portia K. Maultsby, *African American Music: An Introduction* (New York: Routledge, 2006).

14. Albert Murray, *Stomping the Blues* (New York: Da Capo, 1976), pp. 16–17.

15. Muddy Waters, "Walkin' Blues" *The Real Folk Blues,* 1950, MCA Records/Chess 088 112 822-2. The line of argument in this section is understood best in conjunction with listening to the musical examples.

16. Evelyn Brooks Higginbotham, "Rethinking Vernacular Culture: Black Religion and Race Records in the 1920s and 1930s." In *The House That Race Built: Black Americans, U.S. Terrain,* ed. Wahneema H. Lubiano, pp. 157–77 (New York: Pantheon, 1997).

17. Samuel A. Floyd Jr., *The Power of Black Music: Interpreting Its History from Africa to the United States* (New York: Oxford University Press, 1995), p. 6.

18. Sea Island Singers, "Sign of the Judgment," *Georgia Sea Islands: Southern Journey,* vol. 12, Saint Simons Island: 1960, Rounder CD 1712; Joe Washington Brown and Austin Coleman, "Run, Old Jeremiah," *Afro-American Spirituals, Work Songs, and Ballads,* Jennings, LA: 1934, Rounder Records CD 1510.

19. Gunther Schuller was also one of the few writers who drew attention to the importance of timbral innovation in early jazz. See Gunther Schuller, *Early Jazz: Its Roots and Musical Development* (New York: Oxford University Press, 1968), pp. 54–57. Ornette Coleman, "Blues Connotation," *This Is Our Music,* New York, Aug. 1960, Atlantic 7567-80767-2; Jimmy Smith, "Prayer Meetin,'" *Prayer Meetin,'* Feb. 8, 1963, Blue Note CDP 7 84164 2.

20. Olly Wilson, "The Heterogeneous Sound Ideal in African-American Music," in *New Perspectives on Music: Essays in Honor of Eileen Southern,* ed. Josephine Wright (Warren, MI: Harmonie Park Press, 1992), pp. 327–38.

21. More on this point later. In my own work I have stressed that musical grooves simultaneously carry rhythm, harmony, and melody; Ingrid Monson, *Saying Something: Jazz Improvisation and Interaction* (Chicago: University of Chicago Press, 1996), pp. 61–62, 70; Charles Keil and Steven Feld, *Music Grooves: Essays and Dialogues* (Chicago: University of Chicago Press, 1994).

22. David H. Rosenthal, *Hard Bop: Jazz and Black Music, 1955–1965* (New York: Oxford University Press, 1992), p. 6.

23. Bing Crosby, "Pennies from Heaven," *Best of Bing Crosby,* 1936, MCA Records MCAD-11942; Frank Sinatra, "Songs for Swingin' Lovers!" 1956, Capitol CDP 7 46570 2.

24. Billy Eckstine, "Blue Moon" (1948), *Everything I Have Is Yours: The Best of the M-G-M years*, Verve 819 442-2; Nat King Cole, "Sweet Lorraine," *The Complete After-midnight Sessions*, Hollywood, 1946, Capitol CDP 7 48328 2.

25. There is, of course, a ballad tradition in gospel music that features slow tempos and a pleading vocal style that could not be described as crooning. Sam Cooke's "Any Day Now" and Ray Charles's "Hard Times" provide a sacred and a secular example, respectively. Sam Cooke, "Any Day Now," *Sam Cooke with the Soul Stirrers*, Specialty SPCD-7009-2; Ray Charles, "Hard Times," *Ray Charles: The Birth of Soul, 1954–1957*, Atlantic 7 82310-2.

26. Stan Getz, "On the Alamo," *The Roost Quartets*, New York, May 17, 1950, Roulette CDP 7 96052 2; Dave Brubeck, "Pennies from Heaven," *Brubeck Time*, New York, Oct. 14, 1954, Columbia CK 65724.

27. Count Basie, "Tickle Toe," *The Essential Count Basie*, vol. 2, New York, Mar. 19, 1940, Columbia CK 40835.

28. This is a reference to A. B. Spellman's comment that asked of those who called John Coltrane's music "anti-jazz," "Who are these ofays who've appointed themselves guardians of last year's blues?" Quoted in Baraka, *Black Music*, p. 18.

29. This is the linguistic sense of "recursive." The *Oxford English Dictionary* definition is "applied to a grammatical rule in which part of the output serves as input to the same rule; applied to a grammatical feature or element which may be involved in a procedure whereby that feature or element is repeatedly reintroduced." "Reciprocal," on the other hand, implies "alternating back and forth" and mutual sharing. *The Oxford English Dictionary*, 2d ed. (New York: Oxford University Press, 1989).

30. Jon Panish, *The Color of Jazz: Race and Representation in Postwar Jazz* (Jackson: University Press of Mississippi, 1997), pp. xv, ix–xxiii. "Color evasiveness" is a term borrowed from Ruth Frankenberg, *White Women, Race Matters: The Social Construction of Whiteness* (Minneapolis: University of Minnesota Press, 1993), p. xi.

31. Two examples of the many JATP recordings are *Norman Granz's Jazz at the Philharmonic, Hartford 1953*, Hartford, CT, May 1953, Pablo 2308240, and *The Exciting Battle: JATP, Stockholm '55*, Stockholm, Sweden, 1955, Pablo 2310713.

32. Dizzy Gillespie, *To Be or Not to Bop: Memoirs of Dizzy Gillespie with Al Fraser* (New York: Da Capo, 1979), p. 406.

33. Leonard Feather, "The Blindfold Test: Little Jazz Goes Color Blind," *Down Beat* 18, no. 14 (July 13, 1951), p. 12.

34. Pete Welding, "Liner Notes," *Birth of the Cool*, Capitol Jazz CDP 7 92862 2. In 1953 eight of the twelve sides were released on a ten-inch LP titled *Classics in Jazz;* in 1957 eleven of the sides were released on a twelve-inch LP titled *Birth of the Cool*. The Capitol CD reissue from 1989 (listed at the beginning of this note) includes all twelve sides. These details were confirmed in an exchange on the Jazz Research List at jazz-research@yahoogroups.com between Dan Morgenstern, Francois Ziegler, Fabian Holt, and Michael Fitzgerald, June 14–15, 2004.

35. Haig and Davis were recorded with the Charlie Parker All Stars on three radio broadcasts from the Royal Roost in December 1948. Robert M. Bregman, Leonard Bukowski, and Norman Saks, *The Charlie Parker Discography* (Redwood, NY: Cadence Jazz Books, 1993), entries 88–90.

36. André Hodeir reports that Sanford Siegelstein is black, but I believe he is incorrect. Siegelstein played French horn in the Claude Thornhill orchestra.

37. Personnel included Miles Davis (trumpet), J. J. Johnson (trombone), Gunther Schuller (French horn), John Barber (tuba), Lee Konitz (alto), Gerry Mulligan (baritone saxophone), Al McKibbon (bass), Max Roach (drums), and Kenny Hagwood (vocal). See Miles Davis, *Birth of the Cool,* New York, 1949, 1950, Capitol CDP 7 92862 2. The titles from these sessions were originally released as singles.

38. Miles Davis with Quincy Troupe, *Miles: The Autobiography* (New York: Simon and Schuster, 1989), p. 117; Nat Hentoff, "Counterpoint," *Down Beat* 23, no. 17 (Aug. 22, 1956), p. 32.

39. For a more detailed account of definitions of modernism and modernity, see chapter 1 in this volume.

40. On the impact of French jazz criticism on American jazz criticism see John R. Gennari, "The Politics of Culture and Identity in American Jazz Criticism," PhD diss., University of Pennsylvania, 1993.

41. The following discussion is based on André Hodeir, *Jazz: Its Evolution and Essence* (New York: Grove, 1956), pp. 116–36. Discussion of violent and sober sonorities is found on p. 119.

42. Ibid.

43. For an analysis of Miles Davis's *Deception* that points to similar irregular formal features see Lewis Porter and Michael Ullman, *Jazz: From Its Origins to the Present* (Englewood Cliffs, NJ: Prentice Hall, 1993), pp. 239–40.

44. Gennari, "Politics of Culture and Identity," p. 84. Nietzsche's classic opposition (dating from 1872) emerged from his analysis of Greek tragedy. Friedrich Nietzsche, *The Birth of Tragedy and the Case of Wagner,* trans. Walter Kaufman (New York: Vintage, 1967).

45. Dan Gold, "Aaron Copland: The Well-known American Composer Finds Virtues and Flaws in Jazz," *Down Beat* 25, no. 9 (May 1, 1958), pp. 16, 39–40.

46. Ibid.

47. Gunther Schuller, *Musings: The Musical World of Gunther Schuller: A Collection of His Writings* (New York: Oxford University Press, 1986), pp. 18–25.

48. Carl Woideck, *Charlie Parker: His Music and Life* (Ann Arbor: University of Michigan Press, 1996), pp. 171–73, 204–205.

49. See Gendron, "Moldy Figs and Modernists," for a discussion of the dynamic between folklore and European high culture in the assessment of jazz.

50. Woideck, *Charlie Parker,* pp. 205–206.

51. Duke Ellington, "Certainly It's Music," in *The Duke Ellington Reader,* ed. Mark Tucker (New York: Oxford University Press, 1993), pp. 246–48.

52. African American interest in classical music has a much longer history than this. See Eileen Southern, *The Music of Black Americans: A History* (New York: Norton, 1983).

53. For information on Horace Silver and Benny Golson see Lees, *Cats of Any Color*, pp. 77–90, 123–42; Quincy Jones, *Q: The Autobiography of Quincy Jones* (New York: Doubleday, 2001), pp. 120–137; Ted Gioia, *West Coast Jazz* (New York: Oxford University Press, 1992). On the idea of "bridge discourse," see Evelyn Brooks Higginbotham, *Righteous Discontent: The Women's Movement in the Black Baptist Church, 1880–1920* (Cambridge, MA: Harvard University Press, 1993), p. 197.

54. For Mingus's experiences with Tristano see Brian Priestley, *Mingus: A Critical Biography* (New York: Da Capo, 1982), pp. 48–49. The most comprehensive account of Tristano's life and teaching is Eunmi Shim, "Lennie Tristano (1919–1978): His Life, Music, and Teaching," PhD diss., University of Illinois Urbana–Champaign, 1999.

55. Barry Ulanov, "Master in the Making," *Metronome* 65, no. 8 (Aug. 1949), pp. 14, 32.

56. Tristano was especially well known for having students sing complete improvised solos, which they learned by ear and without writing them down, before attempting to play them on their instruments. For a comprehensive account of Tristano's pedagogy see Shim, *Lennie Tristano*, pp. 338–454.

57. Ben Ratliff, "Barry Ulanov, 82, a Scholar of Jazz, Art and Catholicism," *New York Times*, May 7, 2000, metropolitan desk.

58. Barry Ulanov, "The Means of Mastery: Lennie Tristano's Intuition On and Off Records Tells His Musical Story and Perhaps Jazz's Also," *Metronome* 65, no. 9 (Sept. 1949), pp. 14, 26.

59. Lennie Tristano and Warne Marsh, "Intuition," New York, May 16, 1949, Capitol Jazz CDP 7243 8 52771 2 2.

60. Bill Coss, "A New Look at Lennie," *Metronome* 67, no. 11 (Nov. 1951), pp. 13, 22; Al Zeiger, "Lennie Tristano: A Debt of Gratitude," *Metronome* 71, no. 6 (June 1955), p. 23.

61. Leonard Feather, "Feather's Nest," *Down Beat* 22, no. 4 (Feb. 23, 1955), p. 7.

62. Barry Ulanov, "A Talk with Dave Brubeck," *Metronome* 69, no. 4 (Apr. 1953), p. 29.

63. Ted Gioia, *West Coast Jazz* (New York: Oxford University Press, 1992), p. 71.

64. "Brubeck Has Double Life as Jazzman, Classic Composer," *Down Beat* 19, no. 24 (Dec. 3, 1953), p. 6; Nat Hentoff, "Jazz Fills Role of Classical Composition, Brubeck Learns," *Down Beat* 21, no. 11 (June 2, 1954), p. 2.

65. David Brubeck, "Jazz' Evolvement as Art Form," *Down Beat* 17, no. 3 (Feb. 10, 1950), p. 13. Although Brubeck's cultural analysis deploys several clichés that are no longer acceptable (such as the notion that jazz consisted of European harmony and African rhythm), uses the word "primitive" in proximity to "African," and tends to take an evolutionary perspective, the extent to which he refuses to privilege classical music as an evaluative standard at that time is somewhat surprising, given the degree to which he was later called upon to speak authoritatively about the relationship between jazz and classical music. Brubeck's explanation of the move from two to four beats in the measure has nothing to do with West African rhythmic organization. For the principles of African rhythmic organi-

zation see John Miller Chernoff, *African Rhythm and African Sensibility: Aesthetics and Social Action in African Musical Idioms* (Chicago: University of Chicago Press, 1979); David Locke, *Drum Gahu: The Rhythms of West Africa* (Crown Point, IN: White Cliffs Media, 1987); and Simha Arom, *African Polyphony and Polyrhythm: Musical Structure and Methodology* (New York: Cambridge University Press, 1991).

66. Ralph J. Gleason, "Brubeck: For the First Time, Read How Dave Thinks, Works, Believes, and How He Reacts to His Critics," *Down Beat* 24, no. 15 ( July 25, 1957), pp. 13–14, 54.

67. "The Man on Cloud No. 7," *Time* 64, no. 19 (Nov. 8,1954), p. 67. All of the musicians mentioned here are white.

68. Ibid.

69. Don Freeman, "Dave Brubeck Answers His Critics," *Down Beat* 22, no. 16 (Aug. 10, 1955), p. 7; Gleason, "Brubeck," pp. 13–14, 54.

70. Freeman, "Dave Brubeck Answers His Critics."

71. On Brubeck's Native American heritage see Lees, *Cats of Any Color,* pp. 39–61.

72. Gleason, "Brubeck," pp. 13–14, 54.

73. Leonard Feather, "Feather's Nest." *Down Beat* 22, no. 4 (Feb. 23, 1955), p. 7.

74. The term "Third Stream" was coined by Gunther Schuller in 1957 to describe the meeting of classical music and jazz, as well as classical music and other types of vernacular music. "Third Stream," *Grove Music Online,* ed. L. Macy (accessed December, 28, 2005), http://www.grovemusic.com (New York: Grove's Dictionaries, 2002).

75. Higginbotham has provided the most influential theorization of the African American relationships to mainstream moral discourse in *Righteous Discontent,* pp. 183–229.

76. Ralph Ellison, *Shadow and Act* (New York: Vintage, 1964), p. 226.

77. Giuseppe Ballaris, "Milt Jackson," *Jazz Forum* 99 (1986), p. 32.

78. Modern Jazz Quartet, "Vendome," *MJQ,* New York Dec. 22, 1952, Prestige PRLP 7059/OJC-125; Modern Jazz Quartet, "Django," New York, June 25, 1953, Prestige VDJ-1515E; Modern Jazz Quartet, "Concorde," New York, July 2, 1955, Prestige PRCD-7005-2.

79. Bill Coss and Jack Maher, "Record Reviews: Modern Jazz Quartet and Jim Giuffre," *Jazz Today* 2, no. 1 ( Jan. 1957), p. 36.; Don DeMichael, "Record Review: Modern Jazz Quartet, *Odds against Tomorrow,*" *Down Beat* 27, no. 4 (Feb. 18, 1960), p. 34; "Le M.J.Q. Fait-Il Jazz?" *Jazz Magazine* 3, no. 22 (Dec. 1956), p. 20.

80. Ibid. "Je vous étonnerai peut-être en vous affirmant qu'il déteste le jazz. Il peut jouer du jazz formidablement s'il le veut, mais il n'aime pa ça. Ce qu'il aime c'est Bach et Chopin. C'est fou ce que j'ai pu m'ennuyer dans le M.J.Q. Je voulais jouer du jazz et il n'y avait moyen avec ces maudits arrangements. Alors je suis parti. Milt Jackson est un jazzman merveilleux, mais il a les pieds et les poings liées dans le M.J.Q. Il souffre beacoup de ne jamais avoir l'occasion de jouer vraiment. Je pense qu'il finera, comme moi, par s'en aller" [my translation].

81. When he left the group in 1974 he claimed that monetarily he had little to show for his extended stay in the MJQ. See Charles Mitchell, "Modern Jazz Quartet Calls It Quits," *Down Beat* 41, no. 15 (Sept. 12, 1974), p. 9.

82. Bassist Art Davis's suit against the New York Philharmonic provides a different strategy for seeking acknowledgment. See Ortiz Walton, *Music: Black, White, and Blue: A Sociological Survey of the Use and Misuse of Afro-American Music* (New York: Morrow, 1972), pp. 124–34.

83. My account of hard bop builds upon two extremely important books: David Rosenthal, *Hard Bop: Jazz and Black Music, 1955–1965* (New York: Oxford University Press, 1992), and Guthrie P. Ramsey, *Race Music: Black Cultures from Bebop to Hip-Hop* (Berkeley: University of California Press, 2003).

84. Ramsey, *Race Music*, p. 4. Ramsey's use "everyday blackness" builds on John Gwaltney's term, "drylongso."

85. Rosenthal, *Hard Bop*, pp. 62–84.

86. Martin Williams, "The Funky–Hard Bop Regression," in *The Art of Jazz: Essays on the Nature and Development of Jazz*, ed. Martin Williams (New York: Oxford University Press, 1959), pp. 233–38; Baraka, *Blues People*, p. 222.

87. Lees, *Cats of Any Color*, pp. 132–34; Lewis Porter, *John Coltrane: His Life and Music* (Ann Arbor: University of Michigan Press, 1998), pp. 73–76, 93; Rosenthal, *Hard Bop*, pp. 30–31.

88. Blakey's relationship to the African diaspora is discussed more fully in the next chapter.

89. Nat Hentoff, "Blakey Beats Drum for 'That Good Old Feeling,'" *Down Beat* 20, no. 25 (Dec. 16, 1953), p. 17.

90. David Rosenthal's definition of hard bop aesthetic tendencies includes (1) musicians on the border of jazz and popular African American music, such as Horace Silver and Jimmy Smith; (2) musicians such as Jackie McLean, Elmo Hope, and Tina Brooks, whose music was somber and tormented in mood; (3) lyrical players who played with hard boppers in the first group, such as Art Farmer and Bennie Golson, whose aesthetic favored "'saying something' over technical bravado;" and (4) the experimentalists who combined interest in pushing the structural and technical boundaries of the music with an embrace of the "moods and forms" of earlier African American musics; Rosenthal, *Hard Bop*, pp. 44–45.

91. I have published an analysis of riffs in Ingrid Monson, "Riffs, Repetition, and Theories of Globalization," *Ethnomusicology* 43, no. 1 (Winter 1999), pp. 31–65.

92. In the blues, a melodic figure often repeats exactly over the I chord and the IV chord of the blues progression. An example can be heard in the first chorus of Count Basie's "Sent for You Yesterday," *Big Band Jazz*, vol. 2, New York, Feb. 16, 1938, Smithsonian RD 030-2; Count Basie, "Volcano," *Big Band Jazz*, vol. 3, New York: Nov. 6, 1939, Smithsonian RD 030-3.

93. "Horoscope," *Horace Silver Trio*, New York, Oct. 9, 1952, Blue Note CDP 7 81520 2.

94. Thelonious Monk, "Thelonious," *Genius of Modern Music*, vol. 2, New York, Oct. 15, 1947, Blue Note 81511.

95. Examples are "Epistrophy," "Straight No Chaser," and "Bolivar Blues."

96. Art Farmer and Benny Golson, "Killer Joe," *Meet the Jazztet,* Chicago, Feb. 1960, Chess CHD-91550.

97. Lee Morgan, "The Sidewinder," *The Sidewinder,* Englewood Cliffs, N.J., Dec. 21, 1963, Blue Note BST-84157; Wayne Shorter, "Ping Pong," *The Complete Blue Note Recordings of Art Blakey's 1960 Jazz Messengers,* Englewood Cliffs, N.J., Feb. 12, 1961, Mosaic MD6-141. I thank pianist Joan Wildman for, many years ago, having drawn my attention to the importance of the Charleston rhythm.

98. "This Here," Cannonball Adderley, *Greatest Hits: The Riverside Years,* San Francisco, Oct. 20, 1958, Milestone Records MCD-9275-2.

99. See liner notes to *Ray Charles: The Birth of Soul, The Complete Atlantic Rhythm and Blues Recordings, 1952–1959,* Atlantic 7 82310-2.

100. A *montuno* is a term from Latin Music. It most typically describes a two- or four-bar pattern played on the piano that is repeated indefinitely.

101. "Ecaroh," Horace Silver, *Horace Silver Trio,* New York, Oct. 9, 1952, Blue Note CDP 7 81520 2.

102. In *Hard Bop* (pp. 41–61), Rosenthal also argues for the importance of Afro-Cuban music in hard bop. On the Latin tinge in early jazz see Christopher Washburne, "The Clave of Jazz: A Caribbean Contribution to the Rhythmic Foundation of an African-American Music," *Black Music Research Journal* 17, no. 1 (Spring 1997): 59–80. Many white bands also incorporated Latin influences in the 1950s, including Stan Kenton. The Caribbean connection to jazz of the 1950s and 1960s is more fully discussed in the next chapter.

103. Eileen Southern, *The Music of Black Americans: A History,* 3d ed. (New York: Norton, 1997); Dena Epstein, *Sinful Tunes and Spirituals: Black Folk Music to the Civil War* (Urbana: University of Illinois Press, 1977); Ronald M. Radano, *Lying Up a Nation: Race and Black Music* (Chicago: University of Chicago Press, 2003), pp. 180–81, 24.

104. Marshall Sahlins, "Goodbye to *Tristes Tropes:* Ethnography in the Context of Modern World History," *Journal of Modern History* 65 (Mar. 1993), p. 18. Sahlins is trying to talk about the coexistence of sameness and difference in a globalized world: "The very ways societies change have their own authenticity, so that global modernity is often reproduced as local diversity" (p. 2). I thank Williams Bares, who reminded me of the term "indigenization of modernity" by citing the work of Ulf Hannerz, whose work led me back to Sahlins's remarkable essay.

105. By "proclivities to altering the dominant" I mean that the altered notes of the blues scale (♭3, ♭5, ♭7), when played over dominant 7 chords on I, IV, and V, produce vertical sonorities and chords with a wide variety of extensions, including I7♯9, IV7♭9, and V7♭13♯9. Mastery of these chords is at the very core of jazz harmonic practice.

106. An excellent recent commentary on this issue can be found in Scott Saul, *"Freedom Is, Freedom Ain't: Jazz and the Making of the Sixties* (Cambridge, Mass.: Harvard University Press, 2003), pp. 29–96.

107. Krin Gabbard, *Black Magic: White Hollywood and African American Culture* (New Brunswick, NJ: Rutgers University Press, 2004), p. 19.

108. Richard M. Sudhalter, *Lost Chords: White Musicians and Their Contribution to Jazz, 1915–1945* (New York: Oxford University Press, 1999).

109. Rosenthal, *Hard Bop,* p. 118.

110. Sahlins, "Goodbye to *Tristes Tropes,*" p. 3.

CHAPTER 4

1. Succinct biographies of Du Bois, Garvey, and Malcolm X can be found in Henry Louis Gates and Evelyn Brooks Higginbotham, eds., *African American Lives* (New York: Oxford University Press, 2004). More in-depth treatment can be found in David L. Lewis, *W.E.B. Du Bois: The Fight for Equality and the American Century, 1919–1963* (New York: Holt, 2000); Edmund David Cronon, *Black Moses: The Story of Marcus Garvey and the Universal Negro Improvement Association* (Madison: University of Wisconsin Press, 1968); Malcolm X with Alex Haley, *The Autobiography of Malcolm X* (New York: Grove, 1965); Taylor Branch, *Pillar of Fire: America in the King Years, 1963–1965* (New York: Simon and Schuster, 1998).

2. For analyses of the relationship between anticolonialism, the Cold War, and the domestic civil rights struggle see Penny M. Von Eschen, *Race against Empire: Black Americans and Anticolonialism, 1937–1957* (Ithaca, NY: Cornell University Press, 1997), and Brenda Plummer, *Rising Wind: Black Americans and U.S. Foreign Affairs, 1935–1960* (Chapel Hill: University of North Carolina Press, 1996).

3. For a succinct account of Robeson's life see Gates and Higginbotham, *African American Lives,* pp. 714–17; for a full biography see Martin Duberman's fascinating *Paul Robeson* (New York: Knopf, 1988). For Dizzy Gillespie's account of opening night see Dizzy Gillespie, *To Be or Not to Bop: Memoirs of Dizzy Gillespie* (New York: Da Capo, 1979), p. 288.

4. Von Eschen, *Race against Empire,* pp. 17–20, 89, 103–104; Duberman, *Paul Robeson,* pp. 283–85, 397. Although Duberman refers to the "Persian Hotel," he cites a newspaper that may have misspelled the name.

5. Nkrumah became the first president of independent Ghana in 1957, and Jomo Kenyatta became prime minister of Kenya in 1963. Nnamdi Azikiwe was the editor of a chain of newspapers in Nigeria and West Africa and played a prominent role in the struggle for Nigerian independence; see Von Eschen, *Race against Empire,* pp. 54–56.

6. Ibid., pp. 17–20.

7. Ibid., pp. 8, 29, 96–121.

8. Ibid., pp. 78, 83.

9. Gillespie's autobiography spells the name "Azumba"; *To Be or Not to Bop,* p. 289. Elsewhere it is reported as K. O. Mbadiwe and K. Ozoumba Mbadiwe. He later became Nigeria's central minister of communications and aviation; "Overseas Datelines," *Pittsburgh Courier* 47, no. 19 (May 12, 1956), p. 9. See also the Institute for Jazz Studies clippings files, "U.S. State Department."

10. Gillespie, *To Be or Not to Bop,* p. 290.

11. Duberman, *Paul Robeson,* p. 388; Von Eschen, *Race against Empire,* p. 137, 116, 109.

12. I thank Penny Von Eschen for alerting me to the location of the State Department records of the Cultural Presentations Program, which are not in the National Archives, as might be expected, but rather are in the Special Collections Division of Mullins Library, University of Arkansas, Fayetteville, Arkansas. For a more complete treatment of the Cultural Presentations Program see her book, *Satchmo Blows Up the World: Jazz Ambassadors Play the Cold War* (Cambridge, Mass.: Harvard University Press, 2004). I wrote this section before its publication but was stimulated by her work, "Who's the Real Ambassador? Exploding Cold War Racial Ideology," in *Cold War Constructions: The Political Culture of United Sates Imperialism 1945–1963,* ed. Christian G. Appy, pp. 110–131. (Amherst: University of Massachusetts Press, 1997).

13. Virginia Inness-Brown, "The International Cultural Exchange Service of the American National Theatre and Academy (ANTA) and its relationship to the President's Special International Program for Cultural Presentations of the Bureau of International Educational and Cultural Affairs, Department of State," CU, subseries 1, box 2, folder 30, "Wolfe-Larsen Report—Public Comments," Jan. 17, 1961; "Armstrong to Lead the Way in Musical Cultural Invasion?" *Down Beat* 23, no. 1 (Jan. 11, 1956), p. 7; Roy E. Larsen and Glenn G. Wolfe, "U.S. Cultural Presentations—A World of Promise," Report of the U.S. Advisory Commission on International Cultural and Educational Exchange, CU subseries1, box 7 folder 32, "ANTA/Department—General Correspondence, 1962," Dec. 17, 1962; Lisa E. Davenport, "Jazz and the Cold War: Black Culture as an Instrument of American Foreign Policy," master's thesis, Howard University, 1995.

14. The State Department's abbreviation for the bureau is CU.

15. Virginia Inness-Brown, "The ICES and Its Relationship," CU subseries 1, box 2, folder 30, Jan. 17, 1961; "Armstrong to Lead the Way"; Davenport, "Jazz and the Cold War," p. 16.

16. "Projects Completed and Approved for Assistance from Beginning, July 1954, through June 1962: FY1955 through FY1963," CU subseries 1, box 1, folder 39, "GTIC, Cultural Presentations, 1962–1965."

17. Music Advisory Panel minutes, May 3, 1955, International Exchange Program. CU subseries 1, box 12, folder 12, "Music Advisory Panel Meetings, November 1954—December 1956"; Winthrop Sargeant, *Jazz: Hot and Hybrid* (New York: Arrow, 1938).

18. Minutes, Dec. 20, 1955, MAP, CU subseries 1, box 12, folder 12.

19. Larsen and Wolfe, "U.S. Cultural Presentations—A World of Promise," Report of the U.S. Advisory Commission on International Cultural and Educational Exchange, CU subseries 1, box 7, folder 32.

20. "U.S. Government to Send Jazz as Its Ambassador," *Down Beat* 22, no. 26 (Dec. 28, 1955), p. 6. In his autobiography, Dizzy Gillespie recalls the press conference as occurring in early 1956; Gillespie, *To Be or Not to Bop,* p. 413. *Down Beat*'s reportage describes the event taking place in November 1955. Short film clips from the press conference can be

found in *Listen Up—The Lives of Quincy Jones* (video recording), Producer, Courtney Sale Ross; Director, Ellen Weissbro, 1991. The quotes are my best effort at transcribing a sound track that is somewhat difficult to understand.

21. Gillespie, *To Be or Not to Bop*, p. 417. See also "Dizzy to Rock India," *New York Times* (Feb. 2, 1956), IJS clippings files, "U.S. Department of State."

22. The full roster included Dizzy Gillespie, Joe Gordon, Emet Perry, Carl Warwick, Quincy Jones (trumpet); Melba Liston, Frank Rehak, Rod Levitt (trombone), Jimmy Powell, Phil Woods (alto sax), Billy Mitchell, Ernie Wilkins (tenor sax), Marty Flax (baritone sax), Walter Davis Jr. (piano), Nelson Boyd (bass), and Charlie Persip (drums).

23. "History of Jazz Big Feature of Gillespie Overseas Tour," *Down Beat* 23, no. 9 (May 2, 1956), p. 9; "Indians Dizzy over Gillespie's Jazz," Part 1, *Pittsburgh Courier* 47, no. 22 (June 2, 1956), p. 22.

24. Quincy Jones, *Q: The Autobiography of Quincy Jones* (New York: Doubleday, 2001), p. 112.

25. "Indians Dizzy over Gillespie's Jazz," Part 1, p. 22.

26. "Dizzy's Troupe Casts Spell over Mideast Audiences," *Down Beat* 23, no. 12 (June 13, 1956), p. 17.

27. ibid.; "Indians Dizzy," Part 1.

28. Gillespie's words are variously reported. The quote here is from "Indians Dizzy over Gillespie's Jazz," Part 2, *Pittsburgh Courier* 47, no. 23 (June 9, 1956), p. 21, and Marshall Stearns, "Is Jazz Good Propaganda? The Dizzy Gillespie Tour," *Saturday Review* (July 14, 1956), p. 30. Elsewhere Stearns reports that Gillespie said, "Man, we're here to play for the people"; Marshall Stearns, "Turkey Resounds, Reacts to Dizzy Gillespie Band," *Down Beat,* 23 no. 13 (June 27, 1956), p. 16. In his autobiography written in the seventies Gillespie recalls having said, "Man, we're not here to play for any elites! We're over here to make friendships with the small people, the people outside the gates"; *To Be or Not to Bop,* p. 422. "Indians Dizzy over Gillespie's Jazz," Part 2.

29. Jones, *Q: The Autobiography of Quincy Jones,* p. 114.

30. Gillespie, *To Be or Not to Bop,* p. 419; Jones, *Q: The Autobiography of Quincy Jones,* p. 114.

31. Gillespie, *To Be or Not to Bop*, pp. 414, 420–21.

32. Ibid., pp. 421, 415–16.

33. W.E.B. Du Bois, *The World and Africa* (New York: International Publishers, 1965), p. 338.

34. Ibid., pp. 421, 80. Norman Granz was also a member of the Communist Party at one time. Dempsey J. Travis, *Norman Granz: The White Moses of Black Jazz* (Chicago: Urban Research Press, 2003), p. xv.

35. The State Department had been under pressure to increase black employment because its record was among the worst of all of the federal agencies. Although there had been a few visible African Americans in policy-making positions in the department,

including Ralph Bunche (associate chief of the Division of Dependent Area Affairs in the late forties) and Channing H. Tobias (an alternate delegate to the UN appointed by the Truman administration), even with Eisenhower additions in 1953 there were only 55 black employees in a department of 8,231.

36. Stanley F. Morse, "State Department Aids Integration" (letter to the editor), *Savannah Georgia News,* May 5, 1957, IJS clippings files.

37. Most contemporary news reports say the tour lasted ten weeks, but this includes preliminary travel days.

38. "International Exchange Program Contract for Dizzy Gillespie," March 1956, CU subseries 1, box 8, folder 8, "IEP Contracts 1956." Figures in all of the ANTA contracts were for estimated expenses. There are handwritten emendations on the Gillespie contract, which are included in these figures. According to the contract, a few band members were paid more than $200 per week, most likely Dizzy Gillespie and the arrangers, Quincy Jones, Ernie Wilkins, and Melba Liston. Although the actual per diem rate is not included in this contract, a rate of $15 per day was paid to the Wilbur De Paris band in 1957; see Robert C. Schnitzer, "Progress Report No. 43 [to the International Exchange Service]," Feb. 15, 1957, p. 11, CU subseries 1, box 2, folder 13, "Project Proposals 1956–1961"). The total Gillespie figures are somewhat ambiguous since the contract is written differently from those of later tours. Total expenses including salary, per diem allowances, excess baggage, passports, visas, inoculations, and insurance were $6,200 per week (approximately $295 per week per person).

39. "International Exchange Program contract for Dizzy Gillespie," July 1956, CU subseries 1, box 8, folder 8, "IEP Contracts 1956"; "Bandleaders Say State Dept. Tight with Loot," *Pittsburgh Courier* 47, no. 20 (May 19, 1956), p. 21.

40. Schnitzer, "Progress Report No. 43," CU subseries 1, box 2, folder 13, International Exchange Program contract for Glenn Miller, Mar. 18, 1957; CU subseries 1, box 8, folder 6, "IEP Contracts, 1957."

41. "ICES Contract for Herbie Mann," Dec. 3, 1959, CU subseries 1, box 8, folder 2, "ICES Contracts, 1958–1959"; "ICES Contract for Louis Armstrong," Sept. 29, 1960, CU subseries 1, box 8, folder 3, "ICES Contracts, 1960–1961."

42. Robert C. Schnitzer, "Progress Report No. 36," Oct. 29, 1956, CU subseries 1, box 2, folder 10, Project Proposals Book 1, Nov. 1954–Oct. 1956; Robert C. Schnitzer, "Progress Report No. 47," May 31, 1957, box 2, folder 13, "Project Proposals 1956–1961."

43. Among those mentioned in the minutes are Ray Bryant, Horace Silver, Count Basie, Art Blakey, Ahmed Abel-Malik, Sarah Vaughan, Kai Winding, Quincy Jones, and Ornette Coleman.

44. Minutes of the Music Advisory International Cultural Exchange Service of ANTA, 1959–1961, CU subseries 1, "General and Historical Files. Performers," box 12, folders 14–16; Davenport, "Jazz and the Cold War," pp. 24, 39.

45. Minutes of the Music Advisory Panel, Dec. 16, 1959; Apr. 20, 1960.

46. Davenport, "Jazz and the Cold War," pp. 36–41.

47. Press and embassy reports, CU subseries 1, box 2, folder 23, "Performing Arts: General Publicity, ca. 1951–1969."

48. Randy Weston, "Report from Randy Weston on State Department Tour of West and North Africa (1/16/67–4/11/67)," CU S2 subseries 1, box 31, folder 27, "Weston, Randy—Tour Reports."

49. Contemporary new reports called the film *The Saga of Satchmo.* I thank Robert O'Meally of Columbia University and Jazz at Lincoln Center for making a copy of the film available to me. Although Velma Middleton appears with the band in the film, she is not included in the film's credits, which list only the instrumentalists: Louis Armstrong, trumpet; Edmond Hall, clarinet; Trummy Young, trombone; Billy Kyle, piano; Arvell Shaw, bass; and Barrett Deems, drums. There is also a soundtrack recording; Louis Armstrong, *Satchmo the Great* (recorded various locations: 1956), Columbia CK 53580.

50. Reports of the number of people at the outdoor concert varied. The *Pittsburgh Courier, Newsweek,* and *Down Beat* reported 100,000; *Life* magazine, 25,000; and *Time* magazine, 30,000. *Variety* stated a figure of 10,000, which other sources gave for the airport arrival festivities. "Armstrong's 'Axe' Gasses Ghanese Fans," *Pittsburgh Courier* 47, no. 22 (June 2, 1956), p. 23; "Good Will with Horns," *Newsweek* 47, no. 23 (June 4, 1956), p. 50; "Satch's Saga," *Down Beat* 24, no. 4 (Feb. 20, 1957), p. 19; "Satchmo Is a Smash on the Gold Coast," *Life* 40, no. 24 (June 11, 1956), pp. 38–39; "Just Very," *Time* 67, no. 23 (June 4, 1956), p. 23. A short portion of the "All for You, Louis" and the Ghanaian crowd welcoming Armstrong can be heard on Louis Armstrong, *Satchmo the Great,* Accra, Ghana, May 1956, Columbia CK 53580. The CD also includes portions of Edward R. Murrow's narration for the film.

51. "Goodwill with Horns"; Leonard Feather, "Pops Pops Top on Sloppy Bop," *Metronome* 65, no. 10 (Oct. 1949), pp. 18, 25.

52. Dennis Austin, *Politics in Ghana, 1946–1960* (New York: Oxford University Press, 1970), pp. 316–58.

53. Northern Ghana voted on July 12.

54. "MAP [minutes]," Dec. 19, 1956, CU subseries 1, box 12, folder 12, "Music Advisory Panel Meetings, November 1954—December 1956"; Dick Campbell, "Wilbur De Paris Orchestra, Final Itinerary," CU subseries 1, box 9, folder 10, "Performance Records A–f"; "Morocco, Gold Coast, Liberia," *Pittsburgh Courier* 48, no. 9 (Mar. 2, 1957), p. 6.

55. "Scream 'We Want Satchmo' as the 'Saga of Armstrong' Hits Ghana," *Chicago Defender* 52, no. 46 (Mar. 16, 1957), p. 8; "Morocco, Gold Coast, Liberia," *Pittsburgh Courier* 48, no. 9 (Mar. 2, 1957), p. 6; "Nkrumah Couldn't Dance!" *Pittsburgh Courier* 48, no. 12 (Mar. 23, 1957), p. 3.

56. Ethel L. Payne, "World's Notables See Ghana Become Nation," *Chicago Defender,* weekend ed., 52, no. 45 (Mar. 9, 1957), p. 1; Taylor Branch, *Parting the Waters: America in the King Years, 1954–1963* (New York: Simon and Schuster, 1988), pp. 365–66, 368.

57. During these years, many African Americans even emigrated to Ghana. See Kevin Kelly Gaines, *American Africans in Ghana: Black Expatriates and the Civil Rights Era* (Chapel Hill: University of North Carolina Press, 2006).

58. "The *Courier* Salutes Ghana: An Editorial," *Pittsburgh Courier* 48 (Mar. 9, 1957), supplement p. 1.

59. Ibid.

60. Joel A. Rogers, "This Modern City Has Everything!" *Pittsburgh Courier* 48, no. 10 (Mar. 9, 1957) supplement, p. 4.

61. George E. Pitts, "Segregated Audiences Should Be Abolished!" *Pittsburgh Courier* 48, no. 9 (Mar. 2, 1957), p. 22.

62. William G. Nunn Sr., "Stay Out of Dixie!" *Pittsburgh Courier* 48, no. 11 (Mar. 16, 1957), p. 6.

63. "State Dept. Pipes Up with 'Satchmo for the Soviets,'" *Variety* 207, no. 9 (July 31, 1957), p. 1; "'Satchmo' Tells Off Ike, U.S.!" *Pittsburgh Courier* 48, no. 39 (Sept. 28, 1957), p. 3.

64. Norman C. Weinstein, *A Night in Tunisia: Imaginings of Africa in Jazz* (New York: Limelight, 1993).

65. Horace Silver, "Message from Kenya," *Horace Silver Trio,* New York, Nov. 23, 1953, Blue Note CDP 7 81520 2, Art Blakey, drums; Sabu Martinez, conga.

66. Biography, Sabu Martínez Memorial Home Page, http://www.hipwax.com/sabu/. Martinez played with many other jazz performers as well, including Buddy De-Franco and J. J. Johnson.

67. There may be others mentioned as well, but my linguistic abilities are limited to unambiguously recognizing these two.

68. Art Blakey's solo on "Safari," *Horace Silver Trio,* New York, Oct. 9, 1952, Blue Note CDP 7 81520 2.

69. This effect can be achieved by either an elbow or stick held down on the drum head.

70. Machito, *Kenya,* New York: 1958, Palladium PCD-104; Machito, *Afro-Cuban Jazz,* New York, 1947, 1950, 1957, 1958, Saludos Amigos CD 62015. Herbie Mann, Johnny Griffin, and Curtis Fuller also recorded with Machito's band in 1958.

71. Art Blakey, "Art Blakey's Comments on 'Ritual,'" *Ritual,* New York, Feb. 11, 1957, Blue Note CDP 7 46858 2.

72. Jean Clouzet and Michel Delorme, "Entretien: Les Confidences de Buhaina," *Jazz Magazine* 9, no. 6 (June 1963), p. 37. "Pendant deux ans, je me suis plongé uniquement dans les philosophes, les religion et les langues hébraïque et arabes et je n'ai pas le souvenir d'avoir jouer une seule fois d'un instrument pendant toute cette periode" [my translation].

73. Herb Nolan, "New Message from Art Blakey," *Down Beat* 46, no. 17 (Nov. 1979), p. 19.

74. Blakey's recording history is consistent with a six-to-eight-month stay in Africa. Blakey performed in New York in April 1947 and recorded with Thelonious Monk on October 15, 1947. He played with Monk in March 1948 and next appeared at the Royal Roost in October 1948. See Steve Schwartz and Michael Fitzgerald, *Chronology of Art Blakey and the Jazz Messengers,* http://www.jazzdiscography.com/Artists/Blakey/chron.htm (accessed Mar. 13, 2007).

75. Randy Weston, personal communication, Apr. 13, 1999, Cambridge, MA.

76. In the early 1950s Cándido Camero was a member of Billy Taylor's trio. Raul A. Fernandez, *Latin Jazz: The Perfect Combination = La Combinación Perfecta* (Washington, D.C.: Chronicle), p. 79.

77. Art Blakey, *Drum Suite,* New York, Columbia CL 1002. The pieces that included Sabu and Cándido were recorded on Feb. 22, 1957.

78. Dizzy Gillespie, "Afro," New York, May 21 and June 3, 1954, Norgran Records 314 517 052 2.

79. The more typical use of this pattern in Afro-Cuban sacred music is the "short bell" (i.e., beginning the pattern on the fifth stroke of the pattern notated here). If the strokes of the pattern are conceived as longs (L = quarter note) and shorts (S = eighth note), the long bell is LLLSLLS, while the short bell is LLSLLLS.

80. Art Blakey. *Holiday for Skins,* vol. 2, New York, Nov. 9, 1958, Blue Note BST-84005. I thank Elizabeth Sayre and Julian Gerstin for assisting me in the understanding of clave rhythms.

81. Tito Puente, *Top Percussion,* New York, July 19, 1957, RCA 3264-2-RL, with Mongo Santamaría, Willie Bobo, Julito Collazo, and Francisco Aguabella; Tito Puente, *Puente in Percussion,* New York, 1955, Fania TRLP-1011, with Mongo Santamaría, Willie Bobo, and PatatoValdés.

82. Nolan, "New Message," p. 21.

83. Dom Cerulli, "Review of Art Blakey's *Orgy in Rhythm,*" *Down Beat* 24, no. 18 (Sept. 5, 1957), p. 22; Jack Maher, "Review of Art Blakey *Orgy in Rhythm, Volume 2,*" *Metronome* 74, no. 12 (Dec 1957), pp. 25, 28; Don Gold, "Review of Art Blakey's *Ritual,*" *Down Beat* 24, no. 22 (Oct. 31, 1957), p. 24; "Review of Art Blakey's *Holiday for Skins,*" *Down Beat* 26, no. 17 (Aug. 20, 1959), p. 55. See Weinstein, *Night in Tunisia,* pp. 51–53, for a more sympathetic account of these recordings. Selassie and Tubman visited the United States in 1954; Nkrumah in 1958.

84. Vernon Boggs, *Salsiology: Afro-Cuban Music and the Evolution of Salsa in New York City* (New York: Greenwood, 1992), pp. 128–29. My understanding of the histories of Latin music and calypso in the United States in the 1950s is informed additionally by Fernandez, *Latin Jazz;* John Storm Roberts, *The Latin Tinge: The Impact of Latin American Music on the United States* (Tivoli, NY: Original Music, 1985); Steven Loza, *Tito Puente and the Making of Latin Music* (Urbana: University of Illinois Press, 1999); Donald Hill, "I Am Happy Just to Be in This Sweet Land of Liberty," in *Island Sounds in the Global City: Caribbean Popular Music and Identity in New York,* ed. Ray Allen and Lois Wilcken, pp. 74–92 (New York: New York Folklore Society, Institute for Studies in American Music Brooklyn College, 1998).

85. I have not forgotten the French-speaking Caribbean. Its impact on the music of the 1950s and 1960s was just not as prominent.

86. Fernández, *Latin Jazz,* p. 51.

87. George Shearing, *Latin Lace/Latin Affair,* Capitol 7243 4 494993 2 4.

88. It is not used solely in sacred contexts.

89. Randy Weston at the conference, "Miles Davis, the Civil Rights Movement and Jazz," Washington University, St. Louis, May 3, 1997, video recording.

90. Max Roach, interview by author, Cambridge, MA, April 4, 1999.

91. Weinstein, *Night in Tunisia,* p. 41.

92. Weston, "Miles Davis, the Civil Rights Movement and Jazz."

93. Bilal Abdurahman, *In the Key of Time: The Bedford Stuyvesant Renaissance 1940s–1960s Revisited* (Brooklyn: Contemporary Visions, 1993), p. 5. I thank Robin D. G. Kelly for generously making a copy of this book available to me. (The book is not numbered, so this is my pagination, beginning on the first page of the text.)

94. Charles Mingus, "Debut Records Company History" (1965), Charles Mingus Collection, box 57, folder 3, Library of Congress, Washington, DC; *The Debut Records Story,* Debut 4DCD-4420-2 (Fantasy boxed set).

95. Abdurahman, *In the Key of Time,* pp. 5–9.

96. "East Meets West" handbill announcing concert on Jan. 26, 1962. Institute for Jazz Studies, topics files: New York jazz clubs. Abdurahman also appears on Ahmed Abdul-Malik, *Jazz Sounds of Africa,* Englewood Cliffs, NJ, May 23, 1961, and Aug. 22, 1962, Prestige PRCD-24279-2.

97. Brenda Plummer, *Rising Wind: Black Americans and U.S. Foreign Affairs, 1935–1960* (Chapel Hill: University of North Carolina Press, 1996), pp. 247–53.

98. "Islam Covers the Entire Earth," *Muhammad Speaks* 1, no. 2 (Dec. 1961), p. 31. An ad for an African-Asian unity bazaar held in Newark featuring jazz and steel band music can be found in ibid. 3, no. 19 (June 5, 1964), p. 20.

99. Richard Brent Turner, *Islam in the African American Experience* (Bloomington: Indiana University Press, 1997), pp. 109–46; Aminah Beverly McCloud, *African American Islam* (New York: Routledge, 1995), pp. 18–21; Jean Clouzet and Michel Delorme, "Entretien: Les Confidences de Buhaina," *Jazz Magazine* 9, no. 6 (June 1963), pp. 35–42. For a longer discussion of Art Blakey and Islam see also Ingrid Monson, "Art Blakey's African Diaspora," in *The African Diaspora: A Musical Perspective,* ed. Ingrid Monson, pp. 329–52 (New York: Garland, 2000).

100. Clouzet and Delorme, "Entretien," p. 38. "L'Islam a apporté à l'homme noir ce que celui-ci cherchait, une porte de sortie que certains ont trouvée dan la drogue ou la boisson: une manière de vivre et de penser qu'il puisse choisir en tout liberté. C'est la raison pour laquelle nous avons été si nombreux à adopter cette nouvelle religion. Ce fut pour nous, avant tout, une façon de nous rebeller" [my translation].

101. James Feron, "African Nations Shun 'Cold War,'" *New York Times,* Sept. 22, 1960, p. 1; Alfred Duckett, "Why Castro Fled to Harlem, Youth Says Fidel Made Fool of 'White Folks,'" *Chicago Defender,* weekend ed. 56, no. 23 (Oct. 1, 1960), p. 1; Max Frankel, "Cuban in Harlem," *New York Times,* Sept. 20, 1960, p. 1; Branch, *Parting the Waters,* pp. 351–78.

102. Weston, "Miles Davis, the Civil Rights Movement and Jazz," All of the quotes in this section are from this event.

103. Helen Bannerman, *The Story of Little Black Sambo* (London: Grant Richards, 1899).

104. The mid-1960s witnessed a movement to establish Kiswahili as a lingua franca throughout the African continent. See Scot Brown, *Fighting for US: Maulana Karenga, the US Organization, and Black Cultural Nationalism* (New York: New York University Press, 2003), pp. 10–11.

105. Randy Weston, *Uhuru Afrika,* New York, Nov. 1960, Roulette CDP 7945102. All twelve pitches of the chromatic scale are presented in these four bars as well. Shortly after this passage the phrase is completed with "Afrika" articulated in the horns.

106. I thank John Mugane for his help on the Kiswahili language.

CHAPTER 5

1. The full title of the recording is *We Insist! Max Roach's Freedom Now Suite.* Nevertheless, I refer to the piece as the *Freedom Now Suite,* as is usual among jazz musicians.

2. "CORE presents: Freedom Now," Jan. 15, 1961, poster, CORE series 5, box 28, folder 8; Collection of Art D'Lugoff, Max Roach, *We Insist! Max Roach's Freedom Now Suite,* New York, Aug. 31 and Sept. 6, 1960, Candid CCD 9002. The album photo was adapted from widely distributed photos of the lunch-counter sit-ins in early 1960. One example can be found in William H. Chafe, *Civilities and Civil Rights* (New York: Oxford University Press, 1981), p. 84.

3. Amiri Baraka, *Blues People: Negro Music in White America* (New York: William and Morrow, 1963); Frank Kofsky, *Black Nationalism and the Revolution in Music* (New York: Pathfinder, 1970).

4. Stanley Dance, *The World of Duke Ellington* (New York: Charles Scribner's Sons, 1970), p. 21.

5. This list includes information from a detailed search of jazz magazines (among them *Down Beat* and *Metronome*), mainstream newspapers (such as the *New York Times*), African American newspapers *(New York Amsterdam News, Pittsburgh Courier, Chicago Defender),* and handbills from the Marshall Stearns files at the Institute for Jazz Studies in Newark, NJ. The list is, nevertheless, not intended to be comprehensive.

6. Clark Terry, interview with author, Mar. 27, 1997, St. Louis, MO.

7. Amiri Baraka, *The Autobiography of LeRoi Jones* (Chicago: Lawrence Hill, 1997), pp. 298–99. Although I do not have equally detailed documentation of the benefit concerts and politically related events at which avant-garde artists played, many musicians have stated that they played regularly at such events; Roswell Rudd, interview with author, June 28, 1998.

8. Baraka, *Blues People;* John Litweiler, *The Freedom Principle: Jazz after 1958* (New York: Da Capo, 1984); Kofsky, *Black Nationalism and the Revolution in Music.*

9. Abbey Lincoln, interview with author, June 13, 1995, New York.

10. My perspective on the development of the sit-in movement is indebted to Aldon D. Morris, *The Origins of the Civil Rights Movement: Black Communities Organizing for*

*Change* (New York: Free Press, 1984), especially pp. 187–228. Additional information on the sit-ins can be found in Clayborne Carson, *In Struggle: SNCC and the Black Awakening of the 1960s* (Cambridge, MA: Harvard University Press, 1981), pp. 1–18; William H. Chafe, *Civilities and Civil Rights* (New York: Oxford University Press, 1981), pp. 71–101; Taylor Branch, *Parting the Waters: America in the King Years, 1954–1963* (New York: Simon and Schuster, 1988), pp. 271–73; and August Meier and Elliott Rudwick, *CORE: A Study in the Civil Rights Movement* (Urbana: University of Illinois Press, 1975), pp. 101–106.

11. Meier and Rudwick, *CORE,* pp. 188–94, 197–99; Chase, *Civilities and Civil Rights,* pp. 76–77, 80–81.

12. Meier and Rudwick, *CORE,* pp. 199–205.

13. Morris, *Origins of the Civil Rights Movement,* pp. 174–78; Chafe, *Civilities and Civil Rights,* p. 86.

14. Morris, *Origins of the Civil Rights Movement,* pp. 214–20.

15. Ibid., pp. 221–23.

16. Meier and Rudwick, *CORE,* p. 81; "Southern Boycott Spreading North," *New York Amsterdam News* 50, no. 7 (Feb. 13, 1960), p. 11; Marvin Rich, interview with author, Jan. 3, 1997, New York.

17. Nat Hentoff, interview with author, Jan. 2, 1997, New York.

18. Jimmy McDonald to George Haefer, July 25, 1960, IJS topics files: race problems; "Executive Board Minutes," *Allegro* 34 (Aug. 1960), pp. 14–15.

19. Initial coverage in the *New York Amsterdam News* referred to the lunch-counter sit-ins as "sit downs." "The Sit Downs," *New York Amsterdam News* 50, no. 10 (Mar. 5, 1960), p. 8. The sit-down strike was a tactic used by the United Auto Workers in organizing the auto industry in the 1930s. The most famous example is the strike in Flint, Michigan, from 1936 to 1937. See "The Flint Sit-Down Strike," http://www.historicalvoices.org/flint/ (accessed Mar. 4, 2007).

20. Marvin Rich, interview with author; "April 25th Dinner, Financial Report" (May 11, 1965), SNCC subgroup B, series 1, reel 46, frame 1234. In 1960 union scale for a five-piece band for one night at a class A nightclub in New York was $121.64 (three hours); see *Allegro* 34 (Feb. 1960), p. 23.

21. Art D'Lugoff, interview with author, Jan. 5, 1997, New York; Morris, *Origins of the Civil Rights Movement,* pp. 141–55.

22. D'Lugoff, interview.

23. " 'Cabaret for Freedom' New Theatre Movement," *New York Amsterdam News* 50 (Nov. 19, 1960), p. 18; Maya Angelou recalls that all of these performances were held in the summer of 1960. The *Amsterdam News* coverage, however, indicates that they occurred later. See Maya Angelou, *The Heart of a Woman* (New York: Bantam, 1997), pp. 65–81.

24. Don DeMichael, "Urban League 'Festival,'" *Down Beat* 27 (Oct. 13, 1960), p. 20; "Sammy Davis Jr. Brought Friends to Chicago Jazz Bash," *Pittsburgh Courier* (Sept. 10, 1960), p. 23.

25. DeMichael, "Urban League Festival."

26. Harry Belafonte, appeal letter, n.d., check CORE subseries 5, box 28, folder 2; "A Full Evening with Sinatra, Martin, Davis, Lawford, Bishop," *New York Amsterdam News* 51, no. 2 (Jan. 14, 1961), p. 13; Rich, interview; "Joséphine Baker," Oct. 12, 1963 (poster), CORE subseries 5, box 28, folder 8; Howard C. Burney to Val Coleman, Nov. 15, 1963, CORE subseries 5, box 28, folder 8; Val Coleman, interview with author, July 23, 1997. For information on SNCC field secretary wages see "Broadway Comes to Arthur," May 23, 1966, SNCC B, I, reel 46, folder 1257–58; Ella Baker, appeal letter, Jan. 22, 1963, SNCC B, I, reel 45, folder 1086.

27. On funding see Morris, *Origins of the Civil Rights Movement,* pp. 116–19.

28. Both quotes are from "The Messenger of Allah Presents the Muslim Program," *Muhammad Speaks* 2, no. 25 (Aug. 30, 1963), p. 24.

29. All of the quotes from Malcolm X in the next few paragraphs are from George Breitman, ed., *Malcolm X Speaks* (New York: Grove, 1965), pp. 21–22. The Muslim Mosque, Inc., preceded the formation of Malcolm X's Organization of Afro-American Unity.

30. Clayborne Carson, *Malcolm X: The FBI File* (New York: Carroll and Graf, 1991), p. 32.

31. Lani Guinier, *The Tyranny of the Majority: Fundamental Fairness in Representative Democracy* (New York: Free Press, 1994); Michael C. Dawson, *Black Visions: The Roots of Contemporary African-American Political Ideologies* (Chicago: University of Chicago Press, 2001).

32. On racial separatism in SNCC and CORE see Carson, *In Struggle,* pp. 191–211; Meier and Rudwick, *CORE,* pp. 374–408.

33. Some passages of this section were published in Ingrid Monson, "Revisited! Freedom Now Suite," *Jazz Times* 31 (Sept. 2001), pp. 54–59.

34. Many African American composers have chosen to present a historical narrative of African American experience in their works, including Billy McClain's *Darkest America,* a musical theater production from 1896, and Wynton Marsalis's *Blood on the Fields.* See Thomas L. Riis, *More than Just Minstrel Shows: The Rise of Black Musical Theatre at the Turn of the Century,* ISAM Monographs, No. 33 (Brooklyn, NY: Institute for Studies in American Music, Conservatory of Music, Brooklyn College of the City University of New York, 1992), p. 6; Wynton Marsalis, *Blood on the Fields* (sound recording), New York, Jan. 22–25, 1995, Columbia CXK 57694.

35. Nat Hentoff, liner notes to *We Insist! Max Roach's Freedom Now Suite,* New York, Aug. 31 and Sept. 6, 1960, Candid CCD 9002. Personnel on the recording include Booker Little, trumpet; Coleman Hawkins and Walter Benton Jr., tenor saxophone; Julian Priester, trombone; Michael (Babatunde) Olatunji and James Schenck, bass; Mantillo Du Vall, percussion, Max Roach, drums; and Abbey Lincoln, vocal.

36. *We Insist! Max Roach's Freedom Now Suite;* "CORE presents: Freedom Now," (poster), subseries 5, box 28, folder 8; collection of Art D'Lugoff. It is possible that portions of the suite were actually performed at the Village Gate sometime during the summer of 1960; see the later section on Candid Records.

37. Dan Morgenstern, "Freedom Now," *Metronome* 78 (Mar. 1961), p. 51.

38. "Jazz Gallery, N.Y.," *Variety* 222, no. 7 (Apr. 12, 1961), p. 53. Gloster Current reported that Sarah Vaughan also appeared with Lincoln and Roach at the NAACP convention. Oscar Brown Jr. reports that this is incorrect; interview with author, June 29, 1998. See Gloster Current, "Fifty-second Annual Convention Promises a Stepped-up Crusade," *Crisis* 68, no. 7 (Aug.–Sept. 1961), p. 410; "Freedom Now Suite May Go on Tour," *Down Beat* 28, no. 21 (Oct. 12, 1961), p. 13. Ossie Davis and Ruby Dee report that there was also a plan to make a film entitled *Uhuru!* (Freedom!) that used the *Freedom Now Suite* as a soundtrack. The project ran out of money. Ossie Davis and Ruby Dee, *With Ossie and Ruby: In This Life Together* (New York: William Morrow, 1998), pp. 288–289.

39. Brown's father had been an active organizer for the Chicago NAACP's campaign against restrictive covenants.

40. Max Roach, interview with author, Apr. 3, 1999, Cambridge, MA; Oscar Brown Jr., interview with author by telephone, June 20, 1998.

41. Brown Jr., interview.

42. Ibid.

43. "Freedom Album May Be Loaned," *New York Amsterdam News* 42, no. 34 (Aug. 24, 1963), p. 14; "No 'Freedom Now' in South Africa," *Down Beat* 29, no. 13 (June 21, 1962), p. 11; Robert W. July, *A History of the African People* (New York: Charles Scribner's Sons, 1970), p. 500. The *Freedom Now Suite* was performed at a benefit for SNCC in 1965 and on tour in Europe in 1964.

44. Abbey Lincoln, interview with author, June 13, 1995.

45. Dave Brubeck, "Take Five," *Time Out,* New York, July 1, 1959, Columbia CK 65122.

46. Buddy Rich and Max Roach, *Rich versus Roach,* New York, Spring 1959, Mercury 826 987-2.

47. Frank Kofsky accused Orrin Keepnews of suppressing the statement for political reasons on a later reissue. Keepnews found this charge highly ironic since he had written a good portion of the statement to begin with. Keepnews related this information at "Miles Davis, the Civil Rights Movement, and Jazz," a conference held at Washington University, May 3–4, 1997; Kofsky's charges are made in Kofsky, *Black Nationalism and the Revolution in Music,* pp. 50–51.

48. Orrin Keepnews, liner notes to *Freedom Suite,* Riverside OJCCD-067-2 (RLP-258).

49. Nat Hentoff, *Speaking Freely* (New York: Knopf, 1997), pp. 46–53. Hentoff had had some experience organizing sessions for Lester Koenig's Contemporary Records. Among the Candid releases were albums by Don Ellis, Booker Ervin, Lightnin' Hopkins, Steve Lacy, Abbey Lincoln, Booker Little, Charles Mingus, Otis Spann, Clark Terry, Cecil Taylor, and Phil Woods.

50. Lincoln, interview.

51. Charles Mingus, "Original Faubus Fables," *Charles Mingus Presents Charles Mingus,* New York, Oct. 20, 1960, Candid BR-5012. Due to contractual issues with Columbia, Candid could not use "Fables of Faubus" as the title. Russell is probably Senator Richard Russell. The names of the political figures changed in live performance to fit the circumstances of the day. See Sy Johnson, liner notes, *The Complete 1959 CBS Charles Mingus Sessions,* New York, 1959, Mosaic MQ4-143.

52. "Prayer for Passive Resistance," *Mingus at Antibes,* Juan-les-Pins, France, July 13, 1960, Atlantic SD 2-3001. The piece was first recorded on *Pre-Bird,* New York, May 25, 1960, Mercury SR-60627.

53. Hentoff, interview; Gene Lees, "Newport: The Real Trouble," *Down Beat* 27, no. 17 (Aug. 18, 1960), pp. 20–23, 44; Michael Cuscuna, liner notes, *The Complete Candid Recordings of Charles Mingus,* New York, Oct. 20, 1960, and Nov. 11, 1960, Mosaic 111.

54. Lees in "Newport: The Real Trouble" reports that Mingus accused George Wein and the Newport Festival of practicing Jim Crow and chastised Nat Adderley for electing to play the regular festival rather than the one at Cliff Walk Manor.

55. Michael Cuscuna, liner notes, *Complete Candid Recordings of Charles Mingus; Newport Rebels: Jazz Artists Guild,* New York, Nov. 1 and Nov. 11, 1960, Candid 9022; *The Jazz Life,* New York, Nov. 1 and Nov. 11, 1960, Candid 9019. The musicians who appeared on the recording who did not perform at the rebel festival were Benny Bailey, Tommy Flanagan, and Peck Morrison. "Jazz Artists Guild" (advertisement), *New York Amsterdam News* 50, no. 34 (Aug. 20, 1960), p. 13. The personnel listed were Coleman Hawkins, Jo Jones, Max Roach, Charles Mingus, Kenny Dorham, Allen Eager, and Abbey Lincoln. Although no dates are listed in the ad, the "Nightly 8 & 11:30 Mats. Sat. Sun. 2:30" probably refers to Tuesday through Sunday of the following week, August 23–28.

56. Alice A. Dunnigan, "Count Basie Speaks Out, Supports Student 'Sit-ins,'" *Pittsburgh Courier* (Apr. 2, 1960), p. 34.

57. George E. Pitts, "'Cannonball' Blasts Hurok Who Attacked Jazz," *Pittsburgh Courier* (May 28, 1960), p. 33.

58. "The Duke Refuses to 'Second Fiddle,'" *Pittsburgh Courier* (July 16, 1960), p. 23.

59. George E. Pitts, "Belafonte Blasts 'Parlor Liberals,'" *Pittsburgh Courier* (Aug. 20, 1960), p. 23.

60. Chester L. Washington, "'No Intention of Apologizing,' Lena Horne Says," *Pittsburgh Courier* (Feb. 27, 1960), p. 2.

61. "Ray Charles Bucks Bias; Cancels Georgia Concert," *Pittsburgh Courier* (Apr. 1, 1961), p. 23.

62. Portions of the following two sections were previously published in Ingrid Monson, "Miles, Politics, and Image," in *Miles Davis and American Culture,* ed. Gerald Early, pp. 86–97 (St. Louis: Missouri Historical Society Press, 2001).

63. Miles Davis with Quincy Troupe, *Miles: The Autobiography* (New York: Simon and Schuster, 1989), p. 238.

64. The incident was extensively covered in New York newspapers as well as in the jazz and African American presses. See, Martin Burden and Ernest Tidyman, "Jazzman Miles Davis Battles Two Cops Outside Birdland," *New York Post* (Aug. 26, 1959); "Jazz Man Free on Bail," *New York Times* (Aug. 27, 1959); "Police Club Miles Davis for 'Chivalry'," *Pittsburgh Courier* 51, no. 36 (Sept. 5, 1959), p. 2; "This Is What They Did to Miles," *Melody Maker* (Sept. 12, 1959), p. 1; "The Slugging of Miles Davis," *Down Beat* 26, no. 20 (Oct. 1,1959), p. 11.

65. Irving Kolodin, " 'Miles Ahead', or Miles' Head?" *Saturday Review*, no. 12 (Sept. 1959); "Of Men and Miles," *Down Beat* 26, no. 24 (Nov. 26, 1959), p. 6.

66. Les Matthews, "Free Miles, Davis of Cop's Charge," *New York Amsterdam News* (Oct. 17, 1959), p. 1; "Charge Dismissed," *Down Beat* 26, no. 3: (Nov. 12,1959), p. 11; "Aftermath of Miles," *Down Beat* 26, no. 22 (Oct. 29,1959), p. 11.

67. "Judges Dig Baker the Most: Free Miles Davis with Some Cool Sounds!" *New York Amsterdam News* 50, no. 3 (Jan. 16,1960), p. 1, 15; "Miles Files," *Down Beat* 27, no. 7 (Mar. 31, 1960), p. 13; "Miles Exonerated," *Down Beat* 27, no. 4 (Feb. 18, 1960), p. 12; "To Sue NYC, for $1 Million," *Baltimore Afro-American* (Dec. 15, 1959), p. 15.

68. Davis and Troupe, *Miles*, p. 238.

69. The name of the organization has been incorrectly reported as the African Relief Foundation in both Davis and Troupe, *Miles*, p. 253; and Jack Chambers, *Milestones II: The Music and Times of Miles Davis since 1960* (Toronto: University of Toronto Press, 1985), p. 36.

70. Miles Davis, *Miles Davis at Carnegie Hall*, New York, May 19, 1961, Columbia CL 1812. The original LP included only part of the concert. The complete performance was released in 1998 as *Miles Davis at Carnegie Hall—The Complete Concert*, New York, May 19, 1961, Columbia C2K 65027.

71. The African Medical and Research Foundation headquarters is located in Nairobi. See http://www.amref.org

72. Julius Nyerere, *Ujamaa: Essays on Socialism* (London: Oxford University Press, 1977); Scot Brown, *Fighting for US : Maulana Karenga, the US Organization, and Black Cultural Nationalism* (New York: New York University Press, 2003), p. 14-15. See chapter 7 for a fuller description of cultural nationalism.

73. Ronald Moss, interview with author by telephone, Apr. 21, 1995. Moss helped co-found the organzation with Thomas Rees. Davis and Troupe, *Miles,* p. 238, reports the name as "Jean Bock." Jean Bach later directed the film *A Great Day in Harlem*, Image Entertainment, 1995.

74. The mobile unit may have been named for Davis. Ronald Moss, interview with author, April 21, 1995.

75. "Roach Interrupts Davis Concert," *New York Amsterdam News* (May 27, 1961), p. 17; George T. Simon, "Miles Davis Plays Trumpet in Carnegie Hall Concert." *New York Herald Tribune* (May 20, 1961); Institute for Jazz Studies, Clippings Files, "Miles Davis,"

*Someday My Prince Will Come* was cut short. When Miles returned he began with *Oleo*, not *No Blues* as Chambers reports. See Chambers, *Milestones II*, p. 36.

76. Ian Carr, *Miles Davis: A Biography* (New York: William Morrow and Company, 1982), p. 128.

77. Ronals Moss, interview with author, April 21, 1995; Carr, *Miles Davis*, p. 127–28. Carr reports that African nationalist groups accused the ARF of being in league with South African diamond interests.

78. "Riot in Gallery Halts U.N. Debate," *New York Times* (Feb. 16,1961), Sect. 1, pp. 1, 10; "Dizzy to Present New African Work," *New York Amsterdam News* (Feb. 18, 1961), p. 13; "Africa Freedom Day," *New York Amsterdam News* (Mar. 25, 1961), p. 17.

79. Teo Macero, interview with author, May 15, 1995, New York.

80. The LP (Columbia 1812) deleted *Teo, Walkin', I Thought About You*, and *Concierto de Aranjuez*. These selections were released on a separate issue, *Live Miles: More Music from the Legendary Carnegie Hall Concert*, CS 8612 (LP); Columbia CK 40609.

81. My account of the Freedom Rides is drawn primarily from Branch, *Parting the Waters*, pp. 412–85. See also Meier and Rudwick, *CORE*, pp. 135–58; Morris, *Origins of the Civil Rights Movement*, pp. 231–36.

82. Branch, *Parting the Waters*, pp. 413, 415–16.

83. Ibid., pp. 417–18.

84. Ibid., pp. 419, 421–24.

85. Ibid., pp. 427–29.

86. Ibid., pp. 430–31.

87. Ibid., pp. 454–65.

88. Trombonist Roswell Rudd participated in these rides. Roswell Rudd, telephone interview with author, June 28, 1998.

89. Branch, *Parting the Waters*, pp. 469–77, 482–85. Meier and Rudwick, *CORE*, pp. 139–43. The ICC ruling prohibiting segregated facilities in interstate travel was passed on Sept. 1, 1961.

90. Nat Hentoff, liner notes, Art Blakey, *The Freedom Rider*, Englewood Cliffs, N.J., Feb. 12, 18, and May 27, 1961, Blue Note CDP 7243 8 21287 2 4; originally issued as BST 84156.

91. Branch, *Parting the Waters*, pp. 142–44, 148–49. Most of the Freedom Riders served thirty-nine days before bailing out and appealing. This was the maximum time one could serve and still appeal. At the request of the CORE's leadership, some people pleaded nolo contendere, thereby reducing the costs to a $200 fine. In November the NAACP Legal Defense Fund agreed to undertake the actual trial costs and advanced bail money to CORE. Despite tremendous fund-raising efforts, by mid-1963 CORE was $120,000 in debt.

92. Jesse H. Walker, "CORE Telethon 4½-Hour Success," *New York Amsterdam News* 51, no. 28 (July 15, 1961), p. 16; Meier and Rudwick, *CORE*, p. 149. Following the event Walker reports appearances by Billy Taylor, Lena Horne, and Cal Tjader, as well as some folk singers (Leon Bibb). The article advertising the telethon mentions Art Blakey,

Horace Silver, and Oscar Brown as well. It is possible that they were advertised but did not appear. It is just as possible that Walker watched only part of the show. "Big Telethon Set to Aid Freedom Riders," *New York Amsterdam News* 51, no. 25 (June 24, 1961), p. 17. Louis Lomax, journalist and author of *The Reluctant African* (New York: Harper, 1960), was a widely admired writer in the African American community at the time.

CHAPTER 6

Some portions of chapter 6 were previously published in Ingrid Monson, "Monk Meets SNCC." *Black Music Research Journal* 19, no. 2, pp. 187-200.

1. Despite the fact that the movement in Albany, Georgia, was much in the news in December 1961, it does not appear to have affected New York fund-raising events as directly. In addition, since it failed to desegregate public facilities (despite hundreds of people going to jail, continuous demonstrations, and Martin Luther King's presence), it was not a model of victory. Morris ascribes the failure to organizational rivalries between SNCC and SCLC and tactical maneuvers on the part of the white power structure. See Aldon D. Morris, *Origins of the Civil Rights Movement* (New York: Free Press, 1984), pp. 239–50. Clayborne Carson, *In Struggle: SNCC and the Black Awakening of the 1960s* (Cambridge, MA: Harvard University Press, 1981), pp. 70–71.

2. A Salute to Southern Students (invitation), Feb. 1, 1963. SNCC Papers, 1959–1972 (microfilm), subgroup B, part I, reel 45, frame 1097.

3. Minutes of the Steering Committee, New York Friends of SNCC, Dec. 4, 1963, SNCC Papers, subgroup B, part I, reel 46, frames 818–19.

4. Harold Leventhal to William Mahoney, Dec. 6, 1962, SNCC Papers, subgroup A, part IX, reel 27, frame 815; Charles McDew to Max Roach and Abbey Lincoln, Dec. 22, 1962, SNCC Papers, subgroup A, part IX, reel 27, frame 816; "Sponsors of Carnegie Hall, Feb. 1st Benefit for SNCC," n.d. SNCC, subgroup B, part I, reel 45, frame 1094; "Entertainers contacted," n.d., SNCC Papers, subgroup A, part IX, reel 27, frames 856–57, 1163; Ella J. Baker to Harold Lovette, Jan. 7, 1963, SNCC Papers, subgroup A, part IX, reel 27, frames 818–19.

5. Taylor Branch, *Parting the Waters: America in the King Years, 1954–1963* (New York, Simon and Schuster, 1988), p. 713.

6. Bernice Reagon, "Miles Davis, the Civil Rights Movement, and Jazz," conference held at Washington University, St. Louis, MO, May 3–4, 1997, video recording.

7. Leslie Gourse's biography includes a few observations on Monk's views of the "race question." See Leslie Gourse, *Straight, No Chaser: The Life and Genius of Thelonious Monk* (New York: Schirmer, 1997), pp. 220–21.

8. Valerie Wilmer, "Monk on Monk," *Down Beat* 32, no. 12 (June 1, 1965), p. 22.

9. Frank London Brown, "Thelonious Monk: More Man than Myth, Monk Has Emerged from the Shadows," *Down Beat* 25, no. 22 (Oct. 30, 1958), p. 46. Monk later denied ever having made this comment.

10. Duberman, *Paul Robeson*, p. 388.

11. My account of Birmingham is based primarily on Morris, *Origins of the Civil Rights Movement*, pp. 250–74, and Branch, *Parting the Waters*, pp. 725–802. Morris's reading stresses the strategic planning of the movement; Branch implies that the strategy was more emergent and provides a day-by-day account. I list the pages pertaining to specific details in notes at the end of each paragraph. For this paragraph, see Morris, *Origins of the Civil Rights Movement*, pp. 257, 260, 250–51.

12. Morris, *Origins of the Civil Rights Movement*, pp. 263–64.

13. Branch, *Parting the Waters*, p. 740.

14. Ibid., p. 735; "Al Hibbler in Ala.," *Muhammad Speaks* 2, no. 16 (Apr. 29, 1963), p. 22.

15. Project C occurred in the midst of a contested mayoral election between "Bull" Connor and Albert Boutwell. Boutwell (who was considered a moderate despite having been a leader in the local White Citizens Council) won the election, but Connor filed suit. As they awaited legal results, both administrations operated simultaneously.

16. Branch, *Parting the Waters*, pp. 752–54, 756–802.

17. Ibid., pp. 793–802, 824–25.

18. Ibid., pp. 804–806. "Jazzmen Raise Funds at Jackie Robinson's Home," *Down Beat* 30 (Aug. 1, 1963), p. 13.

19. Branch, *Parting the Waters*, pp. 808, 824.

20. Ibid., pp. 872, 874, 876–77; Brian Ward, *Just My Soul Responding: Rhythm and Blues, Black Consciousness, and Race Relations* (Berkeley: University of California Press, 1998), p. 304; "Emancipation March on Washington for Jobs and Freedom" (poster), Aug. 23, 1963. CORE series 5, box 28, folder 8; "Giant 12-Hour Civil Rights Rally," *New York Amsterdam News* 42 (Aug. 24, 1963), p. 14.

21. Branch, *Parting the Waters*, pp. 888–92. Yasuhiro Fujioka with Lewis Porter and Yoh-Ichi Hamada, *John Coltrane: A Discography and Musical Biography*, Metuchen, NJ: Scarecrow Press. Some people dispute the contention that Coltrane's music was conceived with the Birmingham bombing in mind.

22. Jack Chambers, *Milestones II: The Life and Times of Miles Davis since 1960* (Toronto: University of Toronto Press, 1985), p. 60. Davis also performed a benefit concert for the African Research Foundation on May 19, 1961, which is covered in chapter 5. The performance was recorded and released as *Miles Davis at Carnegie Hall*, New York, May 19, 1961, Columbia C2K 65027.

23. August Meier and Elliott Rudwick, *CORE: A Study in the Civil Rights Movement* (Urbana: University of Illinois Press, 1975), pp. 172–74, 222–24; Marvin Rich, interview with author, Jan. 3, 1997.

24. Miles Davis, appeal letter, Jan. 27, 1964, SNCC Papers, subgroup B, part I, reel 45, frame 995.

25. Ibid.

26. Ron Carter, conversation with author, Apr. 23, 1995, New York; Miles Davis and Quincy Troupe, *Miles: The Autobiography,* (New York: Simon and Schuster, 1989), p. 266.

27. Miles Davis, *My Funny Valentine,* New York, Feb. 12, 1964, Columbia CL 2306; *Four & More,* New York, Feb. 12, 1964, Columbia CL 2453. The CD reissue provides the complete performance: *The Complete Concert, 1964: My Funny Valentine + Four & More,* New York, Feb. 12, 1964, Columbia CK 40609.

28. Ian Carr, *Miles Davis: A Biography* (New York: Morrow, 1982), p. 138; Marvin Rich to Miles Davis, Mar. 13, 1964, CORE subseries 5, box 28, folder 8.

29. Charles Neblett, "Miles Davis, the Civil Rights Movement, and Jazz," a conference held at Washington University, St. Louis, MO, May 3–4, 1997, video recording.

30. Bernice Reagon, "Miles Davis, the Civil Rights Movement, and Jazz," a conference held at Washington University, St. Louis, MO, May 3–4, 1997, video recording.

31. Morris, *Origins of the Civil Rights Movement,* p. 264; Clark Terry, interview with author, Mar. 27, 1997.

32. Ward, *Just My Soul Responding,* pp. 289–336.

33. Leonard Feather, "On the Racial Front," *Down Beat's Music '64,* pp. 20–22; Louis Calta, " 'Freedom' Shows in South Planned," *New York Times,* July 11, 1963, p. 21; Milton Esterow, "Birmingham Hall to Be Painted on Date Set for Integrated Show," *New York Times,* July 16, 1963, p. 25.

34. Rich, interview. Chaney and Schwerner worked for CORE, and Goodman for SNCC. See Branch, *Pillar of Fire,* p. 441.

35. "Sunday Evening with SNCC," Apr. 25, 1965. SNCC Papers, subgroup B, part I, reel 46, frame 1226; "Organization of Artists Formed to Raise Funds for Civil Rights," *Down Beat* 32, no. 6 (Mar. 11, 1965), pp. 10–11.

36. Val Coleman, interview with author, July 23, 1997.

37. Ibid.;Terry, interview with author.

38. Ron Carter, interview with author, July 31, 1995.

39. Branch, *Pillar of Fire,* pp. 431–36; Manning Marable, *Race, Reform, and Rebellion: The Second Reconstruction in Black America, 1945–1990,* 2d ed. (Jackson: University Press of Mississippi, 1991), pp. 84–85.

40. Carson, *In Struggle,* pp. 98–99.

41. Ibid., pp. 98–103, 111–18.

42. Branch, *Pillar of Fire,* p. 606. On Martin Luther King's voter registration campaign in Selma, Alabama, which led to the passage of the Voting Rights Act, see pp. 575–84. Meier and Rudwick, *CORE,* pp. 329–30.

43. Meier and Rudwick, CORE, p. 419; Carson, *In Struggle,* pp. 196–206, 215–18.

44. See Carson, *In Struggle,* and Meier and Rudwick, *CORE,* for the details of this debate within each organization.

45. Both Clayborne Carson and James Forman credit Willie Ricks, an SNCC field secretary, with coining the term. Carson, *In Struggle,* p. 209; James Forman, *The Making of Black Revolutionaries* (Washington, DC: Open Hand, 1985), pp. 456–57.

46. Marable, *Race, Reform, and Rebellion,* pp. 96–99.

47. Komozi Woodard, *A Nation within a Nation: Amiri Baraka (Leroi Jones) and Black Power Politics* (Chapel Hill: University of North Carolina Press, 1999), pp. 71–73; Scot Brown, *Fighting for US: Maulana Karenga, the US Organization, and Black Cultural Nationalism* (New York: New York University Press, 2003), pp. 105–13.

48. "The Dinizulu Center for African Culture and Research," 2004, http://www .dinizulu.org (accessed April 19, 2007); "AFSANI," 2004, http://www.afsani.org/ spirituality.htm (accessed Mar. 4, 2007).

49. Babatunde Olatunji, *Drums of Passion,* New York, 1959, Columbia, CK 66011. Gary Stewart, *Breakout: Profiles in African Music* (Chicago: University of Chicago Press, 1992), pp. 87–95.

50. "Of Drums and Drummers," *Muhammad Speaks* 1, no. 14 (Sept. 15, 1962), p. 4; "Michael Olatunji," *Muhammad Speaks* 2, no. 14 (Apr. 1, 1963), p. 21; "African Drummer Entertains Washington Mosque," *Muhammad Speaks* 2, no. 22 (July 19, 1963), p. 14.

51. Jackie McLean, "Miles Davis, the Civil Rights Movement, and Jazz," Conference held at Washington University, St. Louis, MO, May 3–4, 1997, video recording.

52. Ibid.

53. Frank Kofsky, *Black Nationalism and the Revolution in Music* (New York: Pathfinder, 1970), p. 85.

54. Ibid.

55. *Report of the National Advisory Commission on Civil Disorders* (New York: Bantam, 1968), pp. 56–69. Other sources report that twenty-six people were killed. See Brown, *Fighting for US,* p. 101.

56. Brown, *Fighting for US,* p. 100.

57. Ibid., p. 63. Amiri Baraka, *The Autobiography of LeRoi Jones* (Chicago: Lawrence Hill, 1997), pp. 370–73. Woodard, *Nation within a Nation,* p. 80, reports that the police had planted guns in the car.

58. Baraka, *Autobiography of LeRoi Jones,* pp. 331, 336–37, 347, 351.

59. Ibid., p. 337.


CHAPTER 7

1. Of these terms, contemporary periodicals most frequently used the New Thing or the jazz avant-garde. Other frequent terms in contemporary sources were serious music, free jazz, and freedom music.

2. Frank Kofsky, *John Coltrane and the Jazz Revolution of the 1960s* (New York: Pathfinder, 1998), pp. 103–104.

3. Eric Porter, *What Is This Thing Called Jazz? African American Musicians as Artists, Critics, and Activists* (Berkeley: University of California Press, 2002), pp. 149–90; Farah Jasmine Griffin, *If You Can't Be Free, Be a Mystery* (New York: Free Press, 2001), pp. 161–91.

4. The band included Abbey Lincoln, vocals; Max Roach, drums; Coleman Hawkins and Walter Benton, tenor sax; Eric Dolphy, reeds; Mal Waldron, piano; Booker Little, trumpet; Julian Priester, trombone; Art Davis, bass; and Roger Sanders and Robert Whitley, congas.

5. Ira Gitler, "Review: Abbey Lincoln, *Straight Ahead*," *Down Beat* 28, no. 23 (Nov. 9, 1961) pp. 35–36. His reference to the *New Yorker* is Harold R. Isaacs, "Back to Africa," *New Yorker* (May 13, 1961), pp. 105– 43. Muhammad is the correct spelling.

6. Gitler, "Review: Abbey Lincoln."

7. Ira Gitler, "Review: Dave Brubeck, *Time Out*," *Down Beat* 27, no. 9 (Apr. 28, 1960), p. 37; Ira Gitler, "Review: Cannonball Adderley, *The Cannonball Adderley Quintet in San Francisco*," *Down Beat* 27, no. 11 (May 26, 1960), p. 27.

8. Clyde Taylor, "Chords and Discords: A Serious Charge," *Down Beat* 29, no. 1 (Jan. 4, 1962), p. 6.

9. The racial makeup of this group (defined by American racial definitions then operative) was two African Americans (Abbey Lincoln and Max Roach) and six white critics and musicians (four critics and two musicians). Lalo Schifrin was born in Argentina and was a member of Dizzy Gillespie's band at the time.

10. "Racial Prejudice in Jazz, Part 1," *Down Beat* 29, no. 6 (Mar. 15, 1962), pp. 20–26. The quotations in this section with page numbers alone are also from this source.

11. Burton Peretti, *The Creation of Jazz: Music, Race, and Culture in Urban America* (Chicago: University of Illinois Press, 1992), p. 77.

12. This was a new position for Hentoff, who in 1959 had written an article for *Harper's* titled "Race Prejudice in Jazz: It Works Both Ways," *Harper's Magazine* 218, no. 1309 (June 1959), pp. 72–77.

13. Nat Hentoff, liner notes, Abbey Lincoln, *Straight Ahead*, New York, Feb. 22, 1961, Candid CCD 79015.

14. Abbey Lincoln, interview with author, June 13, 1995, New York.

15. Maya Angelou, *The Heart of a Woman* (New York: Bantam, 1997), pp. 169–90.

16. "Riot in Gallery Halts U.N. Debate," *New York Times* (Feb. 16, 1961), pp. 1, 10; Lincoln, interview.

17. "Racial Prejudice in Jazz, Part 2," *Down Beat* 29, no. 3 (Mar. 29, 1962), p. 24. All unattributed quotations in this section are also from this source.

18. Nat Hentoff, interview with author, Jan. 2, 1997, New York.

19. Max Roach, "Max Roach on Jazz," *Muhammad Speaks* 2, no. 6 (Dec. 15, 1962), p. 21. See also Max Roach, "Max Roach on Future of Jazz," *Muhammad Speaks* 2, no. 7 (Dec. 30, 1962), pp. 20, 22.

20. "Racial Prejudice in Jazz," Part 1, p. 26.

21. Gitler liked the *Freedom Now Suite* and thought it was musically successful. He had written a profile of Charles Mingus in 1960 that spoke admiringly of Mingus's reputation for protest. Ira Gitler, interview with author, Oct. 21, 2000, New York; Ira Gitler, "Mingus Speaks—and Bluntly," *Down Beat* 27, no. 15 (July 21,1960), pp. 29–30, 67.

22. Lincoln's four previous albums were *Affair* (1956), *That's Him!* (1957), *It's Magic* (1958), and *Abbey Is Blue* (1959). For more on the place of singers in the jazz tradition see Lara Pellegrinelli, "The Song Is *Who?* Locating Singers on the Jazz Scene," PhD diss., Harvard University, 2005.

23. Gitler, "Review: Abbey Lincoln," pp. 35–36.

24. Fifths in the tempered scale are smaller than their naturally occurring size in the overtone series. Intonation systems, when studied cross-culturally, reveal themselves to be just as constructed as many other features of culture.

25. Lincoln, interview. Singers have only their ears to rely upon in locating pitches. Instrumentalists tend to have fingerings that physically assist them in locating the right pitch.

26. I transcribed these with the aid of Transcribe!, a program that helped me confirm voicings and measure intonation. The harmonies are skeletal and do not include all of the details of the horn parts.

27. The final of the first appearance of the G#4 is a bit less than a quarter tone flat; the second one is in tune.

28. Lincoln, interview.

29. Ibid.

30. At least according to Tom Lord's *Jazz Discography* (West Vancouver, B.C.: Lord Music Reference, 1992).

31. Gitler, interview.

32. Max Roach, interview with author, Apr. 3, 1999, Cambridge, MA. All unattributed quotes of Roach in this section are from this source.

33. Hentoff, interview.

34. Gitler, interview. All unattributed quotes from Gitler in this section are from this source.

35. Ira Gitler, *Jazz Masters of the Forties* (New York: Macmillan, 1966).

36. Lincoln, interview. All unattributed quotes from Lincoln in this section are from this source.

37. See especially Griffin, *If You Can't Be Free,* pp. 161–91; Porter, *What Is This Thing Called Jazz?* pp. 149–90.

38. Abbey Lincoln, telephone conversation, Dec. 4, 2001.

39. Ibid.

40. For an excellent account of Nina Simone at this time see, Ruth Feldstein, "I Don't Trust You Anymore": Nina Simone, Culture, and Black Activism in the 1960s." *Journal of American History* 91 (2005), pp. 1349–79.

41. Lincoln, interview.

42. Nat Hentof, Interview with author, January 2, 1997.

43. "Point of Contact: Discussion," *Down Beat, Music '66* (eleventh yearbook) (1966): pp. 19–31, 110–11. All of the page numbers for the citations in the following two sections are from this source.

44. Amiri Baraka, *Blues People: Negro Music in White America* (New York: W. Morrow, 1963), pp. 200–201, 231.

45. Georgina Born, *Rationalizing Culture: IRCAM, Boulez, and the Institutionalization of the Musical Avant-garde* (Berkeley: University of California Press, 1995), p. 43.

46. Theodor W. Adorno, *Aesthetic Theory* (Minneapolis: University of Minnesota Press, 1997), pp. 1, 6, 21, 23. Originally published in German in 1970, Adorno's treatise on aesthetics crystallized his thinking on art and society, which had been ongoing since the 1930s.

47. Amiri Baraka (LeRoi Jones), *Black Music* (New York: Quill, 1967), p. 15.

48. A. B. Spellman, *Four Lives in the Bebop Business* (New York: Limelight, 1985), p. 4. Although current work has illuminated the limitations of defining U.S. society as a dialectic of black and white alone, discourse in these arguments is generally very binary.

49. *Imagine the Sound,* directed by Robert Mann, New York: Janus Films, 1981.

50. Baraka, *Black Music,* pp. 69–80. Later on, many implied that the term *avant-garde* was imposed by white critics, but Baraka's active use of it before 1963 belies this.

51. George E. Lewis, "Singing Omar's Song: A (Re)Construction of Great Black Music," *Lenox Avenue* 4 (1998), p. 73; John Litweiler, *The Freedom Principle: Jazz after 1958* (New York: Da Capo, 1984), p. 173.

52. Baraka, *Black Music,* p. 70.

53. "John Coltrane: Dealer in Discord," *Muhammad Speaks* 2, no. 9 (Jan. 31, 1963), p. 21.

54. "Cool Scholars Scarce As 'Lockjaw' Blows His Horn," *Muhammad Speaks* vol. 2, no. 10 (Feb. 4, 1963), p. 20.

55. "On the Death of John Coltrane," *Muhammad Speaks* 7 (July 28, 1967), p. 21.

56. Scot Brown, *Fighting for US: Maulana Karenga, the US Organization, and Black Cultural Nationalism* (New York: New York University Press, 2003), pp. 108–115.

57. Ibid., pp. 12–17, 68–73.

58. Dan Morgenstern, interview with author, June 20, 1995, Newark, NJ.

59. Ibid.

60. Other notable club closings included San Francisco's Blackhawk and Chicago's Sutherland Lounge. See Don DeMichael, "The Year in Review," *Down Beat Music '64,* p. 9.

61. For excellent historical accounts of several organizations, including the Association for the Advancement of Creative Musicians (AACM), Union of God's Musicians and Artists Ascension (UGMAA), Collective Black Artists (CBA), and BAG (Black Artists Group), see Lewis, "Singing Omar's Song, pp. 69–92; Ronald M. Radano, *New Musical Figurations: Anthony Braxton's Cultural Critique* (Chicago: University of Chicago Press, 1993); Ronald Radano, "Jazzin' the Classics: The AACM's Challenge to Mainstream Aesthetics," *Black Music Research Journal* 12, no. 1 (1992): 79–95; Porter, *What Is This Thing Called Jazz?* pp. 191–239; Horace Tapscott and Steven Isoardi, *Songs of the Unsung: The Musical and Social Journey of Horace Tapscott* (Durham, NC: Duke University Press, 2001); Litweiler, *Freedom Principle;* Benjamin Looker, *Point from Which Creation Begins: The Black Artists' Group of St. Louis* (Saint Louis: Missouri Historical Society Press, 2004).

62. Morgenstern, interview; "Point of Contact," pp. 24, 28.

63. Spellman, *Four Lives in the Bebop Business,* p. 10.

64. Baraka, *Black Music,* p. 113.

65. This may have been Cecil Taylor or Ornette Coleman.

66. *The New Wave in Jazz,* New York, Mar. 28, 1965, Impulse! GRD-137. Among the participants were the groups of John Coltrane, Archie Shepp, Charles Tolliver, and Grachan Moncur III.

67. Art D'Lugoff, " 'Experimentation' in Public: The Club Owner's Perspective." *Down Beat* 32, no. 8 (Apr. 8, 1965), pp. 14–15; John Coltrane, Grachan Moncur, Archie Shepp, and Charles Tolliver, *The New Wave in Jazz,* New York, Mar. 28, 1965, Impulse! GRD-137.

68. Baraka, *Black Music,* pp. 95–97, 114.

69. The concerts ran from Oct. 1 through Oct. 4, 1964. See John S. Wilson, "Dig That Free-form Jazz," *New York Times* (Jan. 24, 1965), p. X13. Valerie Wilmer reports that the concerts took place over six consecutive nights. Valerie Wilmer, *As Serious as Your Life: The Story of the New Jazz* (New York and London: Serpent's Tail, 1992), pp. 213–15. The "October Revolution" alludes to the Bolshevik Revolution of 1917.

70. Robert Levin, "The Jazz Composers Guild: An Assertion of Dignity," *Down Beat* 32, no. 10 (May 6, 1965), pp. 17–18.

71. Wilson, "Dig That Free-form Jazz"; "Music Notes," *New York Times* (Dec. 28, 1964), p. 34.

72. Spellman, *Four Lives in the Bebop Business,* pp. 25–27; Levin, "The Jazz Composers Guild, pp. 17–18; Wilmer, *As Serious as Your Life,* pp. 214–15; Litweiler, *Freedom Principle,* pp. 138–39.

73. Wilmer, *As Serious as Your Life,* p. 19.

74. All of the preceding quotations in this section are from Spellman, *Four Lives in the Bebop Business,* pp. 18–21.

75. See especially the influential television series by Ken Burns, *Jazz,* vol. 10, PBS Home Video: A production of Florentine Films and WETA, Washington DC, 2000. Cecil Taylor is especially harshly treated.

76. Spellman, *Four Lives in the Bebop Business,* p. 27.

77. Porter, *What Is This Thing Called Jazz?* p. 198.

78. George Breitman, ed., *Malcolm X Speaks* (New York: Grove, 1965), p. 5.

79. See note 60.

80. Morgenstern, interview.

81. *Newport Jazz Festival New York, June 29–July 8, 1973,* program, 1973, p. 62; Gerald C. Fraser, "After a Sour Note, Harmony Reigns on Role of Blacks in Jazz," *New York Times,* July 8, 1972, p. 13. I thank Michael Heller for providing me copies of these two sources.

82. Ibid.

## CHAPTER 8

Some portions of the section on George Russell appeared in Ingrid Monson,. "Oh Freedom: George Russell, John Coltrane, and Modal Jazz." In *In the Course of Performance: Studies in the World of Musical Improvisation*, edited by Bruno/Melinda Russell Nettl, pp. 149–68. (Chicago: University of Chicago Press, 1998.)

1. A. B. Spellman, *Four Lives in the Bebop Business* (New York: Limelight, 1985), p. 30.

2. Liner notes, Ornette Coleman, *Change of the Century,* New York, Oct. 8–9, 1959, Atlantic SD 1327.

3. Ted Gioia, *The Imperfect Art: Reflections on Jazz and Modern Culture* (New York: Oxford University Press, 1988).

4. Jean-Paul Sartre, *Existentialism and Human Emotions* (New York: Citadel, 1985 [1957]), p. 26; Immanuel Kant, *Critique of Judgment,* trans. J. H. Bernard (New York: Hafner, 1951), pp. 150–53. See also Farah Griffin's discussion of genius in *If You Can't Be Free, Be a Mystery* (New York: Free Press, 2001) pp. 14–16.

5. Max Roach, interview with author, Apr. 3, 1999, Cambridge, MA.

6. Among the music theoretical and pedagogical literature exploring these achievements are David Demsey, "Chromatic Third Relations in the Music of John Coltrane," *Annual Review of Jazz Studies* 5 (1991), pp. 145–80; Paul Rinzler, "The Quartal and Pentatonic Harmony of McCoy Tyner," *Annual Review of Jazz Studies* 10 (1999), pp. 35–87; David Baker, *Jazz Improvisation: A Comprehensive Method of Study for All Players* (Chicago: Maher, 1969); Mark Levine, *The Jazz Piano Book* (Petaluma, CA: Sher Music, 1989); Mark Levine, *The Jazz Theory Book* (Petaluma, CA: Sher Music, 1995); Walt Weiskopf and Ramon Ricker, *Coltrane: A Player's Guide to His Harmony* (New Albany, IN: Jamey Aebersold, 1991).

7. Paul F. Berliner, *Thinking in Jazz: The Infinite Art of Improvisation* (Chicago: University of Chicago Press, 1994), pp. 221.

8. Sartre, *Existentialism and Human Emotions,* pp. 13–15, 26, 31; Nichole T. Rustin, "Mingus Fingers: Charles Mingus, Black Masculinity, and Postwar Jazz Culture." Ph.D. diss., New York University, 1999, p. 37.

9. George Russell, interview with author, Aug. 7, 1995, Jamaica Plain, MA. All otherwise unattributed quotes in this section are from this interview. Although in a 1958 interview Davis credited Bill Evans, Gil Evans, and Russell for opening him up to modal approaches to improvisation (Hentoff 1958), he later emphasized the effect on his modal thinking of having seen the Ballets Africains; see Nat Hentoff, "An Afternoon with Miles Davis," *Jazz Review* 1, no. 2 (1958), pp. 9–12; and Miles Davis with Quincy Troupe, *Miles: The Autobiography* (New York: Simon and Schuster, 1989), p. 225. Keita Fodeba's Ballets Africains presented internationally a mixture of traditional musical genres from Guinea and Senegal. As Fodeba explains in the program notes, "stage presentation being different from life, we have had recourse to a slight scenic adaptation" ("Ballets Africans," n.d.). The program notes mention praise songs from Senegal, "Ashanti song," Manding (Mande) music (a picture of a kora player is included), and a "song of the Soudan" as included in the performance.

10. Russell's system is known primarily by its first three editions: (1) George Russell, *The Lydian Concept of Tonal Organization* (New York: Russ-Hix, 1953); (2) George Russell, *The Lydian Chromatic Concept of Tonal Organization for Improvisation* (New York: Concept, 1959); and (3) George Russell, *The Lydian Chromatic Concept of Tonal Organization for Improvisation* (Cambridge, MA: Concept, 1964). The fourth edition was published in 2001 as George Russell, *The Lydian Chromatic Concept of Tonal Organization,* 4th ed., vol. 1: *The Art and Science of Tonal Gravity* (Brookline, MA: Concept, 2001). The page numbers cited in this section are from the 1964 edition except where expressly noted.

11. George Russell, *The Lydian Chromatic Concept,* 1964, pp. i–iv.

12. Russell calls the resolving points "tonic stations"—"tonics to which two or more chords tend to resolve" (Russell, *Lydian Chromatic Concept,* 1959, p. xix).

13. Russell, *Lydian Concept,* pp. 30, 36. I thank George and Alice Russell and Alice for making a copy of the 1953 version available to me.

14. Russell, *Lydian Chromatic Concept,* 2001, pp. 12–19.

15. These are inserted between page 8 and page 9 of the 1964 edition.

16. David Baker, *Jazz Improvisation: A Comprehensive Method of Study for All Players* (Chicago: Maher, 1969); Jerry Coker, *Improvising Jazz,* is also notable, though it covers approximately the same ground as John F. Mehegan, *Jazz Improvisation: Vol. 1. Tonal and Rhythmic Principles* (New York: Watson-Guptill, 1959). For a longer account of jazz theory see Henry Martin, " jazz Theory: An Overview," *Annual Review of Jazz Studies 8* (1996), pp. 1–15.

17. Gurdjieff describes *All and Everything* as "ten books in three series"; see Georges Ivanovitch Gurdjieff, *Beelzebub's Tales to His Grandson: An Objectively Impartial Criticism of the Life of Man,* rev. ed. (New York: Jeremy P. Tarcher Penguin, 2006), p. vii. The first three books are also included in *Beelzebub's Tales to His Grandson* (1973), the second three in *Meetings with Remarkable Men* (1974), and the last four in *Life Is Real Only Then, When "I Am"* (1991). Russell left unspecified the other religious and spiritual ideas he explored but told me that his religious interests were not restricted to Gurdjieff.

18. John Szwed has confirmed that Sun Ra, who read widely in mystical and spiritual literature, was also acquainted with Gurdjieff's thinking. John F. Szwed, *Space Is the Place: The Life and Times of Sun Ra* (New York: Pantheon, 1997), pp. 108–109.

19. James Moore's, biography, *Gurdjieff: The Anatomy of a Myth.* (Rockport, Mass.: Element, 1991), p. 27, describes Gurdjieff's travels in detail. Moore addresses the issue of how Gurdjieff financed his trips accompanied by a group of his followers, called Seekers of the Truth, suggesting that he at points may have worked as a political agent for the Tsarist government.

20. Cornel West, *Prophetic Reflections: Notes on Race and Power in America* (Monroe, ME: Common Courage, 1993), p. 223.

21. Lewis Porter, *John Coltrane: His Life and Music* (Ann Arbor: University of Michigan Press, 1998), pp. 145–58; David Demsey, "Chromatic Third Relations in the Music

of John Coltrane," *Annual Review of Jazz Studies* 5 (1991), pp. 145–80; Jeff Bair, "Cyclic Patterns in John Coltrane's Melodic Vocabulary as Influenced by Nicolas Slonimsky's Thesaurus of Scales and Melodic Patterns: An Analysis of Selected Improvisations," Ph.D. diss., University of North Texas, 2003.

22. Lewis Porter, "John Coltrane's *A Love Supreme:* Jazz Improvisation as Composition," *Journal of the American Musicological Society* 38 (1985): 593–621; Dave Liebman, "John Coltrane's *Meditations* Suite: A Study in Symmetry," *Annual Review of Jazz Studies* 8, (1996), pp. 167–80; Hafez Modirzadeh, "Aural Archetypes and Cyclic Perspectives in the Work of John Coltrane and Ancient Chinese Music Theory," *Black Music Research Journal* 21, no. 1 (2001), pp. 75–105.

23. George Russell, interview with author, Aug. 7, 1995.

24. Lewis Porter, *John Coltrane: His Life and Music* (Ann Arbor: University of Michigan Press, 1998), pp. 296–97.

25. The introduction to "Cubana Be" uses the half-step diminished scale to organize approximately one minute of music. Russell uses staggered entrances in the trombones to introduce the contrapuntally rich theme. "Cubana Be" is included on Dizzy Gillespie, *The Complete RCA Victor Recordings,* New York, Dec. 22, 1947, Bluebird/RCA 07863 66528-2. As in any question of firsts, there are likely other compositions that made use of similar scalar organization. Nevertheless, Russell's was the most prominent.

26. See Lewis Porter and Michael Ullman, *Jazz: From Its Origins to the Present* (Englewood Cliffs, NJ: Prentice Hall, 1993), p. 293, for a transcription of the theme and Davis's solo.

27. An email exchange about modal jazz on the jazz research list (jazz-research@ yahoogroups.com) in July 2001 discussed these issues in detail. Comments were made by Andrew Homzy, Paul Rinzler, Phil Pastras, and Bill Kirchner.

28. Jack Chambers, *Milestones: The Music and Times of Miles Davis* (Toronto: University of Toronto Press, 1985), p. 293.

29. For more on McCoy Tyner's harmony, see Paul Rinzler, "The Quartal and Pentatonic Harmony of McCoy Tyner," *Annual Review of Jazz Studies* 10 (1999), pp. 35–87.

30. Eric Nisenson, *Ascension: John Coltrane and His Quest* (New York: St. Martin's Press, 1993), pp. 111, 185; Lynette Westendorf, "Analyzing Free Jazz," PhD diss., University of Washington, 1994, p. 84.

31. Nisenson, *Ascension,* p. 116; Harold S. Powers, "Language Models and Musical Analysis," *Ethnomusicology* 24 (1980): 1–60. Briefly, Power argues that musics that are subject to fewer ensemble constraints lend themselves more readily to the more expansive type of improvisation found in North Indian classical music (something more akin to a melody type than a scale). Powers contrasts Javanese gamelan and Renaissance music based on a cantus firmus with North Indian alap in making his case for the role of ensemble constraint in shaping the nature of improvisation. Since the former genres are more constrained by the subject of the piece (and the need to coordinate with other parts), they are less free to develop

the open-ended style of improvisation that Powers contends is more linguistic in character (ibid., pp. 37–46). He places jazz improvisation on chord progressions nearer to the Javanese and Renaissance cases. Here the recurrent chord progression functions as the cantus firmus in his thinking. In the modal jazz discussed here fewer chord changes imply fewer ensemble constraints and hence more expansive improvisation, as Powers predicts.

32. An *alap* is a slow unpulsed exposition of the pitches and melodic phrases of a raga that follows a prescribed registral shape.

33. Nisenson offers an invaluable critique of Kofsky in *Ascension,* pp. 179–80.

34. This is a point also made many times in Craig Werner, *Higher Ground: Stevie Wonder, Aretha Franklin, Curtis Mayfield, and the Rise and Fall of American Soul* (New York: Crown, 2004).

35. For an excellent discussion of the contradictory historical claims made about an individual musician's legacy see Gabriel Solis, "Monk's Music and the Making of a Legacy," PhD diss., Washington University, St. Louis, MO, 2001.

36. This is a much larger topic than can be addressed here. For the relationship of American experimentalist composers and jazz, see George E. Lewis, "Improvised Music after 1950: Afrological and Eurological Perspectives," *Black Music Research Journal* 16, no. 1 (1996 ), pp. 91–122.

37. James C. Hall, *Mercy, Mercy, Me: African-American Culture and the Sixties* (New York: Oxford University Press, 2001), pp. 3–10.

38. Paul Gilroy, *The Black Atlantic: Modernity and Double Consciousness* (Cambridge, MA: Harvard University Press, 1993), p. 36.

39. Cornel West, *Prophetic Reflections: Notes on Race and Power in America* (Monroe, ME: Common Courage Press, 1993), pp. 10, 224.

40. Ibid., p. 225.

41. Ibid., p. 164.

42. Ibid., p. 125.

43. Robin D. G. Kelley, *Freedom Dreams: The Black Radical Imagination* (Boston: Beacon, 2002), p. 9.

44. Ibid., p. 192.

45. Suzanne Césaire, quoted in ibid., p. 171.

46. Ronald Radano, "Jazzin' the Classics: The AACM's Challenge to Mainstream Aesthetics," *Black Music Research Journal* 12, no. 1 (1992): 88.

47. Ibid., p. 90

48. Amiri Baraka, *Blues People: Negro Music in White America* (New York: W. Morrow, 1963), p. 231.

49. Theodor Adorno, *Aesthetic Theory,* trans. Robert Hullot-Kentor (Minneapolis: University of Minnesota Press, 1997), p. 78.

50. I discuss Adorno's suspicion of collectivity at greater length in "Riffs, Repetition, and Theories of Globalization," *Ethnomusicology* 43, no. 1 (Winter) (1999): 50–51.

51. John Miller Chernoff, *African Rhythm and African Sensibility: Aesthetics and Social Action in African Musical Idioms* (Chicago: University of Chicago Press, 1979), p. 166.

52. The full text of these principles is available at the organization's website: http://aacmchicago.org/aacmgoals.html (accessed Mar. 7, 2007).

53. George E. Lewis, "Singing Omar's Song: A (Re)Construction of Great Black Music," *Lenox Avenue* 4 (1998), p. 73.

54. John Szwed, *Space Is the Place: The Life and Times of Sun Ra* (New York: Pantheon, 1997); Graham Lock, *Blutopia: Visions of the Future and Revisions of the Past in the Work of Sun Ra, Duke Ellington, and Anthony Braxton* (Durham: Duke University Press, 1999).

55. Szwed, *Space Is the Place,* pp. 109, 141.

56. Ibid., p. 137.

57. Karl Heinz Kessler, "Sun Ra: Music as a Means for Social Transformation," in *Omniverse Sun Ra,* ed. Hartmut Geerken and Bernhard Hefele (Wartaweil, Germany: Waitawhile, 1994), p. 116.

58. Szwed, *Space Is the Place,* pp. 196, 232.

59. Sun Ra, *Holiday for Soul Dance,* 1968–1969, Evidence ECD 22011–2; Sun Ra, *Space Is the Place,* Chicago, Oct. 19–20, 1972, Impulse! IMPD-249; Sun Ra, *The Heliocentric Worlds of Sun Ra,* vol. 2, New York, Nov. 16, 1965, Get Back GET 1005; Sun Ra, *Solar Myth Approach,* New York, 1970–1971, Affinity CD AFF 760.

60. Szwed, *Space Is the Place,* pp. 127, 156.

CHAPTER 9

1. For a very different position on the question of race, essentialism, and the history of African American music, see Ronald Radano, *Lying Up a Nation: Race and Black Music* (Chicago: University of Chicago Press, 2003).

2. W.E.B. Du Bois, "The Souls of Black Folk," in *The Oxford W.E.B. Du Bois,* ed. Henry Louis Gates, Jr. (New York: Oxford University Press 2007 [1903]), p. 122.

3. Adorno, of course, would not have argued this about jazz since he did not view it as true art. Nevertheless, in his view, the authenticity and truth of a musical artwork is carried in its form, not in human agency. Form is, nevertheless, indirectly social because its materials are the product of history and society. Adorno, in other words, focuses primarily on the product and its unfolding rather than its social process of construction and generation of meaning. On Adorno's view of the art work, see Robert Hullot-Kentor, "Right Listening and a New Type of Human Being," in *The Cambridge Companion to Adorno,* ed. Thomas Huhn, pp. 181–97 (New York: Cambridge University Press, 2004), and Max Paddison, "Authenticity and Failure in Adorno's Aesthetics of Music," in ibid., pp. 198–221.

4. A variety of opinions on these topics can be found in Willard Jenkins, "School's In: Wynton Marsalis on What's Right and Wrong with Jazz Education," *Jazz Times,* Sup., *The*

*Jazz Education Guide* (1998/1999), pp. 8–22; Stanley Crouch, *Considering Genius: Writings on Jazz* (New York: Basic Civitas, 2006); Eric Nisenson, *Blue: The Murder of Jazz* (New York: Saint Martin's, 1997), Jerome Harris, "Jazz on the Global Stage," in *The African Diaspora: A Musical Perspective,* ed. Ingrid Monson, pp. 103–34 (New York: Garland, 2000).

5. Stuart Nicholson, *Is Jazz Dead? (or Has It Moved to a New Address)* (New York: Routledge, 2005.)

# Index

Page numbers followed by *f* and *t* refer to figures and tables.

Hammett, Dashiell, 32–33
Hammond, John, 338n15
Hampton, Lionel, 32, 34, 98
Hampton, Slide, 150–151
Hancock, Herbie, 189, 217, 297
Hannerz, Ulf, 351n104
Hanson, Howard, 112
hard bop
    aesthetics of, 98–99, 350n90
    black difference, emphasis on, 106
    cool school vs., 67, 77
    harmony and, 104
    Morgan and, 76
    popular African American music and,
        97–98
    riffs, vamps, and composition, 99–103
Hardmann, Bill, 136
harmonic system, Lydian, 287–293, 289f, 290f
harmony, 103–104, 307–308
Harris, Bill (trombonist), 66
Harris, William (AFM vice president), 52
Harrison, Faye, 21
Harrison, Ira, 21
Harrison, Jay, 112
Hartman, Johnny, 205
Hasan, Bill, 281
Hawes, Hampton, 39, 72
Hawkins, Coleman
    appearances, 36, 109
    benefit concerts, 209
    critics' polls and, 67
    *Freedom Now Suite* and, 172, 177
    Music Advisory Panel and, 126
    Newport Rebel Festival and, 184
Hawkins, Screamin' Jay, 98
Heath, Percy, 95
Heckman, Don, 266
Hegel, G. F. W., 22
Henderson, Bill, 164
Henderson, Fletcher, 314, 338n16
Henderson, Joe, 102
Henderson, Mae, 21
Henderson, Skitch, 41
Hentoff, Nat
    Candid Records and, 182, 184
    in *Down Beat* panel (*See* Racial Prejudice
        in Jazz panel discussion)
    experience organizing sessions, 363n50

*Freedom Now Suite* and, 173, 174
"The Freedom Rider" and, 195
"From Bird to Berg," 85
interview with, 255
on Jim Crow, 61, 62
on Lincoln, 258
on Manuti, 340n44
on sit-ins, 164
*Straight Ahead* and, 239
Taylor and, 278–279
Herbert, Mort, 123
Herman, Woody, 66
Hernández, René, 141
Herskovits, Melville J., 22, 334n38
heterogeneous sound ideal, 75–76
Hibbler, Al, 219–220
Higginbotham, Evelyn, 75, 349n75
Higgins, Billy, 234, 235
Higher Ground benefit concert, 320
Highlander Folk School, 165
Hill, Andrew, 157
Hindemith, Paul, 85, 288
Hinton, Milt, 209
Hodeir, André, 82–84, 347n36
Hodges, Johnny, 66, 72, 77–78
Hogan, G. T., 149
Holiday, Billie, 36, 109
*Holiday for Skins* (Blakey), 138, 140
Holt, Scottie, 234, 235
Holzfeind, Frank, 35
Hopkins, Lightning, 274
*Horace Silver Trio* album, 134
Horne, Lena, 35, 186, 196, 366n93
"Horoscope" (Silver), 100, *100*
House Un-American Activities
        Committee, 45
Howard, Paul, 45
Hubbard, Freddie, 150
Hudgens, Eula, 162
Hughes, Edwin, 112
Hughes, Langston, 148, 149, 165
humanism, 305
Humanist Hall, 44, 45
Huntley, Chet, 246, 341n63
Hurok, Sol, 185
Hurricane Katrina, 319–320
Hyams, Marjorie, 67
hybridity, cultural, 10–13

Monk, Thelonious
  activism and benefit concerts, 164,
    199–201, 205–206, 209, 211
  in polls, 67
  riffs, 100
Monogram, 33
Montgomery, Alabama, 55–56, 119, 194
Montgomery Improvement Association
  (MIA), 55–56
Morgan, Lee, 76, 101, 102, 106, 194–195, 234
Morgenstern, Dan, 172, 259, 266, 268, 279,
  280–281
Morris, Aldon, 161, 163
Moses, Bob, 224
Moss, Ronald, 188, 189, 365n74
MPTF (Musicians Performance Trust
  Fund), 51–52
Muhammad, Elijah, 168, 232f
Muhammad, Sister Clara, 230
Muhammad Speaks, 168–169, 248, 263–265
"mulatto," 8, 9
Mule, Marcel, 86
Mulligan, Gerry, 81, 82, 83–84, 196, 196f
Mundy, Jim, 287
Murray, Albert, 8, 10, 74–75, 90
Murray, Sonny, 259, 266, 274
Murrow, Edward R., 128–129
Music Advisory Panel (MAP), 112, 126
Musicians Committee for Integration, 50–51
Musicians Guild of America (MGA), 51–52
Musicians Performance Trust Fund
  (MPTF), 51–52
Muslim bazaars, 227, 228t–229t, 230, 230f,
  231f, 232f
Muslim Mosque, Inc., 169
Muslim musicians, 147
Muslim program, 168–169
My Funny Valentine (Davis), 216, 298–299,
  299f
Myth of the Negro Past (Herskovits), 22


NAACP (National Association for the
  Advancement of Colored People)
  annual convention (1961), 173, 363n38
  benefit concerts for, 157
  Brown v. Board of Education and, 55
  Freedom Now Suite and, 173
  Legal Defense Fund, 162, 211, 366n92

Nat Cole and, 60, 61
Youth Councils and sit-ins, 161–162
NALC (Negro American Labor Council),
  157, 205
Nanton, Tricky Sam, 143
Nash, Diane, 194
Nashville Christian Leadership Council
  (NCLC), 162–163
National Defaulters list (International
  Musician), 40
National Guard, 236
nationalism, African, 239, 244–245
nationalism, black. See black nationalism
nationalism, cultural and revolutionary,
  226–227, 230
National Liberation Movement (NLM,
  Ghana), 130
national separation, black, 14, 168–169
National Urban League (NUL), 40– 41, 157
Nation of Islam
  black national separation and, 168
  cultural nationalism and, 230
  events (1962–1967), 228t–229t
  Malcolm X defection from, 169, 226
  spirituality and, 265
  unity bazaars and, 146–147
NBC, 40– 41, 246
NCLC (Nashville Christian Leadership
  Council), 162–163
Neblett, Charles, 58, 218
Negro American Labor Council (NALC),
  157, 205
Nehru, Jawaharlal, 109, 114
networks, desegregation of, 40– 41
Newark rebellion (1967), 234–237
Newman, David "Fathead," 101
Newman, Joe, 135
New Orleans, 319–320
Newport Jazz Festival, 184, 280–281
Newport Rebel Festival, 184–185
New Thing, the. See avante-garde expression
  (the New Thing)
Newton, Huey, 227
New Wave in Jazz, The, 303
New York Amsterdam News, 59–60, 140,
  361n19
New York City Police Department, 187
Nicholson, Stuart, 320

Nieto, Ubaldo, 137
nightclubs. *See* clubs
Nixon, E. D., 56
Nixon, Richard, 131
Nkrumah, Kwame, 4, 109, 129–130, 131, 132, 140, 352n5
nonviolence, rejection of, 178
North Indian music, 300–301, 377n31
Nunn, William, 133
Nyerere, Julius, 188, 265

Oakley, Helen, 338n15
October Revolution concerts, 271
O'Day, Anita, 34
Odetta, 165, 209
Ogunde, Hubert, 227
Olatunji, Michael Babatunde
  Africa and, 134, 142
  background, 227–230
  Coltrane and, 303
  *Freedom Now Suite* and, 172, 179
  Mingus and, 231f
  nonpayment claim, 40
  *Uhuru Africa* and, 149
Oliver, King, 94
O'Meally, Robert, 356n49
one-drop rule, 8–9
*Orgy in Rhythm* (Blakey), 137–140, 141
"Oriental and Jazz," 144, 144f
Orishas, 134, 138
Ortner, Sherry, 23
Oserjeman, Baba, 236–237
*Othello,* 36, 108, 109
"outside" musical approach, 160

Pabst, Naomi, 10
Page, Patti, 68
Pahlavi, Shahnaz, 116
Paine College, 186
Pakistan, 117, 118
Palladium, 140
Pan-African Congress (1945), 110
Pan-Africanism, 21, 107–108
Pandit, Vijaya Lakshmi, 109
Panish, John, 78
Parker, Charlie, 66, 67, 72, 83, 86–87, 109, 110, 347n35
"passing for white," 9

Patterson, John, 193, 194
Payne, Cecil, 101, 151
Payne, Don, 121
Payne, Felix, Jr., 32
pay scales, AFM, 38–39
Peck, Jim, 193
pedal points and vamps, 299–303, 302f, 303f
peer pressure, 218–219
Pellegrinelli, Lara, 339n26
Pepper, Art, 104
Peraza, Armando, 141, 142, 149
Peretti, Burton, 242
Persip, Charlie, 115, 149
Peterson, Oscar, 66
Petrillo, James Caesar, 30, 38, 48, 50–52
Pettiford, Oscar, 181
Phillips, Jeanne, 261
Phipps, Kenneth, 187
pitch stability, 251–252, 372n25
Pitts, George, 343n2
*Pittsburgh Courier,* 132–133, 140, 185–186
Pla-Mor ballroom (Kansas City), 32
Point of Contact debate
  "blackness" and, 274–276
  club practices, 267–270
  organizing of, 266
  racial disunity, 277–280
polarization, cultural, 104–106
Pollock, Jackson, 285
polymodality, vertical, 289
popular music, 17–18, 97–98
Porter, Eric, 23, 277
Porter, Lewis, 294
Powell, Adam Clayton, Jr., 110, 112, 113–114, 131, 145–146
Powell, Carleton, 32
Powell, Chris, 98
Powers, Harold, 297, 301, 377n31
Pozo, Chano, 134
practice theory, 26–28, 336n53
practicing, 295
Prado, Pérez, 138
"Prayer for Passive Resistance" (Mingus), 183
Priester, Julian, 172, 179
Priestly, Brian, 89
Prima, Louis, 40
Primus, Pearl, 36, 109
"professional Negro" discussion, 241

Shorter, Wayne, 101, 102–103, 194–195
Shulman, Joe, 81–82
Shuttlesworth, Fred, 193–194, 207, 219
"sidemen," 339n29
Siegelstein, Sandy, 82, 347n36
"Sign of the Judgment" (Georgia Sea
  Islander), 75
Silver, Horace
  *B. Schwarz v. Horace Silver,* 39
  *Birth of the Cool and,* 80
  as composer, 99
  "Ecaroh," 102, 102*f*
  Freedom Riders telethon and, 196,
    367n93
  hard bop and, 79
  harmony and, 104
  "Horoscope," 100
  music theory and, 88
"Simba" (Martínez), 138
Simon, George, 188–189
Simone, Nina, 165, 218–219
Simpkins, George, 162
Sims, Zoot, 209
Sinatra, Frank, 67, 76, 166, 209
singers, 339n26
singing, civil rights movement and, 58
sit-in movement
  background and events of, 161–162
  benefit concerts and, 152–153, 153*f*
  CORE and, 163–164
  musician reactions to, 185–186
  sit-down strikes, 361n19
slaves, 70
Slonimsky, Nicolas, 294
Smith, Carleton Sprague, 112
Smith, Jimmy, 75, 104
Smith, John, 235
SNCC. *See* Student Nonviolent
  Coordinating Committee
social action, practice as, 26–27
  *See also* activism
social categories and aesthetic agency,
  313, 314*f*
social system, differences created by,
  248–249
social theory, 23–27
sonic explorations, 307–310
South Africa, 175

Southern Christian Leadership Conference
  (SCLC)
  benefit concerts for, 157, 209
  Project C (Birmingham, 1963), 57, 206–209
  sit-ins and, 161
  SNCC founding and, 163
Southwide Student Leadership Conference
  on Nonviolent Resistance to
  Segregation" (1960), 163
"So What" (Davis), 296–297
Spann, Les, 150, 151
Spellman, A. B., 234, 269, 273–274, 284,
  346n25
Spirit House, 236–237
spirituality and religion
  avant-garde and, 262, 265–266
  break with tonality and, 307
  non-Western modes of spiritual
    expression, 20
  Russell and, 292–293
  Santería (Lucumí), 134, 138, 141
  utopian visions and, 304–307
spirituals, 103, 317
Spivacke, Harold, 112
State Department, black employees in,
  354n35
State Department tours (Cultural
  Presentations Program)
  administration of, 111–113
  African destinations, 126–128, 127*t*
  demographics, 123–126
  de Paris tour, 130–131
  funding and finances, 111, 120–123, 122*t*,
    355n38
  Gillespie tours, 113–120, 115*t*
  internationalist view and, 108
  jazz tours list, 124*t*–125*t*
  purpose of, 331n6
  Weston's report on, 128
Stearns, Marshall, 113, 116, 126, 354n28
Stevenson, Adlai, 245
Stitt, Sonny, 77
*Straight Ahead* (Lincoln)
  description of, 239
  Gitler review of, 239–240, 251–252
  "In the Red," 252–253, 252*f*
  Langston Hughes poem on, 149
  "Straight Ahead," 244–245, 253, 253*f*

"Toffi" (Blakey), 137, 137f
tokenism, 34, 41
tonal gravity, 289, 298, 301
tonality, break with, 18, 307–308
tonality extender charts, 291
*Top Percussion* (Puente), 138
transcendence of art, 308
travel under Jim Crow, 31
Travers, Mary, 220
Treadwell, George, 32
"Tribute to Martin Luther King," 166–167, 167f
"Triptych" (Roach and Brown), 177–178
Tristano, Lennie, 73, 79, 88–92, 348n56
Tubman, William V. S., 140, 337n8
Turkey, 117–118
Turner, Jessie, 9, 33
Turrentine, Stanley, 75
Tynan, John, 62, 264
Tyner, McCoy, 101, 147, 297, 300, 301

*Uhuru Africa* (Weston), 147–151, 150f, 360n105
Ulanov, Barry, 89–90, 92
underground concerts, 270–272
Unfair list *(International Musician)*, 40
UNIA (Universal Negro Improvement Association), 107, 142
United Nations, 147, 245–246
unity, black, 277–280
unity bazaars, 227, 228t–229t, 230, 230f, 231f, 232f
universalism, 301–303, 306
Universal Negro Improvement Association (UNIA), 107, 142
utopian visions
    inclusion, exclusion, and self-determination and, 310–311
    sonic explorations, 307–310
    spirituality and modernity linked in, 304–307

Valdés, Carlos "Patato" (or Carlos Valdez), 121, 137
Valiente, José, 137
vamps, 99–103, 102f, 300–303, 302f, 303f

vanguardism. *See* avante-garde expression (the New Thing)
Varèse Edgard, 85, 86
Vaughan, Sarah, 32, 67, 68, 363n38
Vee, Aaron, 41
vertical polymodality, 289
Vicente, Chonguito, 138
Vietnam, 223–224
Village Gate
    benefit concerts, 164, 165, 172
    *Freedom Now Suite* benefit, 152
    the New Thing and, 269
Vinson, Eddie "Cleanhead," 98
Vinson, Fred M., 54
Von Eschen, Penny, 109, 111, 353n12
*Voodoo Suite* (Prado), 138
Voter Education Project (VEP), 211
voter registration, 199, 211, 216, 224
Voting Rights Act (1965), 224–225

Walker, Jesse H., 366n93
Walker, Wyatt, 206
Wallace, George, 209
Wallace, Mike, 196
Warfield, William, 112, 123
Warren, Earl (Chief Justice), 54
Warren, Earle (musician), 9
Washington, Booker, T., 226
Washington, Dinah, 209
Washington, Joe, 75
Waters, Muddy, 74
Watkins, Doug, 39
Watkins, Julius, 151
Watts, Isaac, 70
Webster, Ben, 209
Webster, Paul, 33
Wein, George, 184
*We Insist! Max Roach's Freedom Now Suite.*
    *See Freedom Now Suite* (Roach and Brown)
Weinstein, Norman, 133
Wesley, John, 70
West, Cornell, 293, 305
West Coast style, 71–72
Weston, Frank Edward, 143
Weston, Mildred, 145, 146f
Weston, Randy
    "African Lady," 244, 245